Praise for T. H. Watkins's
The Great Depression
America in the 1930s

"Riveting. . . . Watkins scrupulously documents the devastating financial collapse that left an indelible imprint on the nation's collective cultural psyche and evokes that provocative combination of fear, desperation, and hope that characterized the 1930s. . . . More than 100 heartrending black-and-white photographs vivify the sensitive narrative."   —Margaret Flanagan, *Booklist*

"A fine survey. . . . Like it or not, American politics are still polarized around the New Deal. . . . The primal cleft between liberals and conservatives is, in large part, a disagreement about the New Deal; and it was the Great Depression that made the New Deal — so it seemed to contemporaries — inevitable. . . . Watkins is at his best in his ability to recapture the miseries and the hopes, the fears and the ideals, of individual people who lived in a world that may have been physically almost unrecognizable — no interstate highways, no shopping malls. . . . He has used to the full both documentary material turned up by the TV researchers and the incomparable holdings of films, still photography, and sound archives in the Library of Congress and elsewhere."   —Godfrey Hodgson, *Washington Post Book World*

"The decade's legacies, Watkins believes, are the hope and popular cohesion born of the struggle against the era's devastation and a sense of mutual responsibility between Americans and their federal government. It was an era formed by the New Deal's early accomplishments, and it spawned a perception of intimacy between Americans and their president that FDR bequeathed to all his successors, for good or ill."   —Robert F. Nardini, *Library Journal*

"An engaging study of the Depression with numerous news clips, documentary stills, and period photographs."   —*Publishers Weekly*

THE GREAT

America in the 1930s

Back Bay Books
Little, Brown and Company
New York   Boston   London

DEPRESSION

AMERICAN
FLAG SAVED
FROM FIRE
WASHINGTON,
D.C.

T. H. WATKINS

Back Bay Books / Little, Brown and Company
Hachette Book Group
237 Park Avenue, New York, NY 10017
www.hachettebookgroup.com

Originally published in hardcover by Little, Brown and Company, October 1993
First Back Bay paperback edition, January 1995
Second Back Bay paperback edition, October 2009

Back Bay Books is an imprint of Little, Brown and Company. The Back Bay Books name and logo are trademarks of Hachette Book Group, Inc.

Copyright acknowledgments appear on page 376.

Library of Congress Cataloging-in-Publication Data
Watkins, T. H. (Tom H.)
    The Great Depression: America in the 1930s / T. H. Watkins. —
1st ed.
        p.   cm.
    Includes index.
    ISBN 978-0-316-92453-5 (hc) / 978-0-316-92454-2 (first trade pb) /
978-0-316-08043-9 (second trade pb)
    1. United States — History — 1933–1945. 2. Depressions — 1929 —
United States. 3. New Deal, 1933–1939. 4. United States — History —
1919–1933. I. Title.
E806.W34   1993
973.917 — dc20   93-1332

10   9   8   7   6   5   4   3   2   1

RRD-IN

Designed by Barbara Werden

Printed in the United States of America

*To my grandchildren — Aaron Matthew Watkins,
Breanna Mae Watkins, and
Steven John Pless*

CONTENTS

INTRODUCTION
History Shot on the Wing   2

CHAPTER ONE
The Prologue Years   20

CHAPTER TWO
The Shadow of the Hawk   48

CHAPTER THREE
Shades of Revolution   76

CHAPTER FOUR
Redeeming the Hour   108

CHAPTER FIVE
The New Utopians   138

CHAPTER SIX
Ending the Long Darkness   164

CHAPTER SEVEN
Dust, Drought, and Displacement   186

CHAPTER EIGHT
The Politics of Discontent   214

CHAPTER NINE
The Second New Deal   242

CHAPTER TEN
Barricades and Bargains   274

CHAPTER ELEVEN
The Ramparts of Uncertainty   302

CHAPTER TWELVE
Waiting for the Fire   330

FURTHER READING   350

ACKNOWLEDGMENTS   357

PROJECT ACKNOWLEDGMENTS   359

ILLUSTRATION CREDITS   361

INDEX   363

The Great Depression

History Shot on the Wing

Introduction

Overleaf:
A Dust Bowl scene in Cimarron
County, Oklahoma, taken by Farm
Security Administration photographer
Arthur Rothstein in April, 1936.

A GREAT DEAL SEPARATES our own time and the time we call the Great Depression — the six convulsive years of World War II, a phantom conflict called the Cold War that has only just "ended," two real wars in Korea and Vietnam and a television war in the Persian Gulf; nine presidencies; profound explosions of technology and sometimes violent social change; and the rise and fall of entire world governments. To most Americans, then, the story of the Great Depression must stand as history in the most precise and inescapable sense — the chronicle of a time that is so far removed from our world today that its essence should be as difficult to recapture with confidence and accuracy as, say, that of the era of the French and Indian War.

In spite of all that lies between the Great Depression and the present, I think there remains a powerful sense of connectedness, even among those Americans who are comparatively young. Much of that connectedness can be attributed to the stories still told by so many people who survived those times and carry their memories with them. Passed on orally in many families, the experience of having lived through hard times has become part of the common heritage of millions of people. Some of the connectedness can be found in the fact that every single recessionary period in the nation's economic life since the 1950s — including the slump through which we are still struggling as I write this — has been compared in exquisite detail to the years of the Great Depression, quite often to demonstrate that things could be a great deal worse.

But I believe there is something else that contributes to that sense of familiarity, something that evolved out of the time itself. There has always been an inordinate self-consciousness in the American story. From the time the "shot heard 'round the world" started the Revolutionary War at Lexington, Massachusetts, on an April day in 1775, Americans have tended to know they were making history even as they were making it — and knowing that, to document it. Until the middle of the nineteenth century, documentation, voluminous as it was, still was confined to the written word or the drawn or painted observation or memory, both of which put a sometimes distorted screen of subjectivity between the reality of the experience and the perception of those reading or viewing it later. Photography improved the breadth of documentation, beginning with the Civil War, but it was not until well into the twentieth century that the technology of photography had progressed to a point where it could keep up with events at a speed and accuracy that recalls the old definition of journalism as "history shot on the wing."

It is arguable that the era of the Great Depression was the first period of American history to be so fully documented by both still photography and cinematography that the images that were created have literally entered the consciousness of most literate citizens. Photolithography, as reflected in such magazines as *Fortune* and *Life*, had reached high levels of technical quality by the thirties, and photojournalism had achieved the character of an identifiable discipline, particularly in the hands of craftsmen like Albert Eisenstadt, Carl Mydans, and Margaret Bourke-White. Small cameras like the 35mm Leica I and the twin-lens-reflex Rolliflex swiftly replaced the bulky and exhausting Graflex that had typified the twenties, and even the most modestly talented newspaper photographer could sometimes achieve imagery of lasting power. In the motion picture theaters of the nation, weekly newsreels produced by *Pathé News*, *Movietone News*, William Randolph Hearst's *Monotone News*, Henry Luce's *March of Time*, and others gave the audiences the crude cinematic equivalent of the Sunday paper's rotogravure section (though *The March of Time* aspired to higher levels of documentary art).

Americans, in short, were looking at themselves as never before, and to a large degree what they saw then is what we remember now. This would have pleased the New Dealers, for much of the imagery that has become part of the common knowledge of the era was created at their behest. Consider the story of perhaps the depression's most renowned documentary movie. In May of 1935, a twenty-nine-year-old movie critic and erstwhile filmmaker named Pare Lorenz brought an idea to the Department of Agriculture in Washington, D. C. He was not without credentials. A veteran movie reviewer for *Judge*, *Vanity Fair*, *Town and Country*, *Newsweek*, and a former columnist for William Randolph Hearst's Universal News Syndicate, he had coauthored one book, *Censored: The Private Life of Movies* (1930), and been the sole author of another, *The Roosevelt Year: 1933* (1934), a collection of news photographs with extended cutlines that documented the activities of the New Deal. Lorenz wanted to produce a series of film documentaries for the government that would illuminate the full sweep of life in America, good and bad. Through the help of a fellow *Vanity Fair* alumnus, John Franklin Carter, who was by then serving as head of the Division of Information for the Resettlement Administration, Lorenz was introduced to Rexford Guy Tugwell, director of the agency.

Tugwell was a receptive audience. He fully understood the importance of imagery in educating the public — and the Congress — about the importance of the Resettlement Administration's programs. In just two months Tugwell would bring fellow economist Roy Emerson Stryker, a photography buff, down from Columbia University to head up a historical section in the agency's information division. The section's purpose was to create a permanent photographic record of the agency's work, as well as of the lives of the people affected by it, and from July, 1935, until the Resettlement Administration was dissolved and restructured as the Farm Security Administration in 1937, and from then until World War II, such photographers as Dorothea Lange, Walker Evans, Marian Post Wolcott, Carl Mydans, Ben Shahn, Aaron Siskind, John Vachon, Arthur Rothstein, and dozens of others — none earning more than $3,000 a year, when there was even that much money available — produced more than a quarter of a million images of American life in the Great Depression, a pictorial archive that in technical quality, artistic merit, and overall comprehensiveness is unequaled anywhere. (Many of the images in this book are from that collection, which now resides, beautifully catalogued and lovingly kept, in the Prints and Photographs Division of the Library of Congress.)

Tugwell was taken immediately with Lorenz's desire to do in film much of what Stryker and his photographers would be doing in still photography, and the two men agreed upon the Dust Bowl as the first subject. The visual possibilities of "the great vast landscape" under "the huge arc of sky," Lorenz later explained, greatly appealed to him. "I also remembered," he added, "one day in New York when I was working at *Newsweek* and a heavy, slow-moving gray cloud, dust from the drought-stricken Great Plains, blew down in the middle of Manhattan Island and settled like an old blanket over the tower of the *New York Times* building at Times Square."

The film that resulted, *The Plow that Broke the Plains*, was completed in 1936. An unrepentant propaganda piece designed to provide evidence of the need for the New Deal's various agricultural programs, the film nevertheless remains one of the most memorable documents to survive from the years of the Great Depression. Employing a device rarely used in American films at that time, it married powerful images with a simple narration to convey the dimensions of one of the great social upheavals of modern history. "On to the West!" cried Lorenz's narrative, to the accompaniment of Virgil Thomson's original score, while rickety flivvers festooned with worldly goods and packed with children clattered over the landscape:

> *Once again they headed into the setting sun . . .*
> *Once again they headed West out of*
> *the Great Plains and hit the highways*
> *for the Pacific Coast, the last border.*
> *Blown out — baked out — and broke . . .*

Nothing to stay for . . . nothing to hope for . . .
homeless, penniless and bewildered they joined
the great army of the highways.

Lorenz and Tugwell had hoped to get one or more of the big motion picture companies to distribute the thirty-minute film as a regular "short subject." But the large studios which by then controlled nearly every aspect of commercial movie production and distribution had just about given up on anything that smacked of controversy. There had been a brief time in the early part of the depression era when at least a few of the studios had been willing to produce films that attempted to depict some of the darker shadows of these years, as when Darryl F. Zanuck at Warner Brothers had risked a lawsuit from the state of Georgia in 1933 to produce Mervyn LeRoy's *I Am a Fugitive from a Chain Gang*, the adaptation of a convict's true account of his horrific experiences on a Georgia prison gang, from which he had escaped not once, but twice. And even the flashy (and fleshy) Mervyn LeRoy-Busby Berkeley musical extravaganza, *Gold Diggers of 1933*, felt compelled to make a social statement by concluding with "My Forgotten Man," a lament in song for all those who had been dispossessed by war and depression.

By 1936, any remaining desire on the part of the studios to approximate the world as it was had long since succumbed to more immediate realities. The industry was only beginning a slow recovery from the effects of the depression — effects that had come relatively late, but had slammed into the movie colony like one of its own special-effects hurricanes, bending studio executives like so many prop-department palm trees. While the few "social issue" movies the studios had made proved to be profitable, the circumstances did not encourage the taking of chances.

With a few exceptions — the anti-lynching films *Winterset* (1936) and *Fury* (1936) from Warner Brothers, for example — the majors generally confined themselves for the rest of the decade to wholesome products like *Little Women* (1933), peppy Shirley Temple vehicles like *Stand Up and Cheer* (1934), costume epics like *A Tale of Two Cities* (1935) and *Captain Blood* (1936), and such "screwball comedies" as *Mister Deeds Goes to Town* (1936) or *My Man Godfrey* (1936), sprightly films that enfolded the hardships of the depression in a mantle of fast-paced, triumphant humor as a means of both exploiting misery and making it more tolerable. "If 'screwball' comedies successfully turned the world on its ear," social historian Lewis Jacobs noted, "that was perhaps the way it already looked to a Depression generation which felt cheated of its birthright and apprehensively faced further loss in the steady approach of war."

The studios consequently were in no mood to market a somber, realistic view of the Dust Bowl and its refugees, and when *The Plow that Broke the Plains* was offered for distribution in 1936, they turned it down. Only when Arthur Mayer, an independent New York theater owner (most motion picture theaters of the time were locked in monopoly chains like those controlled by Loew's/MGM or RKO) accepted it for his Rialto Theatre, did the public get a chance to see it — and it was entirely symptomatic of the times that Lorenz's classic documentary shared the bill with what many still consider the era's classic screwball comedy, *It Happened One Night*, the Clark Gable and Claudette Colbert romance in which honest poverty and love win out over greed and deception. *The Plow that Broke the Plains* was critically successful and well enough received by the New York audience to encourage other exhibitors around the country to give it screen time. Lorenz went on to launch an even more ambitious film, *The River*, a thirty-minute celebration of the need for and glory of the TVA that was given spectacular authenticity by the inclusion of powerful footage from ruinous floods in the Mississippi River Valley, which providentially, if sadly, struck just as the film was in the middle of production in January, 1937. *The River* premiered at the Criterion Theatre in New York City in February, 1938, and after its own enthusiastic reception was picked up for distribution by Paramount Pictures.

Like *The Plow that Broke the Plains*, Lorenz's *The River* became one of the permanent visual legacies from the decade of the thirties — though both it and the earlier Lorenz film would soon be overshadowed by another film that continues to provide millions of Americans with their first and often most memorable exposure to the character and experience of the Great Depression. Remarkably enough, it was a Hollywood production.

By 1940, tens of thousands of Americans had read at least one of three recent books: John Steinbeck's novel *The Grapes of Wrath*; Carey McWilliams's combination of journalism and sociological treatise *Factories in the Field*; and Paul Schuster Taylor's and Dorothea Lange's powerful documentary mix of words and photographs *American Exodus*. All had as their subjects the Dust Bowl refugees and the migrant labor situation in California, but it was Steinbeck's story of the durable Joad family's travels from their foreclosed farm in Oklahoma to the dim misery and violence of the migrant world of California that had the greatest impact, with its epic narrative form, its deliberate attempt to mythologize the Okie experience, cal power of its language, and such memorably drawn characters as Preacher Casy, the labor agitator, and Ma Joad, the eternal mother figure. "It is easy to grow lyrical about *The Grapes of Wrath*," reviewer Joseph Henry Jackson said at the time, "to become excited by it, to be stirred to the shouting point by it." The novel, he said, "stays with you, beats rhythmically in your mind long after you have put the book down." The book was an immediate best-seller, made John Steinbeck the most famous California writer since Mark Twain left the state in 1867, and won the Pulitzer Prize in May, 1940.

That was good enough for Hollywood, which suddenly decided that Dust Bowl refugees might make box office material after all. Samuel Goldwyn turned the project down, but Darryl F. Zanuck at Twentieth-Century Fox took it immediately. With Nunnally Johnson's screenplay, John Ford's direction, Gregg Toland's cinematography, and Henry Fonda leading a stellar cast, the movie, contemporary *New York Times* critic Frank Nugent said, should be placed on the "one small uncrowded shelf devoted to the cinema's masterpieces." Steinbeck himself found it a "hard, straight picture in which the actors are submerged so completely that it looks and feels like a documentary film and certainly it has a hard, truthful ring." The movie even won the praise of songwriter Woody Guthrie, who had been to the migrants in music what Steinbeck now was to them in fiction. In 1940 the Dust Bowl troubadour wrote a ballad he called "Tom Joad." It was based on *The Grapes of Wrath* and he wrote it, he told folklorist John Greenway, "because the people back in Oklahoma haven't got two bucks to buy the book, or even thirty-five cents to see the movie, but the song will get back to them and tell them what Preacher Casy said."

The story of *The Grapes of Wrath*, whether in book, movie, or musical form, was a fiction, and therefore cannot be read or viewed or heard as history bound by any formal rules of accuracy. But there is no denying its power as image, and with the work of Pare Lorenz and the armies of federal photographers who scoured the land for pictures, as well as the scores of newsreel cameramen and the hundreds of news photographers who had come into their own in the twenties and met their obligations to history in the thirties, it remains an essential part of that resource of memory from which much of modern America's sense of itself has come.

The images are not perfect mirrors of reality, of course. In the hands of true artists, after all, both film and still photography can be fully as subjective as painting, and can even be manipulated deliberately to achieve a desired effect. Margaret Bourke-White, for example, was not above moving the people around in her documentary work for *Fortune* and *Life* to enhance the message her photographs were designed to deliver, and the films of Pare Lorenz, however beautifully crafted as film, were unabashedly propagandistic. Even the photographers of the Farm Security Administration, ostensibly dedicated to the purest documentary goals, were hardly unaware that their work was designed both to sell the need for the New Deal's programs and to celebrate their successes; decisions about what to photograph and how to picture it inescapably were influenced at least subliminally by the imperative of their mission.

But even when manipulated for effect, the imagery was working with the materials of truth; at its core, even *The Grapes of Wrath* portrayed a world that was as real as the sweat and pain of the individuals on whom John Steinbeck had based his book. The images give us access to a time that words alone cannot provide, and they have now become so much a part of the national experience that there are few Americans who cannot conjure up a visual "memory" of those days whether they lived through them or not. Farmland ravaged by erosion and baked by the sun; Hoovervilles, those magpie villages strewn with litter and disappointment; dust storms boiling up in mountainous black clouds over helpless little towns and lonely, hurrying automobiles; homesteads buried in sand; corn dead on its stalks; cattle bawling helplessly for water, each starkly outlined set of ribs forming a cage of misery; ragged, hungry Anglo children drinking from filthy roadside puddles, black children huddled with their cotton sacks in the big lonely fields of the Delta, Hispanic children making adobe bricks in the mountain villages of New Mexico; men sitting on park benches, eyes downcast, standing in dull, uncomplaining ranks in breadlines, piled into the dim recesses of employment offices, waiting, always waiting; ranks of factory stacks outlined against a sky empty of the smoke that once billowed from them in a celebration of industry; the clubs and guns of labor violence, the grim silent marches of the hungry; women drawn down to pure muscle, teeth loose in their mouths, old at thirty, forty; apple sellers smiling desperately; hollow-eyed men with the look of stunned animals; California ditch camps made of tarpaper and tin cans pounded flat, tattered laundry flapping in the wind like flags of surrender; dusty, lonely caravans of automobiles, each vehicle held together by hope and baling wire and Anglo-Saxon curses, piled high with the detritus of lives barely lived; and always, like a talisman, the image of a man, head tilted back, laughing, a cigarette holder jutting from his mouth — myth and propaganda, shame and reality, death and a great stillness on the land, these and the tens of thousands like them are the images that are part of the national memory, perhaps the most permanent and personal legacy we have from that time, proof, perhaps, that it belongs to us now in a way that it belongs to no other people.

■ *A Generation of Memory*

We can look upon these images and find a measure of pride in the psychic durability and character of the men and women who survived the world they reflected; the images are part of what might be called the emotional inheritance of the Great Depression, a demonstration of spirit. But there is another kind of inheritance, one that speaks to what this nation has become as an institution, and it was forged in the heart of the era out of an amalgam of fear, despair, anger, and the passion of idealism.

Make no mistake: if the imagery of the Great Depression is essentially true, it is because there had been nothing in the American experience to prepare its people for the dimensions of what had ripped through the fabric of the nation, and there has been nothing since that truly compares to it. It was the worst of times, a terrible, scarring experience that changed this country and its people forever.

Consider fear. Even if they did not lose their jobs or go hungry themselves, even if the terror of want passed over them without touching them, most Americans felt its passage like a cold, unforgettable wind. We do not always give that impact the weight it deserves, perhaps understandably. The past half-century has witnessed its own share of hard times, of panics and recessions and even a stock market crash of no mean dimensions in October of 1987. And the generations that preceded the thirties were punctuated by the sometimes terrifying vagaries of boom and bust — for example, the panics of 1837 and 1857, or those of 1873, 1893, 1907, or even that of 1921–22. Each of these earlier disasters left the nation's economy staggering, ruined thousands, added to the rolls of pauperdom, inspired labor unrest and all manner of social upheaval.

There were those even in the heart of the Great Depression itself who cautioned Americans to assume a certain cosmic distance from the whole business. "I do not wish to minimize the extreme seriousness of the present situation," the respected historian James Truslow Adams told readers of the October, 1931, issue of *Reader's Digest,* "but I wish to consider it intellectually and not react to it emotionally. . . . When we compare the situation today . . . in relation to the previous great depressions, I think we may say that, instead of giving way to despair, we have considerable cause for thankfulness." But even as Adams wrote, cities were running out of relief money, people were rioting for food, others were suffering all the diseases that malnutrition encourages, still others were starving to death; people were living in culverts, under bridges, on park benches, in anonymous doorways; thousands of jobs were disappearing daily.

There was nothing of the abstract in the pinched and anguished lives of millions of ordinary Americans who would find themselves dead up against it as the depression spun a web of terrible uncertainty through most of the decade. Most would never forget its power, and a whole generation would carry its memory like a shadow that followed them into all the decades of their lives. "The Depression was a way of life for me, from the time I was twenty to the time I was thirty," Chicago schoolteacher Elsa Ponselle remembered. "I thought it was going to be forever and ever and ever. That people would always live in fear of losing their jobs. You know, *fear*."

Fear was the great leveler of the Great Depression. It haunted the dreams of the African-American sharecropper in the South who held a fistful of barren dust in his hand and wondered what the system would do now to cheat him and his family of life. It stalked the middle-class white merchant in Idaho who had seen decades of work destroyed when his once-friendly banker coldly forced him into bankruptcy. It whispered terror into the ear of the Mexican-American foundry worker in Detroit who had put his future in the hands of the *coyote* who brought him north from Mexico into this strange cold place and who now found his job vanished. Fear shattered all the fine Anglo-Saxon certitudes of the Great Plains farm wife who watched black clouds of dust roll up on the edge of the horizon and knew that her dreams would soon be sucked up into that boiling mass. Fear even tweaked the nerves of those too rich to be harmed by economic hardship itself, as they looked around at the financial ruin and entertained dark fantasies of revolutionary hordes boiling up to seize control of their world. Banker J. P. Morgan, for one, decided to put his yacht in mothballs for a while. "It seems very unwise to let the 'Corsair' come out this summer," he wrote a friend in October, 1931. "There are so many suffering from lack of work, and even from actual hunger, that it is both wiser and kinder not to flaunt such luxuriant amusement in the face of the public."

Most middle-class Americans — and those who aspired to the middle class — would not have been overwhelmed by Morgan's sensitivity. Bankers, once considered the pillars of whatever community in which one happened to live (though not always in the usually overmortgaged Midwest), were more often seen now as being among the principal villains of the national disaster. Because of the stock market crash of 1929 and the thousands of bank failures that brought so many of them to ruin, Americans would learn to nurture a permanent distrust of the "financial community" — banks, trust companies, and, above all, brokers of speculation. Workers, farmers, and other identifiable groups had risen up to shout against heartless bankers and rapacious speculators before, but this time faith in the very virtues of thrift and responsibility to which white, middle-class America had given its heart was shattered. The world of money had not merely failed, it had betrayed an implicit trust. One of cartoonist Rollin Kirby's most effective editorial drawings of 1931 depicted an unemployed man ("Victim of Bank Failure") sitting disconsolately on a park bench. He had nothing to feed even the squirrel sitting in front of him begging for peanuts. "But why didn't you save some money for the future when times were good?" the squirrel asks. "I did," the man replies.

Much of the rest of the business world would be tarred by the same brush of betrayal, and over the course of the ten years following the crash of '29, the corporate world would find itself ringed about with restrictions and regulations whose main purpose was not to promote its interests, as government actions in the past had usually done, but to protect the American people from its excesses. If such restrictions would never fully accomplish all that they were supposed to do, and if the federal government would exercise its duty with a diligence that tended to vary according to transient political needs and conflicting ideologies, the fact remained that unfettered capitalism had enjoyed its last hurrah. The Great Depression would witness the blossoming of the regulatory state, whose stipulations have since multiplied to influence the daily activities not only of the stock market and major industry, but small businesses as well, laying down rules regarding interstate commerce, workplace safety, pollution emissions, wages, hours, and working conditions, and all manner of other edicts designed to limit what the business community may and may not do. It is a state which the liberal tradition in America still insists is necessary to ensure that the freewheeling excesses of the past will never be repeated and that the average citizen will be protected from cheats, frauds, and exploitation. The conservative tradition, on the other hand, still rails against the regulatory state as an anathema that has sucked the country dry of enterprise, crippled the production and distribution of goods, and placed an impossible burden on the shoulders of small business and gargantuan industry alike — though not even the antiregulation efforts of the Reagan and Bush administrations were able to seriously diminish the role of federal regulations in the workaday world of capitalism.

If corporate America would lose some power during the Great Depression, "the people" would gain some. Indeed, the very concept of "the people" — that political convenience that had been part of America's electoral grabbag ever since Andrew Jackson's day — would take on a degree of reality it had never before possessed. Up to the era of the depression, even the most significant expression of "pure" democracy in American history — the populism of the 1890s — had been a good deal less than fully inclusive; populism was largely the child of southern farmers, "free-money" advocates, and some labor leaders, and if a few African Americans and others outside the mainstream were given a part in the movement for a short time, the alliance soon enough had succumbed to ancient prejudices.

While there was a certain amount of agitation bubbling even in the generally apathetic twenties, it was not until the years of the Great Depression that people fully began to understand and exercise the political and economic power of cohesion. There is a good deal in the pages that follow of the role of the Communist Party/USA in the turmoil of the thirties, but it should not be understood that the Communists either invented or defined the character of the various reform movements of the era. They helped such eruptions, in some cases even led them, but it was not necessary to invent them. Driven by the terrible imperatives of economic disaster, fear combined with anger to produce perhaps the truest expression of grass-roots activism in American history, and the story of the Great Depression is punctuated by moments when "the people," in one incarnation or another, seized and validated their own measure of hope.

It was hope, after all, that drove people to acts of courage and determination. When black men and women steeled themselves to defy the system that had kept them in slavery and then peonage for three hundred years in the South; when Mexican-American migrant workers put their lives on the line under the relentless sun of California's San Joaquin Valley by striking for decent wages and against living and working conditions that rivaled those of czarist serfs; when a second-generation "bohunk" risked the malevolent wrath of Henry Ford's thugs and put his name on a UAW petition in River Rouge, Michigan; when a poor white "linthead" in a textile mill in South Carolina shut her loom down and walked out, head high and heart pounding — when people rose to moments like this, they were acting not merely in desperation and fury, but in the hope that in doing so they were taking hold of their lives and changing them for the better.

The continuing existence of that hope is one of the most enduring legacies of the Great Depression. It was the same hope that fired the civil rights movement in the fifties and sixties and the American Indian movement, the Chicano movement, and the women's rights movement of the seventies; it was this hope that drove Cesar Chavez and the Mexican-American field workers of California to attempt to replicate in the sixties and seventies the great agricultural strikes of the thirties; it was that hope that gave rise to environmentalism as a modern political power, that gives strength to the movement for gay rights, that continues to fire all the other disparate elements of our society who want the protection or power of law.

That hope has become a permanent part of the national life, and not a little of its durability derives from the fact that in the Great Depression, for one of the few times in American history, a presidential administration would take as its modus vivendi the desire to help the people — *all* the people, including the disadvantaged and disenfranchised. For all their differences, their sometimes massive personality flaws, their moral lassitude at too many points of crisis, their arrogance and self-righteousness, Franklin Roosevelt and most of the agglomeration of individuals collectively known as the New Dealers felt a genuine empathy with the needs and dreams of ordinary Americans and would work hard to relieve their pain and confusion — and in the process would help to change the very character of the democratic process.

For one thing, with their whole-souled dedication to social planning, particularly as represented by such projects as the Tennessee Valley Authority or such social programs as those of the Resettlement Administration, the New Dealers would reinforce the newly discovered faith in the virtues of collective action. The ideal of individualism had marked the world of the twenties; it was the individualistic genius of men like Thomas Alva Edison or Henry Ford that had made them cultural icons, after all, and it was the very *singleness* of his exploit that had made airman Charles Lindbergh the definitive popular hero of the age when he crossed the Atlantic all by himself in 1927. But individualism, it now appeared to millions, had brought disaster upon the nation by encouraging the wildcatters of speculation and endorsing the socially irresponsible actions of self-centered industrialists who cared for nothing but the dimensions of their profit margins — and the people be damned. By the end of the thirties, the great mainstream hero would be the ultimate organization man — the FBI's J. Edgar Hoover, the "G-Man" who led his collectivist cops in pursuit of such rank individualists as John Dillinger. In everything from federal land-management agencies to labor unions, from ethnic self-help groups to

Communist cells, individualism would be stifled by the collectivist urge to join together in common cause for the common good.

Above all, the New Dealers would personalize the federal government. Taken by itself, this was a kind of revolution. Not even the varyingly progressive philosophies that had informed the administrations of Theodore Roosevelt and Woodrow Wilson had put forth the notion that Americans should be affected on so many levels so much of the time by programs conceived and administered in the bureaucratic warrens of Washington, D. C. But during the Great Depression, the federal government would become a living part of American society. Its massive relief efforts in the early years of the New Deal, however frantically administered, were acts of mercy that would be felt and remembered on very personal levels. The work and work-relief programs of the Public Works Administration, the Civilian Conservation Corps, the National Youth Administration, and the Works Progress Administration would make the federal government the primary employer for millions of people. The passage of such landmark legislation as the Social Security Act, with its permanent dent in the paychecks of every American, would make it certain that the government would continue to play a role in the lives of millions for generations to come. And if the national government that evolved from these years is not quite the monolithic welfare state that the conservative tradition would have us believe, it nevertheless has become and doubtless will remain inextricably bound with the everyday life of everyday Americans — largely because in spite of all the speechifying to the contrary that bellows forth from within and without Washington, D. C., that is precisely the kind of government we want.

The role of President Franklin Roosevelt would be a major part of this institutional metamorphosis. The very nature of the presidency itself would change during his activist administration, the executive branch gaining more real power in the function of government than it had previously enjoyed, a power that no president since has seriously attempted to relinquish, though there has been a good deal of rhetoric to the contrary. The nation is still dealing with both the virtues and the problems of what some observers have called "the imperial presidency." Beyond that, however, the personality of Roosevelt as a human being would enlarge (and, some would insist, distort) the character of the presidency as it was viewed by the American people. "My mother looks upon the President as someone so immediately concerned with her problems and difficulties," a man wrote at the time, "that she would not be greatly surprised were he to come to her house some evening and stay to dinner," and the tears that were shed by millions of Americans upon his death in 1945 were those of people who felt that they had lost not merely a President, but a friend.

Whether the emergence of an activist, domestically ubiquitous national government headed up by a fatherly president was good or bad still depends upon the ideological baggage its interpreters bring to the discussion. One thing is certain, however: most Americans would swiftly grow accustomed to a new kind of intimacy between themselves, their government, and, especially, their president. There is something of the depression years in the quadrennial yearning millions of Americans still demonstrate in their desire for the modern equivalent of Franklin Delano Roosevelt — and in the depth of disappointment they still feel when time after time no comparable figure rises up to lead this nation out of whatever economic, political, or moral quagmire in which it finds itself. All American presidents since the thirties, one way or the other, as historian William Leuchtenburg has noted, have been touched by the shadow of Franklin Delano Roosevelt.

Even when the snarl of intimacy became confrontational, the New Deal government and Roosevelt still would be perceived on a deeply personal level — they became *intimate* enemies, held accountable for their actions more directly than ever before in the nation's history. The relationship has survived sporadic attempts to weaken or even obliterate it ever since. Its presence more or less intact helps to explain why Americans still invest so much hope in the possibilities of their presidents and their government and exercise so much anger when they believe either or both have failed them.

Finally, it must be said that if the people found hope again in the New Dealers, the men and women who swarmed to Washington during the bitter late winter of 1933 would bring with them their own baggage of hope. Playwright Sherwood Anderson was not officially one of the New Dealers, but he articulated their expectations as well as anyone. "If there is to be a new world," he wrote in 1932,

> we want it to be an American world. Many of us are looking forward to a new time of restlessness. There is much hidden just under the surface. There may well come soon now . . . a time of protest, of wide discussion, of seeking. There may be a new literature, a new romantic movement, new religious impulses. If the machine has really made for us a new world we may at any time now begin the movement of trying to go into the new world. God grant it may be a better world.

If the Great Depression would begin as a time of horror, then, it would end as an era in which Americans had attempted to make real the possibilities of hope and validate the best that was in us as a society. If too many of those hopes guttered out in disappointment, the fact did not diminish the power they had while alive to help reshape American life, and if this book is about those people in that time, it is very much also about our people in our time — for what we are is what they became.

The Prologue Years

*The future work of the business man is to teach the
teacher, preach to the preacher, admonish the
parent, advise the doctor, justify the lawyer,
superintend the statesman, fructify the farmer,
stabilize the banker, harness the dreamer, and
reform the reformer. . . . The business world is full
of born crusaders. Many of the leaders would be
called martyrs if they weren't rich.*

Edward Earl Purinton,
The Independent, April 16, 1921

CHAPTER ONE

Overleaf:
*On November 11, 1918, after more than four
years of horror, World War I ended. It was
the bloodiest conflict in modern history. A
minimum of 10 million and as many as
20 million people had died, including more
than 100,000 American soldiers out of the
2 million who had been shipped "over there"
after America's entry into the war in the
spring of 1917. Among those who fought and
lived to return and march in relief and
triumph up Fifth Avenue in New York were
the members of the 369th Infantry, the
"Harlem Hell-Fighters."*

N FEW OTHER PERIODS of American history can one find a decade whose beginning and end were more sharply defined by events than the twenties. The era began with the armistice of November, 1918, the climax to the bloodiest war in modern history up to that time, and ended with the stock market crash of October, 1929, beginning the most devastating economic collapse in modern history. Unfortunately, the era that lay between those two gargantuan events is not so easily defined, for it was at once one of the most colorful and least understood periods in the American chronicle. After nearly three generations of popular history, our collective memory has been colored on the one hand by depictions of flappers and lounge lizards, bootleg gin and backseat sin, movie madness and gangland murders, flagpole sitters and Wall Street gamblers, and on the other by portrayals of a stultifying cultural conformism, religious fundamentalism, materialistic self-centeredness, business worship, and rank bigotry.

All of which was true, so far as it went, but it did not go far enough. The fact is, if women marcelled their hair and took up cigarettes, if men learned the fraternal joys of golf and the Kiwanis Club, if millions of people drank perhaps more than they should have in the heady sinful atmosphere of Prohibition, became addicted to the evangelical fundamentalism of cults like Amy Semple MacPherson's Four Square Gospel, bought gramophones and radios and learned the new dance crazes, went to the movies once a week to see the latest Mack Sennett or Harold Lloyd comedy, followed the antics of the rich, flamboyant, adventurous, and criminal in the local press — even if millions of people toyed with any or all of these, most Americans most of the time did not consider themselves part of the parade of the twenties, even though an increasingly garish and inescapable mass media made it nearly impossible to ignore all the noise and circumstance.

They did not keep late hours, most Americans, nor did they race around in the pursuit of sexual liberation. They went to church, got married, and generally stayed married (the divorce rate remained stable throughout the decade). The challenge of getting food on the table and keeping the family going during any given day took up most of the psychological and intellectual resources of most Americans. In 1926, the average worker still spent nearly forty-nine hours a week on the job and brought home only a little over $26. There was neither the disposable income nor the disposable time for ordinary people to jump gaily into the dance of the twenties.

But there was time and energy enough for dreaming; in no previous period of American history had there been such a psychic investment in

Barrels of bootleg liquor are smashed at a New York curbside. "Mother's in the kitchen/Washing out the jugs," a bit of doggerel went. "Sister's in the pantry/Bottling the suds;/Father's in the cellar/Mixing up the hops;/Johnny's on the front porch/Watching for the cops."

In 1926, a sociologist said that the movies, more than any other form of entertainment, created "a reckless lack of appreciation of true values. . . ." In this scene from an obscure jazz-age epic, Alice White cavorts to the reckless appreciation of her cinematic audience.

Like the movies, radio
broadcasting came of age in
the twenties. By the end of
1927, some 680 stations
around the country were
broadcasting to 2.3 million
radio sets. The airwaves
were so overcrowded that
signals interfered with one
another, frequently
becoming entwined to the
point that, the Federal
Radio Commissioner said,
"the listener might suppose
instead of a receiving set he
had a peanut roaster with
assorted whistles." RIGHT:
awed children crowd around
a set in 1923; ABOVE, a
customer checks out the
quality of reception the
latest table-top model gets.

the Lorelei of possibility. World War I may have killed more than 112,000 American soldiers, but it also had accelerated the engines of industry as never before in the nation's history; after a brief postwar recession, the American economy flowered to become a monster of production and profit. The dream that glimmered through much of the decade, then, was that of measureless prosperity, prosperity for all — almost inevitable prosperity, if you were born of the proper color (white) and class (firmly middle). And even if you had not been so blessed, if you were a Polish dishwasher or a Hispanic field hand or a black coal miner, the dream insisted, *some* splash of affluence surely would spill over into your lap from the great pool of wealth whose sources seemed inexhaustible, replenished endlessly by the great world of business, guardian of the national estate. So you were told by the president of the United States himself, Calvin Coolidge, who said that business was "one of the greatest contributing forces to the moral and spiritual advancement of the race." So you were told, over and over again, by newspaper pundits, magazine articles, books, radio broadcasts, and an advertising industry that never stopped selling, day or night. And if that was not enough, there was the evidence of your own eyes and experience — the millions of automobiles that were changing the character and quality of where and how you lived, the ready availability of electricity and tele-phones, the millions of radios that were so cheap now that almost anyone could afford to tune into the world, the mass production of household appliances and conveniences that transformed the meaning of housework. Not all of this, or even most of it, might be yours yet, but there was every reason to hope that it soon would be.

The Death of Progressivism

This self-centered material dream, a bill of goods sold from every secular pulpit, almost completely overwhelmed those progressive instincts that had improved much of American society since the turn of the cen-tury — instincts that had reformed child labor laws, created pure food and drug laws, liberalized the political process, encouraged labor organization, put some restraints on industry and capitalist excess, protected forests and other natural resources, given women the vote. Political and social reform had begun to decline during the jingoistic years of World War I, when a frenzy of patriotism and self-sacrifice exhausted even the progressivism of President Woodrow Wilson, one of the champions of Democratic liberalism. Wilson, who might have been expected to return to his reform efforts after the war, did not do so; he was too sick and too obsessed with his fruitless crusade to get the United States to ratify the Treaty of Versailles and join the League of Nations (predecessor of today's United Nations). By then, most Americans had had their fill of self-sacrifice; they were ready to embrace the individualistic dream of pursuing the main chance. In 1920, the presidency fell to the Republicans under Warren G. Harding, whose administration would prove to be one of the most corrupt in American history, and, after Harding's death in 1923, to Calvin Coolidge, and after him to Herbert Hoover, both of whose administrations were squeaky clean compared to that of Harding, but no less committed to individualism and the material dream.

With daily needs to be met, with the hope of prosperity dangling before them like a carrot, with the memory of the millions of young men who had died for God, country, and idealism during World War I coloring their attitudes with cynicism, millions of adult Americans simply lost interest in reform politics — or politics of any kind, for that matter. "Oh, all this talk is just wasted energy," Dr. Will Kennicott, the male protagonist of Sinclair Lewis's iconoclastic 1920 novel *Main Street*, "told" the author during a fictional return to "Gopher Prairie" for *The Nation* in 1924. "You know and I know that Coolidge is going to be elected. Be better if they called the election off and saved a lot of money, and damn the Constitution! Why, nobody is interested, not one doggoned bit." The cheerful apathy of the fictional Dr. Kennicott was reflected nationwide. In 1920, only 49.2 percent of the electorate had voted in the presidential election, an all-time low up to then; the figure fell again in 1924 to 48.9 percent, and while it rose to 56.9 percent in 1928, that figure was still far below the average of all preceding decades since the 1820s. Part of the decline in percentages could be attributed to women. They had received the right to vote in 1920, after decades of sometimes violent struggle, but during the first few years after suffrage, women voted in far smaller percentages than men.

With few political or social reform movements to restrain them, some of the ugliest tendencies a democracy can foster were left to flourish, among them an almost paranoid isolationism. The thousands of Americans who had died on the battlefields of Europe and the billions of dollars that had been loaned to the allies by this nation, millions of Americans believed, had both been bad investments — wasted on nations who could not control their own people. It was this antipathy that had defeated Wilson's efforts to get the United States to join the League of Nations, and it would color much of middle-class America's attitude toward the torn and bleeding nations of Europe. Safety, this attitude held, lay in keeping ourselves protected from the turmoil and strange political upheavals across the Atlantic, particularly from the horror of Russia, where the Bolshevik Revolution of 1917 had brought socialism to power.

But full "protection" was next to impossible. Some Americans saw in the events of 1917 the last best hope of a world that had been burdened for centuries by the twin yokes of royalism and capitalism, and they embraced the tenets of communism, which held, among other things, that both the machinery and the rewards of production should be taken from the ruling capitalistic class and placed in the hands of those who did the actual producing — the workers, otherwise known as the proletariat. These and other idealistic radicals would be periodically suppressed through official actions like the roundups and deportations instituted by Attorney General A. Mitchell Palmer during the so-called Red raids of 1919, but they could never quite be eliminated. Throughout the twenties an embryonic Communist Party/USA, instructed and at least ostensibly controlled by the Comintern in Moscow, agitated feebly against all the capitalistic certitudes of the material dream, a small but permanently irritating thorn in the side of conservatives everywhere, who tended to react to any challenge from any quarter with charges of "Bolshevism."

The problem, conservatives generally maintained, was all those foreigners. For all the fact that it was founded, settled, and populated by a diverse mix of ethnic and national groups, and in spite of the inspiring words of Emma Lazarus on the Statue of Liberty that told the world to send over their "huddled masses yearning to breathe free," this nation has rarely welcomed strangers with wholehearted enthusiasm, particularly strangers who are not just like the rest of us; even today, when "multiculturalism" has become one of the buzzwords of the politically correct, many Americans turn a jaundiced eye on the arrival of boat people from Cuba and Haiti and "illegals" from Mexico and Central American countries. In the twenties the fear was much more intense, fired by a terror that American institutions would be subverted by uncontrollable foreign elements.

There were, in fact, a great many of the "tempest-tossed" who entered the United States after the end of the war, waves of immigration not unlike the huge populations that had washed up on these shores during the latter third of the nineteenth century and the first years of the twentieth century. Between the end of 1919 and the beginning of 1924, more than 600,000 people from southern Europe, most of them Italians, entered the United States, together with about 150,000 Poles, 50,000 Russians, and 150,000 people from other nations of Central and Eastern Europe — not to mention nearly 175,000 Mexicans. With the exception of the Mexican immigrants, most of whom would drift into the rural areas of the Southwest, the great

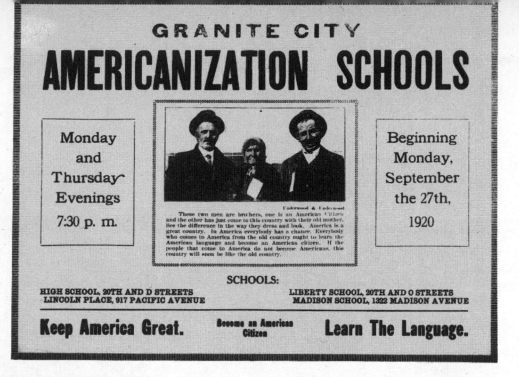

GRANITE CITY
AMERICANIZATION SCHOOLS

Monday
and
Thursday
Evenings
7:30 p. m.

Underwood & Underwood

These two men are brothers, one is an American Citizen and the other has just come to this country with their old mother. See the difference in the way they dress and look. America is a great country. In America everybody has a chance. Everybody who comes to America from the old country ought to learn the American language and become an American citizen. If the people that come to America do not become Americans, this country will soon be like the old country.

Beginning
Monday,
September
the 27th,
1920

SCHOOLS:

HIGH SCHOOL, 20TH AND D STREETS
LINCOLN PLACE, 917 PACIFIC AVENUE

LIBERTY SCHOOL, 20TH AND O STREETS
MADISON SCHOOL, 1322 MADISON AVENUE

Keep America Great.   Become an American Citizen   **Learn The Language.**

To hasten the day when immigrant cultures were supposed to melt into the great American pot, "Americanization schools," like those in Granite City, Illinois, were established all over the country. The melting pot, however, never did bubble fiercely enough; what resulted from the mix of cultures was less a soup than a stew.

During the wartime years and the twenties, a "Great Migration" of African Americans from the Deep South sang "Good-bye Bo, I'm bound for the promised land," and left their tenant farms and plantation hovels to head north — as did this migrating family, photographed in 1917.

In the extraordinary panorama on these and the following pages, a 1924 Ku Klux Klan rally demonstrates the banality of the KKK's particular evil. The scene could be of a county fair or any number of summertime events common to the region — except for the white-sheeted figures marching up and down or running back and forth on mysterious errands. Anxiety over the perceived "Un-Americanism" of an increasingly urbanized

society with its uncertain morals and throngs of foreigners —
especially Jews and Catholics — had combined with bigotry
and racism to revive the old Klan, which by the end of 1924
was claiming some nine million members. Within another year
the organization would be in pitiful decline, betrayed by the
uncertain morals and sordid financial shenanigans of its own
leadership.

bulk of these boatloads of human beings would settle in the urban areas of the Northeast and Midwest.

All these people put considerable pressure on the political, economic, and social systems of the communities in which they lived, many of them already strained by the influx of millions of African Americans from the South during the "Great Migration" of the war and prewar years. This stew of people gave the cities an unsettled and polyglot character that only exacerbated the long-standing distrust that most rural Americans felt for the urban scene, which many rigidly Protestant folk insisted already was dominated by Jews with their presumed sly monetary ways and rumored control over the financial institutions of the country and by Catholics whose obeisance to the Pope was absolute, whose morals were questionable at best, and whose political corruption was legendary.

It was such bigotry that figured largely in the passage of the McCarran Act of 1924, which severely restricted all future immigration to these shores, putting special emphasis on limiting the number of Jews and Poles, Slavs, Russians, Italians, and other insufficiently Anglo-Saxon or Nordic-Protestant types. Somewhat more dramatically, rural fear of urban foreigners also gave rise to a resurgence of the Ku Klux Klan, a collection of bigots who deplored "race-mixing," Jews, and Catholicism in about equal portions, marching around in white sheets and pointed hoods, burning crosses, kidnapping and whipping their victims, and otherwise acting out a perverse version of the affection for fraternal organization that was another characteristic of the twenties. Although it had its origins as a nativist movement against the freedom and empowerment of black people in the years following the Civil War, the reincarnation of the KKK in the twenties was most dominant in the rural and small-town Midwest, where it enjoyed the largest single contingent of a membership that, according to its own numbers, reached nine million (including a 125,000-member women's auxiliary called Women of the Ku Klux Klan). Until its leader, Grand Dragon D. C. Stephenson, fell from power when he was tried and convicted of murder in 1925, after which the organization rapidly declined to a tiny pathological knot, the Klan was a profound influence in the Midwest, completely dominating the state politics of Indiana and striking understandable fear into the hearts of African Americans, Jews, Catholics, and anyone else who did not fit the organization's definition of a true American.

Taking the Golden Bait

While most Americans did not march, demonstrate, or run around dressed up in white sheets, the decade of the twenties was still one of the most thoroughly repressive eras in our history, comparable in its tone, if not its precise nature, to the years that followed World War II, when anti-Communist Cold War warriors like Senator Joseph McCarthy cheerfully trampled on the Constitution in search of subversion. This is not to say that no one was speaking up. Many blacks, Hispanics, Jews, Asians, other ethnic groups, workers, political dissidents, and women refused to suffer the victim's role in silence. The young Communist party was agitating where and when it could, and labor initiated some strikes, like those in the steel and coal-mining industries in 1919. Ethnic groups organized into neighborhood, city, regional, and even national bodies to protect their interests. B'nai B'rith and its Jewish Anti-Defamation League attempted to counter the chronic anti-Semitism that permeated much of this Christian society. Some women founded the League of Women Voters, others began agitation for passage of an Equal Rights Amendment to the Constitution, still others broke into the ranks of business, while Margaret Sanger accelerated her work for birth control. The Brotherhood of Sleeping Car Porters, the most powerful black union in the country, was formed, and the National Urban League and the National Association for the Advancement of Colored People stepped up their work, with W. E. B. Du Bois and his *Crisis* magazine speaking for liberation, while Langston Hughes, Countee Cullen, Alain Locke, and other lights of the "Harlem Renaissance" translated the black experience into literature. In the Southwest, Mexican-American workers carried their organizing skills from the mines, mills, smelters, factories, and farm fields of Mexico to those of their new home.

The results these groups achieved were minimal, at best, and most Americans remained as sublimely unaware of all the agitation as they were of higher mathematics. Even if they had been interested to learn, there were few who were interested in telling them about it. The press in all its forms — including the just-emerging phenomenon of broadcast journalism — took little notice of social unrest, unless it was to deplore or ridicule it. There were more interesting things to talk about in these Roaring Twenties, and not all of them were as monumentally insignificant as the joys of flagpole-sitting, the intricacies of bridge or mah-jongg, the sexual habits of the rich or famous, goings-on in Hollywood, bathing beauty contests, and all the other fads and furbelows that regularly ornamented the columns of newspapers and the pages of magazines.

For years there was a wondrous game to be played, at least for those with the time and money to play it, and the popular press followed and reported its antics with the attentiveness of acolytes. The game was speculation, the definitive material dream of the era of material dreams. Speculation as an enterprise is the child of available capital, and during most of the twenties there was a great deal of capital loose in the land. The richest Americans were very rich indeed, and after buying their homes, automobiles, superheterodyne radio consoles, furs, jewelry, household appliances, fashions, and all the other treasures offered by a mass-production industrial culture, they were still left with a lot of money. Like many less-fortunate citizens, they put much of it away; bank deposits increased from $17.4 billion in 1914 to $52.7 billion in 1928, and many kept their money there, watching it quietly earn interest at 2 or 3 percent.

The less cautious had a look around at more attractive possibilities. At the potential in southern California, say, where a constant barrage of come-hither-to-Paradise advertisements and inducements after World War I would bring no fewer than 1.3 million new residents to the region before the end of the decade — one of the largest internal migrations in American history. Those people needed houses to live in and the houses needed subdivisions to be put in and the subdivisions needed roads and shopping areas to service them. The result was a real estate boom of dizzying proportions: in 1919, the total value of real estate permits in Los Angeles had been $28 million; by the end of 1923 it was more than $200 million, and in the interim fourteen hundred housing tracts had been laid out. Too many, warned the creator of fashionable Westlake Park: "We have enough subdivisions and lots for sale and in process of development to accommodate the cities of New York, Philadelphia, and Detroit." He was exaggerating, but by the end of 1924 there were more lots than buyers; banks pulled in their loans and the boom died amid the rustle of bankruptcy papers.

There was still plenty of money left, so when the glories of Florida real estate began to be touted in the spring of 1925, investors dismissed the California experience as a terrible exception and started pouring money onto the sandy peneplain of the Sunshine State. By the end of the year, Miami sported two thousand real estate offices employing twenty-five thousand agents, each and every one of whom was more than happy to tell the story of the strip of land in Palm Beach that had grown in value from $240,000 in 1923 to $1.5 million in 1924 and an estimated $4 million in 1925. There were many other stories like that, but, as in California, not enough. The inevitable deflation of the boom began to be felt in the autumn of 1926, but before the California experience could be fully duplicated, a hurricane screamed in and wiped out much of the real estate involved, not to mention some four hundred people.

The speculative urge was stalled by these experiences, but not stifled, and it soon enough found an even better arena. "The Stock Exchange,"

After years of lobbying and demonstrations, like this wintertime
suffragette parade in New York City, women had won the vote
in 1920 and were otherwise beginning to assert their rights as
human beings and citizens, which is not to say that a new age
had yet begun. If the work of the American Birth Control
League helped to lower the birth rate from 27.7 per thousand in
1920 to 21.2 in 1929, its leader, Margaret Sanger,
OPPOSITE, TOP (fourth from left), still spent a lot of energy
trying to avoid jail for the crime of promoting contraception.
On other fronts, young women suffered the indignity of arrest
in Chicago in 1922 for daring to challenge the city's ban on
abbreviated bathing suits.

Princeton economist Joseph Stagg Lawrence declared grandly, "is the stage whereon is focused the world's most intelligent and best informed judgment of the values of the enterprises which serve men's needs. It is probable that upon this stage can be discovered the aristrocracy of American intelligence."

Few investors cared to argue with that conclusion, and between about 1923 and the end of 1929, the cathedrals of exchange in Los Angeles, San Francisco, Chicago, Baltimore, Cleveland, Philadelphia, and — the grandest of them all — Wall Street in New York, became the loci of a speculative frenzy that had not been matched since the "Tulipomania" of Holland in the seventeenth century. Indeed, without distending the imagination much, one could have used Charles Mackay's 1841 account of the tulip madness as a description of the stock craze of the twenties:

> The tulip-jobbers speculated in the rise and fall of the tulip stocks, and made large profits by buying when prices fell, and selling out when they rose. Many individuals grew suddenly rich. A golden bait hung temptingly out before the people, and one after the other, they rushed to the tulip-marts, like flies around a honey-pot. Every one imagined that the passion for tulips would last forever.

It was in a similar context that the "Great Bull Market" expanded like a flowering nova in 1928 and 1929, driven by a kind of mass madness not unlike that which had raced through the tulip markets of Holland. In 1927, there had been 577 million shares traded on the New York Stock Exchange; in 1928, the figure was 920 million. The pace accelerated during the first nine months of 1929; indeed, between August and September transactions on the floor of the New York Exchange were already speeding toward the 1.1 billion shares that would end the year. (By comparison, in 1919, the biggest boom year since 1900, total shares had been only 317 million). "There have been bull markets before," the *New York Times* editorialized, "but the present one surpasses them all, having been taken up at a time when brokers' loans had become swollen and when stocks selling at $200, $300, and $400 a share had multiplied tremendously."

Numbers like that may seem insignificant today, when more than three hundred million shares can change hands on any given day and billions of dollars in value go up or down in a matter of hours. But for the time, such figures were extraordinary, magical, intoxicating. What was more, any number could play, and as many as a million did. They were, most of them, amateurs, fair game for the insiders. They bought stock, most of it on margin (10 percent down and learn to pray) through so many broker's loans that by September, 1929, the total amount loaned out by brokers had skittered up from $3.2 billion to $8.5 billion (by comparison, the entire federal budget for that year was only $3.1 billion). On their lunch hours, they crowded into the customer's rooms of the brokerage houses to watch their money, "feverish young men and heated elders, eyes intent upon the ticker tape." Twenty percent of them, it was estimated, were women no less feverish; these sat with other women in special rooms put aside for their use, as if the excitement of watching the ticker tape could explode into sexual frenzy if the sexes were allowed to sit together.

Stock pool geniuses like Michael J. Meehan, armed with investment capital from a variety of individuals, manipulated the hopes of the amateurs like the master of a shell game; during one week in March, 1928, for example, Meehan drove the price of the Radio Corporation of America up from $90 to $109 a share, then quickly sold out, netting his investors a total of $5 million and himself a handler's fee of $500,000 — and the rest of the buyers a handsome loss, as RCA's stock dribbled back down to $87 before those not on the inside understood what was happening. Investment trusts were productive, too. In December, 1928, for example, Samuel Insull, the utility king of Chicago, created Insull Utilities Investments (IUI), traded enough stocks in his other companies to assure control of the trust, then put IUI shares on the market at $12. In January, 1929, the value jumped to $30, by the end of spring to $80, and by the end of summer to $150. Stocks in the rest of his companies rose in a kind of sympathetic increase and by the end of September his personal wealth was estimated at $150 million. "My God," he exclaimed to an associate. "A hundred and fifty million dollars! Do you know what I'm going to do? I'm going to buy me an ocean liner!" Instead, he formed another investment trust. So did a lot of entrepreneurs. By the beginning of 1929, one a day was being organized and by September there were more than five hundred — building nothing, manufacturing nothing, selling nothing but paper shares in their paper selves.

Much of the available capital in the United States and much of that in the entire world was sucked into the market. To an important extent, during the bull months of 1928 and 1929, the market had *become* the economy. This worried some people, like President Herbert Hoover, who in April, 1929, publicly issued warnings against stock speculation while wiring his own broker to sell a number of stocks, "as possible hard times coming." Others were just as wise, if a good deal less honest. In August, Wall Street mogul John J. Raskob wrote an article for the *Ladies' Home*

Journal, "Everybody Ought to Be Rich," which stated that anyone could be worth $80,000 in ten years if he or she invested a mere $15 a week in the stock market. He knew better. Since the turn of the year he had been slowly and quietly dumping most of the stocks in his own portfolio, while making widely quoted public statements that helped to keep prices high enough to maintain his profitable sales.

And none too soon. After tremendous early gains, September's prices began to slide, until by the end of the month the leading issues on the New York Stock Exchange had lost $2.8 million. The market continued to stall, stutter, and surge during the first weeks of October. Still, on October 17, Irving Fisher, professor of economics at Yale, announced that prices had reached "what looks like a permanently high plateau" and said that he was confident that in a few months the plateau would be "a good deal higher than it is today."

No, it wouldn't. One week later, on Thursday, October 24, brokers were overwhelmed with sell orders the minute the doors of the New York Stock Exchange opened. Everything starting dropping ten, twenty, even thirty points. A consortium of large investors managed to stem the tide for a while by buying up large blocks of stock at prices higher than those on the floor; by closing, the average loss among the leading stocks had been held to only ten points. But 12.9 million shares had been traded that day and the tickers did not stop their chattering until 7:08 P.M. Friday and Saturday (a half-day) were relatively calm, but on Monday 9.9 million shares were traded for a loss of $14 billion. Then Tuesday, October 29: in the first thirty minutes, 3.2 million shares were traded; by noon, 8.3 million; by 3:00 P.M., closing time, a staggering 16.4 million.

Loss for the day: $15 billion. Loss for the month: $50 billion. Since Labor Day, the leading industrial stocks in the United States had lost 40 percent of their value.

■■■ *Attack of the Microorganisms*

The ten years that followed the crash of '29 constituted the age of the Great Depression, the effects of which would be found and felt in all levels of American society. But effect is more easily plucked from history than cause, and the truth is, we still do not know with any overwhelming certainty why it was that the biggest and most productive economy on the planet inexorably disintegrated during the three years after the closing gong sounded on the floor of the New York Stock Exchange on October 29, 1929.

Only on one point does there seem to be general agreement: the stock market crash itself did not "cause" the Great Depression. More accurately, as Robert McElvaine has argued,

> When someone becomes ill after "catching a chill," it is not the cold itself that causes the sickness. Rather the cold reduces the body's resistance to microorganisms already present in it, which then are able to cause the illness. Some such role is the proper one to assign to the Crash. The cold wind that swept through lower Manhattan in October and November 1929 lowered the economy's resistance to the point where already existing defects could multiply rapidly and bring down the whole organism.

What, then, were some of the microorganisms that moved to sicken the body economic of the nation? The instability of the world economy created by World War I was one such. Before the war, Great Britain was the world's creditor nation; after the war, the United States assumed that role. Between 1914 and 1918, American loans to the allied nations totalled some $11 billion, and during the postwar years foreign investments by the United States reached $15.7 billion. Nearly a third of that went to Europe, much of it in the form of loans, including a series of loans to Germany that would enable it to make reparations payments to the European allies as called for by the Treaty of Versailles. Those reparations payments, in turn, would enable France, England, and Belgium to pay back the billions in loans the United States had made during the war. Even more important, the loans would stimulate the growth of the European economy and enable it to buy food and goods from the United States.

So the theory went. But that economy was still fragile and neither the reparations payments nor the loan payments had come anywhere near being satisfied by 1928, when the stock market infatuation seriously depleted the amount of capital available for foreign investment. This made it increasingly difficult for European consumers to buy American goods in the numbers American producers needed. The crash itself, of course, depleted American investment funds even more, which further reduced the buying power of the European consumer, which further weakened American exports. In the face of a shrinking market, American industry sprang into action immediately: it demanded protectionism, and got it in the form of the Hawley-Smoot Tariff Act of 1930. The purpose of the law was to prevent foreign goods from undercutting American goods on the domestic market by charging such a high tariff on imports that they would be too expensive to compete. Unfortunately, since an already staggering European market could not ab-

STAGE BROADWAY SCREEN

VARIETY

PRICE
25¢

Published Weekly at 154 West 46th St., New York, N. Y., by Variety, Inc. Annual subscription, $10. Single copies, 25 cents.
Entered as second-class matter December 22, 1905, at the Post Office at New York, N. Y., under the act of March 3, 1879.

VOL. XCVII. No. 3   NEW YORK, WEDNESDAY, OCTOBER 30, 1929   88 PAGES

WALL ST. LAYS AN EGG

Going Dumb Is Deadly to Hostess | **DROP IN STOCKS** | **Kidding Kissers in Talkers Burns**
In Her Serious Dance Hall Profesh | **ROPES SHOWMEN** | **Up Fans of Screen's Best Lovers**

Panic: Wall Street devotees, OPPOSITE, *gather outside the
New York Stock Exchange on October 24, 1929, checking the
early editions to learn the dimensions of the "egg" that Variety
was talking about,* ABOVE.

$100. WILL
BUY THIS CAR.
MUST HAVE CASH
LOST ALL ON THE
STOCK MARKET

*Humorist Will Rogers reminded everybody that Wall Street was
"located in the sharp end of New York. . . ." Among those who
had forgotten was Walter Thorton, who was forced to sell his
snappy roadster.*

sorb its own productivity, much less that exported to it by the United States, the loss of its American market accelerated the collapse of the European financial structure and the Great Depression swiftly became a worldwide disaster, not merely an American one.

Among those American goods that could not be sold at desired levels was agricultural produce. American farmers had enjoyed perhaps the greatest boom in their history during the war years. All farm products had shared in the good times, but nothing had compared to the surge in wheat production and value. In 1910, with prices at an average of 91 cents a bushel, 625 million bushels of wheat had been produced on 45.8 million acres. In 1915, a shade over a billion bushels had been produced (the largest yield in history) on 60.3 million acres. The boom had accelerated still further after passage of the wartime Food Control Act, which had imposed a minimum price of $2.00 per bushel — more than double what the farmers had been getting.

This was the stuff of purest avarice; speculation in land and commodities sped through rural America like a prairie fire gotten out of hand. *Wallace's Farmer*, the industry's bible, complained that farmers had been so busy "sitting around the livery stable and playing games with options" that they had not had time to work the land they had been speculating in. Not that all were experienced farmers. In 1922, an economist examined speculation-farming in eastern Montana and discovered that the tillers of the soil included "two circus musicians, a paper hanger, a sailor, a seagoing engineer, two wrestlers, two barbers, a cigar maker, a race horse man, a bricklayer, a deep-sea diver, six old maids, a milliner, and a professional gambler."

The farmers financed much of the frenzy by mortgaging and remortgaging their properties, encouraged in this excess by equally infatuated local banks. The debt load became horrendous, rising from $3.2 billion in 1910 to $8.4 billion in 1920, with annual interest payments alone increasing from $203 million to $574 million. Still, wheat farmers in particular continued to plant and produce for the rest of the decade as if the boom were going to continue forever. All this might have made some sort of sense if prices had held. They did not. From $2.19 per bushel in 1919, wheat prices dropped to less than a dollar in 1922 and finished 1929 at only $1.05. Other commodity prices suffered similar declines, while taxes on all farm property increased by nearly a third, labor and transportation costs climbed steadily, and the cost of living for farmers as for anyone else continued to rise through the decade. In 1929 the annual per capita income for the nation at large was $750; for farm people it was only $273. Even before the Hawley-Smoot Tariff Act slammed the door on much of its export market, then, the agricultural industry was teetering on the thin edge of collapse — and failure was ready to spread like Spanish influenza when the chill of October, 1929, descended.

Overproduction in general, as a matter of fact, was one of the largest microorganisms whose poisons were set free by the crash. We prided ourselves on being the most productive nation on the planet. More and better goods were produced at greater speed and efficiency during the twenties than at any time in history. In the ten years between 1919 and 1929, the productivity output per worker in manufacturing rose an astonishing 43 percent. But this was a good thing only if the producers could sell what they made or grew — and, increasingly during the twenties, they could not. They could not sell enough of it abroad and, even more significant, they could not sell enough of it at home. Wages increased slowly during the decade, but not at a rate anywhere near the rate of production; increasingly, workers could not afford to buy the very goods they were producing.

The blame for at least some of the widening gap between wages and productivity during the twenties could be laid to the decline in unionism, because without organized labor to exercise some pressure, most employers were not inclined to pay wages any higher than they felt they could afford — and that was nowhere near parity with increased profits. The triumph of industrial Republicanism after the end of the war had nearly killed the labor movement, which had been pictured by the business world and much of the national press as violent, radical, dominated by foreigners and Bolsheviks, antagonistic to the capitalist ideal, inherently un-American, and, not least, expensive. It and its most repellent expression, the closed shop — a factory or business in which all working men and women were required to be members of a union — should be stamped out. "You can hardly conceive of a more un-American, a more anti-American institution than the closed shop," Gus W. Dyer of the National Association of Manufacturers had said in 1920. "It is really very remarkable that it is allowed to exist . . . under the American flag." To put an end to that disgrace, the great industries had put in motion a campaign for what they called the "American Plan" — the universal adoption of the union-free open shop — and had been supported in this ambition at most levels of government. "So long and to the extent that I can speak for the government of the United States," Warren Harding's attorney general, Harry Daugherty, had proclaimed in the days before his own disgrace in the Harding scandals, "I will use the power of the government to prevent the labor unions of the country from destroying the open shop."

The weight of armament brought to bear on unionism and the closed shop had been overwhelming. From the municipal level to the federal level, the judicial system had cooperated by using injunctions to stifle union organizing, strikes, picketing, boycotts, and other expressions of union support with devastating effectiveness. Local police had been more than willing to cooperate with the industry's own security forces to prevent union men from entering the workplace and to break strikes with swift and decisive violence.

Against industry's concentrated determination and the government's anti-union bias the labor movement was as nearly helpless as at any time in its history. Nor could it be said that it presented a solid front of resistance. The American Federation of Labor (AFL), headed by an aging Samuel Gompers, who had stitched it together in 1886 and would rule it until his death in 1924, had established itself as the ruling body over a collection of skilled trades and by the time of World War I had earned an unprecedented measure of cautious respect from both business and government. Union membership under the AFL had climbed to a high of nearly 5.1 million by 1920.

But Gompers and the AFL were essentially conservative, dominated by the traditional crafts and not eager to challenge the entrenched power of postwar capitalism. A more militant faction in the AFL — led by a beetle-browed and roaringly eloquent John L. Lewis, president of the United Mine Workers — began to challenge Gompers's policies, and after the old man's death in 1924 the struggle between Lewis and Gompers's successor, William C. Green, became a corrosive eating at the core of solidarity. Raddled by such internal bickering and under constant assault from without, unionism languished. Membership plunged from its high of 5.1 million in 1920 to 3.6 million in 1923 and would dribble down to 3.4 million in 1929.

If unionism had shrunk, corporate America had blossomed — at least in the size of individual entities and in the salaries and other benefits of those who sat at the top of them. In the decade following the war twelve hundred mergers swallowed up more than six thousand previously independent companies, and by 1929 some two hundred corporations controlled almost half of all American industry. The fewer companies, the less competition, the less competition, the less incentive to keep profit margins down — and federal tax policies took very little of that profit. As a result, most of the personal wealth in the country resided in the pockets, bank accounts, and stock portfolios of a tiny percentage of the population.

But goods had been produced for the millions, not for the thousands, and the millions, in the end, simply could not afford them. The surge of installment buying after the war had obscured the essential weakness in the system for a time, but by 1929 even a burgeoning consumerism had not been enough to carry the burden of overproduction. If you were bringing home a hundred dollars a month or less, there were only so many payments you could make for so many toasters or vacuum cleaners or radio sets or automobiles, no matter how tempting they might be, no matter how cunningly an increasingly sophisticated and ubiquitous advertising industry might present them; you either stopped buying, or you defaulted. And people began to stop buying. During the two months before the crash, production declined at an annual rate of 20 percent, wholesale prices at a rate of 7.5 percent, and personal income at a rate of 5 percent — the first major symptoms of the virulence to come.

Then there had been the banking system. Before World War I, banks had been relatively stable operations; between 1900 and 1920, the number of state and national banks grew from 14,054 to 30,909, and in those twenty years only 1,789 failed. Perhaps it had all been too easy, for hundreds of banks were too slovenly managed to survive the more rapid, complex, and temptingly speculative economic world of the postwar years. From an average of less than 90 a year from 1900 to 1920, the number of failures rose to 505 in 1921, fell to 367 in 1922, and from then until the end of 1929 averaged 691 a year. In 1925, the Louisiana Banking Commissioner took a look at the failures in his state and penned an assessment that could have served as an indictment of the entire system. "[G]ross and evil management," he said, "poor management, promotion of speculative enterprises, loans without security, too large loans, loans to companies in which officers were interested, were the major causes of bank failure."

In 1928, special emphasis could have been placed on "promotion of speculative enterprises" as a poor management tool, for the bankers — who already had encouraged the southern California and Florida real estate follies of 1924 and 1925 — had become willing partners in the stock market extravaganza. The banks, one banker remembered, had "provided everything for their customers but a roulette wheel."

So the wheels of speculation had slowed, then stopped, and the material dream of the prologue years had ended in the silence of ruin. It was up to the survivors now to sift through the wreckage to find what they could that would help them build a new world. There was plenty of wreckage to go around.

The Shadow of the Hawk

Our family are in bad shape children need milk women need nourishments food shoes and dresses — that we cannot get. and there are least 10,000 hungry People in Harlan County daily. I know because I am one of them. . . . I would leave Harlan County if I only had $6.00 to send my wife and boy to Bristol-Va. and I could walk away — But I can't clear a dollar a month that is why I am here. . . . I borrow this postage to send you this informations.

Kentucky coal miner, *The Nation,*
June 8, 1932

CHAPTER TWO

Overleaf:

"[The] way to the nation's greatness is the path of self-reliance," President Hoover intoned in May, 1931, and it remained his fond conviction that free enterprise and individual charity could handle the worst of the depression. Many Americans tried to meet the challenge — including the women shown making contributions to the mayor's "relief barrel" in Detroit, Michigan. In the end, the dream of self-reliance proved a cruel impossibility.

ORDON PARKS WAS sixteen years old in 1929, a young black man trying to work his way through high school in St. Paul, Minnesota, as a bellboy at a downtown club for white businessmen. One Wednesday afternoon, a notice was tacked to the employee bulletin board: "Because of unforeseen circumstances, some personnel will be laid off the first of next month. Those directly affected will be notified in due time." This puzzled Parks until the next day, Thursday, October 24, when the evening papers broke the news of the crash. "I read everything I could get my hands on," he recalled,

> gathering in the full meaning of such terms as Black Thursday, deflation and depression. I couldn't imagine such financial disaster touching my small world; it surely concerned only the rich. But by the first week of November I . . . knew differently; along with millions of others across the nation, I was without a job. . . . Finally, on the seventh of November I went to school and cleaned out my locker, knowing it was impossible to stay on. A piercing chill was in the air as I walked back to the rooming house. The hawk had come. I could already feel his wings shadowing me.

While only a small percentage of the public was directly affected by the collapse of the stock market in October, 1929, it was still a moment of history shared by nearly every American. Like the Japanese attack on Pearl Harbor or the assassinations of John F. Kennedy, Martin Luther King, Jr., and Robert Kennedy in our own time, the crash was a point of reference for those of that time. People took the measure of their era by using the crash as an emotional baseline, and it became the one event on which tens of millions could fix their worry as the full dimensions of the debacle slowly began to be discerned. Gordon Parks was not the only one who felt the shadow of the hawk.

President Herbert Clark Hoover, though, apparently remained oblivious to that shadow — or if he felt it, did not want to acknowledge it. Unemployment had grown from about 1.5 million to at least 3.2 million in the five months since the crash, but on March 7, 1930, Hoover gave the American public the results of his own analysis of the situation. "All the evidences," he said, "indicate that the worst effects of the crash upon unemployment will have passed during the next sixty days."

A more accurate measure could have been found in an unnamed

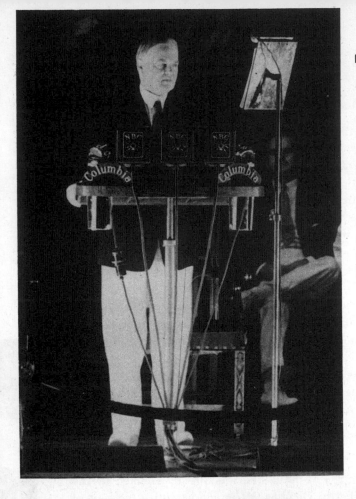

Hoover, campaigning for re-election in 1932, stubbornly refused to believe that the depression was anything but a temporary setback. "We have now passed the worst," he announced in early March, 1930, "and with continued unity of effort we shall rapidly recover." The worst, however, had only begun.

To a middle class that had been reared on the virtues of thrift, nothing was more devastating than a bank failure — and no failure was worse than that of December 11, 1931, when New York's Bank of the United States collapsed.

"No one has yet starved" was a favorite phrase of the comfortable, including President Hoover, and in October, 1930, Republican senatorial candidate Dwight Morrow opined, "There is something about too much prosperity that ruins the fiber of the people." It was, Edmund Wilson said upon reading Morrow's fatuous statement, "a reassuring thought . . . that the emaciated men in the bread lines, the men and women beggars in the streets, and the children dependent on them, are all having their fibre hardened." For millions, soup kitchens provided the only food they would see all day, and some of the hungry and the helpless in Chicago were happy to accept soup and bread from the kitchen established by gangster Al Capone in one of the famous thug's sporadic attempts at public relations.

southern city that Sherwood Anderson visited that same month. The writer spent some time standing outside a big basement soup kitchen, where on a single day he watched seven hundred people go inside to get fed. He was struck by the number of those who did not want him to know their hunger. The man, for example, who approached the soup kitchen three times before swallowing his pride and going down the steps. "I am not here for soup," he told Anderson, who had not said a word. "I came here to meet a friend." Or the young woman who asked him where the soup kitchen was. "I do not want any soup," she assured him when he obliged. She just wanted to say hello to some of the women who were serving the needy. "They are friends of mine."

"They were Americans, such people as you and I," Anderson wrote. "I stood watching them. I was ashamed of my warm overcoat, my stout shoes.

"I made men ashamed standing there."

Most of those who were still coming to the soup kitchen six months later, as the first anniversary of the crash approached, probably would have put little or no faith in anything Herbert Hoover said on the subject of what was now being called, openly and increasingly, a depression. Unemployment had not declined; it had risen, implacably, and in another six months would hit at least 7.5 million. And they would have found plainly incomprehensible the confidence of Rome C. Stephenson, vice president of the American Bankers' Association, if they had heard the pep talk he gave his fellow bankers in downtown Cleveland on September 30. The bankers should not worry, Stephenson said, because business was about to get better. The slump, he insisted, was largely a matter of misperception:

> The depression of the stock market impressed the general public with the idea that it would depress general business. Because of a psychological consequence, it did, but it should not have. There are 120,000,000 persons in the country and at the maximum not more than 10,000,000 were involved in stock-market transactions. The remaining 110,000,000 persons suffered no loss.

The bulk of the American population may not have suffered the loss of stock investments, but there were plenty of other ways to calculate loss, and by the end of 1929, with unemployment rising, with shops and factories suddenly ornamented by Closed or Out of Business signs, and, perhaps most terrifying of all, with scores of banks failing and taking with them millions of dollars in deposits (which were at that time uninsured), the "general public's" confidence in the financial health of the country and the wisdom of its leaders was shaky at best. Confidence fell even further when 256 banks failed in the single month of November, 1930, and further yet on December 11, when the United States Bank, with deposits of more than $200 million, went under. It was the largest single bank failure in American history up to that time, and contributed no little portion to an economic hangover in which, in the words of banker J. M. Barker, "cupidity turned into unreasoning, emotional, universal fear."

■■■■ *Fighting for the Scraps*

There was reason enough for fear. The 1,352 banks that failed in 1930 represented more than $853 million in deposits. In 1931, 2,294 banks went under, with deposits of nearly $1.7 billion. In 1930, 26,355 businesses failed, and the rate of 122 failures per 10,000 was the highest ever recorded up to that time. Both numbers were surpassed in 1931 with 28,285 failures and a rate of 133. The 451,800 corporations still in business in 1932 had a combined deficit of $5.64 billion. The value of all farm property declined from $57.7 billion in 1929 (itself down from a high of $78.3 billion in 1920) to $51.8 billion in 1931. By the end of 1931 unemployment had climbed to 8 million and in a few months would be approaching 12 million.

There had never been such statistics in our history, and there have been none like them since. Their truest meaning, the effect they had on individual human lives, could be seen everywhere, as people struggled blindly and bravely to survive. Which is not to say that everyone was willing to see them for what they were. Like those who attempt to dismiss the homeless of our own day as aberrations, not indications, of the nation's economic condition, many of the pundits of the depression years spent a lot of time explaining away the presence of the poor and the hungry. These were temporary phenomena, it was said, transient indications of a momentary lapse in economic health. Many of the people were not even victims — they were just beggars too lazy or too ignorant to work. But the deprived of the depression years were even more difficult to ignore than the doorway sleepers and street-corner panhandlers of modern America. They could not be explained away, because they would not go away — and their numbers grew day by day, week by week. Like a plague, the disease of deprivation spread with such speed and across so many lines that there were few families in the United States who did not either experience or witness its pain. When neighbors you had known all your life were found one morning with all their furniture stacked on the sidewalk, nowhere to go, no hope in sight, it did not take much imagination to see yourself standing there with them.

You did not even have to be especially vulnerable to feel the power of deprivation. Daniel Willard, president of the Baltimore & Ohio Railroad and in no danger of having his furniture stacked on anybody's sidewalk, for instance, received an honorary doctorate at the University of Pennsylvania in June, 1931, but instead of mouthing the usual platitudes on this happy occasion, burst out with a jeremiad against the very economic system that had made him rich:

> A system — call it what you will — under which it is possible for 5,000,000 or 6,000,000 of willing and able-bodied men to be out of work and unable to secure work for months at a time, and with no other source of income, cannot be said to be perfect or even satisfactory. . . . I would be less than candid if I did not say in such circumstances I would steal before I would starve.

"No one is going hungry and no one need go hungry or cold," President Hoover still insisted in the winter of 1931. Willard would have disagreed. So would Louise V. Armstrong. "We saw the city at its worst," she wrote in *We, Too, Are the People* (1941). "One vivid, gruesome moment of those dark days we shall never forget. We saw a crowd of some fifty men fighting over a barrel of garbage which had been set outside the back door of a restaurant. American citizens fighting for scraps of food like animals!"

"Why does Every Thing have exceptional Value Except the Human being," one destitute person wrote the president, " — why are we reduced to poverty and starving and anxiety and Sorrow So quickly under your administration as Chief Executor. Can you not find a quicker way of Executing us than to starve us to death."

On Chicago's South Side, wandering reporter Edmund Wilson took a look at the old Angelus Building, a tottering, stinking wreck of a place whose owner would have demolished it if he had found the money to do so. It was now stuffed with black people who could afford to live nowhere else. The place, Wilson said, was

> seven stories, thick with dark windows, caged in a dingy mess of fire-escapes like mattress-springs on a junk-heap, hunched up,

hunchback-proportioned, jam-crammed in its dumbness and darkness with miserable wriggling life. . . . There is darkness in the hundred cells: the tenants cannot pay for light; and cold: the heating system no longer works. . . . And now, since it is no good for anything else, its owner has turned it over to the Negroes, who flock into the tight-packed apartments and get along there as best they can.

In an Appalachian Mountains school, a child who looked sick was told by her teacher to go home and get something to eat. "I can't," the girl replied. "It's my sister's turn to eat."

The city fathers over in Muncie, Indiana, did not like to think of people being that hungry in their all-American town. Muncie, after all, was the "Middletown" of the famous 1929 study by Robert S. and Helen Merrell Lynd, and was generally proud of it, too. But by the spring of 1932, the layer of confidence with which the city had consistently blanketed the depression began to grow a little tattered. That year, a Muncie businessman later told the Lynds, "people would go around saying in low tones, 'Have you heard that they're boarding up the so-and-so plant?' And a few days later, 'Have you heard that so-and-so-many trucks of machinery were moved out of town today? They say that half the floor at the plant is stripped already.' It got on our nerves as this went on!" The plant in question was a General Motors assembly plant, and by the end of the summer it had indeed stripped its floors of machinery, closed down, and left Muncie.

New Orleans did its best to keep reality from the door, too. Unemployment was greatly exaggerated, a writer to the letters column of the *Times-Picayune* said in February, 1930, a rumor spread by a "host of fly-speckers, calamity howlers and woe-be-tiders [who] are barnacles on prosperity," but a week later an estimated three to four hundred men showed up to answer a single classified advertisement for work available in Texas. When the advertisement turned out to be a fraud, the crowd started a small-scale riot and the police had to be brought in to put it down.

Out in Yavapai County, Arizona, depression was even harder to ignore for long. Hundreds of men who had been laid off from the copper mines in the southern part of the state wandered north to the vicinity of Prescott. During the summer of 1932, they spread "out into the hills and mountains in the hope of placer mining and getting a few cents a day out of the gravel-bars that were worked fifty years ago," Prescott poet Sharlot

In the mountain communities of the Appalachians, whole families were reduced to dandelions and blackberries for their basic diet. Some children reportedly were so hungry they chewed on their own hands, and even apparently adequately fed children like these shown in a Tennessee schoolroom were almost certainly malnourished; twenty percent of American children were not getting enough of the right things to eat.

"Hoovervilles," tattered communities of the homeless, coalesced in and around every major city in the country, like this vast squalid complex in Seattle, Washington.

By the end of 1930, thousands of schools were operating on reduced hours or were closed down entirely; some three million children between the ages of seven and seventeen had left school. At least 200,000 took to the roads and the rails, like these boys, OPPOSITE, posed as if in the act of hopping a freight. Such wanderers were "vague and lonely," one of them said, "ever on the move." They joined hundreds of thousands of others. "Expectant mothers," Newton D. Baker reported in the New York Times Magazine, "sick babies, young childless couples, grim-faced middle-aged dislodged from lifetime jobs — on they go, an index of insecurity, in a country used to the unexpected. We think of the nomads of the desert — now we have the nomads of the depression."

Hall wrote a friend in June. "Sometimes they really do pan out a few cents — or once in a while get a dollar or more — but the old diggings are very lean of gold. . . ." Others were trying the same thing up in Nevada, where in one lonely canyon a reporter found a man shoveling dirt into a primitive riffle chute to wash out gold. "Me a minin' man?" he replied when asked. "Yes, I'm a miner — all of ten weeks now. Before that, I'd been a sailor all my life. Now it's a simple case of 'root, hog, or die, so I'm rootin'.' "

Hundreds of thousands of people were on the move by then. The Southern Pacific Railroad estimated that its "railroad bulls" had thrown as many as 683,000 transients off its boxcars in a single year. At least 200,000 of the transients were adolescents, most of them male but with no small number of females among them. In the summer of 1932 sociologist Thomas Minehan began a study that took him on the road with young tramps and hoboes. Most of them, he noted, traveled in gangs for safety, an especially important consideration for the young women among them. "Girls in box cars," he wrote, "are not entirely at the mercy of any man on the road whatever their relations with the boys may be. In event of loneliness or illness, the boys and girls have friends to comfort and care for them."

One of the tramps with whom he traveled for a time was a Pennsylvania Dutch boy nicknamed Blink — so named because he had lost an eye when a live cinder blew into his face while he was riding an open car on the Santa Fe railroad. "A bloody socket forms a small and ever-weeping cave on the left side of his face," Minehan wrote. "Tears streak his cheek, furrowing the dirt and coal soot, leaving a strange moist scar alongside his nose." The boy showed Minehan a diary he had been keeping since August, 1932, when he had run away from an abusive father. The entry for September 10 was eloquently typical:

Slept in paper box. Bummed swell breakfast three eggs and four pieces meat. Hit guy in big car in front of garage. Cop told me to scram. Rode freight to Roessville. Small burg, but got dinner. Walked Bronson. N. G. Couple a houses. Rode to Sidell. N. G. Hit homes for meals and turned down. Had to buy supper 20 cents. Raining.

Young and old, male and female, the transient army drifted in a dark caravan of desperation from hobo jungle to hobo jungle, city mission to city mission, begging for leftovers at the back doors of homes, panhandling for pennies on city sidewalks, stealing chickens where chickens could be found, cooking up "mulligan" stews out of whatever could be boiled into edibility, being seduced and raped, thrown into jail, beaten by yard bulls. Those homeless who did not drift — and there were thousands in every city of any size at all — slept in lice-ridden and rat-infested flophouses when they could afford the ten or fifteen cents for a urine-stained mattress on the floor, and on park benches, under park shrubbery and bridge abutments, in doorways, packing crates, concrete pipes, culverts, construction sites, and abandoned automobiles when they could not afford it. The more ambitious among them contrived fragile shelters from scraps of wood and cardboard, old beer signs and fence posts, anything they could find that would keep off the wind and rain of winter and the direct sun of summer. They built them anywhere they could, but most of the time on the outskirts of cities and towns big enough to have outskirts, where outlandish villages began to coalesce like ramshackle suburbs. Everyone called them Hoovervilles; it was not a term of endearment.

▬▬ The Limits of Charity

Like most of his contemporaries — and, indeed, most of the American middle class — if President Hoover believed in anything more profoundly than the virtues of self-reliance and individual initiative, it has not been recorded. This was, after all, the very ethos of a white, Protestant culture, the image that Hoover and his kind held up as the ideal of Americanism. Hard work, honesty, and independence, they believed utterly, had brought this country to the forefront of nations, had built a breed of men (and women, too, some conceded, though not often) who had taken the institutions of the founding fathers and made them the wonder of the world. Anything that might weaken the strength of that tradition would weaken the very character of America and was, by definition, evil. Government charity, especially, by robbing people of initiative, would be the very embodiment of error. The national government should stay out of the personal lives of its citizens, even if they were in trouble. For Hoover and for the millions of Americans who shared his convictions, the idea that people would turn to Washington, D. C., to help them out of a bad spot was nearly unthinkable.

It was a hard theory, but part of the accepted wisdom of the time and difficult for Hoover to abandon even in the face of the present situation.

Still, when the dimensions of the crisis reached proportions that simply could not be ignored, he did not, as is often supposed, coldheartedly refuse to do anything about it. What he did do, for the most part, was call upon the natural generosity of the American people and the paternalism of local governments. Throughout his term he held to the firm belief that direct aid to the individual was not the business of the federal government — unless there were no other course, in which case he made it clear he would act, though almost certainly in great fear of permanently crippling the national character. "This is not an issue as to whether people shall go hungry or cold in the United States," he said in a statement to the press in the winter of 1931.

> It is solely a question of the best method by which hunger and cold shall be prevented. . . . I am willing to pledge myself that if the time should ever come that the voluntary agencies of the country, together with the local and State governments, are unable to find resources with which to prevent hunger and suffering in my country, I will ask the aid of every resource of the Federal Government. . . . I have faith in the American people that such a day will not come.

In the meantime, Hoover authorized the expenditure of about $700 million on various public works projects. He also set up the Reconstruction Finance Corporation, which in early 1932 began doling out the $2 billion that Congress had appropriated to stimulate and prop up industry and agriculture in their time of need. The RFC was one of the few such efforts that amounted to much (it would survive to become one of the most powerful agencies in New Deal Washington). The National Business Survey Conference, for instance, was designed to "market" an optimistic feeling in the business community and as part of this goal its members took a solemn vow not to cut wages. Defections were almost immediate. The National Credit Corporation, for another example, was designed to set up a system whereby healthy banks would assist unhealthy banks; few did, and the NCC virtually collapsed in two years. The Federal Farm Board, created before the depression, was designed to stabilize farm prices through the temporary purchase of surplus farm produce; it managed to lose some $345 million and satisfied no one. The President's Emergency Committee for Employment (PECE) and its successor, the President's Organization for Unemployment Relief (POUR), were largely designed to promote the belief that things were not as bad as they appeared to be and even if they were they would soon get better; neither managed to get the message across with any great success — though the POUR was useful in helping local agencies and private charities raise money by getting pro bono advertisements placed in newspapers and magazines.

It must be said that many Americans tried to sustain self-reliance, as Hoover advised. Probably the best-known examples were the apple sellers who for a time appeared on the sidewalks of nearly every major city. In the fall of 1930, the hard-pressed International Apple Shippers Association came up with the idea of selling apples to the unemployed on credit at $1.75 a crate. The apples would retail on the street at a nickel apiece and if a seller got rid of all the apples in his or her crate, the net could be as much as $1.85. By the end of November, 1930, there were six thousand apple sellers on the streets of New York City alone, crouching, in the words of newspaperman Gene Fowler, "like half-remembered sins sitting upon the conscience of the town." Down in New Orleans, the same device was tried with Louisiana oranges — "Health for You — Help for the Needy," the *Times-Picayune* declared. While people at first responded with sympathy to these peddlers, they were altogether too visible a reminder of the nation's troubles; sales fell off drastically in a few months — not aided in the slightest by Hoover's peculiar public assertion at one point that "many persons left their jobs for the more profitable one of selling apples."

Many people tried to "maintain the spirit of charity" and the dogma of self-reliance in other ways, and many local governments struggled valiantly to meet the crisis themselves, as Hoover so fervently wished. Nothing worked for very long, even in the most successful instances. In Seattle, for example, a few Socialists got together and formed the Unemployed Citizens' League in July, 1931. The organization swiftly grew to a membership of somewhere between forty and fifty thousand. The UCL organized numerous self-help projects — cutting wood on donated land, picking unwanted fruit crops, fishing in Puget Sound, setting up commissaries for the distribution of food and wood, negotiating with landlords to prevent evictions, and putting together a kind of barter economy in which members exchanged services and goods. In response, Seattle mayor Robert Harlin formed the Mayor's Commission on Improved Employment to work with the UCL, and when a million-dollar bond issue was raised to finance it, put the leaders of the UCL in charge of the District Relief Organization. The UCL remained the principal distributor of food and work to the city's estimated forty-five thousand unemployed until the money began to run out.

In Philadelphia, it was the rich who organized, and for a time it seemed that the city would stand as the perfect model for Hoover's vision of private-public cooperation at the local level. On November 7, 1930, the Committee of One Hundred of the city's most influential people met for lunch at the Bellevue-Stratford Hotel and formed the Committee for Unemployment Relief, with Horatio Gates Lloyd, a partner in Drexel and Company, the Philadelphia branch of the House of Morgan, as its chairman. In order to "tide over the temporary distress" of the depression, the committee immediately raised $4 million, which Lloyd parceled out to various private charities. The committee also persuaded the Pennsylvania General Assembly to authorize the city to borrow $3 million for public relief. A municipal Bureau of Unemployment was established and Lloyd himself was put in charge of the distribution of its public funds. Like that of the Socialists in Seattle, the philanthropists' effort in Philadelphia was a great success — for as long as the money held out. The $7 million in private and public money was exhausted by November, 1931. A "United Campaign" raised another $10 million in cash and pledges; Lloyd's committee got $5 million of that, and in three months it, too, was gone, as was the remaining $5 million that had gone to other agencies. In April, 1932, the city got another $2.5 million in direct aid from the state; that was gone in two months. The Lloyd Committee, the *Philadelphia Record* reported on June 20, "is through. For fifty-seven thousand families to whom the Committee has meant life itself, it added, playing on the Hoover administration's assurances that "prosperity is just around the corner," "STARVATION is 'just around the corner.' "

Voluntarism had not worked in Philadelphia, and neither it nor self-reliance would be enough anywhere they were tried. They certainly were not enough in those states in which one of the worst droughts in history gave the overall economic calamity an almost biblical character. The hardest hit was Arkansas, which in July and August, 1930, received only 4.19 inches of rain — 35 percent of what it had gotten during the same two months the previous year — but rainfall in another twenty-two states in the Midwest, Great Plains, and South also dropped by an average of nearly 40 percent in those two months. "The families that are suffering now, or on the verge of it," the Red Cross representative for Arkansas wrote national headquarters in August,

> are not singled out as by flood or tornado or fire, but are just in their homes, with gardens ruined, sweet potatoes not making a crop, the prospect of being in debt to the landlord when the pitiable cotton crop

is gathered instead of having money with which to buy food and clothing for the winter.

Hoover immediately formed another committee — several committees, in fact. At a conference of governors from the affected states on August 14, he told them that they should establish local and state drought committees to handle the problem. For the most part, he insisted, local communities were going to have to carry the burden alone. Furthermore, he believed that the Red Cross should provide the lion's share of any help beyond that. During the terrible floods in the southern Mississippi River Valley in 1927, the Red Cross had stepped in and brought relief to hundreds of thousands of people whose homes and lives had been devastated. The organization had sheltered the homeless, fed the hungry, had helped thousands of people to survive the disaster. Surely, it could do so again.

But the drought of these years was not a single, isolated event like a flood; it had gone on for a long time already and would go on for some time to come, and its disruptive effect was magnified by the larger economic situation which the Red Cross would not have been in a position to do anything about in any event. The organization's institutional inadequacy to accomplish what Hoover expected of it was compounded by the philosophy of its leader, national chairman Judge John Barton Payne. Payne was a close friend of Hoover's and shared the president's reverence for self-reliance. He made it clear from the start that the local and state Red Cross chapters would depend on volunteers and money from the local and state regions, and only under the most extreme circumstances would the national organization step in to help.

The system thus established was more efficient at withholding aid than in furnishing it. The state and local Red Cross chapters, like the state and local drought committees, usually were headed up by the "best people" who had been part of the oppressive plantation system for generations, and were prepared to think the worst of those who sought direct help. Many people worried that if food were distributed, workers might refuse to pick cotton at the wages plantation farmers were willing to pay. "Some, you know," the Red Cross chairman for Monroe County, Arkansas, wrote in early September,

> are ready to let the Red Cross do it all, we think after the cotton is out we can raise some money, and as the worst is to come in the cold winter months, we think it best to postpone doing only what is abso-

"I'll see it through if you will!"

"THEY tell me there's five or six million of us—out of jobs.

"I know that's not your fault, any more than it is mine.

"But that doesn't change the fact that some of us right now are in a pretty tough spot—with families to worry about—and a workless winter ahead.

"Understand, we're not begging. We'd rather have a job than anything else you can give us.

"We're not scared, either. If you think the good old U. S. A. is in a bad way more than temporarily, just try to figure out some other place you'd rather be.

"But, until times do loosen up, we've got to have a little help.

"So I'm asking *you* to give us a lift, just as I would give one to you if I stood in your shoes and you in mine.

"Now don't send me any money—that isn't the idea. Don't even send any to the Committee which signs this appeal.

"The best way to help us is to give as generously as you can to your local welfare and charity organizations, your community chest or your emergency relief committee if you have one.

"That's my story, the rest is up to you. "I'll see it through—if *you* will!"

—*Unemployed, 1931*

THE PRESIDENT'S ORGANIZATION ON UNEMPLOYMENT RELIEF
Walter S. Gifford
Director

COMMITTEE ON MOBILIZATION OF RELIEF RESOURCES
Owen D. Young
Chairman

The President's Organization on Unemployment Relief is non-political and non-sectarian. Its purpose is to aid local welfare and relief agencies everywhere to provide for local needs. All facilities for the nation-wide program, including this advertisement, have been furnished to the Committee without cost.
This advertisement is printed without charge by the Clayton Magazines.

A magazine advertisement produced by the President's Organization on Unemployment Relief.

BELOW: Drought recognized no color line in the heat-ravaged Arkansas Delta, where rainfall for one hundred straight days in 1930 had not "been enough to wet a man's shirt" and where poor African Americans and poor whites suffered equally in the great democracy of bone-deep poverty. "I am near at my row's end," one woman wrote the American Red Cross. "I am asking you for help or advice some way." Hampered by the reluctance of its Washington headquarters to centralize aid, the Red Cross was only partially successful in feeding and clothing thousands of victims as the winter of 1930–31 approached.

ABOVE: "I don't want your millions, mister," a song of the day went, "I don't want your diamond ring./All I want is the right to live, mister./Give me back my job again." Many tried apple-selling to avoid the shame of panhandling. In New York City alone there were as many as 6,000 apple sellers.

lutely necessary at this time, knowing that a person can get along on very little during warm weather.

By November even the planters were calling for direct aid, because they could not feed the families of their workers. Still, most local chapters continued to tell the national headquarters what it wanted to hear and people at headquarters ignored the streams of letters from the desperate, like that from an African-American farmer in Jefferson County, Arkansas:

> There is thousands of collard farmers in Jefferson and Lincoln counties that has not bread. They are Bairfooted and thin closed many has went to the County Judge and to the local Red Cross they Both say that they has no Funds We are planning on sending a Collard men to Washington to lay our Trubles more clearly before you.

Stubbornly holding to his principles, Hoover himself continued to insist that the burden of relief should be carried by the Red Cross, not the government, and he did not even support legislation that would have provided $60 million for feed and seed loans from the Department of Agriculture. And Judge John Barton Payne continued to hold back the distribution of funds from the national Red Cross. But by January the situation was so terrible that even the local chapters had abandoned the pretense that local and state resources could provide sufficient relief, and national headquarters finally responded with a fund-raising drive that began on January 10 and ultimately raised a little over $10 million. Between then and the end of the program in the spring, 2,765,000 people had been fed just enough to get them through the winter. It was pinch-penny charity at best, and no one will ever know how many suffered how much during all the months in which virtually nothing had been handed out. And since records were as carelessly managed as the relief program itself, no one will know how many died.

Some "relief" efforts did not even pretend to charity. Chief among these was the attempted deportation of Mexican Americans, which managed to combine racism with selfishness and desperation in one of the least edifying episodes in American history. By the beginning of the thirties, there was a Mexican-American, or Chicano, population in the United States of about 1.5 million, much of it the result of immigration — some legal, some not (slovenly kept records and conflicting estimates between Mexican and U. S. officials made it impossible to say how many belonged in either category). Thousands of the immigrants had gone north to work the sugar-beet fields of Michigan and the other Great Lakes states, while others had refused stoop labor as a career, moving to Chicago, East Chicago, Gary, and Detroit to look for work in steel mills, automobile plants, and other industries. By 1930 there were 19,362 Mexican Americans living in Chicago, some 9,000 in East Chicago and Gary, and another 8,000 in Detroit, where the allure of the Ford Motor Company had reached into the towns of northern Mexico to call young workers to the "wonderful city of the magic motor."

Most of the immigrants, however, had spilled into the sugar-beet and cotton fields of Texas, Colorado, and Arizona, or on into the huge agribusiness farms of the Imperial and San Joaquin valleys of California. Those who had not joined the stream of migrant labor had gravitated toward the growing Mexican-American settlements in the larger cities. The biggest of these settlements was in Los Angeles, where the Chicano population had increased from 33,644 in 1920 to 97,116 in 1930, making the city the "Mexican capital" of the United States, exhausting the bounds of the older Chicano settlements and spreading out into the neighborhoods of East Los Angeles, where it would remain the largest single segment of the city's minority population.

The bigotry exercised against these people rivaled that endured by African Americans, and when the weight of the depression began to fall upon cities with large Chicano populations, unabashed racism was buttressed by the theory that unemployment among Anglo workers could be blamed on the presence of a labor force willing to work cheap and under conditions that "real" American workers would not tolerate — the Mexican Americans. The answer, some concluded, was deportation — or repatriation, as it was described more benignly. In Gary, Detroit, and other industrial centers, open discrimination, physical threats, racist propaganda campaigns, and free transportation helped to persuade thousands of Chicanos to return to Mexico.

Nowhere was the movement more vigorous than in Los Angeles, however, where the first consignment of 6,024 *repatriados* (songwriter-activist Woody Guthrie would call them "deportees" in one of his most famous songs) left Union Station aboard the cars of the Southern Pacific Railroad in February, 1931. At $14.70 a head, it cost the city and county of Los Angeles $77,249.29 to ship them out, but the savings in relief payments for that year amounted to $347,468.41 — a net gain of $270,219.12. "In the last analysis," historian Rudolfo Acuña writes, "President Coolidge's maxim — 'the business of America is business' — was applicable, and repatriation proved profitable, at least in dollars and cents."

Over the next three years, Los Angeles County would do a pretty good business, deporting 12,688 Chicanos back to Mexico — though Carey McWilliams, who had been on hand to watch the first trainload leave Los Angeles in February, 1931, later pointed out, "Repatriation was a tragicomic affair: tragic in the hardships occasioned; comic because most of the Mexicans eventually returned to Los Angeles, having had a trip to Mexico at the expense of the county."

Elsewhere, there was little comedy, even dark comedy, to be found. In New York City, the apple sellers had vanished by the end of 1931 and by April, 1932, 750,000 people were living on city relief efforts that averaged $8.20 a month per person — about one-fifth of what it took to keep one human being decently — while an estimated 160,000 more waited to get on the rolls as soon as the money became available. In 1930, $6 million had gone for relief in New York; in 1931, $25 million; in 1932, it was estimated, the cost would be closer to $75 million. In Atlanta, the cost of relief for only thirty weeks was estimated at $1.2 million, but by December, 1931, only $590,000 had been raised and no more was forthcoming; in June, 1932, 20,000 people in Atlanta and Fulton County were simply removed from the relief rolls, most of them African Americans. In St. Louis, relief agencies were going through a quarter of a million dollars a month, and in July, 1932, the city had to drop 13,000 families off the rolls. In Fort Wayne, Indiana, the Allen County Emergency Unemployment Committee, formed in December, 1930, managed to raise enough money in its first two years to stay more or less even with the relief load. But in 1932, fund-raising targets were not met and the city's own relief expenditures began to slide. Like those in many other regions, Fort Wayne and other Allen County cities began printing their own scrip and using that as currency for goods and services within their own confines.

In Detroit, the Ford Motor Company was forced to shut down production lines on its spectacularly successful Model A. Introduced to a clamorous public in December, 1927, the Model A had taken the lead in sales away from Chevrolet, and even in 1930 the company had sold 1.4 million cars. But by August, 1931, sales were running at rates only half those of 1930, and Ford simply stopped production. Up to then, Detroit had been carrying a welfare budget of $14 million; it now was cut to $7 million, while the number of those in need of relief swelled. Similarly, a $17 million public works program was slashed to $6 million. Michigan Senator James Couzens offered to start a private relief fund with a personal donation of $1 million if Detroit's other rich people would come up with an additional $9 million; no one appeared interested.

■ *A Private Kind of Shame*

However desperate the measures taken against it by private and public agencies alike, nothing seemed powerful enough to lift the weight of the depression. For those in the middle class or those who might have hoped to work and save their way into the middle class, much of the weight was psychological. "What is surprising is the passive resignation with which the blow has been accepted," newsman Marquis Childs wrote, "this awful pretense that seeks to conceal the mortal wound, to carry on as though it were still the best possible of all possible worlds." Louis Adamic said of American workers, "I have a definite feeling that millions of them, now that they are unemployed, are licked," and many did seem to be finished, burdened beyond the bearing of it by a terrible load of guilt. They had been taught all their lives that hard work and thrift and honesty would be rewarded with at least security, if not wealth. That hope had failed them, and the fault must be in themselves; millions, Studs Terkel remembered, "experienced a private kind of shame when the pink slip came."

The architecture of despair could be seen everywhere, even among those, like most African Americans, who had been at the bottom so long that it might have seemed that nothing could possibly get any worse. But the hopes and psychic toughness of many black people, too, were tried as they had never been tried before — in the black working-class ghetto of Detroit's "Inkster," for example, where Ford Motor Company worker Odie Stallings scratched to keep his family alive.

Stallings, whose story was told in *American Odyssey*, Robert Conot's history of Detroit, had come to Detroit from Virginia after serving in World War I, joining an internal migration that had changed the face of urban America. If World War I had offered the wheat farmer of the Midwest the dream of avarice, it had given the African American of the South the dream of escape. Wartime America had needed bodies, and blacks had responded. Half a million had departed the rural South between 1916 and 1919 alone, and another million or more had migrated during the twenties. Most had found the promised land close to home — in such cities as Birmingham, Alabama, where the black population had nearly doubled in twenty years; or Memphis, Tennessee, where it had more than doubled; or Houston, Texas, where it had nearly tripled. But many of those who joined the Great Migration also had found opportunity winking at them from the Northeast and Midwest. "I'm tired of this Jim Crow," they sang, "gonna leave this Jim Crow town,/Doggone my black soul, I'm sweet Chicago bound," then had boarded trains by the carloads and headed north for Chicago, Detroit,

*Hundreds of thousands of Mexicans entered the United States in the 1920s —
most of them legally, like young Artemio Duarte, whose 1926 emigration
certificate,* OPPOSITE, *shows that he sought the American dream in San
Antonio, Texas. Many more ended up in Los Angeles, whose barrio of nearly
100,000 people in 1930 made it the largest Mexican "city" outside Mexico
itself. When the depression struck, Mexican Americans were accused of taking
jobs away from "real" Americans — and, even worse, of unfairly burdening
local relief efforts. All of this fed the flames of a nativist movement that
encouraged as many as half a million Mexican-American repatriados to return
to Mexico, often with transportation furnished free of charge by Anglo
communities. In Los Angeles, "encouragement" by local authorities often could
not be distinguished from harassment, as reported in the February 27, 1931,
issue of* La Opinion, *the largest Spanish-language newspaper in the city. The
headline reads 11* MEXICANS ARRESTED IN A RAID AT THE PLACITA.

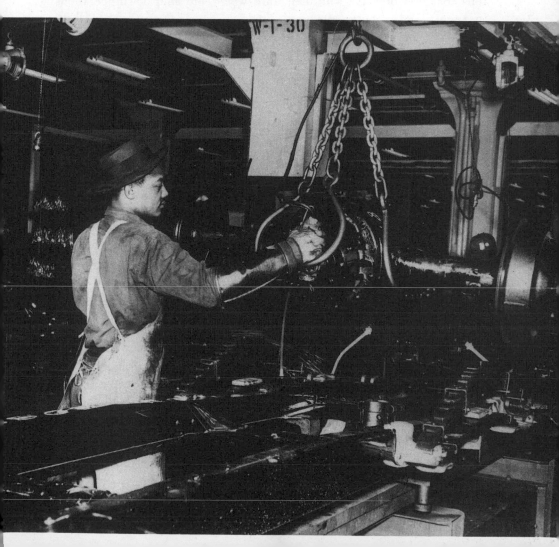

A foundry worker in the "Black Department" of the Ford Motor Company in River Rouge, Michigan. The community in which he and his family probably lived was called "Inkster."

Pittsburgh, Philadelphia, New York. "I should have been here 20 years ago," one transplant had written from Chicago to the folks back home in Hattiesburg, Mississippi.

> I just begin to feel like a man. It's a great deal of pleasure in knowing that you got some privileges. My children are going to the same school with the whites and I don't have to umble to no one. I have registered — will vote the next election and there ain't any 'yes sir' — it's all yes and no and Sam and Bill.

Odie Stallings had been seduced by the same dream, settling in Inkster after finding work in the "black department" at the Ford Plant in River Rouge. He married, and he and his wife, Freda, soon produced two sons. She was pregnant with their third when Ford shut down operations in August, 1931. Shortly afterward, Freda gave birth to another boy. With no income, the Stallings family, like most of those in Inkster, lived on a diet that often was reduced to nothing but starches and water, and Odie dropped from 160 to 125 pounds. His wife was even more wasted, and her breasts were nearly dry; she fed the baby from a bottle filled with flour and water when she could not nurse him herself. Odie trudged the city streets and country roads all over Wayne County in search of any kind of work until his shoes were worn to less than shreds and he could no longer walk long distances. He patched his lightless and heatless shack with newspapers to keep out the cold, but when winter closed down on the ghetto like a fist, the children hacked and coughed incessantly, including the baby, who grew increasingly sick. The parents slept with the infant between them on the narrow bed to keep him warm, but nothing helped, and one morning when they woke he was dead. They put the tiny body in a cardboard box and walking close together under a gray morning sky the family carried their burden up the rutted muddy street and buried it in the makeshift cemetery next to the little community church.

So much, then, for belief in a system whose inherent strengths were supposed to prevent such misery from ever taking place — or if it could not guarantee that, would at least move swiftly and purposefully to repair the damage that had been done. That faith had been tested and had failed — in Detroit, in New York, Chicago, Philadelphia, Seattle, in the farm fields of the Midwest, the cotton plantations of the South, everywhere, resoundingly. What was left, then? Despair, certainly, the bleak anguish of a psychological depression whose dimensions matched the somber statistical dirge of the economic slump. But in human terms, depression often is just another form of anger. And in the end it would be anger, not despair, that would question conventional wisdom, dismantle comfortable assumptions about American society, challenge the machinery of government itself, and bring the first light to the long darkness of the Great Depression.

Shades of Revolution

UNITY OF
WHITE AND
NEGRO WORK
-ERS

I do not say we are going to have a revolution on hand within the next year or two. . . . I hope we may never have such; but the danger is here. That is the feeling of our people. . . . There is a feeling among the masses generally that something is radically wrong. They are despairing of political action. They say the only thing you do in Washington is to take money from the pockets of the poor and put it into the pockets of the rich. They say that this Government is a conspiracy against the common people. . . .

Oklahoma attorney Oscar Ameringer, before a
subcommittee of the Committee on Labor,
House of Representatives, 1932

CHAPTER THREE

PERHAPS ONE OF the most reassuring — if occasionally unnerving — aspects of life during the Great Depression was the fact that millions of Americans, out of work, out of money, sometimes without food and shelter, refused to succumb to despair even in the most harrowing months of the crisis. On Chicago's South Side, for example, Mrs. Willye Jeffries was determined not to curl up and die when the depression came down on her — not even when her husband fell down dead at his job in one of the plants over in Packinghouse Town next to the Union Stockyards. "Well, I had this little girl," she remembered, "and I just thought everybody was pushing me around because my husband was gone. And I was very mean. Very mean." She put her rage to work. When she heard about a run-down apartment building that a landlord refused to maintain for his tenants, she went over and had a look. "You could meet the water coming downstairs. It wasn't fit for anybody to live in. . . . I moved in there to get into a fight. And I got a good fight." She organized the building, encouraging the tenants to stand up for their rights, and together they ultimately forced the landlord to make the necessary repairs to his building. Mrs. Jeffries spent the next several years of the Great Depression organizing tenants, poor people, and workers all over Chicago. "I didn't let them think I was powerless," she explained in later years.

There were plenty of others who refused to let the authorities think they were powerless. In southeastern Arkansas, for example, winter was less than two weeks old when on January 3, 1931, a group of farmers outside the hamlet of England were prodded into action when they could not get enough relief food from the Red Cross. "All you that hain't yaller," one of them shouted, "climb on my truck. We're a-goin' into England to get some grub." Once they got to town they were joined by others, until a crowd of anywhere from three hundred to five hundred people had gathered on the main street of the town, demanding food for their families. The city marshal and a local plantation owner tried to talk to them, but were shouted down. While some in the crowd may have been armed, it was a generally peaceable, if grim, assembly. Merchants conferred among one another and with Red Cross officials, and when they extracted a promise from the Red Cross people that they would be reimbursed, began distributing bread and other foodstuffs to the men to take home to their families. When they were gone, the plantation owner warned city officials that they should not rest easy: "The merchants of England either must move their goods or mount machine guns on their stores!"

The farmers did not come storming back to plunder the town, but the anger that drove them was not an uncommon thing that winter. On January 20, a mob of men and women broke into a grocery store near the city hall in Oklahoma City and began taking goods off the shelves after the mayor rejected a formal petition for food. Twenty-six people were arrested and firehoses were brought out to control the crowd. On February 25, several hundred men and women smashed the windows of a grocery and meat market in Minneapolis and grabbed bacon and ham, fruit and canned goods. When one of the store owners drew a revolver, the crowd jumped him and broke his arm. A hundred policemen were called to the scene and seven people were arrested. Similar "food riots" broke out in many cities at one time or another, from San Francisco to St. Louis.

For many, particularly among those who had invested the most faith in the system to begin with, the frustration and disappointment were almost too much to bear, anger seizing their personalities like an invasive spirit. Oklahoma City attorney Oscar Ameringer told a House labor subcommittee investigating unemployment about a rancher who had stormed into his office in Oklahoma City. The man announced that he was wiped out and, "by God, I am not going to stand for it." When asked just what he had in mind, the rancher reminded Ameringer of the Russian Revolution, and predicted the same for America:

> I just want to tell you that I am going to be one of them, and I am going to do my share in it. . . . If there are enough fellows with guts in this country to do like us, we will march eastward and we will cut the East off. We will cut the East off from the West. We have got the granaries; we have the hogs, the cattle, the corn, and the East has nothing but mortgages on our places. We will show them what we can do.

This was no wild-eyed foreign radical speaking, the committee members understood perfectly well, but a man from the most respected element of society, as society was structured in Oklahoma City in those days — almost certainly a member of the local stockmen's association and probably of Rotary or the Kiwanis as well. When people like that started talking revolution, even if it was done mainly to vent their fury, maybe it was time to take heed.

After all, few of those in the seats of power needed to be reminded of the Bolshevik Revolution of 1917. They could imagine all too vividly (if all too inaccurately) those violent months during which an entire social system had been turned upside down, when rich and powerful people, people just like them, had been driven from their homes by angry mobs, looted of their possessions, even murdered in their beds. For those who had survived the violence, existence had become an agony of dull, plodding conformity and repression of human initiative, all individual dignity and purpose subsumed in the great proletarian dream of "from each according to his ability, to each according to his need." However exaggerated this vision of life in what had become the Union of Soviet Socialist Republics, millions of the comfortable, or formerly comfortable, believed it completely, and as they looked around them at all the turmoil of the early depression years, they saw plenty of reason to fear the same for this country, for themselves.

There probably had never been so many eruptions of public unrest in such a short period of time over so wide a spectrum of geography and population in the nation's history as those that punctuated the months between the winter of 1930 and the winter of 1933, each incident seeming to grow bigger and more menacing than its predecessor — and all of them dutifully and sometimes luridly chronicled in the daily press. Were they merely spontaneous outbursts of anger, or, as many believed, deliberately orchestrated tactics in a kind of sociological warfare — a new American revolution, imported and controlled by the forces of international communism? And even if the revolution did not come through open violence, it might well come through the insidious subversion of American political institutions. There was plenty of reason to fear that, too. In Minnesota, for instance, exasperation had led to the rise of the radical Farmer-Labor party, whose ties to socialism and even communism were identifiable. In 1930 the party's candidate for governor, Floyd B. Olson, was elected, and the party's functionaries were placed in positions of power. Today, Minnesota, and tomorrow — well, who knew?

Minnesota, as it happened, never would become a Soviet state, American style; Olson, who died in office in 1936, was a good deal less of a revolutionary in his deeds than in his words, and the Farmer-Labor party itself would lose power two years later. Nevertheless, Minnesota's fate became a cautionary tale to which American conservatives could and did point with alarm, as the months of the depression ground on; with the economic situation worsening on a daily basis, with Hoover and his people apparently helpless to halt the decline, and with incidents of violence and presumed subversion on the rise, America, it appeared to many, was destined to succumb to revolution. The question at hand seemed to be not whether the revolution would come, but when — and in what form?

■■■ *Organizing Wrath*

The conservative doomsayers were certainly right about one thing: The Communist Party/USA was helping to nurture rebellion industriously where and when it could. The American party, born in a fury of excitement following Russia's revolution, had once claimed a membership as high as sixty thousand (though in reality it was probably less than half that), led by relentless secretive "cadres" of men and women — most of them foreign-born, just as conservatives had claimed — who were every bit as dedicated to the obliteration of capitalism and all its parts as those same conservatives could have feared. But by 1929, dissension in and among those cadres about the party's structure, goals, and philosophy, together with the energetic suppression of anything tainted with the appearance of communism, had brought real membership down to considerably less than ten thousand.

But the party's leaders — chief among them Earl Browder and William Z. Foster — looked upon the crash of 1929 and the subsequent depression and found new hope in what they immediately believed finally must be the beginning of the end for capitalism. By early 1930 the party was busy on a number of fronts, its membership growing. Nor was it or its model — Soviet Russia — quite the bane of civilized eyes it once had been. Communists, after all, were not the only ones who feared that capitalism had failed, and there were plenty of Americans who perceived in the rigid Soviet state the outline of tomorrow — and a good thing, too. Lincoln Steffens, for example, the old "muckraker" who had exposed civic corruption in his famous polemic *The Shame of the Cities*, had gone to Russia and had come back persuaded that the "future is coming; it is in sight; it is coming, really and truly coming, and soon. And it is good."

Many agreed with Steffens, and as we shall see, by the middle of the decade, the American Communists would become almost respectable, at least among some elements of society. But even in the thirties, far and away the most robust and effective period in the party's life, it was a good deal less than the monolithic force to which conservatives of that and future generations pointed as the embodiment of evil itself. Like most American institutions, political or otherwise, the party was characterized by a diversity of interests, individuals, and ideologies quite as much as by a unity of purpose — and that diversity ultimately would undermine even the limited power it enjoyed in the thirties. Nevertheless, in an era in which it seemed to millions of Americans that government, labor, business — all the mainstream democratic institutions in the country — had failed or betrayed their promise, the Communists offered both answers and solutions as noble in intent as they were simplistic in form, and many people were attracted. What was more, particularly in the early years of the depression, the party provided the opportunity to *do* something, to organize diffuse anger into specific action, particularly among working people.

From the beginning, in fact, the party's principal goal had been in dominating and directing the labor movement. Most of this work was done under the aegis of the Trade Union Unity League (TUUL). The TUUL had been founded by Foster, a former Industrial Workers of the World (IWW) organizer, in 1920, and adopted that year as its American trade union wing by the Soviet Comintern — short for the Communist International, a body devoted to promoting worldwide communism. By 1929, the TUUL had already stirred things up in the textile mill town of Gastonia, North Carolina, where workers in the Communist-led National Textile Workers Union had joined an industry-wide strike movement in the spring of the year. Neither in Gastonia or anywhere else in the industry that spring did the workers triumph, but the party tried again in 1931 and 1932, with strikes in the textile factories of Lawrence, Massachusetts, the silk mills of Rhode Island, and, especially, the coal fields of western Pennsylvania and Harlan County, Kentucky, where the Communist-dominated National Miners Union — a dissident group that had splintered from John L. Lewis's United Mine Workers — helped to lead strikes that were met with extraordinary violence even by the standards of the Appalachian coal region, earning the county the name of "Bloody Harlan."

In the meantime, the party attempted to organize the unorganized. In the winter months of 1929 and 1930, TUUL workers walked the streets and haunted the missions and relief centers, parks, and closed factory gates where jobless men stood around out of habit, waiting and worrying and wondering if the gates would ever open again. The organizers stitched together Unemployed Councils patterned after the St. Petersburg Councils of the Unemployed that had emerged during the Russian anti-czarist uprising of 1905. These were designed to be "revolutionary centers" that would organize protests among the unemployed to resist evictions and get food and jobs and otherwise demonstrate proletarian fervor.

What they did better than anything, however, was organize marches, at least for a while. Early in 1930, the Comintern declared that March 6 would be an "International Day for Struggle Against World-Wide Unemployment," and organizers for the TUUL and the unemployed councils put together mass marches that day in New York, Washington, D. C., Baltimore, Chicago, Boston, Seattle, San Francisco, and several other major cities. As many as a million people may have participated, most in relative

Most of the marches and rallies held by the Unemployed Councils of the early depression years were relatively peaceful affairs, but some turned into what a later age would call "police riots," as lawmen attempted to break them up with horses, nightsticks, and sometimes tear gas. LEFT: 1,500 demonstrators are shown clustered in a St. Louis, Missouri, park just before the police moved in. BELOW: In Albany, New York, policemen search people for concealed weapons after some two hundred marchers were met with force when they tried to enter the state capitol to support a proposed New York State Workers Unemployment Conference.

On May 6, 1929 — nearly six months before the stock market crash that year — the USSR's Joseph Stalin ventured a prediction to a small group of American Communists: "I think that the moment is not far off when a revolutionary crisis will develop in America. . . . It is essential that the American Communist party should be capable of meeting that historical moment . . . assuming the leadership of the impending class struggle in America. . . ." It must be said that the members of the Communist Party/USA tried, though not always elegantly. The early American graffiti slathered on the side of the Church of the Heavenly Rest in New York City was a comment on the upcoming state elections in November, 1930.

The Trade Union Unity League (TUUL), the Communist Party/USA's labor arm, helped Mexican-American migrant workers win minor improvements in wages and working conditions, especially in California.

peace — though in Seattle and Washington the police used tear gas to break up what they persuaded themselves were potentially unruly mobs, and in New York City, when some thirty-five thousand people gathered at Union Square on Broadway to hear Foster speak, the police charged into the crowd. "Thousands of terrified people scattered," the *New York Times* reported the next day, "rushing for safety from the flailing police, shouting, stumbling, stepping over one another in their fear and haste to get away."

■ Portending the Future

The party did not confine itself to the streets of the cities, even in the early months of the depression. In California, for example, the TUUL organized and helped to lead Mexican-American migrant farmworkers in agricultural strikes in the Imperial Valley and the San Joaquin Valley, where hundreds of millions of dollars worth of produce was grown and harvested every year in plantation-sized operations that newspaperman and sociologist Carey McWilliams called "factories in the field." Ignored by the labor movement in general — indeed, the AFL, with John L. Lewis leading the way, had agitated for the end of Mexican immigration — local Mexican-American field workers had launched a handful of unsuccessful strikes themselves. These had failed, but had brought them to the attention of the Communists. In the spring of 1930 the TUUL sent organizers into the area to establish the Agricultural Workers Industrial League. In spite of mass arrests and the conviction of eight organizers for violations of criminal syndicalism laws, the TUUL's agents put together yet another union, the Cannery and Agricultural Workers Industrial Union (CAWIU), which not only set about trying to unionize cannery and packing shed workers throughout the industry, but managed to help guide a scattering of small field strikes in 1931 and 1932. These, like the earlier efforts, were failures, but California's Mexican-American agricultural labor movement now was established as a force with which the industry would henceforth have to deal regularly — thanks, in no small part, to a TUUL organizing campaign that had built competently on a foundation of grassroots tradition.

Another large number of the unrepresented and unorganized could be found among the African-American population, particularly among those who had not escaped the bounds of Jim Crow country. The NAACP had softened the radical attitudes that had characterized the organization through much of the twenties, and spent much of its time now attempting to get anti-lynching legislation through the Congress. The National Urban League, even more wedded to moderation than the NAACP, generally confined itself to basic civil rights issues. The Communists had attempted to recruit black members throughout the twenties, though not with much overall success. By 1930, party chief Earl Browder had to admit that "we still have something less than 1,000 Negro members in our Party." The American Negro Labor Congress, the party's first organizing unit for blacks, was dissolved and the League of Struggle for Negro Rights created to take its place, but the LSNR enjoyed little more success in the thirties. Part of the failure doubtless stemmed from the fact that in spite of its rhetoric and its measurable commitment to the cause of blacks, the party's top leadership remained lily white. What was more, there was a strain of traditional bigotry within the ranks of the white membership that no amount of hectoring and "re-education" ever seemed quite able to eradicate. Nor, in the view of some black members, was the party's white leadership willing to do all that it might have done to remove this flaw. "Within Party circles," Harry Haywood, one of the most effective black leaders the party ever had, remembered,

> the [League of Struggle for Negro Rights] became an excuse for failing
> to tackle head-on the Afro-American question and white chauvinism.
> Some even called the LSNR the "Negro Party." This assumed the battle
> for Black rights could be left to a Black party — rather than being a
> priority for both whites and Blacks within one party.

Nevertheless, even if they did not actually join the party, many blacks admired its willingness to put action where its words were, and they had a special reverence for the raw courage many white Communists displayed in challenging the class structure. Carl Murphy, editor of the Baltimore *Afro-American*, for one, became one of the party's most passionate admirers. "The Communists appear to be the only party going our way," he wrote. Rosco Dunjee, editor of the *Black Dispatch* in Oklahoma, while less enthusiastic, was still intrigued. "Yonder stands the poor white with a bomb under his arm," he told his readers,

> — yet love in his heart for me. What shall I do about it? Does that
> unsanitary looking human being hold within his grasp my rainbow of
> promise, and the power which I so sorely need? Is Communism the
> instrumentality through which I am to secure the racial opportunity
> which for years I have longed for and prayed?

To blacks like Murphy and Dunjee, the party's work in the South, where a person of any color could be killed for challenging the system, was especially admirable. At first, the party concentrated its efforts in Birmingham, the most industrialized city in the South, helping people to organize relief committees to obtain food and payments, leading the occasional hunger march, and attempting to unionize local steelworkers. By 1931, it had about five hundred active members in the city, with another several thousand people in various organizations who could be described as sympathetic. Few in either category were white, for the party's deliberate and vocal insistence on racial equality among its membership was no more popular among poor whites than it was among rich whites. Communist agitators, the *Birmingham Labor Advocate* cried in April, 1930, "openly preach social equality for the Black race. . . . Any man who seeks to disturb the relations between the races is a dangerous character, and should be squelched NOW."

It was bad enough that the party had dared to invade the urban precincts of Birmingham, but when it ventured into the countryside it challenged the very essence of the South's economy and social fabric, where nearly sixty years after the abolition of slavery the carefully structured oppression of antebellum life had been replaced by the institutional peonage of the sharecropper and tenant-farmer systems. With the aid of a young African-American schoolteacher in Tallapoosa County named Estelle Milner — one of several women who would play a major part in the movement — the party cobbled together the Croppers and Farm Workers Union (CFWU) in the spring of 1931.

By July, while still generally confined to Tallapoosa County, the new union had grown to about eight hundred members — too many for the comfort of local plantation owners and their captive police and politicians, who responded with anti-union actions whose virulence did not hesitate at murder. Within a few weeks, the little union was all but crushed, and only the stubborn efforts of organizers like Eula Gray, the niece of a union official who had been murdered in his bed, kept it alive through most of the rest of the decade as a skeleton organization renamed the Sharecroppers Union (SCU), whose intermittent attempts at strikes were broken just as surely and swiftly as were those of the migrant farm workers in California.

Still, the fact that the SCU never gained any real power (though it would enjoy a brief resurgence of strength much later in the decade) was less significant than the fact that it existed at all, given the overwhelming power of those who opposed it. This was almost entirely the work of local people like Eula Gray; the party never did invest more than a minimum of its resources in the union. At the same time, the Communists could take no small portion of credit for helping to stir up feelings that had remained dormant or relentlessly suppressed for so long that they were assumed to be all but dead. They were not. The SCU was a testament to the degree to which anger, when focused and organized, could drive men and women to risk everything they had and were in an effort, however hopeless, to win a measure of freedom from a society whose every tradition was designed to keep them suspended in an unchanging oppression. The tiny revolt of the black sharecroppers, then, was more than a depression footnote to the American labor movement — it was a premonitory glimpse of that which would give muscle, bones, and blood to the civil rights movement of the future.

Another, different premonition of times to come could be found in another cause in which the Communist Party/USA played a major part in these years. It was called the Scottsboro case, and for another three decades it would stand as the principal symbol of southern justice, bringing the spotlight of national attention to the glaring inequities and suppression of African Americans in Southern society. On March 25, 1931, a group of five young white male transients got into a fight with several young African-American men while riding a freight from Chattanooga to Memphis, Tennessee, via Scottsboro and other Alabama towns. The white men lost and were thrown from the train. They ran to a local sheriff and complained. The sheriff wired ahead to the authorities in Scottsboro, and when the train stopped there, nine black men were taken from the freight and arrested on charges of assault and battery. During their search of the boxcars, the Scottsboro police discovered two young women dressed as men, as transient women often did. The women immediately claimed to have been raped by all nine black men, and the men were so charged.

All but one of the young men were teenagers, one of them, Leroy Wright, being only thirteen, and they would henceforth be known as the "Scottsboro Boys." Their first trials were swift. In spite of conflicting testimony on the part of the alleged rape victims and the lack of any forensic evidence at all, eight of the defendants were swiftly found guilty; the ninth, Leroy Wright, escaped conviction when the judge declared a mistrial because the jurymen could not agree among themselves whether a thirteen-year-old should be given life imprisonment or the death penalty. There was no hesitancy with regard to the remaining eight. One by one, they were sentenced to die.

Even though the trials were suspect from the beginning, the NAACP had hesitated to become involved in a case that might have threatened the organization's credibility with its large contingent of white supporters. "The NAACP is not an organization to defend black criminals," the *Crisis* had declared primly in October, 1931.

> We are not in the field to condone rape, murder and theft because it is done by Black men. . . . When we hear that eight colored men have raped two white girls in Alabama, we are not first in the field to defend them. If they are guilty and have a fair trial the case is none of our business.

By the time it became apparent to NAACP officials that the charge against the young men was preposterous, the Communist party had seized the verdicts and the sentences and was well on its way toward making them one of the most celebrated causes in modern American history. As early as April 10, 1931, it announced that it was putting the resources of its legal arm, the International Labor Defense (ILD), at the disposal of the Scottsboro Boys. While the ILD's lawyers began filing appeals, the LSNR, the TUUL, and other Communist groups joined to protest the trial, enlisting armies of support from radical, liberal, and even moderate white Americans. Over the next six years, while appeals, reversals, and new trials kept the men alive, sermons on the case were preached regularly in both black and white churches throughout the North, and such prominent persons as Albert Einstein, Thomas Mann, H. G. Wells, John Dos Passos, and many others signed petitions, wrote articles, and gave speeches demanding clemency or pardons. Novelist Theodore Dreiser's National Committee for the Defense of Political Prisoners gave a benefit in Manhattan at which bandleader Cab Calloway performed and a platoon of Communist speakers harangued. The Scottsboro Unity Defense Committee put on another benefit, featuring Paul Whiteman and his orchestra, together with Duke Ellington, Fletcher Henderson, Fats Waller, and other jazz and swing greats.

In the end, the charges against four of the men would be dropped; five others would be convicted and sentenced to long terms (four would later be pardoned and the fifth would escape and never be caught). While the party's ILD would earn encomiums from the American Civil Liberties Union for its work on the Scottsboro case, relations between the ILD and other individuals and organizations that had come to the aid of the men did not run smoothly. The Communists had staked out their territory early and fought to hold it for the party's own purposes, a rigidity which irritated many with an interest in the case, including the latecoming NAACP. It was only after months of bickering that the various parties agreed to the formation of a Scottsboro Defense Committee that included representatives from the ILD, the NAACP, and other organizations and it was this body, not the Communist party, that would guide the conduct of the case over nearly fifteen more years.

Nevertheless, the party could — and certainly did — take credit for being the first group to inspire the national interest that ultimately saved the Scottsboro defendants from summary execution. A chink had been found in the armor of Southern self-righteousness, and while the powers that ruled the region would use all the resources at their command to keep the South invulnerable to change, the seeds of another kind of revolution had been planted whose fruit would be harvested in our own time.

The Battle of River Rouge

The Scottsboro case, for all its national publicity, was still perceived by most Americans as something entirely local, affecting their own lives not at all. If it portended change for the South, it did little to define the character of life in the rest of the country. Other kinds of anger and other kinds of violence struck closer to home, giving greater weight to the continuing fear of millions of people that the system as a whole was in danger of disintegration — or of being destroyed outright. Such worries had flourished ever since the dimensions of the economic crisis had first been perceived, but by 1932 they were epidemic, as the Democratic and Republican parties began to eye the elections coming up in November, attempting to calculate what the continuing economic malaise and public violence might mean to them and to whatever candidates they might choose to lead the country in the heart of this dark era.

It was at this juncture that the early depression's two most dramatic episodes of social unrest flamed into violence, giving such political considerations a rare urgency. It is symbolically convenient that the first of these events could be interpreted as a metaphor representing the failure of capitalism to provide for economic security, and that the second could be seen as representing the failure of government to discover a way to lift the country out of its terrible decline. No two events in the early years of the decade would have greater national impact, and both, whether or not their symbolism was properly appreciated, would be decisive in bringing about the demise of Herbert Hoover and the character of government he represented.

The 1932 hunger march on the Ford Motor Company demonstrated with precision the enormity of the gap between what millions of Americans

There were never many African-American Communists, but some did join up, like these members of the Harlem Unemployed Council, ABOVE, fists raised in an ancestral gesture of defiance and protest.

LEFT: Haywood Patterson, one of the "Scottsboro Boys" accused of raping two white women in 1930, with his International Labor Defense (ILD) attorney, Samuel Leibowitz (on Patterson's right). "I'm going to die," he told the prosecutor, "when you and those girls die for lying about me."

In June of 1932, Angelo Herndon, a nineteen-year-old black Communist, was arrested in Atlanta and charged with attempting to incite insurrection against the state of Georgia, a capital offense. Like Haywood Patterson and the other Scottsboro defendants, Herndon's cause was taken up by the Communist Party/USA's ILD, and in 1937 the U. S. Supreme Court declared his conviction unconstitutional. In the meantime, the ILD repeatedly linked Herndon's case with that of the Scottsboro defendants as one more example of the peculiar nature of Southern justice. Herndon (wearing the white hat) is shown after being released on $15,000 bail in 1934. At his left is Ruby Bates, one of the ostensible rape victims in the Scottsboro case; she had since recanted her original testimony.

wanted and believed they needed and what an entrenched yet suddenly insecure industrial society was ready to give them. By making automobiles so fast and so cheaply that nearly every American family could afford to buy one, Henry Ford had transformed the character of the national life more than any other individual human being since Thomas Alva Edison, and throughout the twenties he had been popularly seen as the definitive American — so much so that he was seriously considered as a presidential candidate in 1924 (he withdrew his name). The assumption was, as it always had been among those who adhered to the go-getters' ethos, that great financial success could not be separated from greatness of character.

Ford himself presented a carefully modest face to the world, but his publicity department had been touting his company for years as the living representative of enlightened self-interest and corporate responsibility. The ballyhoo started in 1914, when the company instituted the eight-hour, "five-dollar" day for its workers. Never mind that the base rate remained $2.34 a day, and that the five-dollar figure could be achieved by a worker only through a complex "profit-sharing" bonus system — and then only if he were at least twenty-two years old, had been with the company at least six months, and could satisfy the company that he was living "a clean, sober, and industrious life." The five-dollar figure, being nearly double the standard daily wage (and for eight hours, not ten), was magical. "GOD BLESS HENRY FORD," the *Algonac Courier* declaimed, and fifteen thousand workers showed up at the Highland Park plant every day in hopes of being hired.

The publicity department beat the drums and blew the trumpets once more in 1926, when Ford instituted the five-day week, and never mind again that if the system gave his workers an extra day off, it also docked them another day's pay. And never mind, too, that to keep his shops union-free and his men sweating every penny of their five dollars through every minute of every hour of the eight hours of every five-day week, Ford hired a natural despot by the name of Harry Bennett to run the company's "service department" as a kind of internal secret police.

Publicity said nothing about Harry Bennett and his gang, but it played ruffles and flourishes again in March, 1931, when Ford announced that he was not only dropping the price of his automobiles but raising the pay scale to a minimum of seven dollars a day for unskilled labor and even more for skilled labor. And never mind this time that in order to do it he had to lay off thousands of higher-paid workers, subcontract work to other companies that paid wages far lower than his (one auto-body factory paid as little as

12.5 cents an hour), and further institutionalize the production-line "speed-up" system that already was driving his workers to blind exhaustion at the end of each day. What was more, the seven-dollar day did not last for long; by the end of 1931, even in those Ford shops that had not been shut down because of poor sales and the need to retool for the production of the first Ford V-8, the pay dropped to six dollars a day and then to four. There was no publicity trumpeting this development.

Altogether, then, there could hardly have been a more logical target for the Communists to set their sights on with another demonstration, and early in 1932 leaders of the TUUL and the Detroit Unemployed Council organized a hunger march on the Ford Motor Company. After being told to be orderly and peaceable by march leaders, about three thousand men and women set out on the brutally cold morning of March 7 to walk the few hundred yards from the outskirts of Detroit to the employment office at the River Rouge plant in Dearborn.

A platoon of Dearborn police met the marchers at the Dearborn city limits and told them to go back. When the marchers continued up the road, the police fired canisters of tear gas among them, then waded in with truncheons. But the police were outnumbered and just as affected by the tear gas as the marchers. They scattered and began to retreat, chased by the now angry crowd, which pelted them with rocks and debris from the roadside fields. By the time the marchers reached Gate No. 3, where the employment office building stood, the Dearborn police had teamed up with a force of Ford's service department security police. More tear gas canisters were thrown and shot into the crowd, while from an overpass near the gate, service department police or firemen (accounts vary) began hosing people down with a blast of freezing water. The crowd continued to throw things, and when Harry Bennett himself sped up, his car was immediately bombarded with stones. Bennett got out of the car, was struck by a thrown object, and fell to his knees, bleeding copiously from a cut on the head. Shots were fired into the crowd from behind the gate and from a submachine gun on the overpass. People began to run in a great confusion of tear gas mist and gunfire, screams and shouts, while some tried to drag the wounded to safety. By the time it was done, four male marchers were dead and more than sixty people wounded. Two dozen of the wounded were taken into custody by the Dearborn police. Some of the injured men were chained to their cots in their cells.

While the police busied themselves by rounding up every radical they could lay hands on and putting them in jail on the grounds of con-

In 1927, the covered conveyor belts and rising smokestacks of the Ford Motor Company's River Rouge plant provided an artistic opportunity for photographer Charles Sheeler in one of his works from "The Rouge Series."

On March 7, 1930, three thousand unemployed workers started to march toward Ford's River Rouge plant. They were attacked by Dearborn police and Ford's company guards. When the fighting was over, four marchers were dead and scores were injured.

The Detroit authorities sprang into action immediately following the battle at the River Rouge Ford plant on March 7: they arrested sixty of the marchers, then rounded up hundreds of Communists, suspected Communists, and assorted other radicals, charging them with "criminal syndicalism." None of this prevented at least six thousand people from joining in a funeral procession through the streets of Detroit on March 12 to honor the four men who had been shot to death during the riot. The procession is seen passing through Grand Circus Park.

spiracy, unjailed radicals organized a funeral procession for the four slain men, and on March 12, six thousand people marched down Woodward Avenue in Detroit under red banners while a band played the "Internationale," the Communist party's anthem. There was no violence. Five years later, Upton Sinclair, the muckraking novelist and Socialist party luminary, published a new novel. Sinclair had once admired Ford greatly, but no more. The new novel was called *The Flivver King: A Story of Ford-America*, and in it Sinclair said that after the violence at River Rouge, Ford cars came in only one color, that of "Fresh Human Blood."

■■■■ A Breathless Silence of Horror

The battle at River Rouge Gate No. 3 was the last such event in which the Communist party would take a significant role, and for all its furious violence, it was no match for the drama that took place in Washington, D.C., in August of 1932 — the greatest single demonstration of its kind in the history of the United States up to that time. It, too, had to do with hunger, though the great majority of those who took part had never done anything like it in their lives before and would have been appalled to hear themselves described as radicals, much less Communists.

In 1924, following four years of lobbying by the newly formed American Legion, Congress had passed — over the veto of President Coolidge — the so-called bonus bill. This legislation authorized the payment of "bonuses" to all veterans of the Great War in the form of adjusted service certificates: $1 a day for each day of service in the United States, $1.25 for each day of service overseas. The money would be put in an endowment fund until 1945, when, after interest, each veteran would receive an average of $1,000. So things had stood until 1929, when Texas congressman Wright Patman introduced legislation to authorize the immediate payment of the bonus. His bill had gotten nowhere in the Congress, but the idea began to pick up steam as the effects of the economic crisis seeped across the country. The Hearst newspapers soon supported the bonus payment, as did the increasingly popular "radio priest" from Detroit, Father Charles Coughlin. Patman introduced new legislation at the opening session in January, 1931. He was soon joined by a number of other congressmen, and by the summer of 1931 President Hoover had another problem on his hands.

He did not want the bonus paid. Among other good and sufficient reasons, he said, it could cost the country as much as $4 billion, which the government could not get its hands on without raising taxes, a recourse he had no intention of supporting. It was not an unreasonable concern, but those who were out of work, and for whom four or five hundred dollars represented as much as five months of food and shelter for their families, tended to look upon his reluctance as plain selfishness. "Pres. Hoover a millionaire," an unemployed tool-and-die maker wrote to an agency in Washington, D. C., "worth about 12 000 000 dollars drawing a salary of 75 000 per year from the government asking some boys to forgo their bonus some of them have not 12 dollars of their own 'Some more nerve.' "

Hoover vetoed a compromise bill that had been passed by both houses of Congress in February, 1931, and he and his supporters in Congress managed to stifle an override, as well as new legislation from Patman. In May, 1932, the House Ways and Means Committee reported out Patman's latest bill with an adverse recommendation, and it seemed the cause was lost. But the idea would not go away. It continued to simmer in the mind of a slender, somewhat sickly, and generally apolitical unemployed cannery worker from Portland, Oregon.

He was Walter Waters, a thirty-four-year-old veteran who had served overseas as a medic with the 146th Field Artillery. After the war, he had drifted from one low-level job to another, finally marrying and settling down in Portland, where he had worked in a canning factory until being laid off in December, 1930. One night in March, 1932, Waters stood up and addressed a meeting of the National Veterans Association. He told the men that they should band together and go to Washington to present their demands for the bonus payment in person — just as big business sent its lobbyists. No one seemed interested that night, but in May, after Patman's bonus bill was rejected, the same group of veterans decided to do as Waters had urged. On May 11, having no other means of transportation, the men blocked the tracks of the Union Pacific, commandeered and boarded a few boxcars, and rattled east across the Cascade range and over the Snake River plain of southern Idaho. By the time they reached Pocatello, Waters had been appointed their "general" and had attempted to give the expedition a quasi-military character on the theory that only military organization would be capable of keeping the men under some sort of discipline, as well as prevent them from being confused with scruffy radical groups. They called themselves the "BEF," the Bonus Expeditionary Force — a gentle parody of the American Expeditionary Force that had been sent overseas during World War I — and they contrived an anthem, of sorts, out of a raunchy old World War I ditty:

We're all the way from Oregon
To get some cash from Washington,
Hinky, dinky, parlez-vous.

We're going to ride the B & O.
The good Lord Jesus told us so.
Hinky, dinky, parlez-vous.

You're going to see a better day
When Mr. Hoover says "O.K."
Hinky, dinky, parlez-vous.

It took the Portland "marchers" eighteen days to get to Washington, picking up fresh recruits all the way. A day out of town, Waters went ahead to talk to officials in the district. His reception was unexpectedly friendly. Pelham G. Glassford, a graduate of West Point and a veteran himself — he· had earned the field rank of brigadier general and a Distinguished Service Cross during the war — had just been appointed chief of the Metropolitan Police after serving time as a lobbyist for the Veterans of Foreign Wars. Glassford had genuine sympathy for the marchers' cause as well as a determination to avoid any violence. He had arranged for the men to be bivouacked in an old vacant building and when they straggled in saw to it that they were provided with food. When even more marchers began drifting into the city to join the Portland bunch, he set up a commissary financed with private donations, including $115 out of his own pocket, and made plans to establish a camp and barracks. When the men took an official vote and made Waters the BEF's commander in chief, they made Glassford its secretary-treasurer.

This relatively serene environment prevailed for weeks, as hundreds, then thousands of marchers made their way to Washington by boxcar, truck, automobile, and foot, responding to the publicity that Waters and the Portland marchers had engendered. Some even brought their families, and with Hoover's secret approval (the president wanted to avoid the appearance of supporting the bonus in any way), Glassford obtained hundreds of tents, a number of field kitchens, equipment, personnel to staff a large dispensary, and other material from government supplies. Hoover also gave his permission to use available government property to house the marchers.

By the middle of June, there were thousands of them — estimates of peak numbers range from fifteen to twenty-five thousand — living in twenty-seven encampments in and around the edges of the District, including several hundred who had been given permission to temporarily occupy a number of buildings currently being demolished for the construction of what would be the Federal Triangle complex across Constitution Avenue (then B Street) from the Mall. The most pleasant of the encampments was "Camp Bartlett" on a plot of wooded land donated by former postmaster general John H. Bartlett about two miles from the Mall and the Capitol building, and the largest was "Camp Marks" on the Anacostia flats directly across the Anacostia River from the city, which housed an estimated fifteen thousand people, including about eleven hundred women and children.

The presence of these thousands of petitioners had the desired effect — at least in the House of Representatives. On June 15, it passed Wright Patman's suddenly resurrected bonus bill by a vote of 209 to 176. The bill was then sent over to the Senate, and on June 17 went to the floor for a vote. As the debate whined on into the evening hours, veterans gathered in the Capitol Plaza, quietly talking, smoking, waiting. There were perhaps twelve thousand of them outside when Waters came out to tell them what the vote had been: 62 to 18 for defeat. Inside, Senator Hiram Johnson, who had been one of the eighteen, had turned to one of his colleagues when the vote was announced. "This marks a new era in the life of our nation," he said. "The time may come when this folderol — these trappings of government — will disappear, when fat old men like you and me will be lined up against a stone wall."

No such melodrama ensued. The men in the plaza outside took the news from their commander calmly. Someone started singing the unofficial national anthem, "America," and when the last notes of that simple, beautiful melody rising from twelve thousand voices drifted off into the summer air, the men disbursed and made their way back to their separate camps.

The question remained of what the men would do now. Waters declared that "We'll stay until 1945," but as the weeks dragged on the coherence of purpose that had kept the BEF together began to dissolve beneath the moist, relentless heat of a Washington summer. Day by day, those marchers who could manage it left the city. One of Waters's lieutenants defied his and Glassford's orders that no more empty government buildings could be used for housing and led a movement across the river and into the city, where they occupied a number of structures in the area of Thirteenth and B streets.

Meanwhile, Hoover quietly supported a transportation loan bill that would provide $100,000 to help the marchers return home, and on July 9 signed it. It set a deadline of July 24 for the men to start leaving. Waters dismissed it as "an effort to send us back to our home towns so we can starve again," and the number of potentially violent demonstrations increased while the number of remaining veterans dribbled down to somewhere between eight and ten thousand. In spite of his best efforts to avoid it, Glassford was forced to make some arrests.

On July 27 Hoover decided that enough was enough: the downtown buildings must be cleared, he ordered, beginning the next day. Even though his secretary of war, Patrick J. Hurley, thought that soldiers should be employed, Hoover insisted that no troops be used in the effort unless absolutely necessary. During the morning hours of July 28, events proceeded peacefully enough; police led men out of the old armory building with almost no resistance. The afternoon was another matter. Waters issued a "call to arms" at the Anacostia camp, and scores of men seized the Anacostia Bridge, while others made their way to the downtown area. There, in two separate engagements, Glassford and his men were pelted with bricks and stones. Several policemen were badly injured and two veterans were shot. One died instantly, the other some time later.

The District commissioners immediately asked Hoover to send in troops and Hoover directed Hurley to issue the necessary order to General Douglas MacArthur, chief of staff of the Army:

> You will have United States troops proceed immediately to the scene of disorder. Cooperate fully with the District of Columbia police force which is now in charge. Surround the affected area and clear it without delay. Turn over all prisoners to the civil authorities. . . . Use all humanity consistent with the due execution of the order.

For the most part, MacArthur ignored the orders. His truest mandate, he told his adjutant, Major Dwight Eisenhower, was to rescue the nation from "incipient revolution in the air." He massed his troops, including a contingent of cavalry and six toylike but nonetheless menacing tanks, along Pennsylvania Avenue. Ex-postmaster Bartlett, he who had donated his land outside the city to house about two thousand marchers, had gone down to the corner of Third and B streets to see what he could see. "A breathless silence of horror," he wrote a few days later, "as in the presence of death, seemed to depress the thousands of bystanders, for it was whispered through the crowd that two veterans had been killed." There was no incipient revolution brewing, he insisted. Then: "But a few minutes later . . . there approached on Pennsylvania Avenue from the direction of the White House (less than a mile away) a force of Cavalry with sabers glistening, making that ominous click of iron feet on the pavement which sounded so much like war."

As the troops advanced, applause and some cheers went up from the crowd, perhaps as an instinctive response. There was soon enough little to cheer about. The mounted soldiers pushed into the crowd, some of them swinging or threatening to swing their sabers. One fourteen-year-old boy suffered a cut on his arm, one veteran had an ear severed, and at least one other got stuck in the hip with a bayonet as the crowd was pushed back several blocks. Bonus marchers in one of the abandoned buildings let fly with bricks. Soldiers responded with tear gas, then moved in and cleared the buildings. Most of the marchers were driven back to the Anacostia Bridge. Through it all, newsman Thomas L. Stokes remembered eight years later, "General MacArthur, his chest glittering with medals, strode up and down the middle of Pennsylvania Avenue, flipping a riding crop against his neatly pressed breeches."

Hoover, meanwhile, was appalled by what he had loosed on Washington. He sent orders through Secretary of War Hurley that MacArthur was not to cross the Anacostia Bridge. MacArthur chose to disregard these orders, too, and early in the evening sent his men across the river and into the BEF encampment on the other side, scattering the few people left with tear gas and physical attacks. Some of the retreating marchers apparently set fires as a final, futile gesture of anger. Troops quickly added torches of their own. "Soon the conflagration was general," Stokes recalled.

> We ventured into the the war zone. Here and there we walked among the fires. Some of the occupants watched their shacks burn quietly, standing beside piles of their few belongings. Then, one after another, they gathered up their possessions and wandered away. The dome of the Capitol was outlined against the flames.

The burning was necessary, MacArthur later insisted, so that the marchers would not be tempted to return and force his soldiers to "bivouac under the guns of traitors."

Among the "traitors" was a family that had taken refuge in a house by the side of the road when the troops crossed the bridge into the Anacostia flats. "The troops came up the hill," the wife said,

It had been a long time since the BEF veterans had marched in formation, but on June 8, 1932, about eight thousand former soldiers managed to put together a somewhat ragged demonstration of parade form.

While the Senate debated the bonus bill that had been passed by the House on June 15, 1932, thousands of BEF veterans rested on the lawn in front of the Capitol Building.

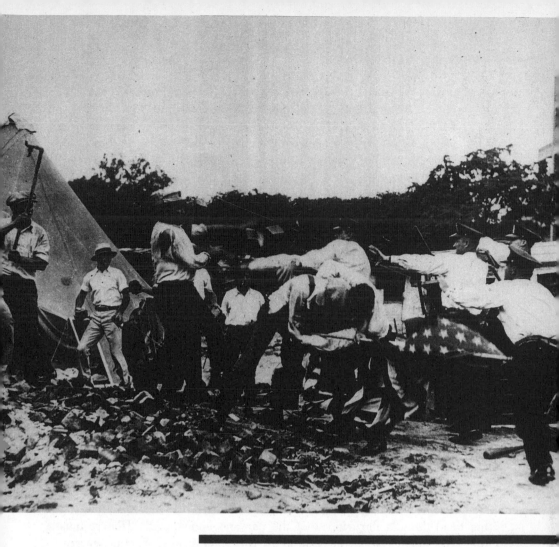

The atmosphere of peaceful assembly that had characterized the presence of the BEF in Washington for weeks was finally shattered on July 28. By the end of the day two veterans were mortally wounded and the BEF driven out of town by Army troops under General Douglas MacArthur. According to an anonymous song that appeared shortly afterward, Hoover and MacArthur were "the Higher Racketeers/Who look on human suffering/With lofty well-fed sneers/And thus will your names be noted/By history's merciless pen:/'They knew how to rise to Power,/But not how to act like men!'"

driving the people ahead of them. As they passed by the house one
of them threw a bomb over the fence into the front yard, which is a
few feet from the door. The house was filled with gas, and we all began
to cry. We got wet towels and put them over the faces of the children.
About half an hour later my baby began to vomit. I took her outside
in the air and she vomited again. Next day she began to turn black
and blue and we took her to the hospital.

Not long after Hoover informed the press that "A challenge to the
authority of the United States Government has been met, swiftly and
firmly," the baby was dead — though the cause of death was never fully
determined.

During the night and into the morning, thousands of men, women,
and children — hot, tired, haggard, bitter, and frustrated refugees from
the "battle" of Washington — dragged themselves to a tatterdemalion
camp at Ideal Park in Johnstown, Pennsylvania. In response to objections
from his town's better class of people, Mayor Eddie McClosky had said
"To hell with everybody! Let them come!" and had offered the stragglers
this sanctuary. The refugees sweltering in the heat of Ideal Park did not
yet know about the baby who would die, but they knew plenty about
dead ideals, *New Republic* correspondent Malcom Cowley reported. "I
used to be a hundred-percenter," a man with a tear-streaked face told
him, "but now I'm a Red radical. I had an American flag, but the damned
tin soldiers burned it. Now I don't ever want to see a flag again." As
Cowley and a companion drove slowly down the road, another man put
his head through the window of the car and announced, "Hoover must
die." Yet another shouted, "You know what this means? This means revolution."

Talk of revolution, Cowley pointed out a few days later, was not
revolution itself. If it came, he said, it would not come from a few thousand
disenchanted veterans and their families: "No, if any revolution results
from the flight of the Bonus Army, it will come from a different source,
from the government itself. The army in time of peace, at the national
capital, has been used against unarmed citizens — and this, with all it
threatens for the future, is a revolution in itself."

Cowley was right. There was revolution in the air, but it was not the
American version of a Bolshevik uprising that the Communist Party/USA
dreamed of or that haunted the imaginings of capitalists. In spite of all the
upheaval that had troubled the nation's life for nearly three years, climaxing
on the sorry field of anger in Washington, D. C., what was about to come

was something entirely different, a peaceful revolution that would emerge from within the great puzzle of government, not be imposed from without, a revolution that even in its failures would enlarge the democratic experience and change the way in which the nation was governed so permanently that it is now almost impossible to imagine government in any other form.

I

Redeeming the Hour

I am a mother of seven children, and utterly heart broken, in that they are hungry, have only 65¢ in money. The father is in L.A. trying to find something to do. . . . O, President, my heart is breaking. . . . O, what a burden and how helpless I am, how proud I am of my children, and how dark a future under this condition. . . . I humbly pray God's Divine blessing on you, for you have tried every way to help the people.

Mrs. H. L., to Franklin D. Roosevelt,
February 1, 1934

ABOLISH BREAD
VOTE FO
ROOSEVE

CHAPTER FOUR

Overleaf:
*While President Herbert Hoover continued
to be blamed personally for the depression
(undeservedly) by millions of voters and
blamed by millions more for the Bonus Army
disaster (more deservedly), Franklin Delano
Roosevelt, the rich, partially paralyzed, and
thoroughly Democratic governor of New York,
shook his head in sadness over Republican
excesses, promised America a "New Deal" if he
was elected president, and took to the campaign
trail. In October, 1932, Roosevelt is shown in
the back of a campaign car in Indianapolis,
Indiana — the very heartland of Republican
hopes — where a clamoring throng suggests
that Hoover's days as president are numbered.*

URING THE FIRST few days after the rout of the Bonus Army, Hoover was given a good press. Reporters dutifully reported his contention that "after the departure of the majority of the veterans, subversive influences obtained control of the remaining men in the District . . . secured repudiation of their elected leaders and inaugurated and organized this attack." He did not use the word "Communists," but that is what he meant, and editorials around the country clucked in admiration of the president's fortitude in putting down revolt. But this happy interlude of approval did not last. Over the next several days, even the conservative press had to accept the evidence that the Bonus Army was as genuine a grass-roots American movement as anything this country had ever seen and that Hoover, MacArthur, and the Army had acted in haste and stupidity in driving the veterans from the city at the point of bayonets, like peasant rabble in some Middle European country. It grated on the average American's sense of fair play. Radio commentator Floyd Gibbons compared the stragglers from the Bonus Army to the World War I refugees whose miserable presence had become one of the permanent memories of the war. But these newest victims, he said, were "American refugees fleeing from the fire and sword of the Great Humanitarian [a nickname Hoover had earned as head of relief efforts for Belgium during the war]." The president, an American Legion Post Commander said, had demonstrated "sadistic principles of government," while the *New York Post* editorialized that cowardice had produced its usual results: "Fear produces cruelty, always, and fear blunders stupidly. What was there to fear?"

Hoover's reelection hopes (he had been renominated in June), already weakened because of the continuing depression, were further damaged by the events of August, and those hopes did not improve over the next several weeks as Hoover, Secretary of War Hurley, Attorney General William D. Mitchell, and others from the administration issued one contradictory and self-serving explanation of the affair after another. Hoover's popular support, thin to begin with after nearly three years of depression, was eroding rapidly.

One man, at least, had seen it coming. Even as the morning light illuminated the still-smoking ruins of the Bonus Army camp at the Anacostia flats the day after the riots, the principal beneficiary of Hoover's miscalculation was sitting in bed in the governor's mansion in Albany, New York, shaking his head over *New York Times* photographs of the previous day's fighting. The pictures, he told an adviser sadly, reminded him "of scenes from a nightmare." He said that Hoover should never have turned

MacArthur loose on the hapless civilian army. The president should have asked a delegation from the BEF to come see him in the White House and talk about the situation. And he should have sent coffee and sandwiches out to the rest.

So spoke the Democratic nominee for the presidency of the United States, Governor Franklin Delano Roosevelt. On the face of it, Roosevelt seemed an unlikely candidate to lead the people of the nation out of the pit of depression and bring about a revolution in the character and quality of government in this country. He was born into great and very old wealth on January 30, 1882, at Springwood, his family's country estate near Hyde Park, New York, not the sort of origins one would expect of a man who would come to be regarded by millions in his own time and even in our own as the "people's" president, a man dedicated to the interests not only of ordinary Americans but of the deprived and persecuted.

The son of an aging but loving gentleman farmer and his young wife, Franklin spent a nearly idyllic childhood, then went on to Groton and Harvard, where his native charm and tall good looks generally overcame his many academic shortcomings. It was in school, by all accounts, that his commitment to the idea of public service began to blossom, a form of noblesse oblige that was no less sincere for being self-consciously aristocratic. At Groton, he was active in the Missionary Society, and while at Harvard he joined the Social Work Society, took time to teach and coach poor boys at St. Andrews Boys Club in Boston, and was an earnest member of the St. Paul's Society, another group devoted to good works. He was suitably proud of his family, which included the Oyster Bay Roosevelts from which his second cousin and the former president, Theodore, had come. While a sophomore, Franklin wrote a paper entitled "The Roosevelt Family in New Amsterdam Before the Revolution," and in it attributed the decline of most of the old Dutch families that had once ruled the region to a lack of "progressiveness and the true democratic spirit." His own family, on the other hand, had true "virility" because of its "very democratic spirit." The Roosevelts, he said proudly, "have never felt that because they were born in a good position they could put their hands in their pockets and succeed. They have felt, rather, that being born in a good position there was no excuse for them if they did not do their duty by the community. . . ." That conviction, tempered and complicated by time and circumstances, would remain at the heart of his political philosophy.

After graduation, Roosevelt was accepted to the bar, but early on had developed an interest in politics and never did spend much time practicing law. Hugely ambitious, he sought to emulate the political career of his older cousin Theodore, a determination given a certain poetic emphasis when he married TR's niece, Eleanor, in 1905. Unlike TR and the other Oyster Bay Roosevelts, who were Republicans — albeit most, like TR, of a strong progressive stripe — Franklin and the Hudson River Roosevelts were Democrats, and it was as a Democrat that he campaigned for and won two terms as a New York State senator (TR had served in the Assembly). In 1913, President Woodrow Wilson appointed him assistant secretary of the Navy (again, a position that had been held once by TR), and after the war he was nominated as James J. Cox's running mate in the 1920 presidential election (TR had been elected vice president with William McKinley in 1900). Defeat that year was followed by an attack of poliomyelitis that nearly killed him and left his legs permanently useless.

Demonstrating an iron will that might have surprised many, Roosevelt refused to let this disaster be anything more than an unfortunate interruption to a career he was determined to take as far as he possibly could. That perseverance, coupled with rare political instincts and undiminished public and private charm, got him elected governor of New York in 1928 (another office that had been filled by TR). And at the end of June, 1932, after a brilliantly managed campaign of primary and state caucus elections and astute arm-twisting and otherwise eloquent persuasion on the part of such allies as James Farley, Louis Howe, and Senators Sam Rayburn and Burt Wheeler, Roosevelt won the Democratic presidential nomination.

Breaking all precedent, Roosevelt flew to Chicago to accept his party's nomination. "I pledge you, I pledge myself," he told the convention,

> to a new deal for the American people. Let all of us here assembled
> constitute ourselves prophets of a new order of competence and of
> courage. This is more than a political campaign; it is a call to arms.
> Give me your help, not to win votes alone, but to win in this crusade
> to restore America to its own greatness.

Now, as July came to an end and the stench from the fires at the BEF Anacostia flats encampment still fouled the air of Washington, Roosevelt told Rexford Tugwell, one of the members of the "Brain Trust" who had helped to direct his campaign, that he was finally certain that he would win. He was right. On November 8, 1932, Franklin Roosevelt received 22,800,000 popular votes to 15,750,000 for Hoover; the electoral college margin was 472 to 59.

Roosevelt's service during two terms as governor of the nation's most populous state in the heart of the nation's most ghastly depression had sharpened his youthful convictions that one of the most important uses of government and government service was to help people who could not help

themselves, and as he had been an activist governor, so was he determined
to be an activist president. As a candidate, he had pledged himself to "a
new deal for the American people," and on Inauguration Day, March 4,
1933, tens of millions of Americans crowded around their radios or the
radios of friends and family to hear him tell them what they might expect
from that promise. Louise Armstrong heard it sitting next to a big console
in the lobby of a Chicago hotel. With her in the room were the desk clerk,
two Filipino hotel workers, and a six-year-old girl who had come up to her
and said, "They told me if I came down here I could hear the president
of the United States talk over the radio." Armstrong invited the girl to sit
with her:

> She sat down beside me and confidingly put her hand in mine. We
> listened for some moments. Then we heard: "President-elect Roosevelt
> is now coming down the ramp —" "Now will he talk?" asked my little
> companion in a stage whisper. "Yes. Very soon now. Be quiet, dear!"
> The Filipino boys had stopped dusting. They stood in front of the great
> French doors . . . immovable. . . . We listened — listened. And at
> last I whispered: "Now! That's the President!"

And this is what they heard him say into a nest of microphones before
a crowd of perhaps 100,000 in the Capitol Plaza in Washington, D. C.,
beneath a dark ceiling of clouds gravid with rain:

> So, first of all, let me assert my firm belief that the only thing we have
> to fear is fear itself — nameless, unreasoning, unjustified terror which
> paralyzes needed efforts to convert retreat into advance. . . .
> [The] withered leaves of industrial enterprise lie on every side;
> farmers find no markets for their produce; the savings of many years
> in thousands of families are gone.
> More important, a host of unemployed citizens face the grim
> problem of existence, and an equally great number toil with little
> return. Only a foolish optimist can deny the dark realities of the
> moment. . . .
> The money changers have fled from their high seats in the temple
> of our civilization. We may now restore that temple to the ancient
> truths. . . .
> I am prepared under my constitutional duty to recommend the
> measures that a stricken Nation in the midst of a stricken world may
> require. . . . But . . . in the event that the national emergency is still
> critical I shall not evade the clear course of duty that will then confront

me. I shall ask the Congress for the one remaining instrument to meet the crisis — broad Executive power to wage a war against the emergency, as great as the power that would be given me if we were in fact invaded by a foreign foe. . . .

The people of the United States have not failed. In their need they have registered a mandate that they want direct, vigorous action. They have asked for discipline and direction under leadership. They have made me the present instrument of their wishes. In the spirit of the gift I take it.

"When it was over," Louise Armstrong remembered eight years later, "the clerk came out from behind the desk and stood beside the radio for a moment. 'God, Mrs. Armstrong!' was all he said. He took out his handkerchief and wiped his forehead."

Armstrong and the hotel clerk knew that they had heard an address of a kind no president had given since Abraham Lincoln had given his own Second Inaugural Address almost sixty years before, calling for a great national healing in the wake of the country's most terrible conflict — its own Civil War. Roosevelt had called for a similar commitment, and had made it clear that if necessary to heal the nation in this latest crisis, he would ask for powers (unspecified, but obviously far-reaching) that no president had ever been given in peacetime. Perhaps Armstrong and the clerk suspected, too, that unlike politicians who mouth words with no real intention of making them real, Roosevelt, like Lincoln before him, meant every word he said.

■■■■ The New Deal Begins

In the months between the election of Franklin Roosevelt and his inauguration on March 4, 1933, fate had seemed determined to prove that things would only get worse before they could get better. Unemployment figures had continued to climb, and by March somewhere between thirteen and fourteen million able-bodied Americans were out of work. That translated to something like forty million people who could not count on a regular source of income. Financial reports after the turn of the year had indicated that in 1932 there had been 1,456 bank failures, with more than $715 million in lost deposits. These were awesome numbers, but they paled in comparison to those of the first two months of 1933, when 4,004 banks with $3.6 billion in deposits had gone down. On March 3, Raymond Moley, one of FDR's advisers, had received an unsettling letter from W. A. Sheaffer, president of the Sheaffer Pen Company, whose fountain pens were

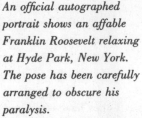

An official autographed portrait shows an affable Franklin Roosevelt relaxing at Hyde Park, New York. The pose has been carefully arranged to obscure his paralysis.

President-elect Roosevelt attempts to make polite conversation with a stone-faced Hoover as they prepare for the trip from the White House to the Capitol for FDR's inauguration, March 4, 1933. Hoover had every reason to be glum; he had been trounced the previous November. "All the money in the world could not induce me to live over the last nine months," he said early in 1933. "The conditions we have experienced make this office a compound Hell." Roosevelt was more than happy to assume the burden, however, and when he found it impossible to get Hoover to chat during the ride, he started waving his hat at the crowds that lined the route.

He campaigned bravely, but as the apple seller and the empty store that flank the Pittsburgh headquarters of the Hoover Club of Eastern Pennsylvania testify, the odds against Hoover were insurmountable.

clipped to the pockets of most literate Americans in that era. "We have today our checks returned and refused from twenty-four states and it looks as though in a few days business would be at an actual standstill," it read. "Therefore, the most urgent emergency in the history of our nation is at hand."

Everywhere in urban America the breadlines were longer, the Hoovervilles more crowded, the stink of hopelessness more rank. In the Midwest, a desperate resentment continued among the farm population, much of it kept at a rolling boil by the Farmer's Holiday Association, founded by a radical Campbellite minister by the name of Milo Reno, president of the militant Iowa Farmers Union. Reno and his union were convinced that farmers, like industrial workers, must be prepared to strike — to withhold not merely their work, but the very goods they produced on their own land — in order to win necessary changes. In May, 1932, the Iowa Farmers Union had organized a national convention in Des Moines to discuss the ways and means of striking, and out of this convention came the Farmer's Holiday Association, with Reno as its president. With the rather stolid slogan, "Stay at Home — Buy Nothing — Sell Nothing," a strike, or "holiday," had been launched in August. It was a messy, turbulent, sometimes bloody, and occasionally sticky business, especially when it came to the marketing of milk. "All the roads leading to Sioux City were picketed," Mary Heaton Vorse reported from Iowa.

> Trucks by hundreds were turned back. Farmers by hundreds lined the roads. They blockaded the roads with spiked telegraph poles and logs. They took away a sheriff's badge and his gun and threw them in a cornfield. Gallons of milk ran down roadway ditches. Gallons of confiscated milk were distributed free on the streets of Sioux City.

"They say blockading the highway's illegal," an old man told her. "I says, 'Seems to me there was a Tea-party in Boston that was illegal too.' "

Small in number (active participants probably represented no more than 10 percent of the farm population in the region), but wrapped in patriotic certitude, the strikers had kept much of the region in a state of sporadic turmoil for months — particularly when they developed tactics that were emulated frequently in other parts of the country where farms and mortgages met. These activist devices were called "penny-auctions" and "Sears-Roebuck sales," and they were simplicity itself.

When news would get out that a neighbor's farm had been foreclosed and was up for auction and all his chattel property subject to sale, handbills would circulate and on the appointed day for the proceedings, scores of farmers would come out to the property, sometimes from as far away as a hundred miles, gather in the farmyard, and by one means or another make it clear to the auctioneer and attending county sheriffs and other officials that this auction was not going to be your normal run-of-the-mill affair — often by dangling a well-noosed rope from a haymow or a tree in a suggestive manner. When the bidding commenced, someone in the crowd would start it off at fifteen cents or so, and it rarely got beyond a few dollars before the bidding stopped and the auctioneer would close the sale. If anyone in the farmyard might be so ignorant of what was going on as to put in a serious bid, a suitably burly man would be likely to step up and put a hand on his shoulder with the words, "That bid's a little high, ain't it?" So it was that in the fall of 1932 an $800 mortgage on Walter Crozier's farm outside Haskins, Iowa, was satisfied for $1.90, or that the horses, cows, and chickens offered for sale at Theresa Von Baum's farm near Elgin, Nebraska, went back to her at a nickel apiece, for a total of $5.35.

Agricultural historian John L. Shover estimates that at least seventy-six foreclosure sales were blocked by such direct action in the months of January and February, 1933, alone. The Iowa state legislature took the point, and on February 17 passed a foreclosure moratorium law, while in Minnesota eight days later Governor Olson issued a decree establishing a one-year moratorium. Many other farm states would later follow suit, but the potential for violence remained high as the members of the new administration got down to work on Sunday, March 5, just a few hours after the band had played the last dance at the inaugural ball in the huge government auditorium down on Constitution Avenue.

It must be said that the new caretakers of government did not let the staggering dimensions of the crisis dim their enthusiasm. Roosevelt brought with him men and women who, for the most part, shared his determination and his reformist convictions. They became known collectively as the New Dealers, and they were one of the most variegated groups ever assembled by any administration any time — from Frances Perkins, who had been Roosevelt's industrial commissioner in New York and now became his secretary of labor (the first female cabinet member in American history), to Harold L. Ickes, a veteran of the urban reform movement in Chicago, who now became his secretary of the interior; from FDR's conservative Hudson River Valley neighbor, Henry Morgenthau, who had been his state conservation commissioner in New York and would become his secretary of the treasury after the resignation of William Woodin, to populist Senator Cordell Hull of Tennessee, who became his secretary of state. With these and dozens of others — intellectuals, politicians, bureaucrats, reformers, educators, planners, analysts, journalists, sociologists, economists, and

Even before the elections in November, 1932, farmers in Iowa had responded to the call of Milo Reno and the Farmer's Holiday Association to "Stay at Home — Buy Nothing — Sell Nothing" in an attempt to force the government to institute a farm program to stabilize prices and give them mortgage relief. "Let's call a 'Farmer's Holiday,' " a ditty in the Iowa Union Farmer ran, "A Holiday let's hold/We'll eat our wheat and ham and eggs/And let them eat their gold" Among other devices utilized by the strikers was the roadblock, like this one set up outside Council Bluffs, Iowa. "If we farmers go down bankrupt," a blockading striker told a reporter for The Nation, "everything in this country goes down"

Between 1930 and 1935 as many as 750,000 farms were lost through bankruptcy or sheriff's sales, as in the quiet courtroom moment captured by photographer Dorothea Lange, OPPOSITE, TOP. More dramatic were "penny auctions," forced sales in which farmers from around a county would gather to assure that a beleaguered neighbor would be able to buy back his own place and goods by holding bids down to pennies, nickels, dimes, or quarters. Those who might have been tempted to make serious bids were soon enough dissuaded — sometimes symbolically, as with the dangling nooses in the auction scene OPPOSITE. "In our part of the country," one farmer said, "when a sale comes on, we warn people that anyone buying a place won't find life worth living there."

labor organizers — together with hundreds, then thousands, of worker bees who swarmed into Washington, Roosevelt began to reassemble the bones of government. "You never saw before in Washington so much government, or so much animation in government," columnist Anne O'Hare McCormick told her readers at the end of April, 1933. "Everybody in the administration is having the time of his life."

They found a Congress that was more than willing to listen to what they had to say. Shaken and nearly as helpless in the face of the crisis as the Hoover administration had been, most members agreed with speaker of the house Henry Rainey when he said that the present situation was similar to that during the first few months after America's entrance into World War I, when "on both sides of this Chamber the great war measures suggested by the administration were supported with practical unanimity. . . . Today we are engaged in another war, more serious even in its character and presenting greater dangers to the Republic." Writing in the March 22 issue of the *New Republic*, "TRB" even accepted the notion that what was going on in Washington was a form of dictatorship:

> As things stand today, Mr. Roosevelt has, in some respects, more power than any President under our Constitution ever had, except perhaps Mr. Wilson in wartime, and while some thoughtful men here are disturbed over what they call a surrender of its constitutional rights by Congress, the shadow of the national emergency stills their protest and controls their vote. And when the facts are considered it seems clear that nothing else could be done.

In spite of popular belief, what was going on in the first few weeks of the New Deal fell far short of dictatorship, but it certainly was opportunity. Such tender acquiescence on the part of Congress would not last forever, and the New Dealers struck swiftly and often while the legislative iron was hot. In the dizzying span of weeks that would come to be called the Hundred Days, Roosevelt and his people set in motion more administrative actions and initiated more legislation than at any similar period of history before or since. The first, however, had not been an idea original with the Roosevelt administration. Earlier, Hoover had urged FDR to join with him in a joint declaration that would impose a brief "bank holiday." Roosevelt had refused. Now, as president himself, he moved, declaring a four-day holiday throughout the nation, beginning Monday morning, March 6, so that Congress could come up with legislation to straighten out the reeling banking system. Many governors had already declared holidays, and at the urging of Roosevelt's people, the rest followed suit on Friday,

March 3. Roosevelt's order of March 6, however, gave the act the weight of something truly momentous. Ted C. Hinckley, whose father was a reasonably affluent lawyer in Pasadena, remembered the first day of the nationwide bank holiday vividly:

> I was seated in our breakfast nook when the back door opened and my father walked in or, I should say, slowly entered. His face was almost ashen. His eyes, usually filled with bonhomie, were filled with fear. My mother rose but, before she could say a word, he groaned, "They have closed the banks."

The elder Hinckley's despair was premature. On March 9, Congress passed the Emergency Banking Act of 1933, and by March 13, banks had started to reopen; by the end of the month three-quarters of them would be back in business. However shocking, Roosevelt's order to close the banks — as well as the Emergency Banking Act — may have been among the *least* revolutionary of the New Deal's programs. However driven he may have been to change the government, Roosevelt, like Treasury Secretary Morgenthau, was essentially a fiscal conservative. Throughout his term, he would repeatedly call for balanced budgets — and if his own social programs would make balanced budgets all but impossible, he nevertheless was utterly sincere in his desire. His clear determination was to refine the capitalist system, not obliterate it and replace it with something new. The order to close the banks and passage of the Emergency Banking Act, then, had been designed not to transmogrify the banking system, but merely to stabilize it by instituting a reorganization plan and setting up loans from the Reconstruction Finance Corporation, among other devices. Indeed, the bill was so conservative that it had startled many members of Congress, who had expected something a good deal more drastic. Possibly with a sense of relief, the House passed it by voice vote the afternoon of its introduction on March 9 after only thirty-eight minutes of debate; the Senate was more cautious — it did not pass the bill until 7:30 that evening, by a vote of 73 to 7. Three months later, Roosevelt would sign another, more complex Banking Act, this one giving the Federal Reserve greater control over the banking system and creating the Federal Deposit Insurance Corporation.

Hunger Is Not Debatable

Few of the financial programs of the Hundred Days possessed quite the emotional and psychological force of the bank holiday. Most — like the decision to go off the gold standard on April 19 or passage of the Federal Securities Act on May 27 — would have long-range impacts on the economic life of the country but less immediate impact on most people. Not so the government's relief programs, which were indisputably direct, massive in scale, and, if flawed and too often confused and confusing, affected the lives of millions at the level of survival itself.

Roosevelt did not share Hoover's faith that individual charity and the efforts of the private sector and local governments would be enough to get people fed and clothed and housed. He had learned better while governor of New York, and among the earliest and most lasting goals of his presidency was to provide federal relief to as many people as possible as soon as possible. To do it, he chose the man who had supervised relief programs for him in New York State — Harry L. Hopkins, a forty-three-year-old horse-playing social worker whose outspokenness, colorful personal habits, and camaraderie with the press would make him perhaps the most visible New Dealer of them all. When Congress created the Federal Emergency Relief Administration (FERA) in May, 1933, funding it with an appropriation of $500 million to be provided by the Reconstruction Finance Corporation, Roosevelt asked Hopkins to come down to Washington to run it.

"I'm not going to last six months here, so I'll do as I please," Hopkins told the press when he started on May 22. By the end of his first day, he had pleased both himself and several states with grants totalling about $5 million. From then on, Hopkins spent freely, if not blindly. Half the $500 million was to be paid to the states as outright grants, as on his first day; the other half would take the form of matching grants — one dollar of federal money for every three dollars of local money allocated for relief. The law required each state to set up and support a local FERA office and raise its own relief funds through taxes, bond issues, borrowing, or any other means at its disposal. When Kentucky, West Virginia, and Ohio, among others, neglected to make such allocations, Hopkins refused to send matching federal funds until their legislatures complied. "Every department of government that has any taxing power left," he said, "has a direct responsibility to help those in distress."

Still, his commitment to satisfying the most basic human needs was absolute. When someone offered up a program that they said would be of benefit "in the long run," he replied, "People don't eat in the long run — they eat every day." The urgency with which he spoke was validated by the reports sent to him from all over the country by FERA officials and a number of roving correspondents. Chief among the latter was a friend of Eleanor Roosevelt's, newswoman Lorena Hickock, who wrote to both the First Lady and Hopkins regularly during several trips into the West. A letter to Mrs. Roosevelt from Bottineau County, North Dakota, in the early winter of 1933 was typical:

> Last winter the temperature went down to 40 below zero and stayed there ten days, while a 60-mile wind howled across the plains. And entering that kind of winter we have between 4,000 and 5,000 human beings . . . without clothing or bedding, getting just enough food to keep them from starving. No fuel. Living in houses that a prosperous farmer wouldn't put his cattle in. . . . They now have 850 families on relief, and applications are coming in at the rate of 15 or 20 a day.

And so they came, in Bottineau County and everywhere else, hands out, angrily, sadly, resignedly, desperately, lining up outside county Emergency Relief Administration offices, filling wooden benches inside, waiting their turn to be interviewed, to testify to their financial shame while case workers doggedly filled out the agonizingly detailed forms that would determine their right to vouchers redeemable for carefully stipulated amounts of food, rent, coal, or heating oil. On client and case worker alike, the stress was terrific. "[You] had people packed into two big waiting rooms, waiting to be called," social worker Augusta Dunbar remembered of the early days of the relief office in Fulton County, Georgia. "Some waited all day and weren't called and had to come back the next day. There were just ten of us. The case load, the number of families you have, was in the thousands. . . ."

Some of the relief was more direct than slips of paper. In September and October, 1933, the federal agricultural program ordered the slaughtering of 6.1 million young pigs as a means to control overproduction and stabilize prices. Much of that meat went to waste, to the outrage of millions of citizens, like Claude E. Thompson of Frankfort, Indiana. "[We] PROTEST THIS ACTION," he telegraphed the president, "AS BEING UNAMERICAN IN PRINCIPLE IN VIEW OF THE FACT THAT WE HAVE THOUSANDS UPON THOUSANDS OF UNDERNOURISHED MEN WOMEN AND CHILDREN IN THIS COUNTRY TODAY WHO ARE UNABLE TO PROCURE A BIT OF MEAT. . . ." In response, the administration established a quasi-public nonprofit entity called the Federal Surplus Relief Corporation to purchase surplus hogs, chickens, livestock, and produce of all kinds — usually by competitive bids in order to guarantee the farmer a fair price. The food was then to be shipped to individual states for distribution to the needy through existing relief programs. Cotton goods were soon added to the distribution system as well. Before its end, the FSRC would distribute 9.4 million pounds of fresh apples, 6.8 million pounds of beans, 290.9 million pounds of tinned beef,

190.5 million pounds of flour, and 297.6 million pounds of pork products.

Whether in the form of vouchers or cans of tinned beef, the straight dole was perceived by most FERA officials to be demeaning and dehumanizing. Roosevelt himself — even as governor of New York — had been constitutionally opposed to the idea of straight welfare, except as an emergency measure. Like Herbert Hoover (though Roosevelt would not have enjoyed the comparison), he believed that the dole was damaging to individual character and that it was better for people to work for what they received. This view was shared in large part by the individuals in question. In her remarkable 1941 memoir of her term as an FERA administrator in a northern Michigan county, *We, Too, Are the People*, Louise Armstrong patched together a doxology of comments from her clients in which the theme of work, work, work ran like a threnody: "It's very hard for me to ask for help," said one. "I don't want charity. I want work — any kind of work. I'll do road work, or anything. . . ." Said another: "I'll do anything, just so it's a job. . . ." And another: "Can't you give me work regular? I got to have a job! . . ." And still another: "Maybe you think I like to come up here beggin'! I don't want no God-damn relief orders! I want work, I tell you! Work! Work! I got to have a job!"

That was the cry that Roosevelt heard, and where he differed from Hoover was in his belief that the government itself could and should provide the work. The FERA had maintained a small work-relief program during its first months, but it was hampered by limitations that relegated most of the jobs to make-work. As the winter of 1933–34 approached, however, Hopkins became more and more convinced that a major work program was going to have to be instituted. By the end of October, he and his aides had devised the blueprint for a wide-scale program that they were convinced could employ four million people over the winter months. Roosevelt liked the scheme and said so during a press conference: "There is a great deal to be said for it. . . . It adds to the self-respect of the country, and we are trying to find out whether a plan of that kind is a feasible thing to do." Hopkins took this as a signal to begin. When an aide asked him later whether the president had approved the plan, he answered, "Approved it, hell! He just announced it at his press conference!"

They called it the Civil Works Administration, and within two weeks 800,000 people were working, with a total payroll of $7.8 million. By the height of the CWA effort in the middle of January, a shade more than the promised four million were in fact working, with a payroll of more than $62 million spent on thousands of projects, among them the construction and repair of highways and roads, bridges, schools, parks and playgrounds, hospitals, airports, flood control facilities, privies, and other public works. Overall, the program was enormously popular, and when the original allocation was gone, Hopkins went to the president and the president went to Congress, and Congress, with an eye on the 1934 elections, provided another $950 million, $450 million to be used to carry the CWA through a phasing-down period, the rest to be used to finance continuing FERA programs. "If Roosevelt ever becomes Jesus Christ," one senator remarked, "he should have Harry Hopkins as his prophet."

"Hunger," Hopkins the prophet said, "is not debatable." Neither was it gender-specific, as Eleanor Roosevelt was swift to point out. As the daughter of an alcoholic father and a distant, critical mother — both of whom had died before Eleanor was ten years old — Mrs. Roosevelt had endured an excruciating childhood, nearly empty of both parental contact and emotional stability. Surviving that bleak upbringing could have embittered her; instead, it had nurtured deep-felt concern for the deprived and downtrodden, which not only had complemented the instincts of her husband but had encouraged and enlarged them. Mrs. Roosevelt was determined to be every bit as much of an activist as her husband, and among her abiding interests was in how the depression was affecting the lives of women — and in how women could be made part of the solution.

Early in the New Deal, Mrs. Roosevelt joined with Mary Dewson, head of the women's division of the Democratic National Committee, and later one of the highest-ranking woman officials in the New Deal, Labor Secretary Frances Perkins, and the leaders of such organizations as the Women's National Democratic Club to knit together the strands of a powerful network dedicated to getting Democratic women their fair share of the patronage pie and significant jobs for all women within the blossoming agencies of the administration. To a degree, at least, they were successful. Ohio supreme court justice Florence Allen was appointed to the U. S. Court of Appeals for the Sixth Circuit, the first such appointment for a woman. Former U. S. congresswoman Ruth Bryan Owen became the first woman foreign emmissary when she was appointed minister to Denmark in 1934, and Democratic committeewoman Daisy Harriman became the second when she was appointed minister to Norway three years later. Josephine Roche was appointed assistant secretary of the treasury in 1934.

Still, the overall proportion of women among the nearly one million employees of the federal government would never rise above 19 percent in the New Deal years, and nearly every federal appointment won had taken a dogged effort that taxed even the uncommon patience of Mary Dewson. "Heavens but the nicest of men are slippery as eels," she wrote Mrs.

Roosevelt after one especially frustrating session with Postmaster General James B. Farley, chief of patronage. The First Lady herself had smoother going with Hopkins, whom she persuaded to create a women's division within the FERA, and in August, 1933, he hired Ellen Woodward, then executive director of the Mississippi State Board of Development, to run it. In consultation with such other women in the Roosevelt administration as Dr. Louise Stanley of the Department of Agriculture, Katherine Lenroot of the Children's Bureau, and Mary Anderson, head of the Department of Labor Women's Bureau, Woodward already had gone a long way toward organizing specific relief and work-relief programs for women when the CWA was created.

To make sure that women became part of the CWA programs and remained in those of the FERA, Mrs. Roosevelt convened a White House Conference on the Emergency Needs of Women on November 20, 1933, and one result of this gathering of women social workers and administration officials was an order from Hopkins that all state FERA directors "pay particular attention that women are employed wherever possible." This somewhat limp instruction was taken by Woodward at face value, and by the middle of February, 1934, more than 300,000 women — 53 percent of those who qualified for relief — were at work on various CWA projects designed specifically for them: sewing, furniture repair, nursing, dental work, public records surveys, highway and park beautification, secretarial work, and such home economics items as canning, housekeeping work, matron services, and school-lunchroom cooking.

For women and men alike, however, the CWA was a temporary expedient, something to carry people through the winter months. True to his word to close down the CWA once the worst of the winter was over, Hopkins began dismantling the program on schedule, and it ended permanently on March 31, 1934. Nevertheless, it had proved so practical and so popular that the FERA's own programs were substantially restructured to include far more work projects than before — and both Roosevelt and Hopkins took comfort from a report given them by Frank Walker, head of the National Emergency Council, designed to monitor New Deal programs. In Montana, Walker wrote, he had seen "men I had been to school with — digging ditches and laying sewer pipe" wearing business clothes because they could not afford work clothes. They did not feel in the slightest demeaned, he said, as he learned when one of his friends pulled a few coins out of his pocket and showed them to him. "Do you know, Frank, this is the first money I've had in my pockets in a year and a half? Up to now, I've had nothing but tickets that you could exchange for groceries." And another told him this:

> I hate to think what would have happened if this work hadn't come
> along. The last of my savings had run out. I'd sold or hocked everything
> I could. And my kids were hungry. I stood in front of the window of
> the bake-shop down the street and I wondered just how long it would
> be before I got desperate enough to pick up a rock and heave it through
> that window and grab some bread to take home.

"I'd pay little attention," Walker advised Roosevelt and Hopkins, "to those
who criticize the creation of C. W. A. or its administration. . . . It is my
considered opinion that this has averted one of the most serious crises in
our history."

▬▬▬ The Soil Soldiers

Frank Walker's assessment was probably true, at least in large part;
the emergency relief program of the CWA did feed and clothe hungry
families through a terrible winter and gave workers a tangible measure of
pride to go along with their relief checks. Designed and operated as a
temporary device to meet a level of crisis that the New Dealers hoped was
temporary, the CWA was a definitive expression of one important aspect
of how the New Dealers tended to function. Much of the legislation that
had come and would come out of the Hundred Days was of the same
character — immediate responses to immediate problems, even when some
of those responses (like the two banking acts of 1933) would end up having
a permanent impact on the national life. For the most part, the New Dealers
had not come to Washington with an agreed-upon agenda of specific programs carefully planned and ready to go; what they brought with them was
spontaneity and inventiveness. "I am for experimenting," Harry Hopkins
said at one point, "trying out schemes which are supported by reasonable
people and see if they work. If they do not work, the world will not come
to an end." Such pragmatic flexibility was not universally shared among
Roosevelt's people (it tended to make Treasury Secretary Henry Morgenthau, for example, more than a little nervous, and mortally offended the
sensibilities of Budget Director Lewis Douglas), but it did characterize
much of their best and most lasting work.

One such experiment would become one of the most durable and well
regarded of all the New Deal's programs — and it came from the president
himself, who had his own share of inventiveness. If the president cared
about the fate of people, he also cared about the fate of trees, having
practiced the arts of silviculture on his Hyde Park estate with such enthusiasm that on various official forms he was fond of listing his occupation

as "tree farmer." It was in early March, 1933, that he proceeded to bring the two concerns together — enlisting young unemployed men in a kind of volunteer "army" to be put to work in the national forests, national parks, and on other federal public lands. When he went to Congress for authorization of the program, he called the new agency the Civilian Corps Reforestation Youth Rehabilitation Movement, but before sinking under the weight of an acronym like CCRYRM, it was soon changed to the Civilian Conservation Corps (known forever after as the CCC). Congress chose not to handle the details itself; it simply authorized the president to create the program and structure it as he saw fit by executive order; it was to last two years. Responsibility was divided up among the Labor Department, which would screen and select the enrollees, the War Department, which would house and feed them in their nonworking hours, and the Departments of Agriculture and Interior, which would design and supervise projects in regional and national forests, national parks, Soil Conservation Service reclamation work, and various other public tasks. The men would be paid $30 a month, anywhere from $23 to $25 of it to be sent to their families.

The CCC officially began on April 5, 1933, calling for an enrollment of 250,000 to be housed in 1,468 camps around the country. The cost for the first year was estimated at $500 million. The men had to be U. S. citizens between the ages of seventeen and twenty-seven (later, twenty-four), out of school, out of work, capable of physical labor, over 60 inches but under 78 inches in height, more than 107 pounds in weight, and had to possess no fewer than "three serviceable natural masticating teeth above and below." They would serve terms of no more than nine months so that as many as possible could be accommodated over the course of time.

Among the earliest enrollees were some veterans who had come to Washington once more, setting up camp and demanding payment of their bonuses for service during the war. While making it clear that he opposed the payments on economic grounds, FDR provided tents, showers, mess halls, and latrines, and, waiving the age restriction for them, invited the members of this new Bonus Army to join his new agency. What was more, Eleanor Roosevelt dropped by one rainy day for a visit, slogging through ankle-deep mud to meet and talk with the men. "Hoover sent the army," said one veteran of the previous summer's BEF disaster, "Roosevelt sent his wife." When it became clear that no bonus would be forthcoming, about twenty-five hundred of the men took Roosevelt up on his offer and joined the CCC.

In the summer of 1934 Roosevelt expanded the size of the CCC to 350,000 and would raise it to 500,000 in 1935. Congress continued to reauthorize it faithfully over the next seven years, and by the time it was closed out in 1942, the CCC had put more than three million young "soil soldiers" to work. In the national forests alone they built 3,470 fire towers; installed 65,100 miles of telephone lines; scraped and graded thousands of fire breaks, roads, and trails, and built 97,000 miles of truck trails and roads; spent 4.1 million man-hours fighting fires; and cut down and hauled out millions of diseased trees and planted more than 1.3 billion young trees in the first major reforestation campaign in the country's history. For the National Park Service they built roads, campgrounds, bridges, and recreation and administration facilities; for the Biological Survey (a predecessor of today's Fish and Wildlife Service) they conducted wildlife surveys and improved wildlife refuge lands; and for the Army Corps of Engineers they built flood control projects in West Virginia, Vermont, and New York State.

In return, the CCC at its best took at least some young men out of the urban tangle of hopelessness where so many resided, introduced them to the intricacies and healing joy of the outdoors, clothed them, fed them simply but better than many had enjoyed for years, taught more than a hundred thousand to read and write, passed out twenty-five thousand eighth-grade diplomas and five thousand high-school diplomas, gave structure and discipline to lives that had experienced little of either, strengthened bodies and minds, and for many provided a dose of self-esteem they had never known. "There may be some people who will say, 'You had to stick it out, there was no other choice,' " enrollee Donald B. Miller wrote as his valedictory in *Happy Days*, the CCC's national newspaper.

> Perhaps you are right, my friends, but an unhappy experience is best forgotten — and we are not trying to forget. . . . We shall all cherish the memory of this brief adventure. We shall be proud to have been members of this army of pioneers, as our forefathers were proud of being the forerunners of a great nation. We say farewell with regret, but face the future with enthusiasm, feeling that we have proven ourselves men.

To Plow Up the Indian Soul

Another generally admired and durable "invention" of the Roosevelt revolution in the early months of the New Deal reached into a corner of American life in which government traditionally had been just another form of enemy — part of an old culture of misunderstanding that had persisted for generations and was alive and well even in the first third of the twentieth century. It was articulated with unconscious humor by the first young man

Eleanor Roosevelt, seen giving a speech at the Hollywood Bowl, was the most publicly active First Lady in American history, and many historians have given her major credit for FDR's sensitivity to human needs.

The New Deal begins: taken on Sunday, March 5, 1933, the day after FDR's inauguration, this picture is the first photograph of a presidential cabinet in session. The first topic for discussion almost certainly would have been the banking crisis.

Some three million enrollees ultimately answered the knock of the "Young Man's Opportunity" touted by this CCC poster. BELOW: FDR and a collection of New Dealers ingest a CCC lunch in Shenandoah National Park in August, 1933.

to qualify and enroll in the CCC. His name was Fiore Rizzo, an Italian American from Manhattan, one of a family of thirteen children whose father had been out of work for three years. After Rizzo took his oath, someone told him that he would be assigned to a camp out West. He scratched his head, looked worried, then spoke for the ignorance of most of his countrymen: "What the hell are we going to do about those Indians?"

What to do about "those Indians" was not a new question in American life, but when Interior Secretary Harold Ickes appointed John Collier, president of the American Indian Defense Association, as commissioner of the Bureau of Indian Affairs, the federal government began looking for answers more earnestly than at any time since the Dawes Severalty Act of 1887 had vainly attempted to make Apollonian dirt farmers out of Dionysian nomads. Collier was swift to make certain that Native Americans were folded into the relief and work-relief programs of the FERA and CWA. He also structured the CCC's Indian Emergency Conservation Work program — more simply known as the CCC's Indian Division — so that it would more accurately reflect the particular needs of the Indians and the cultural imperatives under which most of them lived. There was no age requirement in the Indian Division, for example, and most were given work assignments on their own reservations. Collier and the director of the Indian Division, Daniel E. Murphy, also encouraged the participation of the Indians in the actual management of the program, and more than half of the division's supervisory and salaried jobs ultimately were held by Native Americans.

Possibly Collier's most enduring accomplishment was in reversing the fifty-year insistence on assimilation. The urge to persuade Native Americans to assimilate with white culture in order to save themselves was one of the oldest and least successful impulses of American reform. It had not worked in the 1880s, when the Dawes Severalty Act had tried to codify it in law, and it was not working when Collier took over as Indian commissioner in 1933. For all his arrogant assumptions that he "understood" Indians (as if they were a single people, and not a bewildering mosaic of distinct societies, most with mutually unintelligible dialects and discrete traditions), Collier did understand assimilation's failure. He undertook instead to establish a system that would enable the Indians to survive, if not exactly flourish, within the white society while keeping their tribal identities and cultural strengths more or less intact. "Our design," he said grandly, "is to plow up the Indian soul, to make the Indian again the master of his own mind."

The machinery to implement what would come to be called the "Indian New Deal" was embodied in the Indian Reorganization Act of 1934. The result of months of uncommonly intricate negotiation, maneuvering, and compromise, the act was a good deal less than Collier had hoped, but given

The "Indian New Deal" was generally welcomed by Native-American peoples, but not by the Navajo, who refused to take part in FDR's reform program, in spite of entreaties from BIA commissioner John Collier. He is shown addressing a Navajo gathering in Window Rock, Arizona, 1937.

In spite of the New Deal, most Indians remained bitterly poor, like the three generations of a Navajo family waiting for rations in St. Michael's, Arizona, 1937.

both the complexity of the Indian "question" and the limited ability of white politicians to comprehend nonwhite cultures, it remained a significant break with tradition. It repealed the Dawes Severalty Act; attempted to rationalize and equalize the unworkable land-allotment scheme that severalty had established; organized the reservation tribes into self-governing bodies which, after they had adopted suitable consitutions and by-laws, could police themselves and act as legal entities in their relationship with federal, state, and local governments; established a revolving credit fund for the use of tribal governments; allowed tribes that had adopted constitutions to incorporate themselves, with the power to establish and regulate Indian businesses and, after a ten-year moratorium, to control land sales and leases on the reservations; and, in the most revolutionary of all its provisions, the act stipulated that the Indians themselves had to vote for it by secret ballot before it would become effective for any given tribe — for the first time, Native Americans would be given a choice, however limited, in how they were to be governed. Similar laws were later passed to meet the special needs of the "Five Civilized Tribes" of Oklahoma (many of whom had in fact gone a long way toward assimilation) and those of Alaska (who had simply been forgotten in the writing of the Indian Reorganization Act itself).

From the beginning, this ambitious law was frustrated by recalcitrant members of Congress, many of whom did not like Collier personally and who further feared his "socialistic" tendencies. Collier might have expected that; what he did not expect was that 73 out of 245 tribes that held elections ultimately would choose to exercise their right of self-determination by repudiating the act, for a variety of reasons. The most painful rejection was that of the Navajo, the largest single Native-American population in the country. When government officials instituted a necessary but dreadfully administered reduction in the numbers of sheep on the reservation in order to stop the erosion of overgrazed soils into the drainage of the Colorado River, the Navajo responded to what they perceived as a typically arbitrary assault on their culture and traditions by overwhelmingly voting against participation in Collier's program.

For all the failures of Collier's programs, his determination to preserve the cultural traditions and tribal character of Native Americans remained one of the most important contributions of the Roosevelt era. "The Indian New Deal wasn't perfect," John Echohawk, director of today's Native American Rights Fund, has said, "but its results were fundamentally beneficial for Indian people. The Indian Reorganization Act reversed the direction of American Indian policy. The pattern of history changed from the erosion of Indian sovereignty to its restoration and revival."

▬▬▬ *The New Symbiosis*

The relief programs that marched so bravely through the first two years or so of the New Deal were less than perfect — and especially for people of color, probably not all that much to sing about. However committed the agency heads might be, they could not fully control their programs at the local level. Though it did not deliberately exclude African Americans — and in fact enrolled many — even the Civilan Conservation Corps was raddled by discrimination and bigotry. And no matter what form relief might take, Mary White Ovington, treasurer of the NAACP, pointed out at the time, it "varies according to the white people chosen to administer it, but always there is discrimination."

The CCC and Collier's Indian programs had some durability, but for nearly everyone the work-relief programs were at best temporary and inadequate shields against fate and circumstance. Wages were barely sufficient for subsistence, because Roosevelt and Hopkins did not want to encourage the development of a permanent dependence upon relief — and because local industries voiced powerful objections to wages competitively higher than those they were willing to pay (this fact did not sit all that well with labor, but in this instance objections from that quarter went unsatisfied). The bureaucratic system that had been created worked with just about as much speed and efficiency as most such systems do — which is to say, not much. Nor did the programs ever manage to aid the bulk of the needy; as many as five million unemployed people were left to the inadequate mercies of state relief programs, which in some of the poorer states gave a family less than ten dollars a month on which to live.

That said, there is something else to be said: with all their failings, the FERA, the CWA, and all the rest changed the shape of life for all Americans in this country permanently. We are not talking here about a right-wing shibboleth, the charge that the New Deal had created a so-called "welfare state," with the implication that there was now an underclass of people who would forever be sapped of individuality and independence, parasites living off the very muscle of the Republic. Then as now, few people who were offered work would refuse it. No, the change set in motion during these early years was at once more simple and more profoundly important: what redeemed this hour in American history was the birth of an unprecedented sense of mutual responsibility — of the government for the people, of the people for the government — a symbiosis more intricate and far-reaching in its impact than we have yet learned how to measure.

The New Utopians

Utopian goals? Yes, Utopian indeed, but I do not apologize for suggesting that Utopia is a proper goal for us to strive for and that we are worthy of such a realm if we can achieve it. We are a spiritual people, and life for us would not be worth living if we did not have this urge to reach for what will always seem beyond our reach. If we cannot have it for ourselves, we want it for our children, those projections of ourselves into immortality.

Harold L. Ickes, Secretary of the Interior,
The New York Times Magazine,
May 27, 1934

Chapter Five

Overleaf:

The people of the country, columnist Anne O'Hare McCormick wrote in mid-May, 1933, "are vivified by a strong undercurrent of wonder and excitement. You feel the stir of movement, of adventure, of elation." Whatever else might be said of Roosevelt and the New Dealers, it cannot be denied that they loosed powerful reserves of hope in people who had been functioning on the edge of despair for years — possibly even those hanging around in a pool hall in Muncie, Indiana, photographed by Margaret Bourke-White in 1937.

▰▰▰ *Building Human Happiness*

WE ARE," ROOSEVELT SAID at the beginning of his term, "definitely in the era of building; the best kind of building — the building of great public projects for the benefit of the public and with the definite objective of building human happiness." While the New Deal would build many things, his words were as much metaphor as description. Human happiness was indeed what the New Dealers wanted to build out of the materials of reform, and it was clear to them that the relief programs of the early months, while absolutely necessary to the short-term survival of millions of people, were not the stuff of regeneration. "Happiness lies not in the mere possession of money," Roosevelt had said as part of his inaugural address,

> it lies in the joy of achievement, in the thrill of creative effort. The joy and moral stimulation of work no longer must be forgotten in the mad chase of evanescent profits. These dark days will be worth all they cost us if they teach us that our true destiny is not to be ministered to but to minister to ourselves and to our fellow men.

This was something more than simple inaugural rhetoric; Roosevelt and most of the New Dealers believed in such goals, and believed, too, that the construction of human happiness would require reshaping much of the ways in which Americans then lived and worked — how the financial world functioned, how industry made and sold its goods, how communities grew, how natural resources were protected and used, how human beings could overcome their natural tendencies toward greed and shortsightedness and replace them with an equally natural generosity of spirit and consideration of the future.

No small order, but it did not daunt the movers and shakers of the New Deal — individuals like Raymond Moley, the arid intellectual from Columbia; Rexford Guy Tugwell, Moley's more visionary Columbia colleague; Interior Secretary Harold Ickes, the crusty, short-tempered Progressive Republican from Chicago; Labor Secretary Frances Perkins, the uncommonly observant, voluble, and energetic former industrial commissioner for New York State; Donald Richberg, a radical labor lawyer from Chicago and former law partner of Harold Ickes; Agriculture Secretary Henry Wallace, the slightly quixotic corn geneticist and farmer-philosopher from Iowa; Henry Morgenthau's assistant, Marriner Eccles, an economist who shared the deficit-spending economic theories of the British economic philosopher John Maynard Keynes; and teams of lesser-known thinkers who did much of the actual work, prominent among them Thomas Corcoran and Benjamin Cohen, bright young protégés of the Yale School of Law's liberal-minded Felix Frankfurter, and a trio of radical young reformers in the Department of Agriculture, Jerome Frank, Gardiner Means, and Alger Hiss.

Individuals like these had not come to Washington with fully developed plans tucked into their bulging briefcases, but they arrived ready to start making such plans the minute their trains pulled into Union Station. Whatever else may have differentiated them from one another, most shared a conviction that if enough thought, time, energy, money, purpose, and planning could be brought to bear on a problem, no matter how difficult it might be, it could be solved. That conviction, with the weight of an entire government behind it, would in the next few years transform the public and private landscape of America.

So while Harry Hopkins and his people spent their waking hours in the structuring and administration of the early relief programs of the New Deal, knots of other New Dealers were working industriously to assemble the architecture of social and economic programs that would dwarf anything ever before contemplated in the warrens of government or the backrooms of Congress. By far the most significant of these was an ambitious attempt to fashion and engineer the passage of legislation that would substitute cooperative planning for the free-market piracy and chaos of the nation's industrial economy and at the same time institute a federal public works program that would repair and improve the nation's existing physical infrastructure, create thousands of long-term jobs, stimulate local economies, develop hydropower and irrigation projects to enhance the growth and economic health of entire regions, and generate general industrial recovery by creating markets for iron, steel, concrete, and other products.

The legislation that resulted and was introduced in Congress on May 15, 1933, was called the National Industrial Recovery Act. It was divided into two parts, Title I and Title II. Title I created the National Recovery Administration (NRA), a body designed to get prices and wages under some kind of control. All federal antitrust regulations were suspended for two years and industry-wide panels were authorized to work with the NRA to develop price and wage codes and establish working hours and conditions to which all businesses within each industry would agree to adhere across the board. The agreed-upon codes would acquire the force of law, once approved by the president. Section 7(a) of the act also guaranteed labor the right to organize and bargain collectively, and a National Labor Board was set up to negotiate disputes.

Not since the creation of the War Industries Board of World War I had there been proposed so much government control over industry, a prospect that should have struck horror into the heart of American capitalism. But the business community, like Congress itself, had no idea of how to get the country out of the depression; it was desperate for solutions, and if the answers came from Washington, well, that would simply have to be endured. "If we are to save our traditional freedom for the future," Paul W. Litchfield of the Goodyear Tire and Rubber Company said, ". . . we must make substantial concessions to what we have in the past classified as the more radical school of thought." With no overwhelming opposition from the business community, Congress passed the National Industrial Recovery Act on June 16.

To administer the NRA, Roosevelt appointed Hugh Johnson, a rough-cut, hard-drinking former brigadier general and plow-company executive who in 1933 was serving as a kind of financial utility infielder for Wall Street speculator Bernard Baruch, who called Johnson his "number three man." Described by a fellow New Dealer as "blustering, dictatorial and appealing," Johnson had helped to draft the law, and was nothing if not an enthusiast for what it was supposed to do. "I regard NRA as a holy thing," he said, and used everything from outright bullying to florid publicity stunts to win converts to the cause. He commissioned the famous "Blue Eagle" emblem with its We Do Our Part motto, one of the most enduring images we have from the New Deal years; those who had joined up with the NRA could proudly fly the Blue Eagle as a flag over their factories or tape it as a poster in the windows of their businesses or paste it as a sticker on the windshields of their delivery trucks. Johnson's people produced film shorts extolling the virtues of the NRA that were shown in nearly every movie house in the country, encouraged local chambers of commerce to promote sign-up campaigns, and even staged enormous parades, such as the one for "Blue Eagle Day" in New York City on September 13, 1933, when a blimp trailing a hundred-foot We Do Our Part banner floated over the army of 250,000 NRA acolytes who marched below.

By the end of the NRA's first year, more than 550 codes had been developed and many businesses had signed up, but the success was illusory. Jealousies, disagreements, and plain recalcitrance on the part of many industries and businesses made the code system virtually unworkable. One major problem, social historian Frederick Lewis Allen said later, was "the ingrained determination of business executives to hold down their costs of doing business, to push up prices if they could, and in general to run their companies as they pleased, come hell, high water, or General Johnson."

(Henry Ford, for example, simply refused to have anything to do with the Blue Eagle and got away with it.) Moreover, the economy did not recover noticeably, in spite of Johnson's repeated public assurances that it would, unemployment was still high, and public enthusiasm waned after months of hyperactive promotion. Johnson's own erratic and colorful presence — cheerfully covered by the nation's press — made for high entertainment value but poor administration, and the bureaucracy that was supposed to keep the whole system functioning smoothly jerked and sputtered, losing power and public confidence as it went, until Johnson was forced to resign under a cumulus of notoriety at the end of September, 1934. From then on the raddled agency was administered by Johnson's assistant, Donald Richberg.

The National Recovery Administration ultimately would be dismantled, its goals reappearing later in separate (and more successful) pieces of legislation, but even in its failure it had established a new relationship between government and business and government and labor, one predicated on the assumption that government had a role to play that exceeded the caretaker position it had held in most previous decades — certainly that of the Republican years of the twenties. Much the same could be said, even more pointedly, of Title II of the National Industrial Recovery Act, the Public Works Administration (PWA), whose bureaucratic machine would chug along handsomely through most of the decade, directed with scrupulous care and terrible energy by Interior Secretary Harold L. Ickes, who was given $3.3 billion to fund its operations in June, 1933, had been spending the money ever since, and would continue to do so when the PWA was reauthorized and he was given even more money.

The federal government had supported public works before. Federal bond payments and public-land contributions had financed the building of the transcontinental railroad in the 1860s, for example, and the Rivers and Harbors Act of 1882 had funded the U. S. Army Corps of Engineers in its dredging and flood-control work in the Mississippi River Valley. Even Calvin Coolidge and Herbert Hoover had initiated major public works projects (including the construction of many of the buildings in which the New Dealers now did their work). But never before had there been public works to match the public works of the New Deal. During the six effective years of its life, the PWA would finance a total of 34,508 projects at a cost of a little more than $6 billion, employing in any given year half a million workers or more.

Ickes got his own share of criticism, most of it having to do with the speed — or lack of it — with which he approved projects. Even though it had been created as one more means by which as many people as possible could be put to work as soon as possible (it was, after all, described as an "emergency" agency in the original authorizing legislation), the secretary was determined to ensure that every one of the PWA projects he and FDR (who made the final decision) approved was financially sound and that none was tainted by graft, and he scrutinized each and every one of the proposals with Germanic caution and at a speed his critics considered glacial.

Slowly or not, the projects ultimately set in motion by the PWA were impressive in number. In all but three of the nation's 3,073 counties there would be at least one PWA project. Long Beach, California, got new schools to replace those destroyed in the great earthquake of 1933. The PWA loaned the Pennsylvania Railroad $80 million to electrify its New York-to-Washington route. Atlantic Beach, Florida, got a seawall, Port Heuneme, California, got massive new dock facilities; the Chicago Sanitary District got a $42 million waste treatment complex, Virginia State College for Negroes got a $2 million expansion; Santa Fe, New Mexico, got a new courthouse and so did Kalamazoo, Michigan. There were many court houses, in fact, as well as post offices, hospitals, housing units, hundreds of municipal water systems, and thousands of miles of street and highway projects.

The PWA may have been free of graft, but it was not immune to politics. New York City, for example, got more PWA money than any other city in the country, not least because of the determination of its newly elected mayor, Fiorello H. La Guardia. The stubby mayor had ridden to victory in 1933 as the "fusion" candidate, chosen by reform elements in both major parties to clean up the ancient corruption of the Democratic Tammany Hall and overcome the mossback conservatism of traditional Republicanism. As the president's direct link to the heart of the city's politics, he was enormously valuable to Roosevelt, and the mayor brokered his importance shamelessly to rebuild his city. "Too often," La Guardia told a friend, "life in New York is merely a squalid succession of days; whereas in fact it can be a great living adventure." And, on another occasion: "I am in the position of an artist or a sculptor. I can see New York as it should be and as it can be. . . . But now I am in the position of a man who has a conception that he wishes to carve or to paint, who has the model before him, but hasn't a chisel or a brush." He got many of his artistic tools from the PWA. So did Robert Moses, whom the mayor appointed city park commissioner. In spite of the fact that he despised both La Guardia and the president in about equal portions, Moses shared the mayor's vision for his city and was not at all bashful about using federal

National Recovery Administration (NRA) director Hugh
Johnson had no illusions about the difficulty of overhauling the
entire relationship between government and industry. "It will be
red fire at first and dead cats afterward," he said colorfully, if
a little obscurely. "This is just like mounting the guillotine on
the infinitesimal gamble that the ax won't work." In the end,
the ax did work, especially for Johnson, but not before he had
originated the NRA eagle as the agency's permanent symbol.
ABOVE: San Francisco schoolchildren gather to make a living
NRA eagle at Seals Stadium during a major promotional effort
in September, 1933.

New York mayor Fiorello La Guardia rides with the Roosevelts during a presidential trip to Manhattan in May, 1934. La Guardia used his political intimacy with FDR to get more federal money for New York than was rereceived by any other city in the country. BELOW: *La Guardia officially accepts the federally financed Harlem River housing project, 1937.*

money to build parks, playgrounds, and interborough parkways. Overall, the city received outright grants of nearly $116 million from the agency, and borrowed another $136 million to get the work done, including the biggest single PWA project in the city, the $42 million Triborough Bridge, designed to link the boroughs of Queens, Brooklyn, and Manhattan.

Watering the West

If New York got the most PWA funding of any city, the Great West got more than any region. Politics was less important here than purpose, for it was in the West that the New Dealers saw the opportunity to seize the water and power resources of some of the largest watersheds in the country and make them serve the vision of a new utopia by generating electricity and storing and distributing irrigation water to make the arid interior West "blossom as the rose." Among some of the most ambitious such projects funded almost entirely with PWA money were Bonneville Dam on the Columbia River in Oregon/Washington, Grand Coulee Dam on the Columbia in east-central Washington, Fort Peck Dam on the Missouri in Montana, and most of the dams, canals, and other waterworks of the enormous Central Valley Project in California. The PWA also ensured the completion of Boulder (now Hoover) Dam on the Colorado River in Arizona, a project begun during the Hoover administration but almost out of money by 1933.

Overall, the PWA would spend more than $2 billion to help various federal agencies transform much of the physical character of the West. As historian Richard Lowitt has outlined it, only World War II itself would have a greater impact on the region: between 1933 and 1940, power production would increase from 150,000 kilowatts to almost 3 million; the number of acres being irrigated would rise from less than three million to more than four million; reclamation projects would more than double; and the number of people being served by the irrigation, power, and various municipal water works constructed with the aid of PWA money would grow from less than a million to about five million.

There were those who could (and did, and do) question whether the long-term interests of either the resources or the people of the region were intelligently served by these massive projects, since they helped to encourage population growth in a region that because of its chronic aridity is, as historian Walter Prescott Webb once described it, "a semi-desert with a desert heart." Neither the huge projects put in place or started by the New Deal's engineers nor any of those that followed would be enough to satisfy the overburdened West's everlasting need for water, as two generations of conflict over water allocations among Mexico (over Colorado River allocations), states, regions, cities, the agribusiness industry, the livestock industry, the mining industry, urban boomers, Native Americans, and environmentalists have demonstrated.

There were those who also learned to regret what these projects had done to the natural integrity of the lands and rivers of the West, the last great remnants of the original wilderness America in the coterminous United States — and it is no accident that the central event of the postwar conservation movement was the successful fight in the mid-1950s against the construction of two huge federal dams in Dinosaur National Monument, a national park unit that straddles the border between Utah and Colorado. A more benign legacy for the West — and one that an emergent conservation movement worked closely with the New Dealers to establish — would be the designation of four of the largest national park units in the country: Olympic National Park in Washington, and Kings Canyon National Park and Death Valley and Joshua Tree national monuments in California. With Big Bend National Park in Texas, Everglades National Park in Florida, Shenandoah National Park in Virginia, Cape Hatteras National Seashore in North Carolina, Capitol Reef National Park in Utah, and Great Smoky Mountains National Park in Tennessee/North Carolina, these great parks would expand the national park system by 7.1 million acres — an increase not to be equaled until passage of the Alaska Lands Act in 1980.

■ *For Millions of Yet Unborn*

Fifty million dollars of PWA money also went to help finance the construction of the great showcase of the New Deal's commitment to regional planning, the Tennessee Valley Authority — though the core of the vision first had to be rescued from Henry Ford. The object of Ford's attention was a place called Muscle Shoals on the banks of the Tennessee River in the northwestern corner of Alabama. It was one of the best hydropower sites in the eastern third of the nation, and Ford had not been alone in his admiration. "If I were greedy for power over my fellow-men," former secretary of war Newton D. Baker had said in 1924, "I would rather control Muscle Shoals than to be continuously elected President of the United States."

It was here that the federal government had constructed two plants for the manufacture of nitrate for armaments to be used in World War I and had started construction on two dams to produce the power to operate them. But the war had ended just as the nitrate plant was ready to go on line and construction work on the dams had been halted when Congress refused to allocate enough funding for their completion. So matters had stood in 1921, when Henry Ford tried to get his hands on the project. Out of the goodness of his heart and with no pecuniary interest, as he assured everyone, Ford had proposed to lease the two dams and buy up the nitrate plants and all their facilities and use them to manufacture cheap fertilizer. The lease payment he proposed for the two dams, however, had been grotesquely low, and his offer of $5 million for facilities that had cost the government an estimated $87 million to build was so preposterous that Congress refused it. Ford blamed Congressional refusal on the power monopolies of Wall Street — an entity he once said was firmly in the control of "International Jewry" — but finally retired from the field in October, 1924.

While he rejected Ford's anti-Semitism and had led the Congressional fight against the auto maker's efforts, Senator George Norris, chairman of the Senate Agriculture Committee, shared Ford's antipathy toward such power monopolies as that enjoyed by Samuel Insull in Chicago or that championed by Wendell Willkie, president of Commonwealth & Southern (and future Republican presidential candidate), a company with control over several utility systems in the Southeast and with more than a little interest in the possibilities of Muscle Shoals. If the government did not get into the power business itself in a substantial way, Norris had warned in 1926, "we will find ourselves in the grip of privately owned, privately managed monopoly and it will be extremely difficult to shake off the shackles that will then be fastened upon all of us."

It was that conviction that had fired his own vision for Muscle Shoals, which he saw as the perfect opportunity for the federal government to control the power potential of an entire region to ensure that the resources of nature would be used, in the phrase of the old conservationist, Gifford Pinchot, "for the greatest good of the greatest number for the longest time." Roosevelt agreed — so fervently that it must have startled even the senator. In January, 1933, as president-elect, FDR had visited Muscle Shoals to have a look for himself, and then shared what it had shown him with the world in an impromptu speech in Montgomery, Alabama. Here, he said,

> we have an opportunity of setting an example of planning, not just for ourselves but for the generations to come, tying in industry and agriculture and forestry and flood prevention, tying them all into a unified whole over a distance of a thousand miles so that we can afford better

opportunities and better places for living for millions of yet unborn in
the days to come.

This definitive New Deal fantasy was touched up a little and given
the more official character of federalese in the legislation that Congress
passed and Roosevelt signed on May 18, 1933, but its outlines could still
be seen: the act creating the Tennessee Valley Authority was

> for the especial purpose of bringing about in said Tennessee drainage
> basin and adjoining territory . . . the maximum amount of flood con-
> trol; the maximum development . . . for navigation purposes; the max-
> imum generation of electric power consistent with flood control and
> navigation; the proper use of marginal lands; the proper method of
> reforestation . . . and the economic and social well-being of the people
> living in said river basin. . . .

The Tennessee River Valley, then, would be a great social laboratory, and
to supervise the experiments undertaken there a tripartite board was established. As chairman of the TVA, FDR chose Arthur E. Morgan, a
hydraulic engineer, president of Antioch College, and a more than slightly
visionary thinker who would come to look upon the TVA as a kind of
enormous petri dish in which, through education and example, he and
Roosevelt might "create a new cultural environment" out of the raw material
of the region's two million inhabitants, as Morgan put it in his memoirs.
As his associates in this high endeavor, Morgan chose Harcourt A. Morgan
(no relation), an entomologist and president of the University of Tennessee,
and David Lilienthal, a young Wisconsin attorney recommended to Morgan
by an old friend, Supreme Court justice Louis Brandeis.

The relationship was ragged from the start. Lilienthal's interest was
in public power development as the driving purpose of the TVA and he
would lead the agency's almost constant fight against legal challenges filed
against it by various private power companies, including Commonwealth
& Southern, even as facilities were under construction. Harcourt Morgan's
vision was generally limited to the development, manufacture, and application of new and improved fertilizers. The chairman took under his wing
just about everything else, and while his reforestation, erosion control, and
recreational programs were both practical and generally successful, he
possessed little patience for any idea not his own and, further, had a distinct
tendency to view the inhabitants of the Valley as projects to be improved
through engineering. In later years, he would compare the building of a

Robert Moses, ABOVE, president of the New York State Parks Commission and Commissioner of City Parks in New York, got his own share of federal funds for the city, in spite of the malice he held for both Roosevelt and La Guardia.

"I am surprised to find a place solidly settled with Englishmen," Tennessee Valley Authority director Arthur E. Morgan stated in 1934, "that have not made good." Such attitudes led people of the region to feel that they were being treated as second-class citizens, "untutored inhabitants of some island colony," as one observer put it, "incapable of handling their own destinies." Whatever its social consequences, the TVA did bring jobs. OPPOSITE, BOTTOM: Visibly enthusiastic laborers gather down by the riverside to get their work assignments. Meanwhile, approving critics readied their pens to give proper artistic weight to such structures as Norris Dam, named after the TVA's "father," Senator George Norris, and completed in 1936. "In the Tennessee Valley we have shown (at a time when many doubted it)," one pundit wrote, "that a public architecture can be a great architecture." The Pharaohs, Lewis Mumford said, "did not do any better."

The biggest single Public Works Administration project in New York City was the Triborough Bridge, to which the PWA devoted $42 million in loans and bond purchases.

social order to the building of a bridge: "Personal character in a social order is like the quality of the metal used in bridge building. If personal character is on a low level, then there comes a time when no refinement of social planning and no expenditure of public wealth, however great, will create good social order." He made it clear on more than one occasion that the people of the Tennessee Valley provided pretty poor metal.

Some of the people objected. Writing in the October–December, 1934, issue of *Sewanee Review*, James R. McCarthy took exception to what he called Morgan's "patronizing" tone and suggested that the natives of the region "resented the implication that Washington was the seat of a government which regarded the valley as a colony." Charges of federal arrogance were still being fired nearly two decades later, as in this look back from a Tennessean in 1952:

> It all boils down to this: Dr. "A. E." and his followers, aided and abetted by high authority in Washington, looked upon the Tennessee Valley Authority as a great revolutionary movement which would tend to eliminate state lines, ignore local self-government, and set up a great, centralized, regional body which would dispense the "blessings" of a new social order to the "backward" inhabitants of the Valley.

Humorless, rigid, and unconscious of his effect on others, the chairman so completely alienated his two colleagues that the three men seemed to be locked in constant, very public battle (all three were in the habit of taking the argument to the press). In the end, they would garner so much bad publicity for the program that Roosevelt would be forced to act. In 1938, observing that the chairman was "temperamentally unfitted to exercise a divided authority," Roosevelt removed him. Harcourt Morgan was named chairman in his place, and in 1941 Lilienthal would take over.

By then, many of the structural elements of the TVA were in place, and if the project fell a little short of the glorious vision Norris and Roosevelt had entertained, it remained one of the most impressive public works projects in history. From the appropriately named Norris Dam at the confluence of the Clinch and Powell rivers to the original Wilson Dam at Muscle Shoals, its flood control and hydroelectric dams ultimately would utilize and manage the flow of every major stream in the Tennessee watershed — and when the great floods of 1937 devastated other regions in the Mississippi River Valley, it would be noted with more than a little pride by the TVA's publicists that the Tennessee River and its major tributaries remained under control. Navigation improvements would raise commercial traffic on the river from twenty-two million ton-miles in 1933 to nearly one hundred million ton-miles in 1941.

In the meantime, Harcourt Morgan's fertilizer factories produced and distributed free of charge about 100,000 tons of phosphate fertilizers a year for "demonstration" programs on nearly thirty-six thousand farms in twenty-seven states, while the TVA supervised eighteen CCC camps scattered through the region, most of the work of which was dedicated to the re-forestation of mountain slopes that had been logged over at least twice, and the attempted restoration of some of the most profoundly eroded farm lands in the nation. A good deal of this work had to do with training farmers to utilize contour plowing, terracing, and other techniques to slow the forces of erosion. The difficulty of that assignment was illustrated by the story about a TVA man who offered to show some of these scientific methods to one farmer of the region. "Well, sir," the farmer responded, "I've run through three farms, and pretty well used up this one. You can't tell me nothing about farming."

Above all, however, the TVA would be a celebration of power. By the beginning of World War II the agency would be furnishing more than 2 billion killowatt-hours of electricity to eighty-three municipally owned utility companies in Tennessee and the surrounding states, and another 282 million killowatt-hours to forty-five rural electric cooperatives, 85 percent of whose thousands of miles of lines were bringing light and power to farms and rural communities for the first time. Furthermore, the prices being charged for electricity by the TVA served as excellent "yardsticks" against which the prices charged by private utility companies in the rest of the nation could be measured for fairness. Even more significantly, it was the TVA's ultimate generating capacity of 12 *billion* kilowatts that would make possible the manufacture of much of the aluminum used during the war — and it was the TVA that would furnish the power for the ultra-secret witchery that would be practiced during the war at Oak Ridge, Tennessee, where nuclear physicists busily separated uranium 235 from uranium 238 to build something new under the sun.

An Imperishable Union

Establishing and putting in motion the Tennessee Valley Authority, however complex, at least had been a generally peaceful business. Not as much could be said for the atmosphere surrounding New Deal attempts to resolve the ancient troubles and present crisis in the heartland farms of the Midwest. Agriculture Secretary Henry Wallace may have been fond of strange personal diets featuring cottonseed meal, and may have enjoyed what he considered an almost personal relationship with many of the Old Testament prophets, and may even have had a fondness for the occult, but he had no trouble comprehending the importance of the task that lay ahead of him when he took office in March, 1933: "When former civilizations have fallen," he said, "there is strong reason for believing that they fell because they could not achieve the necessary balance between city and country."

Wallace talked about "balance," but what the average farmer would have talked about was what he considered "fairness." Net farm income had dropped by more than a third in just three years, and the parity ratio — what the farmer paid for his own goods and services compared to what he received for his products — had been cut by nearly half: it now cost the average farmer almost twice as much to support himself and his family as he received in prices. During his campaign in 1932, Roosevelt had maintained on more than one occasion that the depression itself had been caused largely by the decline in farm income, and while that contention was only partly true, there was no denying the fact that if agriculture — the very base on which much of the national economy rested — could not be saved, then neither could the country. And, many believed, there was no time to waste. In January, 1933, John A. Simpson, president of the Farmers Union, had written President-elect Roosevelt to tell him that unless he started "a revolution in government affairs there will be one started in the country. It is just a question of whether or not you get one started first."

Roosevelt certainly wanted to. "That's the fellow you've got to build up," he told people, "the farmer," and one of his earliest directives as president had been to Henry Wallace and his people, asking them to come up with legislation that would build up the farmer and stem the almost constant turmoil in the Midwest. The turmoil could not be ignored; even as Wallace and his advisers worked on the legislation, violence flamed so high it gave the deliberations in the cubbyholes of the Agriculture Building in Washington a certain urgency.

On March 14, just ten days after the inauguration, two hundred farmers marched to the Saline County courthouse in Wilbur, Nebraska, in order to stop the sheriff's sale of a local farm. They crowded into the sheriff's office in the basement of the building, trapping him in his chair behind the desk. The men held him there until a deputy managed to force the door open enough to fire a canister of tear gas into the middle of the mass of men. They cleared out, and the sale took place later that day (and a few hours after that, eighteen of the demonstrators were arrested).

In Iowa, meanwhile, the situation was growing uglier with every passing week. On February 3, a gun battle had ensued when some non-striking farmers tried to run a Farmer's Holiday Association blockade outside Sioux City; five men were wounded and a sixty-seven-year-old man was killed. On March 24, when O'Brien County attorney Jake Moore attempted to serve an eviction notice on a farmer outside Harlan, a group of men held him hostage for several hours until he agreed to accept a rental agreement with the family. On the morning of April 27, farmers invaded the O'Brien County courthouse in Primghar to block another sale, surged up the stairs of the building against a force of club-wielding deputies, and so terrified the attorney for the mortgage holder that he accepted a token settlement. The crowd of farmers still insisted on another symbolic pound or two of flesh; they forced the attorney, the sheriff, and all his deputies to kneel, one by one, and kiss the American flag in front of the courthouse.

The furious climax to Iowa's violence took place in Lemars on the afternoon of that same day, when about a hundred of the farmers who had rioted in Primghar that morning entered the courtroom of Judge Charles C. Bradley, who was hearing a foreclosure case. Bradley ordered the removal of hats and the extinguishing of cigars and cigarettes. "This is my courtroom," he said.

That was not a good idea. Shouting "This is our courtroom, not yours!" the farmers grabbed Bradley from the bench, demanded that he swear not to sign any foreclosure orders, and when he refused slapped him around. They then dragged him from the courthouse and drove him to a crossroads outside town. They threw a rope over a telephone pole, slipped the noose around his neck, yanked it tight, and demanded once again that he promise not to foreclose. The judge was adamant: "I will do the fair thing to all men to the best of my knowledge," was as close as he came to agreeing. The crowd finally stripped his pants from him and flung them into a ditch and left him stranded. Bradley later managed to hitch a ride back to town.

The next morning, Governor Clyde Herring sent national guardsmen into Lemars, and after several hundred farmers charged into a farmyard to break up a chattel sale at a farm outside Denison in Crawford County, the governor sent troops there, as well. Martial law was declared in O'Brien, Plymouth, and Crawford counties and fifty-seven participants in the various events were arrested and held in stockades in Lemars. The situation immediately calmed, and on May 11 the governor revoked martial law. Most of the rioters ultimately received token sentences, the judge in the case generally sympathizing with their point of view.

By then, Wallace and his assistants had come up with what they

There was no mistaking the violent intentions of the horde of
farmers who surged into the courthouse in Primghar, Iowa, on
April 27, 1933, to stop the sheriff's sale of a neighbor's farm.
They beat back a force of club-swinging deputies, surrounded
the attorney for the mortgage holder, persuaded him to accept
a token settlement of the farmer's debt, then took him outside
and made him kneel to kiss the flag. When they were done with
him, they then made the sheriff and his deputies do the same.

Even after Roosevelt's inauguration, explosions of protest continued in the farm country of the Midwest — though usually, as in this scene in Wisconsin, more milk than blood was spilled.

By the end of 1933, the New Deal's agricultural programs had helped to reduce midwestern protest — though baseball bats still waved in Sioux City, Iowa, in November, 1933.

hoped would be the solution. It was called the Farm Relief Act, which was passed by an acquiescent Congress and signed into law by Roosevelt on May 12, 1933. The new law bore, as *Business Week* put it, "all the earmarks of a document hastily drawn to the specifications of divergent and conflicting groups." It gave the president the power to adjust the value of the dollar to implement inflation; a measure long desired by price-hungry farmers, it appalled conservative economists, including FDR's budget director, Lewis Douglas, who said, "Well, this is the end of Western civilization," and later resigned. The act also created the Farm Credit Administration for mortgage relief and the Agricultural Adjustment Administration (AAA), designed to control production (and thereby induce higher prices) by paying farmers to take land out of cultivation or reduce their livestock production, the money to come from a processing tax on food products. Few argued with the need for mortgage relief, but the concept of paying someone for not producing food in a time of great hunger was greeted with horror — not least when Wallace entered into agreements to plow under ten million acres of cotton and slaughter 200,000 sows and 6 million piglets. "A good farmer takes care of his livestock," a "Missouri Farmer" told the readers of the *North American Review* in October, 1934. "I've had that rule drilled into me since I was a boy. It's one of the few rules I've never changed, either in practice or in thinking. However poor I get, I don't intend to slaughter baby creatures or to waste valid property."

Not all farmers were so fastidious. Some three million of them ultimately participated in the programs of the AAA, including the killing of piglets and calves. While some larger enterprises abused the program by taking land out of production, then intensifying their production on unretired land, for thousands of smaller farmers the AAA payments were virtually all they earned. Prices did rise, slightly, and the general effect of the program was to take a good deal of steam out of the protest skirmishes that continued well into 1934. The streets still ran white with milk in some towns, but the power of Milo Reno and the Farmer's Holiday Association was greatly diminished and overall participation was minimal. "Opinion in the grain belt, which was openly sympathetic to the first farm strike a year ago, is now swinging rapidly in the other direction," *Fortune* magazine could report with satisfaction in its January, 1934, issue.

In 1934, Congress and the New Dealers responded to even these reduced levels of agitation with the Federal Farm Bankruptcy Act, the Commodity Credit Corporation, the Federal Surplus Relief Corporation, and the Jones-Connally Farm Relief Act, all of which expanded the government's role in the industry. While overall prices for farm products would not creep back even to the dismal levels of 1929 until the demands of World War II created another boom, the New Deal had effectively satisfied just enough of the farmers' complaints to eliminate any serious challenges to the public peace from that quarter — and with that foundation, the government and the industry would continue to collaborate in the maintenance of a sometimes troubled but always symbiotic and apparently imperishable union. Revised, expanded, sometimes clarified and sometimes made more complex by new laws, that still is the relationship that remains in place today, a complicated tangle of mutual dependencies that, for all its intricacy, still retains the power to diffuse the urge to violence — as it did during the midwestern "farm revolts" of the 1980s.

■■■■■ *Unquenched Fires*

Utopia remained elusive, however, and in spite of all the decent ambitions that had driven the New Deal planners who spent the better part of a decade tearing things down, building things up, and moving things around, for all the improvement to the national estate that resulted, there were human costs that did not always get measured by the calipers and slide rules of the planners. Out in the West, for instance, where the great irrigation projects had brought millions of acres under cultivation, the New Dealers, like all the federal dam builders before them, ignored the provisions of the Reclamation Law of 1902 that were designed to prevent agricultural monopoly and encourage the development of small family farms by strictly limiting the amount of land that could be irrigated with federal water. This stipulation, which struck at the heart of the corporate farms that traditionally had controlled most of the West's land, had been politically inconvenient from the date of its birth and had never been seriously enforced. Nor would it be during the New Deal years. "I work in your orchards of peaches and prunes," Woody Guthrie would sing of the migrants whose lives were played out in the irrigated factories in the fields of the West. "And I sleep on the ground 'neath the light of your moon:/On the edge of your city you'll see us and then/We come with the dust and we go with the wind."

Guthrie wrote this song, "Pastures of Plenty," on assignment for the Interior Department to publicize the Bonneville Dam project and to encourage the raising of local bond issues for rural electrification over the opposition of private power companies in the region. "I made up twenty-six songs about the Columbia and about the dam and about the men," he remembered, and these songs were recorded by the Department of Interior, Bonneville Power Administration, Portland, Oregon. The records were played at all sorts and sizes of meetings where the people bought bonds to bring the power lines over the fields and hills to their own little places. . . . That's how things get done.

Guthrie did do his duty and included a number of laudatory hymns among the twenty-six songs he wrote in the twenty-six days of his little pilgrimage, but the most enduring of them all was the song whose haunting melody and lyric sadness spoke more of human loss than institutional gain: "It's always we ramble, that river and I,/All along your green valley I'll work till I die."

And down in Long Hollow, in the middle of the great experiment called the Tennessee Valley Authority, a family named Lindamood had talked to a reporter from the *Knoxville News-Sentinel* in October of 1934 about another kind of loss. Old Erasmus Lindamood, the family patriarch, had taken the reporter out and showed him the white mark on his cabin that the engineers had placed there to indicate the level the water would reach when the big upstream dam was complete and the reservoir behind it filled. The government was giving the family the money to build a bigger place on higher ground, and on the whole the Lindamoods probably would be better off, what with government scientists helping them to get better productivity from their land, using phosphate fertilizers manufactured right there in the valley, and teaching them how to control erosion. All this and the good chance that they would be getting electricity for the first time — and at rates even they could afford.

Still, something important was being traded here. Old man Lindamood wanted the reporter to know that he was not bitter about having to move from the patch of land on which he had hoped to spend the last of his days and where he had wanted to be buried, like his mother and father before him. "It's one of these here things you've got to make the best of," he said. "It's like a citizen's lot when the country is in war." He would go, he said, and peaceably, too, but in the way of the hill people, he was taking some portion of the past with him. Inside the cabin, he pointed to the fire:

> I was born in this room in the light of this fire seventy years ago. My father built this house in 1859. I won't swear the fire has never once gone out. I do know the ashes in that fireplace seldom, if ever, have got cold in my lifetime.
>
> Winter and summer that fire has been fanned up at night. It was

covered day and night around. A few times I've been off from home two or three or four days at a time. But the old fire, she's been fanned up every night I was here — and I reckon when I wasn't.

There's plenty of matches nowadays. I may be childish. But since I'm going to move out of here, see water lapping around the house and the crib and the smoke-house, and the chicken-house, it'll mean something to take the fire from the old house with me.

Losses as well as gains, then. Still, the government's headlong plunge into the possibilities of the future was extraordinarily heady stuff for those who participated, and even in retrospect, it is sometimes difficult to escape the enchantment of a time when it seemed as if the New Dealers were attempting not merely to revolutionize the nature of the citizen-government relationship, but to restructure entirely the physical character of American society on the same principle embodied in the old Latin phrase *mens sana in corpore sano* — if the nation possessed a healthy body (infrastructure, agriculture, regional development), perhaps a healthy mind (economy, society, politics) would follow.

In the achievement of the first goal, they had succeeded to a remarkable degree. After all, many of the bridges we cross in our automobiles today were built during the New Deal. The vegetables and fruit we put on our tables most of the time were grown on land irrigated by water stored behind a dam constructed during the New Deal — and any one of those dams could also be producing the light by which this book is being read. Much of our urban sewerage is still being treated in sanitation plants given us by the New Deal. Much of our tap water and natural gas come to our homes via pipes laid by the New Deal. We are still driving around on country highways first paved by the New Deal, camping in national parks and national monuments established by the New Deal, strolling on national forest hiking trails laid out by the New Deal under a canopy of trees planted by the New Deal, swimming in public pools built by the New Deal, mailing our letters in post offices constructed by the New Deal, getting marriage licenses in city halls erected with New Deal money. We are still sued in New Deal courthouses, educated in New Deal schools, get well or die in New Deal hospitals, and live in New Deal urban housing projects.

The legacy of the New Dealers, then, is infrastructure as well as politics and government — and if a good deal of it is beginning to disintegrate in our own time, it still stands as the most permanent physical evidence we have of the power of the dreams that fired those people in that time.

Ending the Long Darkness

Maybe I ought to thank you guys for coming down here on our picket line, but why should I thank you? This is your fight. If they lay a hand on one union man . . . they lay a hand on us all. If they bust this strike, they'll bust every strike. We're fighting, you guys and us, for the whole union movement . . . and that means for our kids and our wives and the chance to hold our heads up like men.

Rubber industry strike leader, to picketers in Barbeton, Ohio, April 20, 1934

CHAPTER SIX

Overleaf:

When candidate Roosevelt shook the hand of a Wheeling, West Virginia, coal miner during the campaign of 1932, the symbolism was entirely appropriate. White or black, male or female, no single group of American workers was more thoroughly oppressed than the miners of Appalachia. "They work," Edmund Wilson wrote, "from eight to twelve hours a day, and they get from $2.60 to $3 for it. They are paid not in United States currency, but in chicken-feed specially coined by the companies. . . . The company 'scrip' is worth, on the average, about sixty cents on the dollar." This, in a time when twenty-five or even thirty dollars a week in real money was barely enough to keep an average family decently.

I F MOST OF AMERICAN industry refused to cooperate wholeheartedly in the price and wage structures that the National Recovery Administration had attempted to put in place with its hundreds of exquisitely detailed codes, the American labor movement had little trouble accepting both the spirit and the power of the NIRA's Section 7(a), with its unequivocal stipulation that "employees shall have the right to organize and bargain collectively through representatives of their own choosing, and shall be free from the interference, restraint or coercion of employers. . . ." These words shone like a beacon of promise. For the most part, the labor movement and the working men and women of the rank and file had been trapped in a darkness of neglect and exploitation even during the prosperous years of the twenties, and it was they who suffered first and hardest when the industrial system collapsed. Even in the best of times, wages had never managed to rise proportionately to the cost of living, hours remained long and hard, working conditions were typically abysmal, and in many industries factory work was only a little above the level of peonage. Unionism, strong during World War I, when the nation could not afford labor unrest, had declined in strength and membership, beaten down by the concentrated power of industrial capitalism and a government that serviced its needs and further weakened by conflicts between radical and conservative elements in its own ranks.

Roosevelt had never addressed the question of organized labor's situation during his campaign, confining his remarks to general discussions of unemployment and exploitation as part of the whole web of disaster in which callous Republicanism and uncontrolled industrial capitalism had ensnared the people of the nation. In truth, Roosevelt would never feel particularly comfortable with organized labor. His attitudes were formed in the paternalistic Progressive tradition, which never entirely trusted the worker to control his own destiny. FDR also was put off by what he saw as the movement's tendency toward radicalism and demands that were more often shrill than they were practical.

Nevertheless, millions of working men and women had turned to him as their last best hope. He had promised them a new deal, too, they believed, and they had voted for him in numbers too large to be ignored. While the president had nothing to do with formulating Section 7(a) (it was largely the creation of Donald Richberg and other labor-minded New Dealers, aided and abetted by John L. Lewis and William Green), neither did he put up any significant opposition to its inclusion — though he might have if he had suspected what sprites of turbulence would be loosed when it went into effect.

Roosevelt was not alone in his ignorance; no one had guessed what the dimensions of the rank and file's response to Section 7(a) would be, not even the leaders of the movement, most of whom would be caught napping — just as they had been during the general election of 1932. If the rank and file had voted for Roosevelt, the AFL's William Green had maintained a diplomatic silence that campaign summer about which candidate would get his nod, while John L. Lewis, president of the United Mine Workers and Green's principal rival in the labor movement, had actually given his endorsement to Hoover. The leadership would come around to the administration's side soon enough, and for good reason. In addition to Section 7(a), FDR would later authorize the creation of a Labor Advisory Board and Labor Secretary Frances Perkins would appoint to the five-man board not only three AFL leaders — including, as the board's chairman, John L. Lewis — but Sidney Hillman, the comparatively radical president of the independent Amalgamated Clothing Workers of America.

In the meantime, in the weeks that followed the passage of the NIRA, the rank and file of the movement had scented opportunity just ahead of their leaders and went on to seize the hour with such enthusiasm that their parent organizations often were kept scrambling just to follow. It was one of the purest and most dramatic expressions of rank-and-file labor organizing in American history. In Akron, Ohio, for example, organizers at the huge Goodyear and Firestone plants got union applications and handed them out at the factory gates to anyone who reached for one. Thousands did. "We started talking about the union," one of them remembered, "and I said, 'How long are we going to sit idly by?' People began to organize so that you couldn't write applications fast enough." The rubberworkers, Ruth McKenney wrote in *Industrial Valley*, "believed, blindly, passionately, fiercely, that the union would cure all their troubles, end the speedup, make them rich with wages. . . . Indeed the first weeks of the new rubber union were something like a cross between a big picnic and a religious revival. . . ." Before the end of July, the opportunity that lay untapped in Akron was too obvious for even the AFL leadership to miss, and an organizer was assigned to the town. By the end of 1933, Akron had added 23,000 new members to the roster of the AFL and by 1934 union membership in all trades in Akron had swelled to more than seven times what it had been at the beginning of June, 1933.

Few cities ever got so thoroughly organized as Akron, but nearly every existing union in the country was giddy with the intoxication of sudden growth. David Dubinsky, president of the International Ladies Garment

Workers Union, reported that his membership leaped from less than 40,000 at the beginning of 1933 to more than 200,000 by May, 1934. Sidney Hillman's Amalgamated Clothing Workers doubled from 60,000 to 120,000. But no union matched John L. Lewis's United Mine Workers of America for growth. Lewis (who had helped to write it, after all) was swifter than most to comprehend the import of Section 7(a) and mounted a massive membership drive within days of the NIRA's passage. The act, his *United Mine Workers Journal* wrote, "has given labor the greatest opportunity it has ever had to work out its own destiny." The *Journal* then added: "The bill will only be helpful to those who help themselves." The UMW was willing to lend a hand, though. Sound trucks were sent out into the coal mining districts of Pennsylvania, West Virginia, Kentucky, and Illinois, their sides slathered with signs claiming (a little freely) that "The President Wants *You* to Unionize." By the end of the summer the UMW's membership had risen from about 100,000 to more than 400,000.

The AFL, which for decades had steadfastly refused to dilute the purity of its skilled-trades image by admitting to membership the great masses of unskilled and semiskilled industrial workers, was suddenly confronted with a flood of hundreds of thousands of people clamoring to be let in. The workers would not be denied, and until it could decide just what to do with those who did not fit neatly into one of the existing trade unions, the AFL attempted to maintain control by recognizing and collecting dues from what it called "federal labor unions." In response to demands from those locals for equality, Green and his colleagues counseled patience — a mistake for which the AFL soon would pay dearly.

Until then, there were strikes and work stoppages to be monitored. Not content with merely organizing from the ground up, workers all over the country decided to strike from the ground up, too. Most of these actions were motivated by traditional demands for better wages and working conditions, but a significant number were over the simple question of recognition by employers. Not all of American business and industry, as it happened, embraced the labor provisions of the NIRA with the same enthusiasm as the workers had. The trade journal *Iron Age* warned America of the dangers of "collective bludgeoning," while the *Commercial and Financial Chronicle* raised the specter of ten million potential AFL members rising up to become a class "within the State, more powerful than the State itself."

Some employers, like the Ford Motor Company, simply refused to have anything to do with the NIRA, the NRA, *or* Section 7(a). "I was always under the impression," Henry Ford remarked acidly, "that to manage a business properly you ought to know something about it." Many companies attempted to get around the law in various ways, chiefly by creating "company unions" organized by management itself. The law did not allow employers to force their workers to join such unions, but it usually was not difficult for management to persuade its employees that it would be a good idea to sign up if they wanted to keep their jobs or hard-won promotions.

Ironically, the NRA implicitly encouraged such unions when it stated that it did not "endorse any particular form of organization." What was more, even when a majority of workers in a company had voted to join a true union, management was not obligated by law to treat that union as the principal spokesman for the workers. It could therefore use its own company unions to undercut the authority of the noncompany unions and almost completely subvert the whole notion of "collective bargaining."

The NRA established a National Labor Board (later renamed the National Labor Relations Board and not to be confused with the National Labor *Advisory* Board) to arbitrate the inevitable disputes among labor, management, and competing unions over the question of jurisdiction, but for the most part, the nineteen regional boards it set up around the country were without force or authority and could impose their will only through the art of persuasion. That art was about as effective as it usually is in such circumstances, and between June, 1933, and the end of 1934, more than 1.5 million workers were involved in hundreds of work stoppages and strikes — 1,834 of them in 1934 alone.

■■■ *The Sound of Thousands of Feet*

While the usual clutch of outraged conservatives were ready to charge the Communist Party/USA with responsibility for each and every one of the industrial strikes of 1933–34, the truth was that while TUUL unions were eager and sometimes important participants in any strike that would have them, the labor actions of these years were orchestrated and controlled from beginning to end almost entirely by the workers themselves. This phase of the labor movement was a worker's movement, not one inspired or controlled by ideology or political interest. The Communists were welcome to help out, if they wished, but they were no more in charge of events than was the established union hierarchy. "In 1934," Earl Browder said a year later, "the Red Unions definitely passed into the background in the basic industries, and to some extent also in light industry. The main mass of workers had definitely chosen to try and organize and fight through the A. F. of L. organizations."

With or without the aid of the Communists, many of the industrial strikes that followed passage of Section 7(a) were quite as violent as anything the most militant Red radical might have hoped for. Many seriously disrupted local and even regional economies and social services for weeks, and even when successful many left a residue of bitterness that time could never quite obliterate. In Toledo, Ohio, for example, an AFL local organized under the auspices of 7(a) managed to win recognition, jurisdiction, and a 22 percent hourly wage increase from the Electric Auto-Lite Company in May, 1934 — but only after nearly five months of sporadic violence, the arrival of hundreds of state National Guard troops, and the death of two strikers, with hundreds more injured. At about the same time, in Minneapolis, it took two months of intermittent violence, more troops, four more deaths (two anti-union, two union), and several hundred more injuries before the successful settlement of a strike by the General Drivers and Helpers Union, a subsidiary of the national Teamsters Union, in July, 1934.

But of all the big and little strikes that punctuated the daily life of the country for nearly two years following passage of the NIRA, none more precisely represented the enormous, almost uncontrollable energies that had been loosed than the waterfront strikes that embroiled San Francisco and other ports of the West Coast in the summer of 1934 and the textile strikes that spread across much of the eastern seaboard a few months later. Moreover, while the maritime strikes demonstrated the degree to which the new unionism was freeing itself from the domination of traditional leadership, using Section 7(a) as its lever, the textile strikes illustrated the essential weakness of both Section 7(a) and the Roosevelt administration's overall labor policy.

Just ten days after passage of the act, an AFL organizer named Lee J. Holman began accosting workers on the docks of San Francisco, offering membership in a newly chartered local of the International Longshoreman's Association. The ILA had been moribund in the Bay Area for years, completely overshadowed by the employer-dominated Longshoreman's Association of San Francisco and the Bay District — called the "Blue Book Union" after the color of the little dues book each worker was required to carry if he hoped to find work. While the Blue Book Union paid lip service to the cause of labor, it was generally held by the workers themselves to be little more than "a company controlled union and a racket," as Harry Bridges, an Australian-born seaman, longshoreman, and labor leader described it. Similar systems were firmly in place in all West Coast ports, from Seattle to San Pedro. The Blue Book was bad enough, but the "shape-up" was worse. This crude hiring system forced the men to gather every morning on the docks and hope to be chosen to work any ships ready to be loaded or unloaded. The hiring was in the complete control of the gang

Shortly after her tour of the steel-industry towns, Labor Secretary Frances Perkins joined the other members of the National Labor Relations Board for its first meeting on July 9, 1933. Lloyd Garrison, the board's chairman, is at Secretary Perkins's right, and next to Garrison are Harry L. Millis and Edwin S. Smith. Appointed by Roosevelt to oversee the stipulations of Section 7(a) of the NIRA, the board would in fact prove to be a most reluctant dragon when it came down to actually enforcing the law.

Garment workers joined the organizing frenzy of 1934, and membership in the International Ladies Garment Workers Union swiftly rose from 45,000 to 200,000, including the members of this San Antonio local.

In July of 1933, Secretary Perkins toured the steel towns of
Pennsylvania and West Virginia to discover for herself what
wages and working conditions were. She is seen shaking hands
with a worker at the Homestead plant in Pittsburgh, in 1892
the site of one of the bloodiest labor strikes in American history.
Ever since, the steel industry had kept its factories free of union
activity — by means that included the suppression of free
speech, as Perkins herself learned when the mayor of the town
of Homestead refused to let her use city space to hear
complaints from what he called "malcontents." She was forced
to invite the workers to the local Post Office building for a
hearing.

bosses who chose the working crews each day, and the opportunities for extortion, discrimination, blacklisting, and kickbacks were obvious.

The longshoreman's floating equivalent, the seaman, had his own set of complaints. On shipboard he was exposed to whatever living and working conditions might be deemed appropriate by the captains and the mates. Most seamen were vagabonds by nature and circumstance, and on shore their lives were only a little better than on shipboard, defined and bounded by the waterfront saloons that were their social centers and the boarding houses that were as close to homes as most would ever know — and in both the saloons and the boarding houses they were at the mercy of the shoreside boarding-masters, or crimps, who helped them eat and drink themselves into debt, charged usurious interest rates on their charges, and sent them back to sea in financial bondage.

By 1933, the seaman's recourses were limited to desertion (very common) and the nearly inactive International Seaman's Union, an AFL body founded in 1899 and still dominated by the leadership of conservative Andrew Furuseth, whose commitment to the principles of craft unionism was second only to that of Samuel Gompers himself. He also was a practicing racist who believed that his ISU was "the last great struggle of the white man to maintain himself on the seas." The sailors of the depression years had few problems with the ISU's racism, but the union's conservatism and lack of militancy during the twenties had helped to allow the shipowners to cut wages, raise hours, flood the work force with cheap foreign labor, and maintain the hated "fink book," a device by which boarding-masters kept a record on the "character" (for which was read, "union activism") of each sailor hired in the system. On the whole, the situation was too tempting for the Communist party's TUUL to resist; it was not long before the party's chosen front, the Marine Workers League, found just enough interested seamen in the ports of the nation to bring together delegates in New York City in April, 1930, to form the Marine Workers Industrial Union.

While it enjoyed this small success, the MWIU failed in its bigger ambition — to link seamen, longshoremen, and others into one big maritime union. Among other reasons why such a merger was never achieved was the fact that dockside workers, particularly on the East Coast, had traditionally been divided into clearly defined ethnic and racial entities that held passionately to their territorial imperatives and had no interest in losing their individual identities. Moreover, they tended to look upon the rootless seamen with something approaching contempt — an attitude returned in kind by the seamen. By 1933, Earl Browder admitted, the union was "a small organization isolated from the largest masses."

The MWIU had not been much of a force in San Francisco, either, but it did manage to maintain a loose alliance with a group of dissident ILA members who had banded together to produce a crude but spirited and widely read newsletter, the *Waterfront Worker*. "Why has the ILA not become the fighting organization we want on the front?" the *Waterfront Worker* asked. "Because we have never taken affairs into our own hands. We have from the first left everything in the hands of a few individuals we know little about. . . . We must take the organization into our own hands. The rank and file must run and control the ILA." Led by Harry Bridges, the ILA dissidents welcomed the support of the MWIU, but from the beginning were determined to reshape their union in the image of the workers themselves.

With that conviction and a growing majority of ILA members behind them, Bridges and the *Waterfront Worker* enclave went to work in the fall of 1933. When a locally controlled "special board" of the NRA ruled in September that the Blue Book Longshoreman's Association of San Francisco was a true union, a number of stevedores sympathetic to the ILA publicly burned their blue books on the docks. In October, when a shipping line fired four men for wearing union buttons, the *Waterfront Worker* got four hundred dock workers to walk off the job in a five-day wildcat strike.

In March, 1934, the ILA polled all its West Coast members on whether they would support a strike. The vote was 6,616 in favor of a strike, with but 699 opposed. Nevertheless, the cautious president of the San Francisco Bay District union, Lee J. Holman, refused to authorize a walkout and was backed up by the union's equally hesitant international president in New York, Joseph P. Ryan. Holman was forthwith ousted as president of the ILA local, which, together with district unions in Seattle, Tacoma, and all other West Coast ports except Los Angeles (as rigid an open-shop town as any in America), then issued an ultimatum to the Waterfront Employers Association: begin serious negotiations with the ILA or face a coastwide strike.

The employers refused, and in spite of a telegram from ILA president Ryan urging the workers to cease and desist, about twelve thousand long-shoremen and stevedores in every port but Los Angeles refused to report for work on the morning of May 9, 1934. The ILA was immediately joined by the MWIU and then by some forty-five hundred seamen from the Maritime Union of the Pacific, the regional body of the International Seaman's Union. Four days later, Teamsters Union locals in all port cities but Los Angeles voted to refuse to carry goods to and from the docks. A Joint Marine Strike Committee was organized among all the unions to direct the action and organize pickets. The Waterfront Employers Association and its counterparts in the other port cities brought in strikebreakers, enlisted the aid of local police, formed private police, and employed the usual assortment of devices to keep goods moving and ships in the trading lanes. Union members responded with massive picket lines and violent resistance, and for more than six weeks the West Coast shipping industry was closed down.

When the union rejected two settlements in a row fashioned by National Labor Board negotiators, the Waterfront Employers Association and city officials decided to reopen the port of San Francisco by whatever means necessary. On July 3, seven hundred policemen were armed with tear gas and riot guns and organized into an assault force, freight cars were lined up along the tracks of the Belt Line Railroad as a barrier between strikers and the docks, and five trucks loaded with cargo were escorted down the Embarcadero toward the warehouses with a police captain waving his gun and shouting, "The port is open!" Thousands of strikers attacked the police in an attempt to stop the trucks. Twenty-five people were hospitalized by the end of the day.

Everyone took the holiday off the next day, but on July 5 — "Bloody Thursday" — more goods were moved and the strikers moved again to stop them. The smoky, gunfire-punctuated battle boiled through several square blocks of the waterfront. "[Strikers] surged up and down the sunlit streets among thousands of foolhardy spectators," a reporter for the *San Francisco Chronicle* wrote that night. "Don't think of this as a riot. It was a hundred riots, big and little, first here, now there. Don't think of it as one battle, but as a dozen battles." Something of the terror and confusion that attends all warfare was revealed in the disjointed remarks of the president of the Pacific School of Religion, before a church group in Berkeley on July 19.

> On July 5 at 2:30 P.M. we were standing on four corners, grouped, quiet. All of a sudden, a Ford touring car filled with men drove up into the middle of the intersection — a man in a gray suit got out — he had a riot gun — he shot into the group on the Southwest corner — a striker went "oh" "oh" — stones were *then* thrown by the strikers and the police came up. . . .

Two strikers who had been gunned down during the action died and another eighty-five were injured. Governor Frank Merriam sent seventeen hundred National Guard troops in that night. An enforced truce descended on the Bay Area, and in an atmosphere of martial law a huge funeral procession four days later accompanied the bodies of the slain strikers up Market Street. Throughout the march, one spectator said, there was "an ominous silence among spectators and marchers alike. . . . The sound of thousands of feet echoed up that hollow canyon — nothing else. . . ."

The sorrowing strikers may have been determined, but as Harry Bridges told a reporter for the *San Francisco Examiner* the night of July 5, "We cannot stand up against police, machine guns, and National Guard bayonets." Still, they could make one last resounding gesture of solidarity. On Saturday, July 14, a mass meeting of representatives from 115 Bay Area unions was held at the San Francisco Labor Temple. Bridges offered a motion for a general strike to begin on Monday, July 16, and the motion carried, 315 to 15. On Monday, 127,000 workers stayed home — and most continued to stay home for the next four days. Hospitals were allowed to receive food and gasoline for their ambulances; most hotels were allowed to stay open, as were fifty restaurants; milk deliveries for children and schools were permitted; and doctors were allowed to buy gasoline — but almost every other service in most of the communities in and around the Bay Area was halted.

Back in Washington, Hugh Johnson of the NRA denounced the action, while Secretary of Labor Perkins had her hands full keeping Secretary of State Cordell Hull (sitting in as acting president while FDR and Vice President Garner were both off on vacation) from radioing Roosevelt on the presidential yacht with a request to federalize the California National Guard and put an end to the general strike by force of arms. The AFL's president, William Green, joined in the chorus of outrage, while the ILA's national president, Joseph P. Ryan, told the press that one of the main obstacles to settling the original strike was that "the Communist Party, led by Harry Bridges, is in control of the San Francisco situation." On July 19, much to Bridges's disgust, the General Strike Committee caved in to the pressure and voted to end the walkout, 191 to 174.

After a tumultuous debate, on July 21 the Joint Marine Strike Committee voted to hold a referendum among all ILA workers on the question of accepting federal arbitration of all points of dispute, including control of hiring. On July 25, the members voted in favor of arbitration, 6,378 to 1,471. For their part, the employers agreed to the same arbitration and promised to discharge all strikebreakers and not to discriminate against union members. Twelve thousand longshoremen and thirteen thousand seamen and marine workers returned to work, and in October, the federal mediation board announced a settlement that included wage increases, overtime payments, a five-day, thirty-hour work week, and an agreement that hiring reponsibilities would be shared equally between the union and the employers.

It was less than a complete victory for the union, but a meaningful victory nonetheless, and Harry Bridges claimed it as such. But he could not — and did not — take much pride in the fact that his union had left

OPPOSITE, TOP: *San Francisco waterfront strike leader Harry Bridges talks
with reporters in 1934, and* BELOW *the wiry Australian (in center) waves his
cap during a march down the Embarcadero in San Francisco on May 10,
1934, the day after some 12,000 Pacific Coast longshoremen and seamen went
on strike. Less than two months later, on July 5, 1934, "Bloody Thursday" in
the annals of San Francisco, police started to move cargo from the
Embarcadero by truck. Strikers attempted to block them. By day's end, scores
of people were injured and two strikers were fatally shot, as the battle swept
through waterfront streets. Businessman Donald Brown, who witnessed much of
it, remembered the "insane courage" of the strikers: "In the face of bullets, gas,
clubs, horses' hoofs, death; against fast patrol cars and the radio, they fought
back with rocks and bolts till the street was a mass of debris."* ABOVE: *Police
have fired tear gas to break up a crowd of workers, while spectators gape from
a ridge above the action.*

the seamen's unions in the lurch when it voted to end the strike. The seamen had made the handsome gesture of lending their own strength to the ILA, and now they returned to work with virtually nothing for themselves but the assurance of jobs. It would not be until the rise of the Sailors Union of the Pacific under the leadership of Harry Lundeberg in 1936 that the seamen would begin to attain their own limited measure of power and success.

■■■■ A Month of Flying Squadrons

Limited success, no matter how bloodily won, was better than no success at all — as the United Textile Workers of America learned in September. The industry, which employed hundreds of thousands of workers in plants scattered through most of the eastern seaboard states, had been one of the first to negotiate acceptable wage and hour codes under the rules of the NRA. The United Textile Workers union, an AFL affiliate founded in 1901, meanwhile, took full advantage of Section 7(a) to raise its membership from about 20,000 to more than 300,000 by 1934. That was its membership in May, 1934, when the NRA capitulated to industry pressure for exceptions to the codes, allowing a 25 percent reduction in working hours with corresponding pay cuts. By August, textile workers were averaging $11.50 a week, only a little over half the pay for workers in all other manufacturing industries.

Then there was the matter of the "stretch-out," which the NRA codes did nothing to alleviate. Simply put, this device forced workers to produce more in less time. "They come in there," Katie Lovins, a mill worker in Atlanta remembered, "and wanted people to do more work. . . . And so, if you worked hard and kept that work going, then you got a little more added on to you till you almost got to the place where you had more than you could do." When employers coupled their insistence on the stretch-out with mistreatment of and discrimination against union workers in violation of the NIRA, the UTW ordered a general industry-wide strike to begin on September 3 — Labor Day — 1934. In a few days, at least 300,000 workers had left their jobs in every textile manufacturing state from New England to the Deep South.

In size and overall violence, the Textile Workers strike of 1934 was the largest in American history. In regions in which there were many individual plants, striking workers would walk out of one plant *en masse* and form a "flying squadron" to sweep down on the next plant and demand that its workers come out. The flying squadrons combined with mass picketing, the importation of strikebreakers, and large numbers of public and private police forces to provide all the ingredients for labor warfare.

In Fall River, Massachusetts, an estimated ten thousand strikers surrounded mills, trapping strikebreakers inside. At Trion, Georgia, a striker and a policeman were both killed during strike violence. In Augusta, Georgia, a deputy sheriff shot a picket to death. More than two thousand pickets rioted in Lowell, Massachusetts. In Saylesville, Rhode Island, more than a thousand pickets surrounded the Sayles Company Mill and Bleachery and attacked police and sheriff's deputies. Over in Woonsocket, an estimated ten thousand people rioted in the town, breaking windows and looting stores; one of the rioters was shot and killed. In Honea Path, South Carolina, deputies shot and killed seven strikers. In Danielson, Connecticut, mill owners' cars were attacked by strikers. In Dighton, Massachusetts, police and special deputies turned back a flying squadron from Fall River. In Woonsocket again, thousands of strikers assaulted police and state troopers guarding the Woonsocket Rayon Company plant; one striker was shot and killed.

In state after state, the national guard was called out in an effort to quell the violence. In New England, every state but New Hampshire and Vermont had troops on the street at one time or other during the course of the strike, while in Georgia Governor Eugene Talmadge imposed martial law on the entire state. "The power of the State has been definitely challenged," the governor said. "Men and women who wish only to be let alone at their peaceful employment are being threatened and terrorized. . . ."

In an effort to keep the strike from spilling over into other industries, FDR appointed a special three-man board of inquiry for the cotton textile industry, chaired by John G. Winant, former Republican governor of New Hampshire, early in September. On September 20, the board came up with one of the most ponderously bureaucratic recommendations in labor history: a new Textile Labor Relations Board should be established to serve as the arbitrator of worker disputes, it said; the new board also would create a subcommittee to study workloads to see if they were in fact onerous; meanwhile, the Department of Labor would look into wage levels to judge them for equity, while the Federal Trade Commission would study the capacity of the industry to increase hours and numbers of workers. There was virtually nothing in the proposal for the workers, but on the strength of Roosevelt's request, the officials of the Textile Workers Union acquiesced and called off the strike.

The decision ended the violence, but all but destroyed the union. The workers had risked life and limb and had received nothing in return. The union's membership plummeted and for thousands of workers the

In 1934, the rank-and-file of the United Textile Workers Union voted for an industry-wide strike to begin on Labor Day, September 3. On that day, the first 65,000 workers walked off the job in Gastonia, North Carolina. More than 10,000 of them paraded down the streets of the town, BELOW, while two young workers, LEFT, cheerfully advertised their allegiance.

*During the first few days of the textile strike, superbly
organized "flying squadrons" of union workers swooped down
on one textile mill after another, shutting them down; ABOVE,
a squadron of strikers points in derision at a pair of business-
office employees who refuse to honor the picket line outside the
Cannon company's mill in Concord, North Carolina, on
September 8. Not all strikers stopped at derision, and violence
was widespread and frequent, perpetrated by both sides.*

In Georgia, Governor Eugene Talmadge responded to the textile
strike by declaring martial law and ordering out troops from
the Georgia National Guard. When "flying squadrons" of the
union moved against a mill in Georgia, they were frequently
met by the National Guard's own squadrons, who surrounded
them, scooped them up, and hauled them away to internment
camps, as in this scene outside Newnan on September 18. When
the union's national officers called the strike off at Roosevelt's
personal request, tens of thousands of rank-and-filers were
furious with both the New Deal and the union. "Our local is
gone and it dont seem there is any use to try now as they have
lost faith in the union," one local official wrote headquarters.
"We have had so many promises and nothing done I myself am
almost ready to give up. . . . Please . . . do something that we
may be able to still have faith in our Government." His plea
was never answered.

situation was as bad or even worse than it had been before the strike. Roosevelt had personally asked the mill owners to rehire union workers, but few in fact did, and especially in the mill towns of the South the anti-union traditions of the past remained as firmly in place as ever. "Do you know what would happen to my husband at this mill if he so much as talked union amongst the workers?" one woman asked a federal social worker after the strike. "They'd put him on a new job he didn't know how to do and give him three times more work than he could do. In a day or two his boss man would say, 'Guess I'll have to let you go since you can't keep up with your work.' " The NRA, the Textile Labor Relations Board, the Department of Labor, even the administration, lacked both the power and the will to help the textile workers. It would be more than another generation before union labor would be able to get a decent foothold in the industry again. In some places it still has not.

In the end, then, in spite of all the hope that had been freed up, in spite of the spectacular growth in union membership, in spite of all the sweat, blood, agitation, and excitement, the victories that the auto-parts workers of Toledo, the truckers of Minneapolis, and the longshoremen of San Francisco had been able to engineer after passage of Section 7(a) were the exceptions that tested the rule that the failed textile strike of 1934 proved with such grim clarity: the administration's labor policy, as embodied in Section 7(a) and the toothless bureaucracy that had been put in place to administer it, was simply incapable of rectifying decades of oppression and militant anti-unionism. Had he chosen to do so, Roosevelt could have used the "bully pulpit" of the presidency (as his cousin TR had liked to think of it) far more effectively and energetically to force the issue of union recognition and acceptance by industry of the principle of collective bargaining. He had decided instead to keep his distance from the bloody fray, giving only the most lukewarm support. Every bit as clearly, the limp and indecisive leadership of the AFL had been no less inept in meeting the needs of the workers.

What the workers had won on their own was something worth celebrating — the passion of solidarity among grass-roots organizers, the heady joy that came with the attempt to shape at least some part of the quality of their working lives, the satisfaction of knowing that their presence in the fabric of the nation's economic life would never again be denied or ignored. The long darkness was over. Still, self-help was just not enough; there remained enormous vacuums waiting to be filled in both law and federal action, and sooner or later the Roosevelt administration was going to be forced to fill them, whether it wanted to or not.

Dust, Drought, and Displacement

It was not so much the heat and dryness then as the fear of what they would do. I could imagine a kind of awful fascination in the very continuousness of this drouth, a wry perfection in its slow murder of all things. . . . But this was only for those to whom it was like a play, something that could be forgotten as soon as it was over. For us there was no final and blessed curtain — unless it was death.

Josephine Johnson,
Now in November, 1935

CHAPTER SEVEN

Overleaf:
*Of the thousands of images that emerged
from the drought- and dust-ravaged plains of
middle America in the years of the Great
Depression, few ever matched the simple power
of this Farm Security Administration photograph by Arthur Rothstein. The child, as
anonymous as the patch of ground on which
he stands, was photographed in Cimarron
County, Oklahoma, in April of 1936. "If you
would like to have your heart broken," roving
reporter Ernie Pyle wrote from Garden City,
Kansas, not far north of the Oklahoma border
in June of 1936, "just come out here. This is
the dust-storm country. It is the saddest land I
have ever seen."*

■ *Dry Spell Blues*

F OR A QUARTER of a century, Caroline Boa Henderson and her husband Wilhelmine had raised a family and lived out the hardships and rewards of family farming on a homestead near Shelton, Oklahoma. "We have rooted deeply," she wrote in the summer of 1935. "Each little tree or shrub that we have planted, each effort to make our home more convenient or attractive has seemed to strengthen the hope that our first home might also be our last." But now: "[Our] daily physical torture, confusion of mind, gradual wearing down of courage, seem to make that long continued hope look like a vanishing dream."

In 1930, hail had destroyed their wheat crop. In 1931, terrible prices had undercut a reasonably successful crop. They could endure such drawbacks, as they had before. But then came drought, the worst drought in anyone's memory, day after day, week after week, month after month, year after year of little or no rain, until by 1935 they were facing ruin in a world ruled by the mocking oppression of dust. "There are days," she wrote,

> when for hours at a time we cannot see the windmill fifty feet from the kitchen door. There are days when for briefer periods one cannot distinguish the windows from the solid wall because of the solid blackness of the raging storm. Only in some Inferno-like dream could anyone visualize the terrifying lurid red light overspreading the sky when portions of Texas "are on the air."

The impact of this relentless siege of disaster cannot easily be exaggerated. Agriculture not only was the linchpin of the American economy in the monetary value of what it grew and nurtured — $9.5 billion even in the drought year of 1934 — it produced the very stuff of life on which the rest of the nation's industry, society, and culture fed, physically and even psychologically. In 1934, nearly 30 percent of all Americans still lived on farms, and a good part of how the nation viewed itself was rooted in its agricultural traditions and experience. Henry Ford, for one — a titan of modern industry if ever there was one — was so obsessed by his own and the country's rural origins that he spent much of his adult life collecting old houses, barns, farm implements, buggies, and other rural paraphernalia from the countryside, moving them to Michigan, and assembling them in a kind of living museum he called Greenfield Village, outside Dearborn. "The land supports life," he once wrote. "Industry helps man to make the land support him. When industry ceases to do that and supplants the land,

and the land is forgotten and man turns to the machine for sustenance, we find that we do not live off the work of our hands but off the fruits of the land."

Now, both the image and the reality of the land were under assault. Natural cycles had combined with human miscalculation to produce the most devastating agricultural disaster in American history — and little the New Dealers could produce in the way of legislation or emergency measures would do more than provide intermittent and inadequate relief. Drought was nothing new, in this country or any other, but that of the 1930s, which continued through most of the decade — combining in some years with unprecedented heat waves — was "the worst in the climatological history of the country," according to a Weather Bureau scientist. It struck first in the eastern third of the country in 1930, where it crippled agriculture from Maine to Arkansas and where only Florida enjoyed anything that approached normal rainfall. It had been drought that had aggravated the terrible desperation of those farmers who had invaded the little town of England, Arkansas, in January of 1931, demanding food for their children, and drought that in 1930 had given the great Delta bluesman, Son House, the theme for "Dry Spell Blues": "Them dry spell blues are fallin', drivin' people/from door to door,/Dry spell blues are fallin', drivin' people/from door to door./Them dry spell blues has put everybody on/the kindlin' floor."

In 1932, the center of the drought started heading west, and by 1934 it had desiccated the Great Plains from North Dakota to Texas, from the Mississippi River Valley to the Rockies. In the northern Rockies in the winter of 1933–34, the snowpack was less than a third of normal, in the central Rockies less than half, and in areas of the southern Rockies barely a dusting of snow had been seen.

Providence, fate, or some other cosmic force might be blamed for the drought itself, but not for the phenomenon that accompanied it over hundreds of millions of acres: most of that was inescapably man-made. The speculative dance of the war years and the twenties had abused millions of acres of farmland in the South and Midwest, as farmers plowed, planted, and harvested as much as they could as often as they could. Much of the topsoil was left so exhausted it could barely support the most undemanding ground cover, much less productive crops. Careless plowing had rutted the fields, leaving the land open to gullying from erosion. "Since the cover was first disturbed [in the nineteenth century]," a state commission of the National Resources Planning Board reported, "Iowa has lost apporoximately 550,000 tons of good surface soil per square mile, or a total of thirty billion tons." Iowa was not alone. "Approximately 35 million acres of formerly cultivated land have essentially been destroyed for crop production," the 1934 *Yearbook of Agriculture* reported, adding that "100 million acres now in crops have lost all or most of the topsoil; 125 million acres of land now in crops are rapidly losing topsoil. . . ." At the same time, decades of overgrazing by cattle and sheep ranchers in the western plains and valleys had left one former rich grassland after another stripped clean of ground cover, vulnerable to rampant wind and water erosion. Grass, a Texas sheepherder of the time commented, "is what counts. It's what saves us all — far as we get saved. Men and towns and such as that, don't amount to a particular damn anyhow. Grass does. Grass is what holds the earth together." Not everyone had understood that simple fact. Since the first great cattle and sheep herds had been turned out in the last third of the nineteenth century to feed on the rich grasslands of the plains and mountain pastures of the interior West, the grass had been steadily, ruthlessly overgrazed, until the earth over enormous stretches of land was no longer held together by anything but inertia. After the wartime and postwar booms of the teen years and the 1920s, more than half the grazing land in the western states was in a condition of soil depletion described by the Department of Agriculture as "extreme" or "severe."

The soil, loose and dry, lay unprotected from the winds, which repeatedly swept down on the ruined grasslands of the west, scooped them clean and carried the dust into the air, moving east to the exposed and waiting farmlands of the plains. Here, the winds deposited much of it, moved it around, added to it, filled the air now with the western grasslands dust and the plains farmland dust in a great choking geographic mix. Beadle County, South Dakota, November 11, 1933:

> By mid-morning, a gale was blowing, cold and black. By noon it was blacker than night, because one can see through night and this was an opaque black. It was a wall of dirt one's eyes could not penetrate, but it could penetrate the eyes and ears and nose. It could penetrate to the lungs until one coughed up black. If a person was outside, he tied his handkerchief around his face, but he still coughed up black. When the wind died and the sun shone forth again, it was on a different world. There were no fields, only sand drifting into mounds and eddies that swirled in what was now but an autumn breeze.

The dust did not always stay west of the Mississippi. When conditions were right, the wind would carry it east on the jet stream in enormous clouds and drop it in the form of filthy unseasonal snow on Chicago, Indianapolis, Washington, New York, and even on the gently rolling decks of Atlantic liners. During just one storm between May 9 and May 11, 1934, an estimated 350 million tons of soil disappeared from the West and reappeared in the East. Chicago got four pounds of it for every person in the city, and Washington, New York, Boston, and other cities burned their streetlamps in the middle of the day.

The government did what it could. Interior Secretary Harold Ickes established the Soil Erosion Service under Hugh Hammond Bennett in August of 1933; the agency later moved over to the Agriculture Department as the Soil Conservation Service and Bennett and his people diligently organized farmers into soil conservation districts, but not all the reeducation, preventive measures, or reclamation work in the world could repair the damage of generations. In June of 1934, Roosevelt signed the Taylor Grazing Act, which authorized the president to withdraw up to 140 million acres of federally owned public land from application under any one of the three thousand or so public land laws on the books and to establish grazing districts whose use by the cattle and sheep industry was to be carefully monitored by a new Interior Department agency, the Grazing Service. The Service would be marginally successful in stabilizing the situation, but could do little to repair historical damage. Between 1933 and 1934, the Federal Emergency Relief Administration would spend $85 million to purchase and attempt to rehabilitate ruined farmland, but this program, too, was nearly helpless to reclaim land that nearly a century of abuse had left ruined.

Little helped. Human strength failed. Hope died. "[The] longing for rain has become almost an obsession," Caroline Henderson wrote in 1935. "We dream of the faint gurgling sound of dry soil sucking in the grateful moisture . . . of the fresh green of sprouting wheat or barley, the reddish bronze of spring rye. But we wake to another day of wind and dust and hopes deferred. . . ." The Hendersons toughed it out and continued to work their land for more than two decades, but for thousands of other farm families the drought alone was more than they could endure.

▆▆▆ The Dynamics of Dispossession

Many people simply pulled up stakes and abandoned their land, and even for many of those who might have stuck it out in spite of all that nature could do, financial circumstances would make it all but impossible. Resident and absentee owners alike lost their lands to foreclosure proceedings; according to Department of Agriculture reports, nearly two hundred out of every thousand farms in the states of the Midwest, the Central South, and the Plains succumbed to forced sales between 1930 and 1935. And when landlords failed, so did croppers and tenant farmers, and to the ranks of dispossessed owners were added thousands of men and women who were forced off land they had worked as if it were their own. Often, they were forced off the land even when their landlords were doing reasonably well, thanks to the Agricultural Adjustment Administration's scarcity program, particularly in the cotton-growing regions of the South.

After the center of drought had moved west, plantations in Alabama, Arkansas, Mississippi, East Texas, and other areas had a bumper crop of cotton on their hands. But there already was a surplus of 12.5 million bales left over from the 1932 season, and prices had fallen to 6.5 cents a pound. More production would, it was felt, lower prices even further and destroy the industry. So it was that the AAA instituted its scarcity program: the cotton planters would plow under anywhere from a quarter to a half of their cotton plants in order to increase the value of existing and future supplies. "To have to destroy a growing crop," Agriculture Secretary Henry Wallace admitted as he launched the program, "is a shocking commentary on our civilization." But destroy the landlords did, and for the most part did so with hearts full of gladness. The program not only raised the price of cotton by about four cents a pound, as promised, it also compensated the landlord for his plowed-up cotton with an amount equal to anywhere from six to eight cents a pound. "The tighter the government control the better," one landlord rejoiced. "[We] never want to see a relaxation of governmental control. The more inspectors Washington puts on the job, the happier we'll be!" One impediment to their complete happiness was the fact that the law required them to share the government payments with their plantation help — half of what they received was supposed to go to sharecroppers, a quarter to tenant farmers. That was rectified in 1934 with another adjustment: under a complex system of "rental" and "parity" payments, the compensation was deliberately skewed in the landlord's favor — so much so that landlords were making more money for *not* growing cotton than they had for growing it, while tenants and sharecroppers lost money.

From the landlord's point of view, the system worked even better because the local administration of the program remained in the hands of locally elected production control committees who were, unsurprisingly, dominated by owners and their friends and relatives, with only occasional oversight by county agents — almost all of them chosen from the same gene pool as the landlords. The opportunities for various forms of theft were irresistible to many owners, who persuaded their croppers and tenant farmers to sign away their shares by threats or subterfuge, or underpaid them, or simply kept the government's payments for themselves without bothering to resort to any special tactics. On one typical plantation, a later government report would say, the owner's gross income had increased from $51,554 in 1932 to $102,202 in 1934, while that of his sharecroppers and tenant farmers had fallen from $379 to $355.

Further, with cotton acreage reduced from 35 million acres in 1932 to 26.5 in 1934–35, the labor force required to plow, plant, and pick the crop was sharply reduced, particularly in those instances when acreage reduction was combined with a rise in the use of tractors and other mechanized equipment. As a consequence, thousands of sharecropper and tenant families found themselves forced off the land — "displaced," as the federalese of the time put it. "I let 'em all go," one Oklahoma landlord frankly admitted.

> In '34 I had I reckon four renters and I didn't make anything. I bought tractors on the money the government give me and got shet o' my renters. You'll find it everywhere all over the country that way. I did everything the government said — except keep my renters. The renters have been having it this way ever since the government come in.

No one knows precisely how many families were displaced in the early years of the New Deal — or just how many had left the land as the direct result of crop reductions or tractor use. However many, there was not much in the way of employment the affected states could offer these suddenly landless and workless thousands; in Arkansas, for example, the unemployment rate was 39 percent in 1933, and in Missouri, Oklahoma, and Texas it ranged from 29 to 32 percent. People began to leave their home states in growing numbers after the terrible summer of 1934. Oklahoma had a net loss of more than 440,000 people in the 1930s. Kansas lost 227,000. Throughout the Plains states, 2.5 million people ultimately would leave for other parts. Most of those parts were nearby; the greater portion of the internal population movement in the American middle in those years was from one state to a neighboring state. But some 460,000 people moved to the Pacific Northwest, where they found work on the building of Bonneville and Grand Coulee dams, found abandoned homesteads they could work in southern Idaho and the eastern valleys of Oregon and Washington, went into the ancient forests of the region as lumberjacks or joined the migrant workers in the hop fields and beet fields — or simply settled in the cities and collected relief checks where and when they could.

■■■■ A Paradise to Live in or See

Other thousands, particularly from the southwestern Plains states, headed for California. All logic dictated the move, so it seemed. After all, between 1910 and 1930 an estimated 310,000 southwesterners had already moved to the Golden State, lured by the promise of opportunity that had bathed California in the glow of hope ever since the Gold Rush of 1848–52. Residents of Oklahoma, Arkansas, Texas, and other states who had fallen upon hard times now thought of all the cheerful letters they had been receiving from friends and relatives in California, took a look at the tormented land and overburdened cities of their own regions, and put together the wherewithal to get themselves and their families across the plains and deserts to the golden valleys of the West Coast. In one fifteen-month period alone, some 86,000 did precisely that, individually and as families, by car and by bus, most of them taking no more than three or four days to rattle down Route 66 to the border crossing at Yuma, Arizona. By the end of the decade another 220,000 or so would do the same.

If many of these people were hard-pressed by farm failure or urban unemployment, most were less than destitute or without family support. They had relatives waiting to house and feed them, if nothing else, and some even had jobs waiting for them. That still left tens of thousands who legitimately could be described as rural refugees, and one thing they soon learned was that land monopoly and agriculture on an industrial scale was a California tradition and the opportunities to engage in family farming were limited to the point of nonexistence. More than 100,000 of the migrants consequently did not gravitate toward the state's farming regions, but to the city of Los Angeles, with some going down to San Diego or up to San Francisco.

Authorities in Los Angeles were less than pleased. The city's relief program was among the best in the country, but it was stretched to its limits and the last thing the city needed — or at least wanted — was another influx of potential welfare recipients, particularly when it was having at least some success in moving trainloads of Mexican-American *repatriados* out of town. "As the migration began to gather momentum," Carey McWilliams remembered, "strenuous efforts were made to check or deflect it. At that time, we had a handsome, daring chief of police in Los Angeles who had no great respect for the Constitution." The chief's name was James

OPPOSITE, TOP: *In an Arthur Rothstein photograph taken in Kaufman County, Texas, in August, 1936, a cotton-plantation owner's daughter weighs cotton sacks while transient pickers wait to be told what they have earned at the end of a long day. A few years before, the pickers might well have been among the 581,000 white and 486,000 African-American sharecroppers or tenant farmers who then worked the plantations of the Deep South, but one of the unintended consequences of the New Deal's agricultural programs was the displacement of tens of thousands of such people. The group of evicted sharecroppers huddled in a makeshift camp* ABOVE *was just one of hundreds that lined a hundred miles of highway between Sisketon, Missouri, and the Arkansas state line in the winter of 1935–36. Another cause of displacement was a labor-saving tractor,* OPPOSITE, *used on an all-electric, all-mechanized demonstration farm established in Virginia by the Interior Department in the summer of 1936.*

E. Davis, and in February, 1936, he would send 125 Los Angeles city policemen to patrol the borders of Arizona and Oregon (eight hundred miles north of Los Angeles) in an effort to keep transients out. All this exercise accomplished was to inspire the American Civil Liberties Union to file a suit against the city, generate much nationwide ridicule at the city's expense, and give songster Woody Guthrie one of his best lyrics:

> Lots of folks back east, they say, leavin' home every day,
> Beatin' the hot old dusty way to the California line;
>
> 'Cross the desert sands they roll, gettin' out of that old Dust Bowl,
> They think they're goin' to a sugar bowl, but here is what they find:
> Now the police at the port of entry say,
> "You're number fourteen thousand for today."
>
> Oh, if you ain't got the do-re-mi, folks,
> If you ain't got the do-re-mi,
> Why you better go back to beautiful Texas,
> Oklahoma, Kansas, Georgia, Tennessee.
> California is a garden of Eden,
> A paradise to live in or see,
> But believe it or not, you won't find it so hot,
> If you ain't got the do-re-mi.

Most of California's new population would become irretrievably urban, whether it had started out that way or not, scattering through poor and middle-class white Los Angeles neighborhoods and out into the bungalow-and-apartment-building suburbs of Long Beach, Compton, Encino, Gardena, Covina, Southgate, Downey, and other towns. But some of those with rural roots would seek the work that was most familiar to them, joining California's drifting population of about 200,000 migrant farm laborers — the largest regional segment of the great army of migrant farm laborers in the United States, a constantly moving and nearly invisible population of as many as two million men, women, and children who cut cane in Florida and dug potatoes in Maine, picked peaches in Georgia and apples in Pennsylvania, plucked strawberries in Louisiana and dug sugar beets in Michigan, and harvested wheat from central Texas to northern Montana.

Some 110,000 people from the new migration would move to agricultural areas of California — more than seventy thousand of them to the San Joaquin Valley alone. Not all these new arrivals would become migrant laborers, of course, but most did, taking their place in the cheap labor pool that California's agricultural industry had come to expect as its due; for more than eighty years, it had capitalized upon successive waves of Chinese, white native Americans from earlier periods of economic stress, Japanese, Indian (from India), Filipino, and, most recently, Mexican-American laborers.

The new farm laborers found most of the agricultural regions still reverberating from the labor battles of the previous three years. Agriculture workers had been excluded from the provisions of Section 7(a), but in California the Communist party's TUUL nevertheless had organized the Cannery and Agricultural Workers Industrial Union (CAWIU), and it would be this union — sanctioned by no law but the uncodified law of worker consent — that would launch and lead some of the most dramatic, if lesser known, of the strikes that punctuated the labor movement's resurgence.

Of the thirty-seven individual strikes affecting the production of everything from walnuts to cherries recorded in these months, twenty-four of them were led by the CAWIU. Most were touched with violence, but none more so than the San Joaquin Valley cotton strike that began on October 4, 1933. Involving at least eighteen thousand and perhaps as many as twenty thousand workers and embracing virtually the state's entire cotton-growing industry, it was the largest agricultural strike in American history — and easily one of the bloodiest. Before it ended twenty-four days later, two Mexican-American strikers, a man and a woman, had been shot and killed during a siege of the union hall at Pixley, another man killed in nearby Arvin, and hundreds of strikers and nonstrikers injured during these and other attacks. Nevertheless, CAWIU leaders managed to negotiate a settlement that included a 25 percent wage increase and grower recognition for the union.

Overall, the California farm strikes of 1933–34, involving as many as fifty thousand workers at one time or other, raised the wage throughout the agricultural industry in the state by as much as twenty-five cents an hour. This was more than the state's agribusiness establishment had ever thought would be necessary. It responded by forming its own organization, the Associated Farmers of California, which in 1934 persuaded state authorities to help them out with a major crackdown. In July of that year, Carey McWilliams reported, "Raiding parties, armed with sawed-off shotguns, handcuffs, blackjacks, rubber hoses, billies, riot clubs, gas bombs, and accompanied by news reporters and photographers from the *Sacramento Bee*," smashed into (and smashed up) the CAWIU's headquarters in Sacramento and arrested more than two dozen union members and leaders they

An estimated 2.5 million people left their home states in the South and the Great Plains during the depression years. The hitchhiking couple ABOVE was photographed by Walker Evans outside Vicksburg, Mississippi, in 1936. The family in the overloaded sedan BELOW was captured by Dorothea Lange in 1935; the family had joined a bitter migration that took hundreds of thousands vaguely westward.

"The exploitation of farm labor in California," Carey McWilliams *wrote in 1939,* *"is one of the ugliest chapters in the history of American industry. . . . Sources of cheap labor in China, Japan, the Philippine Islands, Puerto Rico, Mexico, the Deep South, and Europe have been generously tapped to recruit its ever-expanding ranks."* BELOW: *Japanese packing broccoli;* RIGHT, *Filipino orchard workers.*

found there. Eighteen were tried on the standard charges of criminal syn-dicalism and eight would be convicted after a long trial in 1935. By then, the movement had entered a new phase. Except for a month-long strike of lettuce workers in the Salinas Valley in the late summer of 1934 and a particularly violent strike in the same area two years later, labor strife in the fields of California generally subsided. With its leaders in jail and its small resources exhausted, the CAWIU faded.

Part of the reason for the union's decline was the lack of any real involvement on the part of the new migration from the Southwest. Most of these people came from fundamentalist cultures. They had little experience in or sympathy for the notion of unionism and nurtured a strong nativist distrust of communism. Furthermore, they carried a full load of bigotry with them and were not inclined to mix with the Mexican-American workers who had populated the union movement. Indeed, as often as not, their participation in the migrant farm labor struggle was as strikebreakers, not strikers.

Before long, this latest resource of cheap labor would account for nearly half the total of all the state's migrant workers. Like their prede-cessors, most Anglo migrants confined themselves to journeys up and down the state, following the cycles of planting and harvest from the Imperial Valley to the Sacramento Valley and all the valleys in between, though some backtracked to the cotton fields and other irrigated crops of Arizona or continued straight up California to Oregon and Washington to work the hop fields and beet fields of the north. The average distance traveled from crop to crop every year, the State Relief Administration calculated, was 516 miles. The migrants frequently traveled and worked as families, living in the squalor of work camps either erected by themselves wherever they could with whatever they could or provided by the farmers. Whether self-built or furnished, these feculent little communities, often called "ditch camps" because they were located on the side of roads along which ran filthy water ditches, were disease-ridden and indisputably unfit for human beings. At one point, Carey McWilliams reported, fifty babies died of diarrhea and enteritis in one county during just one picking season; children in Tulare County were reported dying at the rate of two a day; and during an inspection tour of eighteen camps in the vicinity of Kingsburg in Kings County, one social worker found "dozens of children with horribly sore eyes; many cases of cramps, diarrhea, and dysentery; fever, colds, and sore throats." Hookworm, pellegra, and rickets were common.

Pay was better than it was in the depressed regions of the South and the Midwest, but whether by the day or by the amount of fruit picked or vegetables dug, wages were still far below what a family needed for decent upkeep. What was more, the seasonal character of the job made it impossible to accumulate a significant stake even when one or more members of the family made up to $3 a day, as many did. The recorded need for seasonal labor in the California fields over one two-year period, for example, ranged from a low of 48,173 workers in March to a high of 144,720 in September. Average annual farm labor income, as a consequence, never got much above $1,300 for each family — nearly $500 less than other Anglo California families (though $315 more than the average for *non-Anglo* Californians).

Huddling to wait out off-season unemployment in makeshift "shack-towns" and "Little Oklahomas" perched on the outskirts of agricultural service centers like Bakersfield, Fresno, and Modesto, collecting state relief, sending their children to local schools, the migrants soon earned the pious contempt of their neighbors in the traditional manner of humans rejecting outsiders who are unfamiliar and therefore vaguely threatening. Whatever their origin, they became known collectively as "Okies" and "Arkies," with a few "Texies" thrown in for good measure, and were subject to the kind of abuse and discrimination that the state's Mexican-American, Filipino, and African-American field workers had endured as a matter of course for decades. "These 'share croppers,' " one woman complained, "are not a noble people looking for a home and seeking an education for their children. They are unprincipled degenerates looking for something for nothing." Interviewing customers at several Sacramento Valley bars, a reporter collected a good run of comments: "Damned Okies." "No damned good. Don't do a damned thing for the town." "Damned shiftless nogoods." "Damned Okies. Damned bums clutter up the roadside."

They possessed a terrible patience, however, these despised migrants, as well as a burning determination and an anger to which someone would be forced to answer sooner or later. But it would be another season or two before the New Dealers would comprehend the full dimensions of what had fallen on these wanderers and begin, slowly and indecisively, to give them sanctuary.

■ *The True Proletariat*

There were others who waited, too, but who had not possessed the means or often the inclination to join the migration west — though they had more than a fair share of anger. Many of these, particularly those African Americans trapped in the relentless misery of the Deep South,

Migrant laborers in California could expect no help from the American Federation of Labor, one of whose California leaders had summed up the AFL's attitude nicely: "Only fanatics are willing to live in shacks or tents and get their heads broken in the interests of migratory labor." Those who were willing to get their heads broken (and often did) were the Communist organizers who created the Cannery and Agricultural Workers Industrial Union (CAWIU) in 1931. Of the dozens of strikes and other work actions led by the union in its short life, none was more dramatic (or met with more violence) than the San Joaquin Valley cotton strike of October, 1933. A striker uses a cornet to call nonunion workers out of a cotton field near Tulare, while union picketers and California Highway Patrol officers look on.

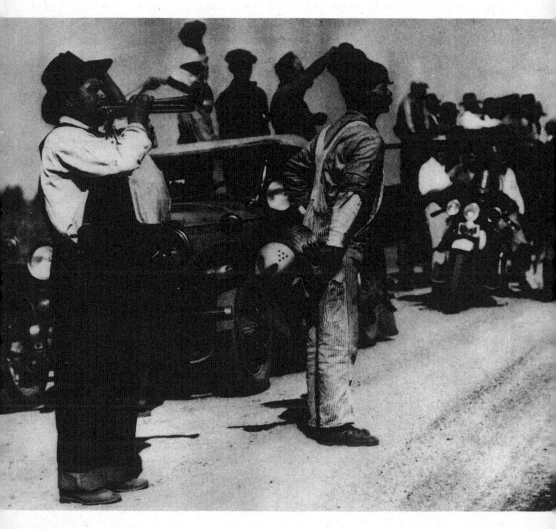

California's cotton strike, the largest such strike in American history, involved entire families; a group of Mexican-American women is trucked out of the Corcoran strikers' camp to join a picket line.

In Texas, among those looking out for migrant labor interests was Emma Tenaycuca, state secretary of the Communist Party/USA. She is seen talking to reporters in the Federal Building in San Antonio, where she has filed a complaint against U.S. border police for the beating of several Mexican Americans.

turned once again to the nearly moribund Sharecroppers Union as the only thing in sight that seemed to offer any kind of hope, however limited. The scarcity program of the Agricultural Adjustment Administration, one SCU organizer in the battered town of Camp Hill, Alabama, said, had given "new life" to the union. "The SCU in places where [it] has been slack [is] beginning to wake up and people don't wait for the comrades to come as they used to." Nevertheless, the little African-American union, like the largely Mexican-American CAWIU in California, was not sanctioned either by the AFL or by law as stipulated in Section 7(a) of the National Industrial Recovery Act. It had virtually no financial or psychological support beyond that provided by its own people, and after a series of brief picking-season strikes that resulted in some wage increases and a resurgence of membership that rose briefly to a high of eight thousand, the full weight of the supremely racist and preeminently violent plantation society was allowed to come down in full force on the union. Union meetings were disrupted repeatedly by local whites, leaders were beaten and arrested by local police, and jailed by the local judiciary. The union was simply overwhelmed and soon sank into obscurity once more.

In the Delta region, meanwhile, a slightly more durable and better-known agricultural union had appeared. The Southern Tenant Farmers Union (STFU) was the child not of the Communist party, as the SCU had been, but of the Socialist party — though the new union's origin and structure were entirely local and its leadership infinitely more democratic than the party-directed SCU even pretended to be. Norman Thomas, the peripatetic Socialist leader, helped to give it birth and would remain by all odds its most dedicated national supporter, but at no time did he or the Socialist party's national headquarters exercise anything that smacked of control.

In the autumn of 1933, Thomas, who had been criticizing the AAA regularly since its inception, received a letter from Dr. William Amberson, a professor of physiology and a Socialist party member in Memphis, who told him that two active Socialists from Tyronza, Arkansas, had come to him with the proposal that he do a survey of sharecropper working and living conditions. The two Tyronza Socialists were Henry Clay East, town constable and owner of a small service station, and Harry Leland Mitchell, owner of the dry-cleaning shop next door.

Mitchell had come to Tyronza out of Tennessee already converted to socialism and had managed to bring East around to his way of thinking, and the two had organized an "Unemployment League" in 1932 that helped local people pry state welfare benefits out of the hands of the plantation owners who ordinarily administered the program to the benefit of those nearest, dearest, and most useful to them. East and Mitchell were certain that if Wallace and his people just had enough information about what was happening to the croppers and tenant farmers they would do something about it, and they came to Amberson, the most educated man they knew, to assemble and organize the material.

Amberson proposed that Thomas finance the report and lend his name to it. Thomas agreed, and even before *The Plight of the Sharecroppers* was issued in May, 1934, he traveled down to Tyronza in February, meeting with local sharecroppers and with East and Mitchell. It was during this trip that the subject of organization first came up, as Clay East remembered it:

> When Norman Thomas was there . . . we had dinner at my home, and during the meal Norman was the first one that planted that idea in our heads. He told me at that meeting, "What you need here is a union." In other words, the Socialist Party wasn't going to be any help to these tenant farmers. This was after we had taken him out and shown him the conditions in the country and all. And that is where the idea originated, when Thomas told us that. So, after he left, we talked the thing over.

Thomas returned home and continued a barrage of letters to Henry Wallace wondering when the Department of Agriculture might be getting around to rectifying the blatant lawlessness and discrimination revealed in *The Plight of the Sharecroppers*, while East and Mitchell and a few local Socialists put together the skeleton of the Southern Tenant Farmers Union. It was a pretty thin business at first, but the creation of the union, together with the publication of *The Plight of the Sharecroppers*, immediately caught the attention of Chester Davis, director of the AAA, and Cully A. Cobb, head of the AAA's Cotton Division. Both men were sympathetic to the needs of the plantation owners and mistrustful of anything that might threaten their welfare, so after Cobb asked a local county agent to fill him in on Mitchell, East, and Dr. Amberson, they were ready to believe the worst when it came via telegram: "DOCTOR WILLIAM B. AMBERSON ON STAFF MEDICAL DEPARTMENT UNIVERSITY OF TENNESSEE CHIEF OF POLICE RE-PORTS HIM FULL FLEDGED COMMUNIST HAS MADE NUMBER EFFORTS TO START UPRISINGS AMONG NEGROES ALL THREE INDIVIDUALS LOCALLY RE-GARDED VERY DANGEROUS."

Just to be sure that the whole business of tenant displacement and other embarrassments was nothing more than propaganda being spread by Mitchell and his radical friends, Davis and Cobb sent an investigator down to look into things. After talking to several planters, the investigator reported that the landlords were operating the program fairly and indeed generously. An unfavorable report issued a few weeks later by Calvin B. Hoover of Duke University and the AAA's economics staff, however, forced Davis to launch yet another hard-hitting investigation in May, 1934. His instructions to the investigative team were firm:

> The work which you are to do in investigating and adjusting difficulties must be done in such a way as not to reflect unfavorably upon the work which has already been done by these local leaders. . . . Nothing must be done which might cause them to feel that their actions are being questioned. . . . [No] small minority should be permitted to cast a cloud upon the whole program and bring criticism upon the South and upon the Agricultural Adjustment Administration.

This was a man, clearly, who did not want to hear any bad news. Nor did he — at least not from this team: after looking into 1,457 complaints of mistreatment, cheating, and illegal evictions, the investigators found 1,040 to be without merit, and those cases in which some wrongdoing had actually been discovered (or at least admitted) resulted in the revocation of only twenty-one AAA contacts.

While Davis sent his carefully instructed investigators into the region to avoid discovering anything that would reflect badly on the AAA, STFU president Mitchell and his fellow organizers had been busy dealing with the racial question. One of the principal weaknesses of the SCU had been its racial homogeneity; from the beginning, it had been a black union. This had done much for southern African-American pride and sense of solidarity, but black power was not yet political power, not in the American South, at least, and the union's work had gone largely unnoticed outside the South. The leaders of the STFU knew they could not afford to leave white people out of the equation, even though the great majority of sharecroppers and tenant farmers in the Delta were black; this would be an organization built on class, not race. As practical southerners, the organizers knew that they could not force the creation of an openly integrated union, whether blacks and whites were being badly used together or not. The device they came up with was to establish segregated locals — but with integrated, interlocal meetings. Soon, it was possible to discern whether a meeting was that of a black local or a white local only by the color of the officers up on the platform or at the head of the room of whatever church basement or living room or abandoned building the meeting was being held in. It even found its own anthem, one derived from an old camp-meeting hymn and destined to resonate at the heart of another movement in another time:

> *The union is a-marching.*
> *We shall not be moved.*

> *The union is a-marching.*
> *We shall not be moved.*

> *Just like a tree that's planted by the water,*
> *We shall not be moved.*

One of the union's first significant acts as an organization was to hire a lawyer to file suit against the AAA for allowing a local plantation owner, Hiram Norcross, to evict from his five-thousand-acre plantation all tenants who had joined the union, replacing them with nonunion hands. The suit ultimately would be denied, but in the meantime Mitchell decided to go up to Washington and argue the STFU's case before Henry Wallace himself early in January, 1935. Two black men were included in the carful of five people who made the trip without stopping (no hotel or roadside-cabin motel would have taken in an integrated group): the Reverend E. B. McKinney, vice president of the union, and the Reverend N. W. Webb, a union organizer from Birdsong, Arkansas.

If Mitchell had hoped to gain sympathy from Wallace by demonstrating the biracial character of the STFU, he might have been overestimating the secretary's devotion to the welfare of African Americans, which was not much. Wallace had resisted instituting any programs devoted specifically to black farmers on the grounds that it would do "more harm than good" and throughout his tenure the fifty-two thousand employees of the Department of Agriculture never included more than eleven hundred blacks, most of these in custodial positions. As late as 1940, he would in all innocence ask an African-American colleague, "Will, don't you think the New Deal is undertaking to do too much for the Negro?"

In any case, Wallace was not expecting the integrated crew from

LEFT TO RIGHT: H. L. Mitchell, founder of the Southern Tenant Farmers Union; Socialist Norman Thomas, the union's national spokesman; and Howard Kester, an STFU organizer.

"[T]he ties that bind us are deeper than those that separate us," Richard Wright once said. The STFU demonstrators waving their signs in Washington, D.C., gave validity to the black writer's words — at least briefly. Note the reference to a missing report that was critical of plantation owners: it never has been found.

What gave the STFU its particular strength was its firmly integrated nature. "There was no difference, and some of 'em was beginning to see that there was no difference," J. R. Butler, president of the union from 1935 to 1942, remembered. "Of course, there still was a lot of prejudice among the white people in those days, but hard times makes peculiar bedfellows sometimes, and so some of them were beginning to get their eyes open and see that all of them were being used. . . . As soon as we began to tell people what the situation was and what might be done about it, well, they could see . . . they were all in the same boat and they all had to pull together." Blacks and whites attend a union meeting together.

Arkansas when it showed up at his office at nine o'clock in the morning. "We went right into the Secretary's office," Mitchell remembered,

> and the receptionist asked us who we were and we told her we were a delegation from the Southern Tenant Farmers' Union and we wanted to see the Secretary. She asked if we had an appointment. Of course we did not. I never heard of having to make an appointment to "see" anybody before. I hesitated and didn't know what to say. McKinney stepped up and said, "Ma'am, we will just sit down here. If Mr. Wallace is busy, we'll just wait until he gets through and we can talk to him then."

Eventually, Wallace did consent to see the group. He was polite but non-committal about any shortcomings in the AAA program, though he did promise to send down yet another investigator to look into the situation.

True to the secretary's word, a third investigation was instituted, and this time Chester Davis had nothing to do with it. A few days after the STFU visit, Jerome Frank, general counsel of the AAA and a New Deal liberal, sent attorney Mary Conner Myers to Arkansas. Unlike the other investigators, she spent time talking to members of the SFTU and to tenant farmers and sharecroppers, as well as plantation owners and managers and county agents. Her report probably substantiated the charges that Thomas, Mitchell, and the other agitators had been making all along, for when she passed it on to Davis, it went from him to the AAA's Cotton Division, where, without anyone else ever seeing it, the report promptly and permanently disappeared (in his history of the SFTU, *Cry from the Cotton*, Donald H. Grubbs reports that it was still missing from the National Archives as late as 1965).

This apparent coverup was enough to gag a bureaucrat — or at least some bureaucrats — and in February, without consulting Davis or anyone in the Cotton Division, Frank, Alger Hiss, Gardner Jackson, and a few other liberal officials in the AAA's legal division tried to implement an interpretation of the law that would require all landlords receiving federal payments not only to retain the same number of families on their plantations, but the same *individuals*. When Davis learned what Frank and the others were up to, he went to Wallace and demanded that he be allowed to fire them. Wallace agreed, and followed up by issuing his own ruling to the effect that the law "does not bind owners to keep the *same* tenants."

By the middle of February, 1935, then, AAA policy was back on track. The Southern Tenant Farmers Union could — and did — feel itself abandoned by the New Dealers, while the plantation owners could — and did — feel encouraged to begin yet another effort to reaffirm their power and destroy the union. Like the displaced and dispossessed migrants living in the ditch camps of California's agribusiness empire, the subjugated croppers and tenants of the plantation South were left to wonder when and if their patience would ever find a harvest of hope.

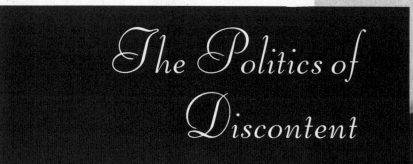

The Politics of Discontent

CHAPTER EIGHT

To what extent do nine out of ten workers — let out by dividend-paying companies and knocked about for the past four years . . . agree with all these . . . Santa Claus newspaper articles about the vast re-employment activities? . . . To what extent they disagree will be shown in coming elections, even as it was shown in 1932, unless this administration . . . gets busy in a hurry, right now, and does what it has its mandate to do, namely, take this squirming capitalistic class vigorously in hand and force the bitter dose of re-employment down its mulish throat. . . .

Johnny Q. Public, to radio commentator Boake Carter, 1934

Overleaf:

Roosevelt and most of the New Dealers would have described themselves as enlightened when it came to race relations. By comparison to every administration that preceded them (and a few that followed), the sentiment was generally true, but there were plenty of African Americans who were willing to point out how far the administration still had to go to achieve perfect grace. This speaker hammers home the point during an anti-lynching rally in New York City; the logo on the podium seems to charge that for all its aspirations, the New Deal remained oblivious to the essential horror that continued.

■ Unintended Consequences

While the New Dealers were industriously pouring concrete, hanging steel, and rearranging the nation's social and economic furniture, the same anger, frustration, and fear that had brought them to power was bubbling up into a stew of discontent. "Sooner or later in life," Robert Louis Stevenson once wrote, "we all sit down to a banquet of consequences," and according to historian Alan Dawley, what the New Dealers were presented with as they neared the middle of the sometimes roisterous banquet table of the thirties was "the unwritten law of unintended consequences." For all their defects and inconsistencies, the New Deal's programs had opened a door to possibilities that had not been seen for many years, if ever. Nevertheless, Roosevelt and his people were just not moving far enough and fast enough to satisfy many of the discontented. The administration had raised the expectations of those who had enjoyed little or no hope at all for too long — and for all their moving and shaking, the New Dealers had not managed to keep pace with the aspirations they had loosed among millions of people. They certainly had fallen short of what the dispossessed migrants of the Dust Bowl and the suppressed croppers and tenants of the South had hoped of them. Viewed in the light of unmet expectations, the New Dealers had even failed the labor movement, and the bloody violence of 1934 unmistakably had been one of the "unintended consequences" of the New Deal's efforts.

Altogether, then, the political landscape of this election year of 1934 was enlivened by more than just rich Republican conservatives — those whom Roosevelt would later denounce as "economic royalists" — bewailing the administration's "socialistic" and/or dictatorial excesses and Democratic liberals touting the New Deal's accomplishments. The American political scene had always been various, but now it included a bewildering mosaic of interests, some of them being heard from significantly for the first time, and each clamoring for a share of the New Deal's pie.

Even as the election campaigns started heating up, for example, a collection of disaffected conservative Democrats — many of whom, like GM executives John J. Raskob and Alfred P. Sloan, were as rich as any Republican in the land — was beginning to coalesce around former New York governor and FDR ally Alfred E. Smith to create the so-called Liberty League, a coalition determined to prevent the nomination of Roosevelt in 1936. The League was too new and too ill-defined in the fall of 1934 to be a major force yet, but its presence and continuing growth put a load of worry on many New Deal backs.

Then there was the unhappiness being expressed among women. For all the public glamour that attached to those few women in the administration who had attained genuine power, like Secretary of Labor Frances Perkins, millions of working women both inside and outside government service had found relatively little significant progress to cheer about. From the beginning, the New Deal's various work-relief programs had accepted a double standard with regard to both opportunities and pay scales that no amount of persuasion, gentle or otherwise, from Eleanor Roosevelt or anyone else could ever quite eliminate. More than 25 percent of the vaunted wage codes of the NRA, for example, consistently set lower rates for women than for men, in spite of Hugh Johnson's early public promise that "where women do men's work, they should get equal pay." The trouble was that the work codes were defined in such a way as to exclude coverage for many jobs that ordinarily fell almost entirely to women. And even in some of the covered jobs, such as those in the coat and suit industry, the wages established for specific jobs included a ten-cent-an-hour difference between men and women doing the same work.

The situation inspired the Women's Trade Union League, the National Consumers League, the General Federation of Women's Clubs, the YWCA, the National Association of Women Lawyers, the Women's Joint Congressional Committee subcommittee, and other organizations to join in protests to the NRA. But Roosevelt's determination to get the codes established and on the books as rapidly as possible overcame any notion of fairness, and the inequities remained in place for the life of the NRA. Many women consequently felt it appropriate to wonder aloud about "the forgotten woman" as a mordant commentary on Roosevelt's famous gubernatorial radio address of 1932: "These unhappy times call for the building of plans . . . that put their faith once more in the forgotten man at the bottom of the economic pyramid."

◼ A Durable Racism

There were plenty of forgotten women at the bottom of that pyramid, and some of the women were black — a condition that had its own, additional burden of deprivation. The New Dealers were, at least in principle, color-blind, and by the middle of the decade most African Americans had severed their old ties to the Republican party and joined the Democrats. Having done so, they became increasingly insistent that the New Dealers live up to their pretentions — a call that came not just from the traditional leadership of the NAACP and the Urban League but from such outspoken young intellectuals as Abram L. Harris, Charles H. Houston, and Ralph J. Bunche of Howard University, E. Franklin Frazier of Fisk University, and Harvard Law School graduate John P. Davis — who in July of 1933 had persuaded the NAACP and the Urban League to support the creation of the Joint Committee on National Recovery, an organization designed to "speak with authority for the major organized forces among Negroes, that can speak quickly and intelligently."

All African Americans could and most did take pride in seeing black leaders like Mary McLeod Bethune consorting with Eleanor Roosevelt on a regular basis, Robert C. Weaver working as an adviser on "Negro affairs," William Hastie installed as assistant solicitor in the Department of the Interior, and Robert L. Vann functioning as assistant to the attorney general. Indeed, by 1934 there were enough African Americans holding significant positions in the New Deal for an unofficial "black cabinet" to coalesce around Mrs. Bethune and the others; it would later be institutionalized as the Federal Council on Negro Affairs. Meanwhile, Interior Secretary Harold Ickes (who had been head of the Chicago branch of the NAACP for a brief period in the early twenties) had become so firmly established as the chief spokesman for black interests in the administration that he often seemed to be, as historian Arthur Schlesinger has said, "Secretary of Negro Relations." The dream of equality even burned in the bosom of Franklin Roosevelt, if a statement he once made to Mrs. Bethune could be taken at face value: "People like you and me are fighting and must continue to fight for the day when a man will be regarded as a man regardless of his race or faith or country."

Nevertheless, the government was hardly putting its full weight behind the goal of equal treatment for blacks. Even the New Deal's most universally admired innovation, the Civilian Conservation Corps, was marred throughout its life by a not very subtle racism. Congressman Oscar De Priest, a black Republican from Illinois, had offered and Congress had accepted an amendment to the CCC's authorizing legislation that stated that "in employing citizens for the purpose of this act no discrimination shall be made on account of race, color, or creed," but it was a stipulation too often observed by being breeched. An unofficial quota of 10 percent black enrollment had been established, on the theory that this represented, roughly, the percentage of blacks in the general population. In fact, though, only about two hundred thousand African Americans were enrolled during the life of the program, about 6 percent of the total enrollment. And because the Labor Department had decided that the most efficient means of selecting enrollees was to utilize the already existing state relief agencies, local

Many unemployed single women, like these demonstrators, held that hiring married women was unfair to them. Most men agreed, and discrimination against married women was common, both officially and unofficially.

The members of the Federal Council on Negro Affairs — Roosevelt's "black cabinet" — photographed in 1938. Their spiritual head — and the only woman among them — was Mary McLeod Bethune, (front row, center).

The CCC workers in this photograph, shown in barracks with their white officer, demonstrate one of the failures of the New Deal. Robert C. Fechner, vice president of the International Association of Machinists, was appointed head of the CCC to mollify labor leaders. He was a white man born in Georgia and his union specifically excluded blacks. It was not surprising, then, that while legislation prohibited discrimination in the recruitment of CCC enrollees, many southern officials were allowed to ignore the law, while Jim Crow regulations issued by the U.S. Army were condoned — including an order that "colored companies" were to be "employed in their own states" and that "complete segregation" was to be maintained wherever possible.

prejudices made it inevitable that in the states of the Deep South, especially, only a paltry number of black men would ever be allowed to participate.

Furthermore, rigid segregation was maintained in all but those few states — mostly in New England and scattered parts of the West — where there just were not enough black enrollees to make up full companies. All black companies except two (one, appropriately enough, at Gettysburg National Military Park) were in the command of white officers, as might have been expected, since it was ancient Army custom; still, the custom extended to other supervisory personnel as well, including teachers, and not even some unshirted hell raised by Interior Secretary Ickes, whose Department of Education was in charge of teaching programs in the camps, was enough to alter the situation significantly. Jim Crow remained in place — which was fine with the scores of local communities that constantly petitioned Robert C. Fechner, head of the CCC, to move all-black camps to areas near somebody else's town. There were so many such complaints, both in the South and elsewhere, that most of the black camps eventually ended up being relegated to areas of national parks or national forests well removed from the nearest towns.

If the institutional racism of the CCC was regrettable, the quasi-legal racism of southern lynch law was indefensible. After all, lynching was not merely a matter of social inequity and economic oppression. It was plain murder, and in its most extreme forms took on a vicious character — including torture, mutilation, burning — that seemed to bubble up from some of the deepest and most savage pits in the human psyche. Lynching had been a plague on black people for decades, but surely now, in this new age of enlightenment and social progress, an end could be made of it. So many African Americans hoped and believed, and their leaders — particularly those in the NAACP — were not long in calling for the New Dealers and the Congress to do so once and for all.

It seemed possible. By 1934 a great deal of white support had been added to the crusade, even in the South. "Of all present Southern social phenomena, the tendency to resort to lynch law for the punishment of alleged crimes of Negro offenders is the most dangerous and the most inexcusable," George Fort Milton, editor of the *Chattanooga News* and chairman of the Southern Commission on the Study of Lynchings, had written in the *Virginia Quarterly* in April, 1932. "Whenever a lynching has occurred, one can say definitely: The crust of civilization has given way to the blind anger of the animal." In the South, at least, the "blind anger" traditionally was rationalized as the natural fury of white men whose women had been insulted, assaulted, raped, and murdered. Nonsense, the

Milton Commission had concluded: "The popular opinion that most lynchings are for the punishment of crimes against women is wide of the fact. Of 3,693 persons lynched during the 41 years ending with 1929, only 23 were accused of actual or attempted crimes against women."

The chore at hand, the Milton Commission had warned, was largely a matter of education — to change "the social viewpoint of the South, so that justice rather than hysteria, hate, and fear will control the adjudication of responsibility for crime. This involves a long and tedious process." The willingness of white southerners to work patiently for the cause was commendable, but others were not much interested in waiting — certainly not the black community. As with so much else, it had been waiting for a long time. The first federal anti-lynching legislation had been introduced as far back as 1899 by George H. White, a black congressman from North Carolina. The bill had gone about as far in the Fifty-sixth Congress as one would have expected, and it was not until 1919 that Missouri's splendidly named Congressman Leonidas Carstarphen Dyer introduced the second such bill, largely crafted by James Weldon Johnson, then executive secretary of the NAACP. The bill did not reach the floor of the House that year, nor the next, nor the next — but in 1922 Dyer managed to get it out of committee and up for a vote. It passed 230 to 119, but died in the Senate when even those northern senators who favored such legislation proved reluctant to offend their outraged southern colleagues.

Anti-lynching legislation had remained a priority with Walter White, Johnson's successor at the NAACP, as well as with Mary White Ovington, a white cofounder of the organization and chair of its governing board. In January, 1934, they persuaded Colorado Senator Edward P. Costigan to introduce an anti-lynching bill that had been drawn up by the NAACP's legal committee. It stipulated that a lynching case should be tried in a federal court if a state had taken no action against its perpetrators within thirty days; that if the federal court found that the police authorities had been derelict in their duty to protect their prisoner, the appropriate officers would be subject to fine and imprisonment; and, finally, that damages of not less than $2,000 and not more than $10,000, to be paid by the county in which the crime had occurred, could be sought by the victim's heirs in the same federal court.

The bill was reported to the Senate Judiciary Committee, and the NAACP brought a platoon of witnesses to testify at subsequent hearings, explaining that 5,053 lynchings had occurred since 1882 (a figure considerably higher than that cited by the Milton Commission in 1932), 277 of them in the previous twelve years; that 3,513 African Americans had been murdered in such incidents; that among the dead black people were ninety-four women; that in only one-sixth of the cases had rape or attempted rape even been the alleged cause of action; that less than 1 percent of the lynchings had resulted in the arrest and conviction of anyone by local or state authorities; and that the Fifth and Fourteenth Amendments to the Constitution and the power vested in Congress to legislate for the peace of the citizenry all validated the proposed law's constitutionality.

The bill was reported favorably on March 28 — and promptly began a long exile that lasted the rest of the 1934 session, stalled by the threat of filibuster from such southern senators as James Byrnes of South Carolina, Josiah Bailey of North Carolina, Tom Connally of Texas, and the Senate's preeminent bigot, Theodore Bilbo of Mississippi. Senator Costigan worked closely with Eleanor Roosevelt in an effort to get her husband to put the legislation on his "must" list, hoping that the president's influence would be enough to overcome southern resistance and the continued reluctance of many northern and western senators to challenge them. FDR had gone on record against lynching, calling it "a vile form of collective murder," but in this election year of 1934, with his New Deal programs barely under way and his finely tuned antennae picking up disconcerting peeps and whistles from the political ether regarding the anti-lynching legislation, that, unfortunately, was as far as he was willing to go.

Anti-lynching legislation would be reintroduced in the new Congress in 1935; in the meantime, blacks were counseled to exercise patience in this and other hopes. The day of equality would come, FDR assured Mrs. Bethune, "but we must pass through perilous times before we realize it."

■■■■■ Voices Made for Promise

Among those who were doing their best to keep the political situation in a state of agitation during the midterm year of 1934, of course, were the Socialists and the Communists. Internal disunity and fratricidal tendencies prevented these diverse leftist agglomerations from manipulating the American political process with anything near the competence they professed and right-wing conservatives nearly always believed. While still superior in numbers to the Communists, the Socialist party was in a period of decline, weakened by an endless fight between a cautionary "Old Guard" and a younger, more militant faction of left-wingers led by Norman Thomas, the party's sometime presidential candidate.

On the face of it, by contrast, the Communist Party/USA seemed reasonably healthy in 1934, claiming a firm membership of more than 25,000 in its main body, another 6,000 in the Young Communist League, and 500,000 "sympathizers." Over the objections of conservatives and intransigent isolationists, Roosevelt had formally recognized the USSR in 1933, and diplomatic relations between the two countries had been reestablished, encouraging a more favorable public perception of the Soviet state. In 1934, after the Comintern in the USSR decided that the rise of Hitler and fascism was an even greater threat to proletarian goals than capitalism, Earl Browder, the American party's general secretary, began building a "Popular Front" — also called "the People's Front" — which literary critic and party member Malcolm Cowley remembered "seemed to offer vast possibilities. It might bring together all factions on the left and then win over the wavering middle class. . . . It might introduce broad social reforms (and note the emphasis on reforms; the word "revolution" was losing its glamour)." Communism, Browder would say, was just "Twentieth Century Americanism," and for a brief while in the thirties the party lent some measure of support to New Deal policies and acquired a kind of shaky respectability. Thousands of young people, particularly those of the relatively well educated middle class, joined the Young Communist League, agitating against fascism and otherwise exhibiting levels of idealism and commitment similar to those that would characterize the nationwide student movements of the 1960s and 1970s, when young people challenged "the establishment" on every question from free speech to the Vietnam War.

Still, the Popular Front of the 1930s remained a profoundly loose-jointed affair in which not even the Socialists could be persuaded to participate on any significant level. And the party itself was only a little more coherent than its Socialist competitor. It was in a state of constant intellectual ferment, particularly among the writers, artists, and other creative types who clustered in Trotskyist, Stalinist, and other ideological knots to wrangle over philosophy and policy. At the same time, Browder and the relatively conservative elements of the party were locked in a constant struggle for dominance with hard-liners, led by the party's labor specialist William Z. Foster, who had run for president in 1932 on a platform he had outlined himself in a book titled with unmistakable clarity, *Toward a Soviet America*. "Mr. Roosevelt," he had written elsewhere during the campaign, "is nothing more or less than a lightning rod for capitalism to protect it from danger," and while he generally held to the party line on the question of the Popular Front, Foster never really changed his mind. He remained comparatively militant — and within the radical core of the labor movement and among those who did the work in the field it was Foster, not Browder,

National Association for the Advancement of Colored People secretary Walter White (far left), with NAACP leaders Charles Houston, James G. Tyson, Leon A. Ransome, and Edward P. Lovett.

Politics and flags of protest — like that flying outside NAACP
headquarters in Manhattan, OPPOSITE *— were not enough;*
on July 19, 1935, Rubin Stacy of Fort Lauderdale, Florida,
was lynched for "threatening and frightening a white woman."

who stood tallest. "In our eyes he remained the authoritative public spokes-man on issues confronting the labor movement," California farm labor organizer Dorothy Healey recalled. "It is an oversimplification to assume that just because Browder was general secretary and he said or did some-thing, that's what filtered down to us in the rank and file as the last word on Party policy."

Meanwhile, and in spite of squabbles and internal discontinuities, for many young and not-so-young people the Communist party was a fear-fully exciting thing to be part of in the 1930s, an orthodoxy in which passion fed conviction and all of life was honed to a sharpness never again experienced. "I was vain, shallow, pretty, and energetic," one woman recalled of her postcollegiate days in the party. "But I was a Communist. And being a Communist made me better than I was. It was the great moral adventure of my life." As one of its "unintended consequences," the New Deal provided plenty of opportunity for such moral adventurers to exercise their passionate agitation, and while their effectiveness would range from significant to nil, depending upon where and how they operated, the Com-munists would remain a presence to be reckoned with wherever people sought to organize hope and anger to annihilate despair and fear.

In 1934, however, there were even louder political rumblings for the New Dealers to worry about. There was, for instance, the loutish and irrepressible former governor of Louisiana, Senator Huey ("Kingfish") Long, who had ridden into office in 1930 on a wave of his own creation — a state political machine erected and held together by a combination of rare po-litical intelligence, intimidation, ruthlessness, an intuitive sensitivity to the needs and dreams of the poorest and most bitter of his constituents that ensured him their adulation, calculatedly expansive welfare and public works projects designed to continue that adoration, oratorical gifts that had not been witnessed in those or any other parts in years, and a vision for the future of the nation that was no less genuine for being as messy and intemperate and dramatic as its creator.

On February 23, 1934, Long went on nationwide radio to explain his vision to the whole country. The goal, he said, was to decentralize wealth, and to further this effort he had created an organization called the Share the Wealth Society. Its slogan was Every Man a King. Simply put, Long would impose a system of graduated income taxes that would prevent anyone in the country from keeping a fortune of more than five million dollars or earning more than one million dollars in any one year. The revenue from the taxes would provide every family in the country with a "homestead" of five thousand dollars, or "enough for a home, an automobile, a radio, and the ordinary conveniences." Every family would be guaranteed an annual income of from two to three thousand dollars a year. There would be old-age pensions, free college education for deserving students, a thirty-hour work week and a month of paid vacation for every worker, and the government would purchase most surplus agricultural products.

Share the Wealth was immediately greeted with charges of socialism at best and insincerity at worst. Long denied both, claiming that his plan would save the system, not destroy it. As for sincerity: "My enemies believe I'm faking. Let them think it. That's in my favor. All the time that they fight me, they fight upon a mistaken basis." Those who chose to dismiss Long out of hand, journalist John Franklin Carter noted, would be making a mistake:

> Long is a demagogue, no doubt, as well as a slick politician, but he
> has been making the same speech for seventeen years. He can fairly
> claim to have been consistent in advocating these fundamental issues,
> which did not become visible to others of our leading statesmen until
> the depression was biting deep into an unsound economic structure.

The powers that were had no cause for complacency. Long's office claimed to be receiving as many as sixty thousand letters a week, and Share the Wealth clubs began to spread, helped along by the vigorous proselytizing of the Reverend Gerald L. K. Smith, a minister of radical bent who had been fired from the First Christian Church in Shreveport, Louisiana, for preaching Long's gospel from the pulpit. Long subsequently had hired him and turned him loose. By the end of the year, Share the Wealth headquarters would claim a membership of more than 4.6 million people in 27,431 clubs representing every state in the nation. The White House began to appear obtainable.

Long was not the only one receiving sackfuls of mail that year. In Royal Oak, Michigan, a depressed little suburb of Detroit, a stubby "radio priest" with a magical voice was claiming as many as a million letters a week. His name was Father Charles Coughlin, and his career stood as a singularly pointed example of how the economic crisis had begun to alter even the character of religion in the United States. The depression, historian Page Smith has noted, "posed a special challenge to the Christian churches." To many of the evangelistic and fundamentalist sects, the economic calamity was the signal that the Second Coming was indeed at hand and that all good Christians should stop worrying about present circumstances and prepare to meet their Maker at any moment. Most Protestant,

Catholic, and Jewish religious leaders, however, responded — much as did society as a whole — with increasingly vigorous entreaties for the government to play the Samaritan's role and tend to the hungry and the homeless directly. For most of the New Deal years, FDR could count on substantial levels of support for his social programs from virtually all of the Jewish clergy and most of the Catholic and Protestant clergy.

But there was a healthy population among the clergy that saw the need for even more drastic measures and for whom the New Deal would never go quite far enough. In a national poll early in the decade, 28 percent of the Protestant clergy responding said that they advocated some form of socialism. Among students at the various theological seminaries, the proportion was much higher and some, like the young man met by Communist organizer Elizabeth Bentley at the Union Theological Seminary, went even beyond socialism to the belief that "Communism is the Christianity of the future" and that he, "as a potential Christian minister, must *per se*, be a Communist. . . ." Somewhat milder proponents of change called for a revitalized form of the old Social Gospel that had played such an important part in the last years of the nineteenth century and first years of the twentieth, while Reinhold Niebuhr, the dominant Protestant philosopher of the era, reminded capitalists that "we can no longer buy the highest satisfactions of the individual life at the expense of social injustice."

Socialism and the Social Gospel were a good deal less rampant among Catholics, but they were not unknown. The activist instincts of Dorothy Day, for instance, a former newspaperwoman and novelist and devout lay Catholic, were close to the Protestant mold of religious socialism. With Peter Maurin and a handful of similarly militant Catholic philosophers in Manhattan, she had started the Catholic Worker movement with the publication of a weekly newspaper of the same name whose first number she and a young associate had handed out personally during the May Day parade down Broadway in 1933. Later, she would found a kind of settlement house — she called it a "house of hospitality" — on Mott Street in the Bowery, and from then until her death in 1980 the Bowery would remain the home of the *Catholic Worker* and of the works of personal mercy in which the movement specialized, providing beds to a constant stream of "guests" and feeding as many as a thousand hungry people a day.

It was to varieties of religion, too, that many African Americans turned for solace, release, and relief. The urban storefront churches in the black enclaves of Chicago, Cleveland, New York, and other eastern cities, for example, spawned the Don't Buy Where You Don't Work movement, a frequently successful campaign to boycott local merchants who did not hire local help. In Chicago, Elijah Poole, who had been converted to the Islamic religion in Detroit, changed his name to Elijah Muhammad and became the patriarch of the "Black Muslim" movement of the Nation of Islam, which slowly grew into a subcultural force that in another thirty years would capture the heart and imagination of the young activist who would become known as Malcolm X.

No black religious movement of the period, however, could compare to that of the Reverend Major Jealous Divine, Father Divine, whose integrated — though predominantly black — Peace Mission movement, founded in 1919, had acquired a membership of some two million people by the middle of the 1930s. "God is here on earth today," his followers sang, "Father Divine is his name," while his sermons preached an end to racism, peace on earth, and food for all. Father Divine's dedication to the hungry did not stop at the pulpit; the enjoyment of food was a major part of the ritual of his form of Christianity, and all were welcome to share. "Oh, my Lord, he fed a lot of people," longtime Harlem resident Naomi Washington remembered. "And when I tell you it was good food — I went. As much as you could eat. If you were hungry when you went in, when you came out, if you didn't eat for two days, you had enough."

Father Coughlin, who in 1934 already was enjoying the fruits of the good life his popularity as a radio personality had brought him, did not claim to be God, as did Father Divine. Similarly, he would have drawn the line at Dorothy Day's level of commitment to selfless socialism — though even he once told his listeners, "I believe that wealth, as we know it, originates from natural resources and from the labor which the children of God expend upon these resources," and called for the nationalization of all such resources. That was early in his public career, though, not long after the young priest had become pastor of a small parish in 1923. The parish was so poor that it did not even yet have a church building, but with money borrowed from the Archdiocese of Detroit, Coughlin had built a church and had christened it the Shrine of the Little Flower in honor of St. Therese, the "Little Flower of Jesus," canonized in 1922. A few months after completion of his church building, Coughlin had begun a weekly radio sermon over local station WJR as a means of expanding his tiny parish and raising money.

The tactic worked very well indeed. "His distinction," Wallace Stegner remembered, was

> a voice of such mellow richness, such manly, heartwarming, confidential intimacy, such emotional and ingratiating charm, that anyone

Some called him a raw demagogue and others a mountebank, but few could deny that Huey Long was a political genius of the first order. LEFT: He passes out $15,000 in $7 chits to enable LSU students to attend the big football game with Vanderbilt in 1934.

Father Charles E. Coughlin, the "radio priest" of Detroit, who founded the Union for Social Justice in November, 1934. Within a few years, his finely tuned egalitarianism would be supplanted by bigotry, virulent anticommunism, and plain anti-Semitism.

In 1934, Francis Townsend, a California doctor, had a brainstorm called Old Age Revolving Pensions (OARP), which advocated the payment of a monthly stipend to old folks, providing they spend it all within the same month. Within a few months, thousands of "Townsend Clubs" sprang up. BELOW: The good doctor waves to a crowd of enthusiasts in St. Louis; LEFT, a Townsendite in Kansas links OARP and unionism.

California gubernatorial candidate Upton Sinclair gets off an unrecorded but clearly effective quip during his startling campaign of 1934. All Republicans and most moderate Democrats (including FDR himself) looked upon Sinclair's run unenthusiastically, for his End Poverty in California (EPIC) program, if instituted, would have eviscerated traditional economics and politics alike. So his opponents believed, in any case, and in their own campaign California's Republicans went to extraordinary lengths to ensure his defeat — including the distribution of thousands of snide fabrications called "Sincliar" dollars; the two sides of these are shown.

THE RED CURRENCY

ONE

SINCLIAR DOLLAR

10U   10U

GOOD ONLY IN CALIFORNIA OR RUSSIA

I, GOVERNOR OF CALIFORNIA, HEREBY ISSUE THIS LABOR CREDIT WITH THE DEMAND THAT IT BE ACCEPTED AS FULL PAYMENT OF WAGES FOR LABOR PERFORMED, AND FOR ALL MERCHANDISE.

NOT VERY GOOD ANYWHERE

Tom Phoney
SEC'Y OF FINANCE

50
© 1934

Utopian Sinclair
GOVERNOR OF CALIFORNIA

10U   ENDURE POVERTY IN CALIFORNIA   10U

ONE

SINCLIAR DOLLAR

10U   10U

ISSUED BY UPPY & DOWNY BANK

Nº 0000

EASY PICKINGS IN CALIFORNIA

REDEEMABLE IF EVER, AT THE COST OF FUTURE GENERATIONS

Tom Phoney
SEC'Y OF FINANCE

Utopian Sinclair
GOVERNOR OF CALIFORNIA

10U   ASSETS, IF ANY, GUARANTEED BY I, GOVERNOR   10U

tuning past it almost automatically returned to hear it again. It was
without doubt one of the great speaking voices of the twentieth century.
Warmed by the touch of Irish brogue, it lingered over words and
enriched their emotional content. It was a voice made for promises.

Coughlin was soon picked up by CBS, and by 1930 the "voice made for
promises" oozed out over seventeen network stations across the East and
Midwest, with numerous hookups from independent stations. When the
listeners of Philadelphia's WCAU were asked to choose between the New
York Philharmonic and Father Coughlin for their Sunday afternoon enlightenment, 112,000 chose Coughlin's music and only 7,000 that of the Philharmonic. With an audience estimated at ten million, Coughlin soon
organized his listeners, creating the Radio League of the Little Flower.
Contributions were welcome, and there were plenty. In 1932, he replaced
the little church of 1923 with a big new one, featuring a seven-story tower
with a huge depiction of the crucified Christ on one side. He began investing
in silver futures.

Popularity was power, and after 1930, when the full impact of the
depression hit the Detroit area, Coughlin lashed out with increasing anger,
combining contempt for "predatory capitalism" with a fiery hatred of communism and all its works and winning a swelling audience of worshipful
listeners. "Let not the workingman be able to say," he sang in one of his
radio cantos, "that he is driven into the ranks of socialism by the inordinate
and grasping greed of the manufacturer." The priest was an ardent supporter
of Roosevelt in 1932 and remained a friend of the New Deal through the
first months of FDR's presidency, but by the middle of 1934 he was beginning to show his impatience with the New Deal's reluctance to carry
banking reform and other measures as far as he wanted them carried. He
now used terms like "international bankers" with a regularity that hinted
at the anti-Semitism that would later characterize most of his public utter-
ances. "The Democratic Party," he warned at the end of the year, "is merely
on trial. Two years hence it will leave the courtroom of public opinion
vindicated and with a new lease on life, or will be condemned to political
death if it fails to answer the simple question of why there is want in the
midst of plenty." It would soon enough be clear that if the radio priest did
not quite have an eye on the White House himself, he was willing to believe
himself to be one of those who would determine just who it might be who
would sit there after 1936.

Meanwhile, there was another quarter to be heard from. At about the
same time that Huey Long had decided to go public with his Share the

Wealth program, Francis Townsend, a slender, elderly, and largely unremarkable doctor who had gone into semiretirement in Long Beach, California, like so many other aging refugees from midwestern winters, wrote a letter to the *Long Beach Press-Telegram* announcing his own program to save the country. His was called Old-Age Revolving Pensions, Ltd., and if it was designed principally to provide for the security of people of Townsend's generation, the scheme, or so it was imagined, would have stimulated the national economy to the benefit of all ages. Like Long's Share the Wealth, the Townsend Plan, as it came to be called, was simple: every person sixty years old or older would be paid the sum of $200 a month — provided, first, that they did no other salaried work and, second, that they spend the entire $200 within a month after having received it. The money to pay for all this would come from a 2 percent tax on all goods at each stage of production.

Within months, Townsend's message had spilled out of California and into the nation at large, and by the end of 1934 there would be more than five thousand Townsend Clubs with a membership of about two million old folks who were entranced with the notion of being given spending money that they had to spend in order to get some more money to spend, and so on.

That was a lot of people, and there soon developed speculation over the possibility of some kind of political union among these three voices of promise — Townsend, Coughlin, and Long. They all were in sympathy with one another's goals to a greater or lesser degree and all three went out of their way to speak well of one another for the public press. Together, they represented millions of supremely discontented Americans who seemed to have dismissed or were nearly ready to dismiss not only traditional politics but socialism and communism as well and embrace a new kind of demagoguery.

■■■ *Uppie and Downey*

No one may have known just what might come of an alliance among Long, Coughlin, and Townsend, but in California, where 1.25 million people were still on the relief rolls in 1934, the unlikely political rise of Upton Sinclair was making it abundantly clear that nearly anything was possible in this year of discontent. Sinclair was a practicing Socialist and a prolific author of muckraking novels that attempted to rip the lid off various industries and institutions in American life — *The Jungle* on the meat-packing industry, *Oil!* on the Teapot Dome affair, *Boston* on the Sacco-Vanzetti affair, dozens more. Like millions of other Americans, he thought the New Deal was fine, as far as it went, but it had not gone nearly far enough, and in October, 1933, he published yet another book: *I, Governor of California, and How I Ended Poverty: A True Story of the Future*. The book sold handsomely, not least because Sinclair timed its publication to coincide with his filing as a candidate for the Democratic nomination for governor in the 1934 election.

His economic theories were laid out in detail in the book. The overarching theme was "production for use," not profit, and like the Long and Townsend scenarios, it had a seductive simplicity. To raise revenue, the general sales tax would be replaced by a graduated income tax and heavy taxes on corporations, banks, and insurance companies. Unused land — land assumed to be held for speculative purposes — would be taxed at 10 percent. The money raised from these taxes would be used to purchase idle land and establish agricultural colonies made up of unemployed laborers and bankrupt farm families. The colonies would grow everything they needed and trade their excess production for goods manufactured in state-owned factories. The whole program would be bound together by an internal system of credits and scrip to give it economic autonomy within the capitalistic system around it — said capitalism, of course, ultimately to be overwhelmed by this new creation.

Sinclair's End Poverty in California (EPIC) campaign was launched to the jeers of millions, but hundreds of thousands of Californians were more than ready to accept the artful simplicity of its program. A newsletter, *EPIC News,* soon reached a circulation of 1.4 million. When Democratic funders refused his solicitations, Sinclair sold *I, Governor* by the tens of thousands and EPIC clubs — more than two thousand of them — sprang up to raise money door-to-door and street-corner-to-street-corner. And on August 28, 1934, Sinclair and Sheridan Downey ("Uppie and Downie" they were called), his choice for lieutenant governor, overwhelmed contender George Creel and his running mate to capture the Democratic nomination.

Conservative and moderate Democrats were amazed and appalled, and while Sinclair assiduously sought his support, FDR, smiling, affable, but determined not to get tarred by the brush of radical failure if Sinclair lost, never quite came out and publicly approved the novelist's candidacy. During a long meeting with Sinclair at Hyde Park on September 4, however, he apparently gave the candidate every indication that he ultimately would do so. "I talked with one of the kindest and most genial and frank and open-minded and lovable men I have ever met," Sinclair burbled to reporters after the meeting.

Republicans of all stripes were in no way ambivalent; they were horrified. More than a year of intermittent agricultural strikes, not to mention the general strike in the San Francisco Bay Area earlier in 1934, had left them convinced that the state teetered at the precipice of Red revolution already. A Democrat, they might have been able to live with, if just barely — but an avowedly *socialistic* Democrat? They soon waded in with the most comprehensive, best-organized, and best-financed state-wide campaign anyone had yet seen.

Funded through a front organization called United for California, the campaign was a media effort from the beginning, the first in which virtually all forms of popular communication available would be brought into play — and, as in campaigns today, where on the television sets of America toothy candidates become as noisily ubiquitous as the visual soap operas that have supplanted those of radio, much of what spilled forth could have been most accurately described as "negative campaigning" long before the term itself was invented. In southern California, the campaign of Sinclair's Republican opponent, incumbent governor Frank Merriam, was handled by Don Francisco, head of the West Coast office of Albert J. Lasker's pioneering advertising agency, Lord & Thomas; in the north, similar duties were performed by Clem Whitaker, founder of Campaigns, Inc., the first political consulting firm in history.

With the aid and advice of Francisco and Whitaker, the state's principal newspapers — most of whose owners were Republicans — regularly packed their "news" stories with such open lies as those included in a *Los Angeles Times* "exposé" to the effect that from EPIC-sponsored "motion pictures, plays, shows, rodeos, food and other merchandising, auction sales, banquets and what nots" Sinclair was expecting a personal profit "to the potential tune of a quarter of a million dollars." Editorials viewed with alarm stentoriously and repeatedly and editorial cartoons relentlessly lampooned EPIC and its leader.

At Don Francisco's behest and with Albert J. Lasker's blessing, Lord & Thomas wrote and produced radio shows like "Weary and Willie," which followed the adventures of a pair of mythical hoboes as they journeyed to California to live the good life of parasites in a California under EPIC, or "The Bennets," in which a family of ordinary Californians sat around and discussed the terrible fate that awaited them if EPIC were to pass. In Hollywood, Irving Thalberg and Louis B. Mayer of Metro-Goldwyn-Mayer financed the production of "California Election News," a series of three film shorts that appeared in hundreds of California theaters during the course of the campaign. Ostensible newsreels, these cunning fabrications featured an "Inquiring Cameraman," who traveled about interviewing actors playing solid American businessmen who worried about revolution and intoned their support of Merriam, confused little old ladies who confessed to being misled by Sinclair's oily rhetoric, panhandlers eager to cash in, and hairy radicals with vaguely Yiddish accents who proclaimed EPIC as the wave of the socialistic future.

Given the size and horsepower and spectacular sophistication of the machine that had gone into action against him, it is noteworthy that Sinclair lost the election on November 5 by as few as 260,000 votes — 1,138,000 for Merriam, 879,000 for Sinclair. What remains intriguing is what the outcome might have been had not Progressive candidate Raymond Haight been running against both Sinclair and Merriam; Haight received 302,000 votes. In any event, the *New York Times* joined its namesake in Los Angeles in approving the results. Wherever such radicalism might appear, the newspaper said, "the only way, the American way, is to challenge the whole thing directly, face it squarely, and make an end of it for good and all."

■ *Winning in the Middle*

If the nation seethed with seemingly uncontrollable labor violence during much of this election year, if women, blacks, and other factions were putting pressure on his administration, and if strange new eruptions were confusing political certainties, Roosevelt faced some unsettling diversity within his own ranks, as moderate and radical forces were urging him now in one direction, now in another. Raymond Moley, the founding member of the Brain Trust and a moderate, declared in the spring of the year, "The New Deal is practically completed." A few weeks later, Rexford Tugwell, another Brain Truster and a radical, disagreed with some force. "This battle for a New Deal is not yet over," he said, "indeed, I suspect it has just begun." Elsewhere in the administration, Secretary of the Treasury Henry Morgenthau and Budget Director Lewis Douglas (who would resign at the end of the summer) urged fiscal caution, while Interior Secretary Harold Ickes and FERA director Harry Hopkins advised the expansion of existing programs. Donald Richberg, who had taken over a troubled NRA after Hugh Johnson's resignation, cautioned Roosevelt to go easy on the business community in his public statements, while presidential assistant Thomas Corcoran urged him to hammer business relentlessly.

If any or all of this confusion worried Roosevelt, he was not admitting it. He was convinced, he said, that the New Deal was safely negotiating a middle course between the right and left wings of national political thought. In his opinion, he told a meeting of his administrative oversight agency, the National Emergency Council, in August, opposition to his administration came from "about ten to fifteen percent of people whose mental slant might be described as being at the extreme right of modern philosophy, and the rest of it is from ten to fifteen percent of the mental slant that belongs to the extreme left." Therefore, he said, he was not worried about the continuation of a strong Democratic majority after the election, and took comfort from the predictions of both Postmaster General James Farley, his 1932 campaign manager, and John Nance Garner, his vice president — Farley said that the Democrats would lose no seats in the House and the Republicans would win none, Garner that the Republicans would gain no more than thirty-seven seats, which would still leave the Democrats with a healthy majority.

Election-year Congressional guessing games have always been notoriously unreliable, even when undertaken by those with the political expertise of Farley and Garner — and those of 1934 did not prove the exception. Both Farley and Garner guessed badly. On November 6, 1934, the Democrats actually gained nine seats in the House, while the Republicans lost fourteen to Democrats, Socialists, and other radicals; just as remarkably, the Democrats now ruled the Senate with sixty-nine out of ninety-six seats — the largest single-party senatorial margin in history up to that time. Roosevelt had been dead right in his assumptions that the great middle portion of the electorate was still persuaded that the Democrats held out more hope than the Republicans. In spite of all the discontent and discombobulation, then, the New Dealers could anticipate the new year with considerable pleasure, knowing that Roosevelt had one of the largest margins of congressional support in the history of the presidency.

What Roosevelt did not have, however, was a Supreme Court that was willing to endorse his most ambitious designs to restructure the relationship between the government and the people. Four of the nine justices, led by the aging James McReynolds, were hidebound conservatives. Chief Justice Charles Evans Hughes and Justice Owen J. Roberts could have been described, at best, only as moderates. The remaining three — Louis Brandeis, Harlan Stone, and Benjamin Cardozo — were liberals, but not even this trio could be counted on to support every New Deal challenge that came its way. What the New Dealers could expect from its mix of ideologies and attitudes was indicated as early as January 7 of the new year, when the Court declared unconstitutional Secton 9(c) of the National Industrial Recovery Act, a stipulation that authorized the president to prohibit the shipment of illegally produced "hot" oil across state lines. Over the next several weeks, the Court followed this decision with several others that invalidated various New Deal measures, a campaign that came to a climax on May 27 — "Black Monday," in New Deal memory — when in its decision on *Schecter* v. *United States* the court effectively invalidated all of the code-making and price-fixing powers of Title I of the NIRA. In his cloakroom after the decision, Justice Louis Brandeis, a sometimes ally-sometimes enemy of New Deal policy, told Thomas Corcoran, "This is the end of this business of centralization, and I want you to go back and tell the President that we're not going to let this government centralize everything. It's come to an end."

Justice Brandeis spoke too soon, underestimating the determination and ingenuity of Roosevelt and his people and the continuing depth of the administration's popular support — all of which would combine to produce one more innovative chapter in the chronicle of the Great Depression.

The Second New Deal

I had seen these people at the relief station, waiting for the investigating machine to legalize them as paupers. Now they had work cards in their hands. . . . They had risen from the scrap heap of the unemployed, from the loneliness of the unwanted, dreaming of regeneration, together. The new job look lighted the most ravaged faces. . . . We were as hilarious as slum children around a Christmas tree. Men who hadn't had a job for years fondled five- and ten-dollar bills with the tenderness of farmers rejoicing over a new crop of grain.

Anna Yezierska,
Red Ribbon on a White Horse, 1950

CHAPTER NINE

Overleaf:

One of the most durable of the institutional beliefs of the Roosevelt era was that human dignity was diminished under direct relief programs but enriched by programs that provided work in exchange for relief — and that workers knew it. "They were accustomed to making a return for their livelihood," Federal Emergency Relief Administration (FERA) director Harry Hopkins said. "It was a habit they liked, and from which they chiefly drew their self-respect." That sentiment ruled in the Works Progress Administration (WPA), the "Second New Deal's" massive work-relief program, as illustrated by this promotional poster.

OOSEVELT, NEWSPAPERMAN William Allen White declared in his
Emporia (Kansas) *Gazette* after the Democratic triumph in the elections
of 1934, "has been all but crowned by the people." Perhaps, but the
Democratic victory could not be taken to indicate unanimity in Congress, as FDR knew perfectly well. Within the House and Senate there
would still be a constant ideological dispute going on among old-line Progressives, such as Senator George Norris of Nebraska and Senator Burton
K. Wheeler of Montana; younger, more militant Progressives and Democratic liberals, such as Senator Robert M. La Follette, Jr., of Wisconsin
or Congressman Maury Maverick of Texas; a few self-proclaimed radicals,
such as Congressman Vito Marcantonio of New York; some products of old
Democratic city machines, such as Senator Robert F. Wagner of New York,
a Tammany Hall graduate, or the new senator from Missouri, Harry Truman,
who had come to Washington courtesy of the Pendergast machine in Kansas
City; and moderate southern Democrats, such as Senators Joe Robinson of
Arkansas and Jimmy Byrnes of South Carolina, whose seniority gave them
domination over many of the committees who did most of the work of
Congress and great influence over the outcome of floor votes.

However diverse this Democratic Congress, it could still be made to
do the work that Roosevelt wanted to have it do, because outside the
Congress a coalition had appeared whose power could not be ignored —
and for the most part, it was a Roosevelt coalition. Except for those of the
extreme Left and Right who would have shucked the system entirely, the
discrete and divided segments of the Democratic party who clamored for
change understood that they had no other political venue in which they
could legitimately hope to further their interests, no matter how disappointed they still were in the New Deal's accomplishments, no matter how
frustrated they remained at the slowness and seeming timidity of government.

Roosevelt had always had most working men and women on his side,
but he had organized labor now, too, in spite of the imperfections of Section
7(a), and would gain it even more firmly in the coming months, as John L.
Lewis and William Green both endorsed his programs. He had a healthy
contingent of women, an "interest group" whose hopes were nurtured by
the presence of Eleanor Roosevelt. He had most blacks, who continued to
desert the Republican party that had freed their ancestors. He had virtually
all segments of Catholicism, from Irish to Polish to Italian to Mexican-American; most Jews, from New York's Lower East Side to Chicago's Twelfth

Street; and a fair share of Protestants of all shapes and sizes, save the rich and Republican. He had the farmers of the Midwest, the ranchers of the West, even the plantation owners of the South, who just loved the AAA's programs. He had, in fact, poor people and beleaguered middle-class people just about anywhere they could be found and were allowed to vote.

How long he might be able to keep them was another matter, for in spite of all the legislative and administrative activity, the economic situation for ordinary Americans was still not anything Roosevelt and the New Dealers could point to with much pride. Unemployment at the end of 1934 still stood at about twelve million. The average worker's income was $1,099, more than $800 less than it took to maintain a family of five decently, and if the industrial economy appeared to be slowly but steadily recovering, the gap between the haves and the have-nots was at least as wide as it had ever been. "In December, 1934," Senator Wagner pointed out in Congress in May, 1935,

> payrolls registered only 60 percent of the 1926 level, while dividend and interest payments were fixed at 150 percent of that level. Total wages have risen only 28 percent in the last two years, while 840 corporations have increased their profits from $471,000,000 in 1933 to $673,000,000 in 1934, a gain of 42 percent. Net profits of 1,435 manufacturing and trading companies increased from $64,000,000 in 1933 to $1,071,000,000 in 1934, or 64 percent, while their annual rate of return rose from 2.7 percent to 4.5 percent.

And if the president had any doubts as to the effect the depression was still having on millions of people, he could have turned to any one of the thousands of letters the White House still received every month, most similar in their anguish to the letter Eleanor Roosevelt got from "One of the Unwashed" on February 28, 1935:

> I am sending you a plea for the dirty bunch, we are getting tired of being so termed. . . . We do not dare to use even a little soap when it will pay for an extra egg a few more carrots for our children, pale and woebegone they look. . . .
>
> But our faith must not falter when these children ask will Roosevelt give us work to-morrow, we must answer with conviction in our voices, I am just sure he will. . . . We know that our President is doing his utmost for us and all this could be adjusted so easily and our country happy again. . . .

The "adjustment" would not in fact be easily done, but Roosevelt was willing to try it as 1935 began — and so were the rest of the most militantly dedicated of the New Dealers, whose readiness to take reform another big step forward was typified by Harry Hopkins. Born in modest circumstances himself, he had considerable empathy for those in need, and after graduation from Grinnell College in 1912, he had been a social worker in New York City, a Red Cross administrator, director of the city's health agencies, head of New York's Temporary Relief Administration during Roosevelt's gubernatorial years, and now was director of the New Deal's FERA programs. A thin, slightly frazzled chain-smoker and coffee swiller, Hopkins possessed a swift tongue and a manic energy that belied the fact that he suffered throughout his adult life continuous stomach and intestinal problems that would put him in the hospital more than once. If it could be said that he possessed a credo, it would have been encompassed in his remark that every man in the country should "have access to the opportunity to provide for himself and his family a decent and American way of living." True to that conviction, shortly after the elections of 1934 Hopkins turned to a few members of his staff as he and they were driving out to a local race track. "Boys," he said, "this is our hour. We've got to get everything we want . . . now or never. Get your minds to work on developing a complete ticket to provide security for all the folks of this country up and down and across the board."

With such enthusiasm firing the work of the reformers in the White House and the Congress, some of the most important and long-lasting of all the administration's programs would be launched between the beginning of January and the end of September, 1935. Among those who participated and those who merely watched with great interest, this surge of reform would come to be called the Second New Deal.

■■■■ *A Measure of Self-Esteem*

Sacrifices, of course, would have to be made, and one of the most significant was the anti-lynching bill that had been reintroduced in the first session of the Seventy-fourth Congress early in 1935. For weeks, the bill sat in the Senate, unattended, while the NAACP did everything it knew how to do to apply public pressure, to no avail. In his annual message in January, Roosevelt had included lynching in his list of crimes that "call on the strong arm of Government for their immediate suppression," but, as in 1934, he was reluctant to put the arm on Congress. Not even a face-to-face appeal from Walter White at a meeting arranged by Eleanor

Roosevelt could move him. "As was his custom when he wished to avoid discussing a subject," White remembered, "he told many gay and amusing anecdotes to postpone an anticipated ordeal." After some time, White finally was able to broach the subject of the meeting.

"But Joe Robinson [Senate majority leader] tells me the bill is unconstitutional," Roosevelt said.

When White carefully refuted this claim, as well as other objections to the bill that FDR raised, the president snapped, only half in jest, "Somebody's been priming you. Was it my wife?"

It had been Mrs. Roosevelt, as a matter of fact, but White evaded a direct answer to the question — and in the end got an honest answer to his own. "I did not choose the tools with which I must work," Roosevelt finally said. "Had I been permitted to choose them I would have selected quite different ones. But I've got to get legislation passed by Congress to save America. The Southerners by reason of the seniority rule in Congress are chairmen or occupy strategic places on most of the Senate and House committees. If I come out for the anti-lynching bill now, they will block every bill I ask Congress to pass to keep America from collapsing. I just can't take that risk." White had no effective argument with which to counter Roosevelt's remarks, save that of simple morality and justice — which, then as now, carried a good deal less political weight than pragmatism. The anti-lynching bill would not be revived again seriously until 1938.

Probably highest on Roosevelt's list of the legislative priorities to which anti-lynching had been sacrificed was a new work-relief program called the Works Progress Administration (WPA), which — in spite of its nonsensical name, which Roosevelt invented and refused to change — may have been the best known of all New Deal inventions, perhaps because it affected more individual lives more directly than any other. It was the most massive and comprehensive effort ever undertaken in the nation's history up to that time to ensure that every able-bodied American male — and even some able-bodied American females — would be able to earn at least the basic needs of life for themselves and their families. Even more than the New Deal's earlier relief programs, it was responsible for the creation of a new and immutable intimacy between the people and their government — an intimacy so thoroughly in place today that it is difficult to remember that once it was a revolutionary concept.

After the success of the CWA program in the winter of 1933–34, Hopkins was convinced that a major work program was the only form of federal relief that would put food on the tables of workers and their families without starving them of their pride, and in the middle of September, 1934, he had gone to Roosevelt with a proposal to expand the FERA's work program by another four million jobs. The expansion, he thought, might cost as much as an additional $250 million. But Roosevelt, for once moving several steps ahead of his eager New Deal colleagues, had an idea of his own, one involving many more jobs and many more projects and costing many more hundreds of millions of dollars than Hopkins's comparatively modest notions — so sweeping a change that Hopkins came away from his meeting with the president spinning with excitement. "The big boss is getting ready to go places in a big way," he told a fellow worker. "Three to five years and going strong by two years. We are talking of five billion a year actually spent." His colleague wondered if it could really be done. "It can be done," Hopkins replied. "We have to prove it."

It would be easier to prove after the results of the Congressional elections that November 6, and it is probably a good measure of Roosevelt's power at that moment in history that when he went to Congress early in 1935 and asked for $4 billion in new money — most of it to be spent on his new project — and did so while providing only the vaguest outline of what he had in mind, he got it. He signed the WPA's authorizing legislation, the Emergency Relief Appropriations Act, on April 8, and by early summer the new agency, with Hopkins at its head, was spending the first of the more than $11 billion the agency would go through before being canceled in 1943.

No other single idea that Roosevelt ever conceived himself — not even the CCC — had greater scope than his vision of a proper work-relief program. Over the course of its life, the WPA would employ more than 8.5 million people in three thousand counties across the land on 1.4 million individual projects. The workers of the WPA, according to historian Edward Robb Ellis, "built 651,087 miles of highways, roads and streets; constructed, repaired or improved 124,031 bridges; erected 125,110 public buildings; created 8,192 public parks; built or improved 853 airports." They did so at an average salary of only $41.57 a month, but it was better than utter joblessness and the thin and demeaning comfort of the dole. It also helped more women more directly than any other relief program — though again not on an equal basis with men — even though its administrator at least gave the notion of equality his initial support. Hopkins, the story went, asked at an early WPA staff meeting whether women should be paid at the same rates as men. Every man in the room (there were no women at this particular meeting) but Hopkins's assistant, Aubrey Williams, was opposed. "Well, fellows," Hopkins said, "thank you very much. Aubrey's right about this, and that's what we'll do."

It did not work out quite so smoothly. Ellen Woodward, director of the FERA and CWA women's programs, took over similar duties in the WPA, where she found that options for women were severely limited by the determination of both Roosevelt and Hopkins to put men to work first. Despite the fact that 680,000 women had been adjudged eligible for WPA work, she was able to employ only 405,700 in the peak year of 1938 — just 13.5 percent of all WPA employees that year. And while 85 percent of those eligible had experience in a wide variety of trades, only sewing projects and recreation work were at first declared appropriate activities for working women. In time, Woodward would be able to expand women's projects to include bookbinding, home nursing care for the elderly, school lunch programs, nursery school work, and a marginally successful Household Workers' Training Program. But for all Hopkins's good intentions regarding salary equity, the nature of these jobs, as well as the sewing and recreation programs, guaranteed that women would be paid as little as half of what most men received on construction jobs, and for the duration of the WPA the opportunities for working women remained much more limited in scope, variety, and remuneration than those for men.

During an early restructuring of the agency, however, Woodward persuaded Hopkins to combine her Women's Division and the Professional Projects Division, and in this new format professional women, at least, acquired a greater degree of equality with their male counterparts. This was especially true after her division took over what was called "Federal Number One," a department that included the Federal Art Project, the Federal Music Project, the Federal Theater Project, and the Federal Writers Project.

These programs carried the work-relief concept farther than many, even among FDR's supporters in Congress, thought it should reasonably go. In previous years, the federal government's role as a supporter of the arts had been minimal, at best, generally being confined to the production of statuary, bas-relief, and suitably patriotic or otherwise high-minded portraits and murals for the ornamentation of public buildings and public places — efforts supervised, with perhaps unconscious symbolism, by the Department of the Treasury. The ethos of work and respectability that informed much of the nation's institutional character did not encourage art for art's sake — indeed, art and artists in any medium were generally held to be unreliable types with loose morals and questionable ideological convictions. Why encourage them by supporting them? Hopkins's answer to such criticism was simple: "Hell! They've got to eat just like other people." So they did, and the WPA fed tens of thousands of them through employment in their fields — and if the quality of their contributions to the cultural enrichment of the nation was mixed, there was no gainsaying their energy and enthusiasm. Government subsidy, Federal Art Project director Holger Cahill insisted, "was the next logical step in the development of American art [as a] functioning part of our national life," and to that end his agency sponsored the eventual completion of 2,566 murals and 17,744 pieces of sculpture that adorned the walls, halls, and niches of public buildings all over the country. Most of these tended to be basically neutral, if exquisitely idealized, depictions of American life, history, and industry in the classical tradition (noble farmers, ethereal mother figures, and muscular working men were prominent), though a few highly politicized artists borrowed freely (if not necessarily competently) from the radical and communistic visions of Diego Rivera and other militantly revolutionary symbolists and took the opportunity to denigrate capitalism in various subtle ways.

The Federal Theater Project, led by Hallie Flanagan, founder of the Experimental Theater at Vassar, was equally determined to make theater arts a functioning part of the national life, and to that end launched thousands of productions in church basements, school auditoriums, and tiny local theaters to enlighten the culturally deprived. Most such productions were standard fare, with the works of Shakespeare and other classics predominating. One innovation, however, was the creation of sixteen "Negro units" in which African Americans took on roles normally reserved for white actors. The most spectacular single black production was the "voodoo *Macbeth*," produced by John Houseman, director of the Harlem Negro Unit, and directed by Orson Welles. The setting was not Scotland, but Haiti.

Other innovations were to come. Eleanor Roosevelt, who had been among those who recommended the appointment of Flanagan, had herself noted that "the time has come when America [may] consider the theatre, as it [is] considered abroad, a part of education." Flanagan agreed — and carried it a step further with her own belief that "the plays we do should be informed by the consciousness of the art and economics of 1935." The result of this conviction was *The Living Newspaper*, a lively attempt to give dramatic form to the issues of the day. *Triple-A Plowed Under*, for example, was a defense of the New Deal's agricultural programs and a call to eliminate the hated middle man; *Injunction Granted* lambasted the court system's role in the stifling of union organization and the suppression of strikes; *Power* celebrated the construction of hydropower dams and featured marching construction workers singing such stirring refrains as "Oh, see them boys a-comin'/Their government they trust,/Just hear their hammers

The slightly sardonic expression presented by Harry Hopkins in a portrait camouflaged the substance of a man utterly committed to the notion that the government's principal job was to help people.

BELOW: A small army of WPA workers cut firewood for sale at the District wood yard in Washington, D.C., in 1935, one of thousands of similar job projects around the country.

Under the direction of Ellen Woodward, the women's programs of the WPA expanded to embrace everything from bookbinding to nursing care for the elderly, but the dominant "industry" represented was sewing. By the end of 1937, nearly 300,000 women were employed in more than nine thousand sewing units, like that in New Albany, Indiana, BOTTOM. These units, ranging in size from as few as ten in rural areas to as many as 1,500 in urban areas, were turning out more than 122 million articles a year, among them nurses' uniforms and house dresses, like those modeled, TOP, by workers in the Milwaukee Sewing Project.

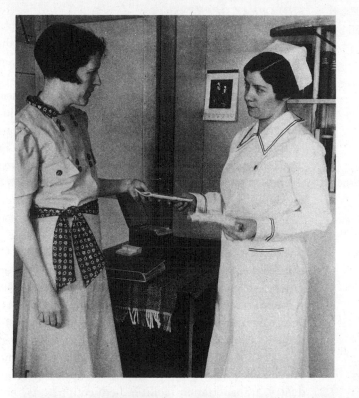

ringin',/They'll build that dam or bust"; perhaps the most unusual of all, *Spirochete*, an offering of the Chicago production company, told the story of the fight against syphilis.

The Federal Music Project was not so message-ridden. Under the direction of Nikolai Sokoloff, the longtime conductor of the Cleveland Symphony, the project created thirty new city symphony orchestras, as well as hundreds of smaller musical groups. Under its aegis, some twenty-five thousand public performances were produced, from the New York City Orchestra playing Carnegie Hall to Tommy Watkins and His Western Band playing the little desert towns of southern California.

The Federal Writers Project had a number of writers, editors, and researchers who went on to considerable fame — among them John Cheever, Kenneth Rexroth, Maxwell Bodenheim, Conrad Aiken, Edward Dahlberg, and Richard Wright — and along the way produced an extraordinary body of work. Jerre Mangione, one of its officials and author of the standard history of the project, says that "to this day no one knows exactly how many published items it produced." The best known of the Writers Project publications, however, were the still-useful state-by-state *American Guide* volumes, descriptive guides to each of the forty-eight states, featuring introductory essays that outlined the state's geology, history, growth, industry, transportation facilities, education, arts, entertainment, and folkways. The essays were followed by detailed highway-by-highway, road-by-road, and street-by-street tour routes for each state and its principal cities. Taken as a whole, the guides offered a mosaic of American life duplicated nowhere else in our history or literature. "None of the common generalizations about America and the American temperament seem to fit it," critic Robert Cantwell wrote in 1939,

> least of all those attributing to Americans qualities of thrift, sobriety,
> calculation or commercial acumen. On the contrary, it is doubtful if
> there has ever been assembled anywhere such a portrait, so laboriously
> and carefully documented, of such a fanciful, impulsive, childlike,
> absent-minded, capricious and ingenious people. . . .

The WPA's art, theater, music, and writing projects did not, as their adherents earnestly hoped they would, transform the cultural landscape of America, instilling in every citizen a thirst for the higher things of life. The citizenry generally remained more interested in the size and frequency of its weekly paycheck or monthly relief payment than in the character and quality of the arts. Nevertheless, these programs did bring more art to more people than at any other time in our history, allowed at least some artists, writers, musicians, and actors to continue to practice their crafts while surviving economically, and, not incidentally, helped to spread the word about the programs and policies of the New Deal throughout the land. Moreover, they established a precedent for the federal government's support of the arts that would flower into today's National Endowment for the Arts and National Endowment for the Humanities programs (both of which occasionally have come in for much the same kind of conservative criticism — from the likes of Senator Jesse Helms and others — that the New Deal's programs would suffer).

From street repair to street guides, the WPA was not without genuine flaws and inconsistencies. As noted, its wages, like those in the earlier work-relief programs, were barely sufficient for subsistence. Its bureaucracy often was staggeringly inefficient, and WPA files were swollen with complaints about late or incorrect checks. "Laborers" became such a generic term in the sometimes limited vision of WPA officials that workers were too often assigned to jobs for which they had no experience and passed over for jobs in which they were experts. Training programs for future employment were scarce at best. Nor did the WPA ever manage to aid the bulk of the needy — as many as five million unemployed people were left to the inadequate mercies of state relief programs, which in some of the poorer states gave a family less than $10 a month on which to live.

For all this, and for all the things it built, the public buildings it ornamented, the music it played, the theater it produced, and the words it published, the importance of the WPA to the well-being of the nation could most accurately be measured in the maintenance of self-esteem, as validated by the workers themselves. In February, 1936, a working man was driven to express himself in block-print poetry and send it off to Roosevelt: "I THINK THAT WE SHALL NEVER SEE," it read in part, "A PRESIDENT LIKE UNTO THEE. . . . POEMS ARE MADE BY FOOLS LIKE ME,/ BUT GOD, I THINK, MADE FRANKLIN D." The author of this tender screed signed himself "W. P. A. worker 81058," and his opinion was widely shared among WPA workers, like those in Battle Creek, Michigan, who in April, 1936, begged FDR to "Please continue this W. P. A. program. It makes us feel like an American citizen to earn our own living." Not the least of the gifts of the Second New Deal, then, was a measure of pride.

■■■■ *Now What Are You Going to Say to Our Youth?*

So far, none of the New Deal's programs, including the CCC, had done much to meet the needs of about 3.3 million young people who were

In 1935, John Houseman set up a WPA Federal Theater Project in Harlem's Lafayette Theater. Over the next four years, the Harlem Theater Project performed numerous plays written by and for African Americans, including Frank Wilson's Walk Together Chillun, *Rudolph Fisher's* The Conjure Man Dies, and William Du Bois's Haiti. But no production matched the spectacular success of the all-black-cast Macbeth, *directed by the young Orson Welles, who set the story not in Scotland, but in Haiti during the age of King Christophe. The "voodoo Macbeth," as it came to be called, opened on April 14, 1936, and ran for eighteen weeks in New York before going on the road for appearances in WPA theaters scattered from Chicago to Dallas.*

The WPA's Federal Art Project put some four thousand artists to work and in the process, according to Ben Shahn, one of the best of them, "begot an enlightened public art for today" and fostered "the first widespread indigenous art movement that the country has known." Even Shahn had to admit, however, "In quality, the average, through sheer weight of numbers, had to be low." That could not be said of the work of Selma Burke, shown ABOVE with her Art Project bust of Booker T. Washington (in later years, she would design the Franklin D. Roosevelt dime); nor could it be said of Lucienne Block, seen at work on one of her best murals, "Cycles of a Woman's Life," for the Women's House of Detention in New York City.

out of work, out of school, and out of luck, struggling on the thin edge of poverty and often succumbing to vagabondage. "The Civilian Conservation Corps," Thomas Minehan wrote in his 1934 book, *Boy and Girl Tramps of America*, "has done little to check the exodus of children. It enlists only boys and not all of them. . . . What we need is a new Child Conservation Corps, which will have as its purpose the saving not of our forests a hundred years from today, but of our boys and girls growing into the men and women of tomorrow."

Eleanor Roosevelt would have agreed, had she read the book, and she very well may have. She may even have read erstwhile novelist Martha Gellhorn's report to Harry Hopkins from Rhode Island just before Christmas, 1934. If so, it would only have reinforced her already powerful conviction that something had to be done for young people, for it was the psychological condition of adolescents, Gellhorn wrote, that she found particularly agonizing:

> I would find it hard . . . to describe the understandable and terrifying cynicism of these children. One said to me, "I'd steal if I had the guts." A very pretty Italian girl of twenty one, saying, "I'm young; it seems to me I got a right to something; if it's only one new dress a year. . . ." I don't know whether this hopelessness will turn into suicidal depression, or into recklessness. . . . I don't want to howl doom, but it really is a horrible mess.

"Now what are you going to say to our youth who are not wanted in industry?" Mrs. Roosevelt had asked in an article for the May, 1934, issue of *Woman's Home Companion*. "We have no plans for you! We offer you nothing, we simply restrict your activities. . . . I would like to see us institute a volunteer service to the country open to both boys and girls." To this end she worked on a reluctant FDR, who was firm in his belief that "his" CCC was the only practical answer to the youth problem — in spite of the fact that it excluded young women — and finally persuaded him to issue an executive order in June, 1935, that established the National Youth Administration, to be funded by $50 million in relief money. Aubrey Williams, Harry Hopkins's principal assistant, was placed in charge and would head the new program until it ended in 1943.

The NYA operated at two levels. The first was a student work program, which offered various campus work assignments designed to give students enough money to stay in school. High school students were paid an average of $6 a month and college students an average of $15. The amounts may have seemed minimal, but for many students the tiny salaries were crucial. Helen Farmer, who entered the program at John H. Franklin Polytechnic High School in Los Angeles, remembered it fondly:

> I lugged . . . drafts and reams of paper home, night after night. . . . Sometimes I typed almost all night and had to deliver it to school the next morning. . . . This was a good program. It got necessary work done. It gave teenagers a chance to work for pay. Mine bought me clothes and shoes, school supplies, some movies and mad money. Candy bars, and big pickles out of a barrel. It gave my mother relief from my necessary demands for money.

An estimated two million young people ultimately took part in the NYA's school work program, and it remained well regarded throughout its life. The out-of-school program was less well defined. During its first year, it concentrated on make-work jobs in local communities that would keep the young people in their homes — painting public buildings, cleaning and maintaining city parks, and performing other tasks that benefited the participants and local governments about equally. In later years, the out-of-school program, while continuing the work projects, shifted emphasis to vocational guidance, placement programs, and job training, most often in workshops located in urban centers but also in resident centers in which the participants took part in cultural and educational enrichment programs as well.

The out-of-school program was less successful than the school work program, mainly because no amount of training in job skills as seamstresses or carpenters or any other trade was of much use if the jobs were not there when the skills had been learned. A group of NYA girls wrote to Eleanor Roosevelt, complaining that while their stay in the Camp Jane Addams resident center at Bear Mountain State Park in New York had been most enjoyable and enlightening, now that they were back in the concrete reality of Manhattan, few had been able to find work. "Now after four weeks of tramping through the streets more than one girl says there is nothing left except suicide or tramping on the roads." It was disaffected young people like these women who joined the Young Communist League or who made up the membership of the American Youth Congress, a generally leftist agglomeration of youth groups from around the nation which sporadically lobbied for an American Youth Act and with which Aubrey Williams and both Roosevelts maintained a somewhat nervous relationship until World War II.

"I have moments of real terror when I think we may be losing this generation," *Eleanor Roosevelt said in May, 1934. The solution devised was the National Youth Administration (NYA).* BELOW: *High school students are put to work by the NYA in their school library in Hopewell, Virginia;* RIGHT, *an NYA-paid Virginia Union University student (standing) supervises a game room for underprivileged youths in Richmond, Virginia.*

Whatever else might be said of the NYA, racism was not a charge that reasonably could be leveled against it. Unlike his fellow southerner, Robert Fechner, Aubrey Williams was committed to the pursuit of equal rights for African Americans, and with the full support of Mrs. Roosevelt made the NYA probably the most color-blind of all New Deal agencies. To make sure it remained that way, he appointed Mary McLeod Bethune director of the NYA's Division of Negro Affairs. Mrs. Bethune, who also founded the National Council of Negro Women in 1935, was an indefatigable lobbyist for African-American causes and even in Georgia the NYA proved itself particularly useful to African-American children. In November, 1940, the *Crisis*, the NAACP's journal, acknowledged that while the lack of jobs was, if anything, more critical for black participants than white, the NYA in Georgia nevertheless "managed to serve, in sheer numbers, more Negro young people than any other state."

▇ *Thinking Big*

However ambitious in scope, the WPA and the NYA possessed a certain practicality. Sometimes, however, the administration's social and economic planners dreamed a little too big for reality — as in some of their earliest attempts to deal with rural displacement, the terrible consequence of drought, dust, economic pressures, and the AAA's scarcity program. The FERA's Rural Rehabilitation Program had spent some $85 million to purchase and rehabilitate wrecked farmland but had been able to save only the tiniest fraction of land that needed rescue. Another solution put forth had been simmering as a philosophical notion in the mind of FDR himself for some time, his own amplification of the "back to the land" movement that since the turn of the century had sporadically envisioned the restoration of a Jeffersonian Arcadia as a kind of antidote to all the ills of industrial society. The vision was still real to him when he became president, and on April 17, 1933, FDR wrote Senator George Norris of Nebraska: "I would really like to get one more bill, which would allow us to spend $25 million this year to put 25,000 families on farms at an average cost of $1,000 per family. It can be done. . . . Will you talk this over with some of our fellow dreamers on the Hill?" The result was called Subsistence Homesteads and at first was placed in Harold L. Ickes's Department of the Interior.

Ickes thought the program too poorly planned to be of much use and was irritated by what he felt was undue interference by Eleanor Roosevelt and FDR's personal adviser, Louis Howe, both of whom had become enamored of the project. He was perfectly happy when Roosevelt decided to fold all rural rehabilitation efforts into a new agency, the Resettlement Administration, in May, 1935, and appoint Rexford Tugwell to run it. Tugwell was not much happier about Subsistence Housing than Ickes, but the program managed to limp along, until by World War II, 10,938 homestead dwellings would be constructed in a handful of subsistence projects — Arthurdale in West Virginia, Westmoreland in Pennsylvania, Cumberland in Tennessee, Tygert Valley in West Virginia, and Aberdeen Gardens, an all-black community near Newport News, Virginia — that managed to become functioning communities.

Tugwell had his own favorite schemes for the Resettlement Administration, among them the goal of moving as many as 500,000 farm families from overworked land and giving them fresh starts elsewhere. Only 4,441 families ever did get resettled, however. Tugwell's other idea was only a little more successful. "I'm for decentralization," he once wrote, "for simplicity of life, along with a recognition of the complexity of industrial and scientific civilization." His attempt to reconcile these contradictory impulses resulted in a projected system of "Greenbelt" towns. "My idea," Tugwell said, "is to go just outside centers of population, pick up cheap land, build a whole community and entice people into it. Then go back to the cities and tear down whole slums and make parks of them." Only three such towns were actually built — Greenbelt, Maryland, just outside Washington, D. C.; Greenville, Ohio, near Cincinnati; and Greendale, Wisconsin, near Milwaukee. The government continued to own them until 1955, when they were sold, lock, stock, and dream, to private developers.

If the Greenbelt, Resettlement, and Subsistence Homestead programs — overplanned, underfunded, and poorly administered — fell short of what the administration had hoped, the Rural Electrification Administration still stands as one of the most elegantly conceived and permanently effective agencies the federal government ever created. As late as 1935, only 12.6 percent of all American farms were electrified, since private utility companies were reluctant to invest in transmission lines and the construction of local facilities to service scattered customers — nor were banks eager to make loans to rural cooperatives to construct their own lines and facilities, since the cooperatives could not pay interest rates the banks found attractive. But one day in the spring of 1935, Senator George Norris, a champion of public power and rural electrification, went to Roosevelt with a scheme to break the impasse. Roosevelt listened, then called in Jesse Jones, chairman of the Reconstruction Finance Corporation. According to Jones, in just ten minutes the three men came to an agreement: Roosevelt would create a Rural Electrification Administration as part of the general relief program; the RFC would loan the new agency $40 million a year for ten years at 3 percent interest; the REA would, in turn, use the money to help finance the construction of rural electric delivery systems, either by private utility companies or by rural cooperatives, making loans at interest rates below the normal levels. In May, the agency was created by executive order.

When, by May of 1936, it became clear, first, that the REA would function more efficiently as an entity independent of the relief program and, second, that private companies still were reluctant to cooperate, Congress restructured the agency as an independent body that would make its preferential loans only to cooperatives. By the end of the year, 29 rural systems were in place — and by the end of 1941, there would be 773 systems with 348,000 miles of transmission lines serving more than nine hundred thousand customers representing 35 percent of all farms (by the 1970s there would be more than 1,000 systems, 1.7 million miles of lines, and nearly seven million customers representing more than 95 percent of all farms).

The Reluctant Dragon

It is one of the enduring ironies of the Second New Deal that perhaps the two most important pieces of legislation that ever came out of the Roosevelt years were neither conceived by nor vigorously pushed through Congress by Roosevelt himself, who feared both their political and their economic ramifications. And even when he finally could not avoid direct action, he was a most reluctant dragon.

The first of these was comprehensive labor legislation, much more the child of Senator Robert F. Wagner than of Roosevelt. As chairman of the original National Labor Board appointed by Roosevelt in August, 1933, Wagner had learned of the inadequacy of the NIRA's Section 7(a) firsthand. Among other shortcomings, the law could be effective only if the NRA's administrators were willing to withhold the Blue Eagle of endorsement from any business or industry that did not abide by the law's stipulations. "[U]ntil the promises made by the Recovery Act," Wagner warned, "are given definite meaning, we can not have happy and contented workers." Hugh Johnson, director of the NRA, and his general counsel, Donald Richberg, were equally certain that economic growth could not be achieved unless they had happy and contented industrialists; consequently, they did not force the issue of compliance.

The president refused to put pressure on Johnson or Richberg to

All his life, Franklin Roosevelt believed in the blessings of rural life. "The country has . . . advantages that the city cannot duplicate," he had said while still governor of New York. "There is contact with earth and with nature. . . . There is an opportunity . . . to establish a real home in the traditional sense." The outcome of this sentiment was the New Deal's Subsistence Homestead project, an effort to build and populate self-sustaining towns in rural settings. Only a few of these survived mismanagement and underfunding, among them Cumberland, Tennessee, where Eleanor Roosevelt is shown addressing workers from the bed of a truck.

The Subsistence Homestead towns were built, as Interior Secretary Harold L. Ickes put it, as "a demonstration of the social benefits of a sound community life," but near Newport News, Virginia, one of the projects took on an added value of pride. This was the 150-family Aberdeen Gardens community, the only Subsistence Homestead project built for and by African Americans. William R. Walker, Jr., the community's manager, was black, as was William C. McNeill, the project's chief construction engineer, and every laborer on the job (all supplied by the WPA), from the construction workers, TOP, to the office clerks, BOTTOM.

enforce the law. Moreover, when the two NRA executives arbitrarily issued a "clarification" of the law to the effect that the NRA would support "the right of minority groups or of individual employees to deal with their employer separately," he did not repudiate the statement, even though it clearly undermined the ability of any union elected by a majority of workers to act as the primary representative in any given industry. By the end of 1933 Wagner was thoroughly disillusioned by the administration and had started drafting a more useful "Labor Disputes Act" that would create a permanent National Labor Board with powers roughly equivalent to those of the Federal Trade Commission. The bill was introduced early in 1934, but Roosevelt, responding to pressure from Hugh Johnson and others in the administration — not to mention the howls of protest that the National Association of Manufacturers sent up the minute Wagner's bill was introduced — not only did not give the Wagner legislation his support, he submitted a joint resolution drafted by Richberg and the Labor Department that would take the place of any comprehensive law. The resolution gave FDR the power to create a "Board or Boards authorized and directed to investigate issues, facts, practices or activities of employers or employees in any controversies arising under Section 7(a)." Roosevelt then spent some time appealing to Wagner's sense of loyalty to him and the party, asking that he withdraw his own legislation and support the administration's weak-kneed resolution. Reluctantly, Wagner did so, and the Roosevelt resolution passed.

That did not stop the senator permanently. In February, 1935, he drafted and introduced another labor bill. It was similar in many respects to his 1934 legislation, but the National Labor Relations Board (NLRB) that the new legislation proposed would amount to a Supreme Court for labor. Not only could it validate the authority of individual unions and supervise the elections by which workers chose their representation, it was empowered to hear complaints from workers, issue "cease and desist" orders when necessary, and petition the courts for the authority to enforce its decisions. This time around, while he did not actively support the legislation, Roosevelt did not actively oppose it, either — probably because he wanted to see how far it might get in the new Congress elected in 1934.

That was quite a distance, as it turned out. The Wagner National Labor Relations Act was sent to the floor of the Senate for a vote on May 16, 1935, and passed comfortably, 63 to 12. On May 19, House Democrats inquired of the president if he would be agreeable to having them consider the Wagner bill in that body. FDR said yes, and the bill was reported out of committee favorably on May 20. Four days later, the president publicly announced that he favored the "principles" embodied in the Wagner bill. "By preventing practices which tend to destroy the independence of labor," he said, "it seeks, for every worker within its scope, that freedom of choice and action which is justly his." The bill probably did not need any more help to be pushed over the top, but it got some anyway on May 27, when the Supreme Court struck down the provisions of Title I of the National Industrial Recovery Act, including Section 7(a). Roosevelt forthwith put the Wagner Act on his priority list, and on July 5 it was on his desk, ready to be signed.

The National Labor Relations Act, in Wagner's opinion, was the only hope that management-labor relations would ever take place in an atmosphere in which both parties negotiated on a basis of genuine equality. And it was not just labor's future that was at stake here, he emphasized, for "the cultivation of collective bargaining is not merely an abstract matter of freedom for the worker, but rather a concrete foundation for the general welfare." Over the next ten years, the NLRB would hold some twenty-four thousand elections in which more than six million workers took part. In the same period, it would hear thirty-six thousand cases of alleged unfair labor practices, would invalidate two thousand company unions, reinstate three hundred thousand employees who had been dismissed for union activities, and force guilty industries to pay back wages amounting to more than nine million dollars.

With the Wagner Act as its fundament, the labor movement would grow in both size and power throughout the years of World War II and become a major participant in the boom years that followed the war. Nor did the law in action bear out the darkest imaginings of the industrial and business communities, most of which considered it an ax blow at the fragile base of the free enterprise system. Quite the contrary: the activities of the NLRB, even conservative labor historian Foster Rhea Dulles has written, "greatly helped to stabilize industrial relations."

Another "foundation for the general welfare" was being poured even as the Wagner Labor Act was being debated — though its history was even longer and more troubled. The movement for old-age security began at the turn of the century, when Isaac M. Rubinow and the American Association for Labor Legislation started what he called a "continuous and obstinate agitation for social insurance." In 1924, Rubinow's obstinacy was joined by that of Abraham Epstein, who founded the American Association for Old Age Security.

Working in a loose alliance, Epstein, Rubinow, and others pushed the individual states for the passage of a handful of social insurance laws, but these were so weak as to be insignificant. The old-age pension movement did not achieve a major success until 1930 and passage of New York State's Old Age Security Act, signed by then Governor Franklin Roosevelt on April 10. Meanwhile, Epstein had begun to look to Congress for passage of national legislation, and by the time of Roosevelt's inauguration in 1933 the indefatigable lobbyist had helped to craft several versions of an old-age security measure, only to see each stalled in a slough of disinterest. During 1933, the situation improved markedly. By then, a broad-based foundation of support for such legislation had been built in Congress, and old-age bills were reported favorably out of both the House Labor Committee and the Senate Pensions Committee in early January, 1934. Congress needed only FDR's open support for final legislation to be crafted and passed. For reasons still not fully understood (though they most likely stemmed from Roosevelt's fear that the program would cost too much) that support did not come, in spite of Roosevelt's enthusiasm for old-age security as governor of New York. For a time it seemed that both old-age security legislation and workman's compensation legislation — this, too, wallowing in presidential neglect — would never become part of the New Deal's legacy.

Then along came the California doctor, Francis Townsend, with his outlandish pension plan and, less outlandish, his millions of letter-writing members, who began to exert so much pressure on both Congress and the administration that FDR could no longer put off action — though it cannot be said that he moved with much speed. At the end of June, 1934, he appointed a committee to study and draw up proposals for comprehensive social security legislation that would include an old-age pension system, workman's compensation, national health insurance, and unemployment insurance. As is usual with anything invented by a committee, the legislation that was finally cobbled together and signed by Roosevelt on August 7 as the Social Security Act of 1935 was a mess of compromises that had only gotten messier as it went through the amendment process in Congress. One of the first items to be dispensed with was national health insurance. Harry Hopkins had believed that "with one bold stroke we could carry the people with us . . . for sickness and health insurance," and he may have been right; but the opposition of the American Medical Association to anything that smacked of what it already was calling "socialized medicine" was overwhelming. Not until our own day would national health insurance for every American appear to be an idea whose time finally had come.

The Social Security Act was imperfect in other ways — not least in its workman's compensation provisions, which were bound in ganglia of federal-state regulations that would render them fiendishly difficult to understand, much less administer. But the most pernicious compromise, in the view of many, was Roosevelt's insistence that the program be self-supporting through a payroll tax. This, Abraham Epstein lamented in anger, was "a system of compulsory payments by the poor for the impoverished" that conveniently relieved "the well-to-do from their share of the social burden" — and it would later be cited as one of the causes of the recession of 1937–38, as people began to feel the effects of the first payroll deductions. Furthermore, as we have seen in our own time, the nature of the system produced some nasty unanticipated political repercussions. As the number of Social Security recipients has swelled over the years, the cost of maintaining the system has forced the government to raise the payroll deductions of those who are still working in order to make payments to those who are not. Those being hit by ever-increasing deductions resent what they believe to be an unfair burden, especially when speculation abounds that the whole system might be bankrupt by the time they become eligible for payments. At the same time, the huge numbers of Social Security recipients comprise the single most powerful "special interest" in the nation — and it has little sympathy for the notion that Social Security payments should be cut or the system overhauled in any significant fashion.

However flawed a legacy it may have been and however ambivalent FDR himself may have felt toward it, the act was, as historian Kenneth S. Davis has written,

> one of the major turning points of American history. No longer could "rugged individualism" convincingly insist that government, though obliged to provide a climate favorable for the growth of business profits, had no responsibility whatever for the welfare of the human beings who did the work from which profit was reaped.

■■■■ Beating the Odds

If the successful passage of social security legislation deprived Francis Townsend's movement of some of its logic, it did not seem to slow it down much — at least, not in 1935. What did decline, however, was speculation that Townsend, Father Coughlin, and Senator Huey Long would somehow forge an alliance and put together a viable third-party challenge to FDR's reelection in 1936. Such talk ended when Long was gunned down by an assassin in the rotunda of the Louisiana State Capitol Building in Baton Rouge on September 8, 1935 — though the circumstances of his death

There was no denying the success of the Rural Electrification Administration (REA), which brought light and power to millions of rural people for the first time, including the folks in Tom Green County, Texas.

MORE SECURITY FOR THE AMERICAN FAMILY

THE WIDOW OF A QUALIFIED WORKER WILL RECEIVE MONTHLY BENEFITS AT AGE 65. IN CERTAIN CASES, AN AGED DEPENDENT PARENT MAY GET BENEFITS. ...

FOR INFORMATION WRITE OR CALL AT THE NEAREST FIELD OFFICE OF THE

SOCIAL SECURITY BOARD

LEFT: *For all the defects its critics discovered, including taxes that still nick millions of paychecks, and despite his own lukewarm support during its formulation, FDR remembered the Social Security Act of the Second New Deal as one of his proudest moments. "I guess you're right on the economics," he once told a critic of the payroll tax, "but those taxes were never a problem of economics. They are politics all the way through. We put those payroll contributions there so as to give the contributors a legal, moral, and political right to collect their pensions and the unemployment benefits. With those taxes in there, no damn politician can ever scrap my social security program." And no politician ever has.*

The three main political impulses of the 1936 elections ornament the street banners of this scene in Hardwick, Vermont: the Unionists (supported by Townsendites), the Republicans, and, overwhelmingly dominant, the Democrats.

immediately got the national rumor mills grinding on another subject. The assassin was shot to tatters by Long's bodyguards and the unconscious Long was rushed off to the hospital, where he apparently might have recovered had not an inexperienced surgeon botched the operation. These details (and, for the New Deal, the convenience) of his death pricked the eternal American fascination with conspiracy theories, in spite of the lack of any supporting evidence. To the day of his own death in 1976, Gerald L. K. Smith, Long's worshipful lieutenant, was convinced that there was something to it. "It cannot be proved," he said in 1966, "that Roosevelt ordered the assassination of Huey Long, but it can be proved that those who discussed his assassination were positively of the opinion that it would please the president."

While it is too cynical to say that Long's death pleased the president, it unquestionably gave him relief. The only serious danger to his re-election had been removed from the political scene — though a feeble effort would still be mounted by the late senator's erstwhile allies. A bereft Gerald L. K. Smith disappeared for a few months after his hero's death, then showed up in May, 1936, as Townsend's new associate. Coughlin, in the meantime, had been thinking ahead to a third-party candidacy for someone under his management. To that end he established what he called the Union party and in June, 1936, chose a candidate to challenge Roosevelt and whomever the Republicans might pick as their standardbearer. The lucky Union party candidate was Congressman William Lemke of North Dakota, who had gained some small attention as a relatively radical agrarian reformer. Before the end of June, Smith held a press conference to announce that he and Francis Townsend and the whole weight of the Townsend movement would support Lemke and the Union party in November.

The Democrats, as fully expected, once again gave Roosevelt the nomination. The Republicans, for their part, settled on Governor Alfred Landon of Kansas as the man of the hour. Genial, vaguely progressive (he had been an early admirer of FDR and the New Deal), but essentially stolid and unimaginatively Republican to the core, Landon enjoyed the full support of all of the Republican Old Guard, most of whatever was left of the old Independent Republican faction, much of the disaffected Democratic contingent, especially those who had joined forces with Alfred E. Smith and the Liberty League, most of the nation's press, most of the nation's industrial establishment, most of the nation's business community, most of the nation's advertising industry, most of just about everything it was assumed it would take to get him elected. Roosevelt, on the other hand, had a stubbornly persistent economic slump, four years of turbulence, a failed NRA, rejection by the Supreme Court, labor strife, Communist agitation, rebellion in the ranks of the Democratic party, general and continuing dissidence and dissatisfaction among wide portions of his constituency, and the irritation of sundry lunatic fringes to hamper him.

None of it mattered. By the end of October, it was obvious to Landon himself and all but the most blindly stubborn Republicans that Roosevelt was going to win. It was merely a question of by how much. As it happened, quite a lot: the victory on November 3 was even more complete a triumph than that of 1932, with 27,476,673 popular votes and 523 electoral votes going to Roosevelt and 16,679,583 popular votes and only 8 electoral votes to Landon. Lemke got no electoral votes, and fewer than a million popular votes.

In spite of everything, in spite of mixed results on just about every New Deal program, in spite of the fact that his efforts had yet come nowhere near ending the depression, in spite of all the power arrayed against him, Roosevelt was still the president of the people — who would have understood in their bones what writer Richard Wright had told a group of fellow WPA writers one summer afternoon in 1935. "Folks," he had said, "Where I come from, they're all singing 'Roosevelt! You're my man!/When the times come/I ain't got a cent,/You buy my groceries/And pay my rent./Mr. Roosevelt, you're my man.' "

Which is not to say that the people were not perfectly willing to continue kicking up their heels and giving their president and his administration whatever grief seemed appropriate. Increasingly now, people would be exercising the new power that the government, in the curious symbiosis that characterized the New Deal, had given them, and quite often doing so without the blessings of the administration — indeed, over its opposition. At the same time, circumstances and Roosevelt's own peculiar hubris would soon combine to seriously weaken the strength of the very coalition that had brought the New Deal to power and kept it there.

Barricades and Bargains

I got in the mills in 1936, and I [was] fortunate to be caught up in a great movement of the people in this country. . . . [A] movement of the kind that we had . . . in the CIO was a movement that moved millions of people, literally, and changed not only the course of the working man in this country, but also the nature of the relationship between the working man and the government and between the working man and the boss. . . .

Steelworker John Sargent,
oral interview, 1973

CHAPTER TEN

Overleaf:

*United Mine Workers president John L. Lewis
dominated the labor movement from 1935 to
the beginning of World War II. His origins in
the dismal coal-mining town of Lucas, Iowa,
gave his kind of unionism a singular power,
according to reporter Jonathan Mitchell:
"Unionism in the Welsh and Scottish coal-
mining areas has a special quality. . . . It has
always been hopelessly tangled up with
evangelical religion. Possibly the horrors of
the early Welsh coal mines, where half-naked
mothers acted as draft animals in the black,
suffocating galleries, served to identify
unionism with the path to heaven." Lewis
spills a fair measure of evangelical passion
over a crowd of 10,000 textile workers in
Lawrence, Massachusetts, during an organizing drive in May, 1937.*

■■■ *A New Kind of Unionism*

"D EPRESSION," *BUSINESS WEEK* had written as early as April, 1935, "is a forgotten word in the automobile industry, which is forging ahead in production, retail sales, and expansion of productive capacity in a manner reminiscent of the 'twenties.'" Sales had continued high through 1936. General Motors — one of the "big three" that included the Ford Motor Company and the Chrysler Motor Company — alone would produce more than 1.7 million cars and trucks that year, and its $7 million loss of 1932 would rebound to a profit of $163 million in 1936. With this in hand, after taxes and dividends, the company planned a major expansion program that would enable it to dominate the industry in 1937. Some of the money also would go to the Pinkerton Detective Agency for the employment of spies in the company's shops to sniff out union activists. General Motors, Senator Robert M. La Follette's Committee on Civil Liberties would later say, "stands as a monument to the most colossal super-system of spies yet devised in any American corporation." On the face of it, then, with nearly seventy plants in thirty-five cities in fourteen states, assets of $1.5 billion, and the best anti-union program in the business, General Motors had little to worry about from a labor movement still finding its sea legs after passage of the National Labor Relations Act of 1935.

The company underestimated the unhappiness of workers who, even if not quite ready to join a union, were still willing to demonstrate solidarity when properly stimulated. "General Motors was the best organizer we had," a plant activist recalled. If the company had not "pushed the guys around so much" and if it had been "just the least bit more liberal in concessions to the workers, the strike would never have happened." But a strike did happen — and swiftly. On December 26, after two union men were demoted, a shift of 135 workers sat down at the Fisher Body Plant in Cleveland. Four days later, on December 30, when word got around inside Fisher Body Plant No. 1 in Flint, Michigan, that the company was going to start moving equipment out of the place before the workers could emulate their friends in Cleveland, the workers shut the plant down, asked the security police to leave the premises, and took over the property. One of the workers later recalled that while probably not one in four of the men thought that GM could actually be beaten, many felt, with him, that his "job was no good anyway so that if I had lost it I hadn't lost anything."

As 1937 began, then, a few American workers were giving a special meaning to something Franklin Roosevelt would say during his Second

Inaugural Address on January 20. "Shall we pause now and turn our back upon the road that lies ahead?" he would ask. "I see one-third of a nation ill-housed, ill-clad, ill-nourished. It is not in despair that I paint for you that picture. I paint it for you in hope, because the nation, seeing and understanding the injustice in it, proposes to paint it out. . . ." The striking GM workers had seized not merely a couple of the physical plants of an automobile company, they had taken hold of hope itself, and before it was over, their exploit would reverberate with greater force than any other single act of organized labor in the years of the Great Depression.

The GM labor action was called a "sit-down," and while dramatic enough in itself, it was significant for a bigger reason: it represented a new kind of unionism, one that would soon be the dominant force in American labor. To a very large degree, it could be attributed to the single-minded obsession of one man — John L. Lewis, president of the United Mine Workers, a union over which he had reigned as one of the most visible, vocal, and intellectually volatile men in public life for more than fifteen years, with his bulldog body, his explosive mane of hair, his lively black eyebrows, his air of pugnacity even when standing perfectly still, and above all, his growling voice and sometimes convoluted oratorical eloquence.

There was nothing convoluted about his view of the AFL's shortcomings, however. The most important of these, he believed, was its failure to capitalize on the opportunity Section 7(a) of the NIRA had provided to build a large, cohesive body of labor organized not vertically along the lines of individual crafts, but horizontally across whole industries. If, he wrote,

> the labor movement in this country cannot fulfill its mission unless the basic, mechanized, mass production industries are organized upon an industrial basis, it is clear that the American Federation of Labor, so long as it permits craft unions to possess jurisdiction over skilled workers in these basic industries, cannot meet the proper requirements of an organized labor movement in America.

Lewis and his allies in the labor movement — principally, David Dubinsky of the International Ladies Garment Workers Union, Sidney Hillman of the Amalgamated Clothing Workers of America, Charles Howard of the International Typographical Union, George L. Berry of the Printing Pressman's Union, and Thomas McMahon of the United Textile Workers of America — decided in the fall of 1935 that their efforts to force open the gates of the AFL to the great mass of workers probably was hopeless. AFL President William Green remained as devoted to the primacy of craft unionism as ever, and some of his own supporters were openly contemptuous of the people who wanted in. "My wife," an AFL organizer once told Norman Thomas, "can always tell from the smell of my clothes what breed of foreigners I've been hanging out with."

In October, following the conclusion of the AFL's annual convention in Atlantic City, New Jersey, Lewis and the other dissidents met and put together the outlines of a semiautonomous organization that would, in effect, burrow from within the AFL body to promote the unionization of industrial labor in spite of the parent union's objections. They called it the Committee for Industrial Organization and ten days later the embryonic CIO opened an office on K Street in Washington — across the street from the United Mine Workers office, appropriately enough.

When William Green and the AFL executive council, suspecting insurrection, ordered the CIO to cease and desist whatever it was up to, Lewis sped off on an organizing junket, traveling to Detroit, Cleveland, Toledo, Kansas City, Milwaukee, and other industrialized areas where the workers gathered in enormous crowds to hear the thunder of his voice, cheering until their own voices were hoarse, pledging their allegiance to the CIO. On January 19, 1936, he appeared in Akron, Ohio, where in spite of blizzard conditions, thousands of rubber workers crowded into the big assembly hall of the national armory building to hear him speak. " 'Organize!' Lewis shouted, and his voice echoed from the beams of the armory," Ruth McKenney remembered. " 'Organize!' he said, pounding the speaking pulpit until it jumped. 'Organize! Go to Goodyear and tell them you want some of those stock dividends.' " The speech, McKenney said, "made a profound impression in Akron. His audience went out of that chilly hall to make John L. the most talked of man in town. A hero to his listeners, he was next morning a hero to every second man in the rubber shops." The groundwork of a relationship having been laid, the CIO was quick to step in and offer help when the rubber workers struck the big Goodyear plant a few days later, while the AFL largely ignored the strikers' pleas for help, and after the strike was settled to the workers' satisfaction in March, the United Rubber Workers Union formally declared its allegiance to the CIO.

By then, Lewis had turned his attention to the steel industry. In March, 1936, he suggested to Green that the AFL join with the CIO to help the Amalgamated Association of Iron, Steel and Tin Workers launch a massive organizing drive. Green waffled. After waiting until the middle

By 1938, John L. Lewis and other AFL dissidents had split off to form the Congress of Industrial Organizations (CIO), whose brash organizing skills are demonstrated by this recruiting poster.

Strikers take their leisure by sitting down for a news photographer during the great sit-down at GM's Fisher Body Plant No. 1 early in 1937.

LEFT: Roy Reuther, brother to Walter and Victor, has to shout to get his message across to a crowd of strikers gathered at Fisher Body Plant No. 2 on January 8, 1937.

In both GM Fisher body plants, the men insisted that women workers leave during the strike. Most of the women resented it, but joined with nonworking women outside the plants to form a daily parade.

of April, Lewis then offered the CIO's services to the AA directly and was accepted. The AA formally joined the CIO and agreed to function as part of a Steel Workers Organizing Committee (SWOC) appointed by Lewis himself.

Green and the AFL executive council were livid. On August 3, the AFL officials met in special session, discussed various charges against the CIO, then sent the leaders of all unions that had affiliated with Lewis the order to abandon the CIO or face expulsion. Four days later, Lewis convened the CIO's own executive board, made up of those very same union leaders, all of whom voted to ignore the AFL order. While the split would not be formally ratified by both bodies until 1938 (at which time the CIO would become the "Congress of Industrial Organizations"), there now were two major organizations representing the interests of labor.

▆▆▆ Labor's Epiphany

Among those on hand in Akron to witness the victorious end of the URW strike against Goodyear Tire at the end of March, 1936, were members of yet another new union, the United Auto Workers, formed the previous year. "We'll be next," one of the men told a jubilant Rose Posetta and Powers Hapgood, two CIO organizers. "Will you come and help us?" Posetta and Hapgood assured him that they and the CIO unions would indeed be there to help.

The UAW already had within its ranks a number of skilled and determined organizers, among them Walter, Victor, and Roy Reuther, three young unashamed Socialists (Walter and Victor had even gone to work in an auto plant in the Soviet Union for a while) who would soon become so ubiquitous in the UAW movement as to become something of a legend. At one point, so the story went, one employer all too familiar with Walter Reuther's name saw that of Roy in a newspaper story. "Jesus Christ," he said, "is there another Reuther?" He was told there was indeed another Reuther. At that moment, a voice on a bullhorn outside the employer's plant started bellowing encouragement to strikers. "Who the hell is out there?" he asked. He was told that it was the voice of yet another Reuther — Victor. "My God," the man groaned, "how many of those Reuther bastards are there?"

By the fall of 1936, the omnipresent Reuther brothers and their fellow organizers had brought only about twenty-five thousand auto workers out of a total of one million in the entire industry into the UAW. No matter — with some $25,000 in the union kitty, the UAW set out to organize everybody else. One of the first plants targeted was one that turned out brake drums for the industry, most of them going to the Ford Motor Company. That fact redounded to the union's benefit, for when Walter Reuther organized the plant and led a sit-down strike in December, 1936, Ford soon put pressure on the owners of the company to settle so that it could continue to get its parts.

Elsewhere, the union did not do as well — until the sit-downs that started at GM's Fisher Body plants in Cleveland and Flint at the end of December, 1936. Knowing drama and opportunity when he saw it, John L. Lewis would soon bring the full weight of the young CIO to bear on the struggle, not to mention his incomparable instincts for public relations. From the beginning, the sit-downs captured the interest of the general public, which — even among those who opposed such anarchic tactics — marveled at the initial orderliness of the whole business. Inside the Flint plant, for example, the men organized themselves neatly. A "mayor" was elected, along with a council of ten men to help run the community of fifteen hundred workers. A sanitary engineer was appointed. Strikers were divided into "families" of fifteen, each with its own leader and its own specified area of the plant, or "apartment." There was a barber shop, a game room, organized sports, even a "post office." Bruce Bliven, editor of the *New Republic*, was one of several writers allowed into Fisher One from time to time for publicity purposes. "Fifteen hundred men had lived for two weeks in a building never intended to be lived in at all," he reported,

> yet the place was remarkably neat and tidy, at least as clean as it is under normal conditions. Beds were made up on the floor of each [unfinished] car, the seats being removed if necessary. . . . I could not see — and I looked for it carefully — the slightest damage done anywhere to any property of the General Motors Corporation. The nearly completed car bodies, for example, were as clean as they would be in the salesroom, their glass and metal shining.

There were no women left inside, although Fisher One had employed many women, especially in the upholstery shops of the plant. Some of these were union members and many were married to male workers. The union leaders had persuaded the women to leave — both to protect them should violence ensue and to avoid snide commentary from management and its captive press — and the women had marched out in their overalls and working caps, many of them resentfully. Most of the women organized and joined committees to gather and smuggle food and medicine into the plant.

Others helped to prepare meals for the pickets, and still others served six hours a day of picket duty themselves throughout the strike. "I found a common understanding and unselfishness I'd never known in my life," one of them said in words that ring with a certain modernity. "I'm living for the first time with a definite goal. . . . Just being a woman isn't enough any more. I want to be a human being with the right to think for myself."

The peace that prevailed for the first two weeks of the strike did not last. General Motors declared its intention not to deal with the strikers so long as they occupied company property. That resolve was restated when about one hundred workers sat down at Fisher Body Plant No. 2. On January 2 the company got an injunction ordering the union to evacuate the plants, but it soon became known that the judge in question was a General Motors stockholder to the tune of more than $200,000. The embarrassed judge was forced to rescind the order and recuse himself.

While the company shopped around for another judge, it decided to make a move against Fisher Two, held by the fewest number of strikers. Company officials ordered the heat turned off in the plant at noon on January 11, and when outside strikers attempted to deliver dinner to the men on the inside, company guards locked the gates. A group of sit-downers went out and broke the locks. The guards called the Flint Police Department, which responded that night with a tear-gas attack. Workers drove the police back with door hinges, bottles, stones, ice balls, and anything else they could lay hands on. Once more, the police attacked, and when they were driven back again, turned and opened fire with pistols and riot guns. Fourteen strikers and two bystanders were wounded, but the union men still held their ground — and the plant — when the "Battle of the Running Bulls" was done.

The battle inspired Michigan Governor Frank Murphy, a prolabor man, to send in National Guard troops to keep the peace and to use his influence to get UAW and GM officials to sit down and start talking. A truce was reached when the company agreed to negotiate only with the UAW and the union agreed to have its workers leave the plants. William Knudsen, GM's chief executive officer, tried to arrange secret talks with company unions, however, and when word leaked out, the UAW called the truce off. Labor Secretary Frances Perkins then stepped in, talking first to Lewis, then to Alfred P. Sloan, GM's president, trying to get them together. Lewis demanded UAW recognition as his prerequisite; Sloan demanded the evacuation of the plants as his; nothing happened.

The tension increased on February 1, when CIO strategists decided to capture GM's Chevrolet Plant No. 4, the biggest in the company's com-

plex. It was appropriately guarded, but the union made an elaborate pretense at making preparations for a sit-down takeover of the smaller Chevrolet
Plant No. 9, being careful to arrange for the news of the imminent takeover
of No. 9 to leak out, and when police, National Guard troops, company
guards, and unaware union sympathizers all rushed to the smaller plant
for the impending battle, leaving No. 4 unprotected, a contingent of union
men walked into the now unguarded plant, turned the machinery off, and
seized it. The company obtained yet another injunction — this one un-
tainted by judicial investments — but the men refused to move from any
of the three plants now occupied and only National Guard soldiers could
have hoped to force them out. Governor Murphy was profoundly reluctant
to use them.

By now, General Motors was losing serious amounts of money. Its
weekly production had been about 15,000 cars before the strike; in the
first ten days of February it dropped to a paltry 151. Negotiations between
Lewis and Knudsen and their entourages, with Governor Murphy watching
over them nervously, finally began in earnest on February 4. Newspapers,
the National Association of Manufacturers, and the business community at
large all demanded that Murphy send in the troops. If the governor seriously
thought of complying, he was soon dissuaded, according to a story pro-
mulgated by Lewis himself. At one point during the negotiations, Lewis
told an interviewer in later years, he scribbled down the message of a
telegram he told Murphy he was prepared to send the governor (and the
newspapers) if troops were ordered to attack:

> I shall personally enter General Motors plant Chevrolet No. 4. I shall
> order the men to disregard your order, to stand fast. I shall walk up
> to the largest window in the plant, open it, divest myself of my outer
> raiment, remove my shirt and bare my bosom. Then when you order
> your troops to fire, mine will be the first breast that those bullets will
> strike.

The governor, Lewis said, turned white and fled the room.

Since the political repercussions would have been ghastly, Murphy
almost certainly would never have used troops. Lewis knew this perfectly
well, so his little drama, if it actually took place, was more along the lines
of a charade. In the event, on February 11, it was done. In the settlement
signed by all parties that day, GM recognized the UAW as the exclusive
bargaining agent for its members, promised not to interfere with or discriminate against any union members, and pledged to start negotiations
over various workplace issues on February 16. In exchange, the UAW

promised to evacuate the plants and not interfere with production while a contract was being negotiated.

The UAW took on Chrysler next, sitting in at the Dodge and Plymouth plants and ringing the rest of the company's main plants with masses of pickets until Chrysler officials accepted the General Motors agreement as their own. The unionization of the Ford Motor Company was more difficult. The unionization of the Ford Motor Company, in fact, would not be possible, not yet — as Walter Reuther and three other UAW organizers learned when they tried to lead a rally of union men outside Ford's River Rouge plant on May 26, 1937. At the same overpass at which the hunger marchers had been beaten back in 1932, Reuther and the rest of the union leaders were set upon and badly beaten by a gang of Harry Bennett's legbreakers. Not until the spring of 1941, with war impending and the courts, the government, public opinion, his son Edsel, and even much of the rest of the industry arrayed against him, would Henry Ford capitulate and allow a union election in his company. When he finally did, 69.9 percent of his seventy-eight thousand workers joined the UAW.

If Henry Ford had not been ready to read the lessons of Flint, Michigan, "Big Steel" had. In March, just a few weeks after the settlement with General Motors, the president of U. S. Steel suddenly agreed to accept the CIO's Steel Workers Organizing Committee as a legitimate bargaining agent, increased wages by 10 percent, and established a forty-hour week with overtime. "Little Steel," led by Republic Steel in Chicago, was less tractable. Republic's president, Tom Girdler, met an attempt to strike his plants that summer of 1937 with the importation of strikebreakers and the cooperation of local authorities. On Memorial Day, when workers and their families tried to combine a picnic with a rally and demonstration outside Republic's South Chicago plant, they were attacked, suddenly and without mercy. Black steelworker and union organizer Jesse Reese was among them when the police opened fire:

> I began to see people drop. There was a Mexican on my side, and he
> fell; and there was a black man on my side and he fell. Down I went.
> I crawled around in the grass and saw that people were getting beat.
> I'd never seen police beat women, not white women. I'd seen them
> beat black women, but this was the first time in my life I'd seen them
> beat white women — with sticks.

When it was over, ten people were dead and dozens wounded in what immediately was called the "Memorial Day Massacre." A smaller "mas-

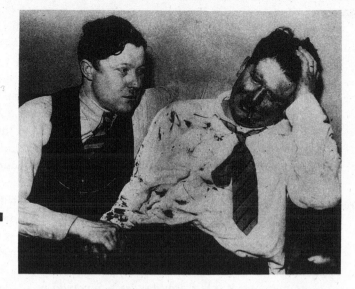

On May 26, 1937, Walter Reuther (left), Richard Frankensteen (right), and two other UAW organizers were beaten by Ford's hired police. "It was the worst licking I've ever taken," Frankensteen said later that day.

During what would come to be remembered as the "Memorial Day Massacre," ten people were killed when police opened fire on a group of men and women near the gates of Republic Steel on May 30, 1937. Policemen begin clearing the battlefield of the dead and wounded.

sacre" took place at the same time at the Republic plant in Youngstown, Ohio, where company police fired into a crowd of pickets from passing trucks, killing two and wounding dozens more.

The National Labor Relations Board (NLRB), established by the Wagner Labor Act in 1935, had been generally silent up to the spring of 1937, fearing that in a pending test case the Supreme Court would declare both the act and the NLRB unconstitutional, as it had the NIRA in 1935. But in April of 1937, to the surprise of many, the Supreme Court upheld the law, and now, armed with the validation of the court, the NLRB ordered Tom Girdler to begin negotiations.

By the time the federal government forced Girdler to start bargaining with his employees instead of shooting them, the membership of CIO unions had grown to more than four million, and the success of the sit-down strikes in Flint and Detroit had inspired other organized and unorganized workers to go and do likewise. The U. S. Bureau of Labor Statistics reported that as many as 400,000 workers were involved in sit-down strikes before the movement ran its course. The press tended to look upon many of these actions as little more than the expressions of a fad — the photograph of a group of striking waitresses "sitting in" at the lunch counter of a Woolworth's store proved irresistible, for instance — but to the workers themselves the strikes were serious indeed, and sometimes dangerous. They indicated with drama and precision the degree to which working people finally had chosen to take control of their own fate.

The drama of the sit-downs helped to illustrate why it was that the CIO's Packing House Workers Organizing Committee could take on the gigantic killing houses of Armour and Swift in Chicago and persuade Middle European and Mexican-American immigrant workers not only to organize and strike but to go against the Catholic Church, many of whose priests vilified the CIO and unionism in general from their pulpits every Sunday on the grounds that both were the agents of Godless communism. It helped to explain why women office workers would fight the male dominance of the CIO and successfully petition for the inclusion of the United Office and Professional Workers of America as a certified CIO union, or why men and women textile workers in the South, even as they remembered the violence and sorrow and failure of the 1929 and 1934 strikes, would still respond to Sidney Hillman's earnest, if doomed, attempt to rebuild the United Textile Workers Union through the CIO's Textile Workers Organizing Committee.

In the years since this decade of incandescent violence and painful victory, the historians have come along to point out some hard truths. John

L. Lewis would prove himself in time to be as infatuated with his own power as he was concerned with the fate of his workers. The CIO would be riven for years by vindictive struggles between Lewis and his many enemies, as well as among clots of conservatives, Socialists, radicals, and Communists. Neither it nor the AFL would give what it should have given to women and blacks and other minorities. In spite of the growing power of the union movement, most American workers would remain badly represented when they were represented at all (and most were not). While the federal government's efforts to mitigate the cruelty of labor warfare and achieve balance between labor and industry would be at least partially successful, much of its activity was smothered in an enervating bureaucracy. And the Roosevelt administration itself would demonstrate time and again that its support of working men and women was ringed about with conditions and exceptions and special circumstances.

All of this was true, and none of it mattered. This is why: Mary Sweet was an African-American organizer for the International Ladies Garment Workers Union, and in her later life she told a story from her union days in Harlem that serves as a parable to illustrate the almost mystical power that unionism held for many people in the thirties. A Jewish manufacturer, her story went, opened up a little factory in Harlem, hiring thirty black women and one experienced Jewish cutter. "Before very long," Sweet said,

> the ILGWU organized the girls . . . and a strike was called. The Jewish cutter joined the union, too. The strike went on for several weeks and the workers were having a real tough time. . . . But they stuck it out and the boss cracked first. The union and the boss sat down to negotiate and the boss gave in to almost every demand, but one thing he wouldn't do. He wouldn't take the Jewish cutter back to work. He felt that the cutter should have stuck by him because they were both Jewish. Well, they called a meeting of the crew, the thirty girls and the Jewish cutter, and the strikers were told what the boss offered and they were to vote on it. Mind you, they were all dead broke, but they voted unanimously to stay on strike until every one of them was taken back. And they won.

That one brave moment of absolute solidarity in a small dress factory in Harlem, New York City, was an epiphany that illuminated the truest and most enduring legacy of the labor movement in the Great Depression.

■ *Paupers Bargaining with Paupers*

The sad paradox of labor's rise to triumph in the 1930s, of course, was the fate of the unionized migrants of California and the southern agricultural workers represented by the Southern Tenant Farmers Union. Neither group would ever achieve anything close to the strength enjoyed by unions in the industrial sections of the country, not even when they cast their lots with the CIO, and neither would ever be fully recognized by the New Deal itself as genuine participants in the organized labor movement.

While Section 7(a) had not specifically excluded agricultural labor, for example, the Roosevelt administration had chosen to interpret the law as if it had, offering as justification the theory that in the long run agricultural labor would benefit more fully from the provisions of the Agricultural Adjustment Act. When Section 7(a) was invalidated along with the NIRA by the Supreme Court in January, 1935, the National Labor Relations Act that followed in the summer was very specific indeed; thanks to lobbying efforts on the part of the American Farm Bureau Federation and the National Grange, the act stipulated that any rights granted by the new law "shall not include any individual employed as an agricultural laborer." And after the Supreme Court declared the AAA itself unconstitutional on January 6, 1936, the administration responded with the Soil Conservation and Domestic Allotment Act, a law that attempted to duplicate the crop-production stipulations of the old law — but did no more than the AAA itself to protect the rights of those who worked the land as laborers, not owners. No New Deal law ever would; when the government finally chose to recognize the travails of the agricultural worker, it would treat the situation as a social problem, not a labor problem.

All of which left organized agricultural labor in a no-man's land that assured its powerlessness — though it would continue the fight stubbornly for a while. In California, the arrival of the new wave of Anglo migrants after 1934 had helped to diffuse worker unity in an industry formerly dominated by Mexican-American and Filipino laborers. And if many residents of the state did not like the Okies much, the Associated Farmers of California were more than willing to tolerate them as a means of undercutting the unions. Consequently, labor organizers found their efforts frustrated by the influx of a relatively docile labor force and a comfortably financed and superbly organized cryptofascist alliance between the Associated Farmers of California, local police departments, the California Highway Patrol under Chief Robert Cato, a fierce anti-unionist, and the California State Department of Criminal Identification — not to mention a court system ready and willing to issue search warrants, bench warrants, and injunctions against picketing and other strike activities at the drop of a gavel.

In an effort to make some power of their own, union representatives from agricultural regions all over the country gathered at a national convention in Denver in July, 1937, to form the first national agricultural union: the United Cannery, Agricultural, Packing, and Allied Workers of America (UCAPAWA), which allied itself with the CIO. While it received little beyond transient moral support from the leadership of the CIO, the UCAPAWA had better luck organizing the new migrants than had any of its predecessors — largely because of the field work of the Communist-led Workers Alliance, which had risen in 1936 and now functioned as a kind of unofficial organizing arm of the union — but the weight of history was moving against the effort. Most migrants continued to ignore the union, and the Associated Farmers and their official and unofficial allies remained nearly invulnerable to change. The union would manage to lead short-lived and violently suppressed cotton-field strikes in 1938 and 1939, however, and a more successful cannery workers strike against the California Sanitary Canning Company in Los Angeles in August, 1939 — an episode notable for the fact that scores of Mexican-American and Jewish women laborers in Local 75 combined to play a major part in organizing and leading the strike whose overall tactics were under the guidance of another woman — Jewish UCAPAWA organizer Dorothy Healey. "We wore down the Shapiro brothers' [the plant owners'] resistance," Healey remembered,

> by organizing picket lines in front of their homes. They were big poobahs in Jewish organizations in L.A., so we got all kinds of Jewish organizations to adopt resolutions condemning their refusal to bargain. Finally they agreed to meet with us, and at a dramatic midnight bargaining session they gave in and recognized the union.

Recognition, as it turned out, was just about all that either Local 75 or the national UCAPAWA ever would get in California — and by the beginning of World War II, organized labor in the state's great "factories in the field" was in a torpid condition.

Among the early members of the UCAPAWA was the Southern Tenant Farmers Union, which had been going through hard times itself. Beginning in January, 1935, arrests, raids, vigilante actions, and other anti-union turmoil in Arkansas drove many of the union leaders (especially the African Americans among them) across the river to Memphis. For many croppers, a reporter for the *New York Times* had written in the middle of April,

The success of the sit-down strikes in Detroit early in 1937 brought forth hundreds of imitations, and for a time during the spring and summer of the year "sitting down" took on the character of a fad. Among the sittees were the cooks for the Willard Hotel in Washington, D.C., TOP, and the waitresses in a Detroit nut shop.

As the white faces sprinkled through this portrait of laundry workers on strike in 1937 indicate, during the labor movement's finer moments the concept of solidarity could transcend ancient prejudices. In Chicago, a white union member walked into the credit union office of the Armour packing company one day and offered to co-sign a loan for a black fellow worker. He was urged not to do it. The black man was his friend, the worker replied angrily: "He works with me. He's a union brother and I guess maybe you're surprised to hear that I'm in the union, too! So you just save that advice of yours for somebody don't know no better."

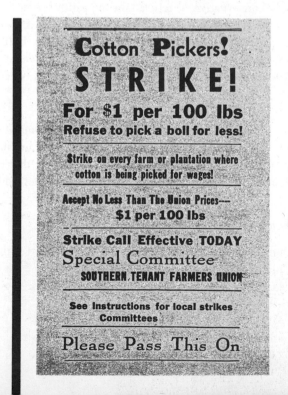

Cotton Pickers!
STRIKE!
For $1 per 100 lbs
Refuse to pick a boll for less!

Strike on every farm or plantation where cotton is being picked for wages!

Accept No Less Than The Union Prices— $1 per 100 lbs

Strike Call Effective TODAY
Special Committee
SOUTHERN TENANT FARMERS UNION

See Instructions for local strikes Committees

Please Pass This On

The strike sign documents the essential failure of the STFU strike of September, 1935. The strike did raise the price for a hundred pounds of picked cotton — but only to 75 cents, not a dollar.

the "Three A's" have spelled unemployment, shrunken incomes, and a lowered standard of living. . . . Attempts to better their lot through organization in the Southern Tenant Farmers' Union have taught them that they have few rights under the laws of Arkansas and no more security under the New Deal than they have had in the past. Scores have been evicted or "run off the place" for union activity, and masked night riders have spread fear among union members, both white and Negro.

In spite of this atmosphere of continuing terror, STFU president Harry Mitchell still called for a rank and file strike vote at the end of August, 1935, and after the membership approved the proposal, thousands of cotton pickers that season grew suddenly too sick to work or had gone off fishing and hunting. Landlords and managers responded with scabs, threats, and some scattered violence, but when the strike was finally called off at the beginning of October, the pay for a hundred pounds of picked cotton had been raised from an average of fifty cents to seventy-five cents.

It was the closest thing to a genuine labor victory the union had ever achieved — or ever would achieve. It helped to boost the membership to more than thirty thousand in 328 locals by January, 1937, but numbers never would translate into real power and the STFU would never break the grip that the plantation system continued to hold on the lives of its workers. A strike in the picking season of 1938 failed, and an internal conflict between the relatively conservative Mitchell and his followers and a more radical element led by the Reverends E. B. McKinney and Claude Williams ended the same year with the expulsion of the two radicals. Mitchell pulled the STFU out of UCAPAWA entirely in 1939, and by the eve of World War II it was down to a few scattered locals. "We were paupers trying to bargain with paupers," Mitchell would later say.

No method can be devised whereby an organization of economically insecure people such as tenant farmers, sharecroppers, and farm laborers on southern plantations can bargain with an industry that is disorganized, pauperized, and kept alive only by Government subsidy.

■■■ An Unwholesome Spectacle

In the end, then, the story of farm labor in the migrant culture of California and the plantation culture of the South would stand as one of the principal failures of the New Deal and the organized labor movement in the years of the Great Depression. Both would largely ignore these workers, and even when the government finally chose to move, in its inchmeal fashion, to address the misery and violence of their lives, it did so less out of any deliberate commitment than because the constant glare of publicity had made it impossible to ignore the situation any longer. It was as early as the October, 1934, issue of Henry Luce's *Fortune* magazine, after all, that photographer Margaret Bourke-White presented for a national audience some of the first and most powerful images of drought, while one of the magazine's unnamed writers produced captions as powerful as anything on the subject that had yet appeared in print:

> You won't understand the evil in this season unless you know the large land in the time of its health. . . . You couldn't understand unless all your life was in that land and the land lay long past death all around you. Then, gentlemen, you might begin to know what it can mean to watch the wind play a death rattle on corn such as this, in the year nineteen hundred and thirty-four, when much of the northern half of the earth was no better than a turning hearth, glowing before the white continuous blast of the sun.

And three years later, Bourke-White would team up with southern writer Erskine Caldwell to produce *You Have Seen Their Faces*, a popularly successful book whose words and pictures illuminated the excruciatingly personal character of the misery that attended the life of the cropper and tenant farmer.

By then, the plantation society had generated its own measure of publicity, albeit unintentionally, after violence spiraled into increasingly vicious episodes, including the murder of Willie Hurst, a black sharecropper who had been prepared to testify that he had seen sheriff's deputies beating union members, and in June, 1936, the kidnapping of the Reverend Claude Williams, a Vanderbilt graduate and founder of the New Era School — a "workers' school" — in Little Rock, Arkansas, and Willie Sue Blagdon, the Socialist daughter of a well-known Memphis family. Seized by six men while driving together from Memphis to Earle, Arkansas, Williams and Blagdon had been taken into a field and flogged.

Blagdon was not bashful about showing her welts to the press, and the uproar around the country was spectacular. Hundreds, perhaps thousands, of poor blacks and poor whites — including women — had been flogged, shot, hanged, and otherwise brutalized over the years with no significant upwelling of fury from the general public, but this time it was a white woman of genteel circumstances who had been beaten, and the incident was too much for even some southern newspapers to swallow without objection. Norman Thomas, who continued his ties to the STFU, and Gardner Jackson — who, after his dismissal from the Department of Agriculture during the "purge" of 1935, had organized the National Committee on Rural Social Planning — publicized the Blagdon incident at every opportunity, joined now by the American Civil Liberties Union, church figures Reinhold Niebuhr and Dorothy Day, columnist Drew Pearson, and Supreme Court Justice Louis Brandeis, among many others.

In the fall of 1936, Roosevelt reacted by appointing a Special Committee on Farm Tenancy with Henry Wallace himself at its head and a representative of the STFU as a member. In early 1937 the report issued its conclusions that the plight of sharecroppers and tenant farmers was indeed a terrible thing, "an unwholesome spectacle," in fact. It recommended that the Resettlement Administration be scrapped and a new agency established in its place — and that among the new agency's provisions should be a program to finance the purchase of small family farms for those who had been forced off the land by natural disaster, economic necessity, or human iniquity. In July, 1937, Congress answered with the Bankhead-Jones Farm Tenancy Act, which set up a three-year, $85 million loan program to help tenant farmers buy their own land, animals, seed, feed, and machinery, as well as help existing land-owners to rehabilitate their properties. To administer the program, Agriculture Secretary Henry Wallace established the Farm Security Administration, which absorbed all the programs and responsibilities of the Resettlement Administration.

The law was much too little and much too late to be much help. There was so little money — just $10 million had been appropriated for the first year of the program — that farmers in only 20 percent of the counties in the nation could even get loans, and these were limited to ten per county. The fund was increased to $25 million in the second year and $50 million in the third, but no more than a fraction of the landless would ever receive any help. For the rest, their condition would remain generally as dim as it always had been.

As for the migrant laborers of California, many remained homeless, living in miserable roadside camps and shacktowns, incurring the wrath, contempt, or indifference of the larger population. Soon enough, though, the plight of these, too, would be part of the national news stream, for not everyone looked upon them with the kind of loathing that on the East Coast used to be reserved for recently arrived European immigrants. There was, for instance, the Simon J. Lubin Society, organized in April, 1936, and named after the man who had created and headed the California Division of Immigration and Housing from 1913 until 1923. Under the direction of Omer Mills, Fred Soule, and Jonathan Garst, the Society attempted to establish housing and health reforms for the migrants and issued a feisty little publication, *The Rural Observer*, under the editorship of a young radical named Helen Hosmer, who meticulously documented the outrages of the Associated Farmers of California and then heaped scorn and ridicule upon their associated heads.

There was, for another example, photographer Dorothea Lange. One rainy afternoon in March, 1936, she remembered, she was driving through the San Joaquin Valley when a sign, "Pea-Pickers Camp," unaccountably caught her attention and would not let it go. She turned back, drove into the camp, and pulled up in front of a ragged tent with a woman and several children in it. "I saw and approached the hungry and desperate mother," she said,

> as if drawn by a magnet. I do not remember how I explained my presence or my camera to her, but I do remember she asked me no questions. I made five exposures, working closer and closer from the same direction. . . . There she sat in that lean-to tent with her children huddled around her, and seemed to know that my pictures might help her, and so she helped me. There was a sort of equality about it.

And in the *San Francisco News* on March 10, 1936 (just above Eleanor Roosevelt's regular "My Day" column, as it happened), Lange's poignant "Migrant Mother" photographs appeared under the headline, "Ragged, Hungry, Broke, Harvest Workers Live in Squallor [sic]."

Then there was John Steinbeck, the author of two well-received novels of California, *Tortilla Flat* (1935) and *In Dubious Battle* (1936). In August, 1936, after Lange's "Migrant Mother" images had been published to a gratifyingly large public response, the *News* sent Steinbeck on assignment in the San Joaquin Valley to produce a series of articles on the migrant labor camps. The series appeared in successive issues of the newspaper from October 5 through October 11 under the running title of "The Harvest Gypsies." A few months later, Helen Hosmer of the Simon J. Lubin Society gathered the articles up and published them in an edition of 100,000 copies as *Their Blood Is Strong*. "In their heads, as they move wearily from harvest to harvest," Steinbeck wrote of the migrants he had seen and talked to,

Largely ignored by the government and the labor movement
alike, the migrant labor population of the United States
continued to wander the country like an invisible army. Even at
the end of the decade, estimates put the number of migrants at
four million people nationwide. Whether they were housed in
filthy company shacks, like the cannery workers of Dania,
Florida, 1937, OPPOSITE, BOTTOM, or in ghastly ditch
camps of California, like the migrant mother and her children
found by photographer Dorothea Lange in a pea-pickers camp
in 1936, OPPOSITE, TOP, the living conditions of these
migrant families were dreadful — as another 1936 Lange
photograph, ABOVE, demonstrates with brutal simplicity. For
the vast majority, things never got any better, even after the
federal government instituted its migratory housing program.

there is one urge and one overwhelming need, to acquire a little land again, and to settle on it and stop their wandering. One has only to go into the squatters' camps where the families live on the ground and have no homes, no beds and no equipment; and one has only to look at the strong purposeful faces, often filled with pain and more often, when they see the corporation-held idle lands, filled with anger, to know that this new race is here to stay and that heed must be taken of it.

The Simon J. Lubin Society and concerned government workers spread Lange's photographs and the words of Steinbeck and others throughout the state and, to the extent they could, throughout the country. By the spring of 1937, the Resettlement Administration had responded by taking over the operation of two migrant labor camps first established by the State Emergency Relief Agency in 1931, and then starting construction of four new federal camps. After creation of the Farm Security Administration in the fall of 1937, twelve more federal camps were constructed in an attempt to provide at least decent living conditions for the workers and their families. The government publicized these model communities with its usual gravity. And the camps *were* clean, and relatively healthful, and in the lives of some families they made a very real difference — but they were pitifully few, housing only hundreds of families when thousands of families needed food, shelter, and health care. They were not, as Carey McWilliams warned as late as 1939, the answer to the problems of agricultural labor:

At the present time, the camps are wholly inadequate; they provide shelter for only a small portion of the workers involved. It should be pointed out, moreover, that the camps enable the residents to work at very low wages and, to this extent, they have probably tended to keep farm wages at a sub-subsistence level. The solution of the farm-labor problem can only be achieved through the organization of farm workers.

Unfortunately, as the farm workers of California and the South had already learned after much sweat, blood, and pain, union organization was a dream that circumstance would never make real enough to lift them from peonage to dignity. The South would never see the creation of a viable agricultural union. And not even the California farm labor movement that began anew in the 1960s under Cesar Chavez and the United Farm Workers of America, while somewhat more successful in gaining improvements in wages, hours, and working conditions on some of the state's biggest farms, could fully overcome the weight of tradition and government indifference. Power remains as fragile a dream for the African-American, Mexican-American, Cuban, Salvadoran, Ecuadoran, and Guatemalan farm worker of today as it was for the oppressed croppers and wandering migrant laborers of the Great Depression.

The Ramparts of Uncertainty

Have always been on the Democratic side of the question
. . . but lying [sic] all politics aside I am writing on a
far more important subject. . . . It is the subject of
dealing with the vital point of the Welfare in life. . . . It
is just going from bad to worse, as far as I can see. I
have been trying to keep my nerve and patience, and also
my confidence in the administration, but now . . . I am
afraid I am losing it, and am beginning to think I am
only kidding myself, and what is the use of
doing that any longer.

Mrs. N. G., to the Roosevelts,
June 22, 1938

CHAPTER ELEVEN

Overleaf:

The sedate Texas couple pictured sitting with their handsome console in 1939 do not appear to be likely candidates for radio hysteria. Still, they could have been among the thousands of Americans who were persuaded through the genius of Orson Welles and the peculiar immediacy of radio broadcasting that the United States had been invaded by Martians on the night of October 30, 1938. "Aunt Grace, a good Catholic," one man recalled a week later, "began to pray with Uncle Henry. Lillie got sick to her stomach. I don't know what I did exactly, but I know I prayed harder and more earnest than ever before."

O N THE EVENING of October 30, 1938, radio listeners who had not been paying sufficient attention were startled when a musical program featuring "Ramon Raquello" and his orchestra was cut off by a news flash: "Ladies and gentlemen, we interrupt our program of dance music to bring you a special bulletin from the Intercontinental Radio News." Mysterious explosions of "incandescent gas," the announcer said, had been observed on Mars through the telescope at the "Mount Jennings Observatory" in Chicago. A few minutes later, further bulletins told of strange aerial vehicles landing in various parts of the country and of even stranger creatures that were seen emerging from them. Soon, as reports began filtering in from New Jersey, New York, Washington, D.C., and elsewhere, it was clear that the United States and perhaps the entire world had been invaded by Martians bent on taking over the planet.

Thousands of listeners succumbed to panic. The *New York Times* received 875 telephone calls in a matter of minutes. A woman was barely prevented from taking poison in order to escape being seized alive by the Martians. "My God," one caller asked the police in San Francisco, "where can I volunteer my services? We've got to stop this awful thing!" In Newark, New Jersey, families in one neighborhood ran into the street, mouths covered with handkerchiefs. When the electricity suddenly went out in a town in Washington, the residents assumed the Martians had just blown the power complex at Bonneville Dam to smithereens. Sailors were called back to their ships. "I was really hysterical," a teenager remembered. "My two girl friends and I were crying and holding each other and everything seemed so unimportant in the face of death. We felt it was terrible we should die so young."

No one died at Martian hands (or tentacles) that night, of course, for what these and millions of others were listening to was an uncommonly realistic radio dramatization of H. G. Welles's *The War of the Worlds* on the CBS drama series "The Mercury Theatre of the Air." The hysteria that resulted was, to a large degree, a tribute to the power that radio had acquired in the eighteen years since Pittsburgh's KDKA had begun regular broadcasting. Nearly 27 million American households (out of a total of less than 34 million) possessed radios in 1938, which meant that as many as 97 million people out of a population of 128.9 million exposed themselves to a daily aural kaleidoscope of serials, soap operas, comedy shows, serious drama, farm reports, country music, big band music, symphony music, opinion shows, amateur hour contests, breakfast shows, sermons, political speeches, and millions of hours of commercial pitches, jingles, and promotions that spilled out of 743 individual stations, many of them affiliated with the three main national networks — CBS, NBC, and Mutual. Radio had become to Americans of the 1930s what television would be to a later generation.

But if the panic over "War of the Worlds" illustrated radio's dominance, it also demonstrated something troubling that lay at the heart of the nation's life in the last few years of the decade. It was, poet W. H. Auden had said, "an age of anxiety," and when the fictitious Martians began landing, they stirred up fears and uncertainties that had never been fully conquered, for all the resurgence of hope that the New Dealers had inspired. The desperation of the early depression years had been alleviated, but its memory remained fresh and the thin cloak of recovery could never quite obscure it. Every twitch and dip of the economy carried with it now a reminder of the original crash. What was more, both Europe and the Far East seemed to be sinking ever deeper into a totalitarian quagmire whose implications for this nation were unclear but increasingly worrisome. The years that followed the elections of 1936, then, were marked by a growing sense of political confusion and division, economic unpredictability, and vague fears of international violence, the whole leading to an ugly rise in levels of intolerance and a weary impatience with problems that simply would not go away. Americans, Harry Hopkins said in an article for the *New Republic* in 1937, had become "bored with the poor, the unemployed and the insecure." The inarticulate sense of community that had been personified by the people and programs of the early New Deal, the quality of mission that had given millions of people the feeling that they were sharing in a great moment of history, was beginning to diminish slowly, and nothing Roosevelt and his administration tried to do seemed enough to bring it back.

◼ *The Switch in Time*

The years 1937 and 1938 could not have been among Franklin D. Roosevelt's favorites. He had won reelection in November, 1936, with one of the largest pluralities in presidential history, gathering in every state but Maine and Vermont. Democratic candidates had won 331 seats in the House, an all-time high, while the Republicans had gotten only 89, with 13 going to those of other persuasions, some of them radical. The Democrats also gained another six seats in the Senate. The situation seemed ideal for the president to carry the New Deal's energy into a fresh term.

But the election results of 1936 could not be read as an unmixed triumph any more confidently than could those of 1934. The people had given the president a vote of confidence of astounding proportions, but it was a limited mandate, more of a personal endorsement of FDR than a blanket approval of everything the New Dealers had done or might do. Within the House and Senate, similarly, the diversity of interests and priorities that the Democratic victory of 1934 had represented was, if anything, even more complex in the membership that was elected in 1936; by no means could the president count on Congress to support his every notion.

As, for example, his attempt to restructure the United States Supreme Court in 1937. For nearly two years, Roosevelt quietly held a massive grudge against the Supreme Court, whose conservative majority, coupled with the honest fear of centralization expressed by such as Justice Louis Brandeis, was industriously disemboweling his most ambitious programs. Not only had the court invalidated Title I of the NIRA in June of 1935, in the spring of 1936 it had declared as unconstitutional the Bituminous Coal Conservation Act — designed as a "little NIRA" for the coal industry — then struck down major portions of the AAA, and shortly after that decided that a New York State minimum-wage law was invalid, which suggested that the National Labor Relations Act might be in trouble when challenged. Since 1936 was an election year, Roosevelt refused to make a public issue of the situation. The most he would say was that the Supreme Court had created a "no-man's land" with respect to labor legislation. When asked by a reporter what could be done about it, Roosevelt merely replied, "I think that is about all there is to say about it."

With the election behind him now, he had more to say on February 5, 1937 — at least to his cabinet and the House and Senate Democratic leaders he called to a special meeting that morning. It was then he announced his intention to ask Congress that afternoon for legislation that would give him the power to appoint one additional judge to the federal judiciary for every judge who had reached the age of seventy but who had declined the opportunity to retire. The proposed bill applied to the entire federal judicial system, but no one in the cabinet room that morning had any doubt at all about who the real targets were: six of the nine justices on the Supreme Court of the United States were over seventy years old. By appointing another six justices, Roosevelt could guarantee himself a liberal majority. "Mr. Attorney General," Vice President Garner later said he told Homer Cummings, "before that law comes back up here for the Boss's signature, many, many moons will pass."

There would never be enough moons; indeed, the president's effort set in motion events whose increasing vindictiveness would help to dismantle the structure of his relationship with Congress and condemn the New Deal to a long legislative twilight. The president's friends in Congress faithfully did what they could, but his motives were all too transparent. The bill's objective, Colonel Robert McCormick's Roosevelt-hating *Chicago Tribune* pointed out in tones of sweet reason, "is to enable Mr. Roosevelt to command a majority of the Supreme Court. The question raised," it went on, "Shall the Supreme Court be turned into the personal organ of the President . . . is fundamental because, if Congress answers yes, the principle of an impartial and independent judiciary will be lost in this country." Walter Lippmann did not even pretend to sweetness. Roosevelt, he said in his newspaper column, was "drunk with power."

Nor was it just the press lords and the conservative pundits of the country who found themselves horrified by what they saw as a wholesale assault on one of the oldest and most important institutions in the nation's history. One of Senator Pat McCarran's constituents in Nevada pleaded with him to defy the kind of tyranny that "Cornwallis and Howe fought for in 1776," while another cheered North Carolina Senator Josiah Bailey's opposition to FDR's plan: "Bully for you! Oh bully for you! *Don't*, don't let that wild man in the White House do this dreadful thing to our country."

Arms were twisted, old obligations were called upon, and the president himself used all his arts of charm and cajolery, but the actions of the Supreme Court itself over the next several months made an already difficult ambition nearly impossible. On March 29, in a decision involving a minimum-wage law in Washington State, the Court effectively reversed an earlier decision regarding a similar law in New York. On that same day, it upheld the constitutionality of the Amended Railway Act of 1934, which had authorized employee elections for the choosing of a union — a decision that validated the position of the largest black union in America, A. Philip Randolph's Brotherhood of Sleeping Car Porters. On April 12, the Court upheld the constitutionality of the Wagner National Labor Relations Act, and then on May 24 upheld a Wisconsin law that prohibited the use of court injunctions to stifle labor picketing, and approved the Social Security Act of 1935. The same Supreme Court that had appeared to be the New Deal's most rigid enemy was suddenly on the right side of things. Whether the threat of FDR's "court-packing" scheme, as it was called, had anything to do with this apparent reversal of attitude is still open to debate among scholars of the Supreme Court, but a "switch in time saved nine," one cynic of the day remarked, and in truth, the Court's sudden conciliatory tone had taken a good deal of steam out of FDR's campaign.

The final blow came when Senator Joseph Robinson, who had been staunchly carrying the fight in the Senate against a growing body of opposition, died suddenly on July 14, 1937. Without Robinson to persuade his colleagues otherwise, on July 22 the Democratically controlled Senate voted 70 to 20 to recommit the legislation to the Judiciary Committee for further review. The vote was less a matter of parliamentary procedure than a form of burial.

Over the next several years, deaths and retirements among the older justices would enable Roosevelt to liberalize the Court with the appointments of men like William O. Douglas, Felix Frankfurter, Hugo Black, and Frank Murphy (the Michigan governor who had struggled to settle the UAW sit-down strike in Flint). But his short-lived vendetta against the Court had left a taint of malevolence and anger in the political firmament that would remain — and a serious doubt in the minds of millions of voters who wondered if Roosevelt's actions did not bear out Lord Acton's old dictum that "power tends to corrupt, and absolute power tends to corrupt absolutely." The president's opposition in Congress would soon be playing to that doubt vigorously.

▆▆▆ The Roosevelt Recession

Uncertainty over his relationship with Congress was not the only domestic problem besetting the president in the years of 1937 and 1938, a fact he alluded to during a Fireside Chat broadcast on June 24, 1938, putting as good a face on things as he could. "It makes no difference to me whether you call it a recession or a depression," he said.

> In 1932 the total national income of all the people in the country had reached the low point of $38 billion in that year. With each succeeding year it rose. Last year, 1937, it had risen to $70 billion. . . . This year, 1938, while it is too early to do more than give a mere estimate, we hope that the national income will not fall below $60 billion and that's a lot better than $38 billion.

Well, yes, some listeners might have wanted to respond, $60 billion *was* better than $38 billion — but what had happened to the $10 billion that was lost between the end of 1937 and the middle of 1938? A good many people were asking that very question, or versions thereof, as a matter of fact. After all, from the spring of 1933 to the fall of 1937 the economy had enjoyed a steady, if undramatic, recovery, particularly after 1934. As Roosevelt noted in his speech, personal income had indeed risen since

1932 (though modern figures put the numbers at $50.2 billion in 1932 and $74.1 billion in 1937). Employment rose in the same period from 27.9 million to a shade over 36 million, while unemployment finally dropped from an all-time high of 12.8 million (25.2 percent of the labor force) to 7.7 million (14.3 percent). The annual average wage of factory workers increased from $1,086 to $1,376, and in spite of the thousands of strikes, work stoppages, and general turmoil, the manufacturing labor force grew from 6.9 million to 10.8 million. There were 31,822 business failures in 1932, but only 9,490 in 1937. Finally, corporate income rose from $5.3 billion to $13.2 billion.

By the standards of precrash America, of course, many of these figures were still weak — and people remembered 1929 and the years that followed with a certain grim clarity. That, it appears, was part of the problem. If profligate investment in the twenties had been one of the impulses that had sapped the strength of the economy, the opposite instinct may well have helped to damage the recovery of the mid-1930s. People were paying down their debts now, as best they could, and saving more: out of the $9 billion in higher income they received between the end of 1935 and the end of 1936, for example, individuals put $3 billion in the bank; and between the end of 1936 and the end of 1937, while income rose only $4.2 billion, savings remained high at $2.3 billion. People who had been boiling grass for food a few years ago and who were now earning a relatively decent income were understandably inclined toward caution. This cast of mind was further encouraged when the full impact of the payroll tax to finance the Social Security System began to be felt in 1937; some $2 billion was taken out of the paychecks of working Americans during that year — while no retirement benefits had yet been paid out.

One of the results of these suddenly cautionary instincts was that while consumer spending remained stable, it did not suck up all the goods that were being produced by growing businesses and an expanding labor force. Things started piling up in warehouses as inventory, as they had in the late twenties, and the value of unsold goods was estimated at $5 billion by the middle of 1937 — the highest figure in history up to then.

Federal actions did not help. Roosevelt had never really abandoned the idea of a balanced budget, and while by the spring of 1937 this was largely a philosophical concept — the federal deficit had risen to $3.6 billion in 1936 and it would fall below $1 billion only once, in 1937, during the rest of the decade — he was still sensitive to conservative demands that he start reducing federal spending. Between his second inauguration and September, 1937, Roosevelt's orders cut the total number of those employed on WPA and other emergency employment projects from 3.7 million to 1.9 million. Private employment offset the full effect of this, since it had increased by 4.7 million between March, 1936, and September, 1937, but the sudden loss of income from federal jobs was nonetheless a powerful depressant. So was the fact that funding for PWA projects was severely curtailed over the same several months. Not only was the administration no longer priming the pump, it was, according to one observer, even "taking some water out of the spout."

Beginning in August, 1937, these elements combined to produce an economic crisis whose emotional impact was reminiscent of that from the crash of 1929, precisely because recovery, on the face of it, had appeared to be proceeding slowly but steadily. The stock market began to sag, then dropped with a sickening thud on "Black Tuesday," October 19, when 7.2 million shares were traded — the biggest one-day volume since 1933. The Dow Jones average stood at 190 when the slide began; after the October crash, it stood at 115. The decline continued into 1938; stocks on the New York Exchange that were worth $20.3 billion at the end of 1936 dropped in value to just over $11 billion by the end of 1938. The Federal Reserve Board's adjusted Index of Industrial Production slid from 117 in August, 1937, to 76 in May, 1938 — in nine months it lost almost two-thirds of what it had gained since 1933. In March, 1938, unemployment rose by another four million, bringing the proportion of unemployed in the total labor force to nearly 20 percent.

The president's enemies were not long in calling this the "Roosevelt recession" and laying about them with some mean joy in "I told you so" declarations. Hugh Johnson, who had never quite forgiven FDR for forcing him to resign as director of the NRA, was downright gleeful. "The old Roosevelt magic has lost its kick," he wrote in his newspaper column. "The diverse elements in his Falstaffian army can no longer be kept together and led by a melodious whinny and a winning smile." On March 25, the stock market took another plunge, and early in April Harry Hopkins and Aubrey Williams drove down to the president's enclave at Warm Springs, Georgia, and persuaded him to launch a new federal spending program as the only sure way to boot the economy back into recovery.

On April 14, Roosevelt asked Congress to authorize $3.75 billion in new spending. Legislators, with an eye on the elections in November, swiftly complied. Hopkins and the WPA got more than $1.4 billion; Ickes and the PWA got almost $1 billion; and the remainder was spread through a baker's dozen of federal programs. Sure enough, by the summer economic indicators were slightly on the rise. The stock market improved, and a sluggish recovery seemed underway once again by the end of the year. At the same time, there was little to indicate that the country would be coming back to full economic strength anytime soon — not when unemployment had risen to more than nine million by the end of the year and seemed destined to bear out the truth of a gloomy prediction by Harry Hopkins in 1937 that it was "reasonable to expect a probable minimum of 4,000,000 to 5,000,000 unemployed even in future 'prosperity' periods."

■ They'll Be Sorry Yet

Democratic unity, if such a thing could be said to still exist by then, took another blow when Roosevelt, who was not a man to take political disloyalty lightly, finally decided to vent his spleen over what Congress had done to his Supreme Court plan. Even while Congress was endorsing his economic pump-priming efforts in the spring of 1938, he was planning his revenge. According to Postmaster General James Farley, early in 1938 the president began to summon various senators and congressmen up to the White House for informal chats about whom he might or might not support in the November elections, after which they would leave with worried looks. "I've got them on the run, Jim," FDR chortled. "They go out of here talking to themselves, memorizing my lines to repeat them up on the Hill. I'd like to see the faces sag over my mumbo-jumbo. They have no idea what's going to happen and are beginning to worry. They'll be sorry yet."

It was not enough to throw confusion into his enemies; Roosevelt decided to challenge the conservative wing of his own party directly by attempting to swing voters toward liberal candidates and away from conservative candidates in the various primary elections that spring and summer. FDR's resolve only intensified when the House killed an administration reorganization bill that would have given the president great freedom to move departments about and otherwise consolidate power in the executive department; the bill squeezed through the Senate by a vote of 49 to 42, but even after weakening amendments were included, the House voted by 204 to 196 on April 8 to recommit the legislation. In Florida, liberal Senator Claude Pepper got a ringing endorsement from Roosevelt in February and won his primary by more than 100,000 votes. With that to bolster his confidence, the president renewed his old attacks on the Republican minority in Congress during his Fireside Chat of June 24. He called them "Copperheads," referring to those congressmen who had opposed Abraham Lincoln's conduct of the Civil War, then toward the end of the speech slid into a weakly disguised call to arms against conservative Democrats:

In the coming primaries in all parties, there will be many clashes
between two schools of thought, generally classified as liberal and
conservative. Roughly speaking, the liberal school of thought recog-
nizes that the new conditions throughout the world call for new rem-
edies. . . . The opposing or conservative school of thought . . . does
not recognize the need for government to step in and take action to
meet these new problems. . . . Assuming the mental capacity of all
the candidates, the important question which it seems to me the primary voter must ask is this: "To which of these general schools of
thought does the candidate belong?"

In what would be called an attempted "purge" of the party's conservatives,
Roosevelt then publicly involved himself in several Democratic primaries
around the country, targeting such conservative Democrats as Maryland's
Senator Millard Tydings for defeat and such liberals as hopeful congressional candidate Lyndon Johnson of Texas for victory. The effort failed.
Besides Claude Pepper, the only other candidate endorsed by Roosevelt
who won was Johnson — and all but one of those he had wanted to defeat
went on to win nomination (Tydings by more than sixty thousand votes).

The situation did not make for an amicable working relationship
between the Congress and the president as the legislative season of 1938
wore on. One prime indication that the mutualism that had carried so much
of the New Deal's legislation through Congress was beginning to fade was
the sudden success of Congressman Martin Dies of Texas, a conservative
Democrat with a special interest in investigating things that might be un-
American. Sit-down strikes, for instance, which in a resolution offered in
the spring of 1937 he said were "sweeping the nation and threatening the
very foundations of orderly government." He wanted to investigate them at
the time, but Roosevelt was able to quash the proposal. A few months later,
however, Dies was at it again, this time asking for a special committee to
investigate

the extent, character, and objects of un-American propaganda activities in the United States [and] the diffusion within the United States
of subversive and un-American propaganda that is instigated from
foreign countries or of a domestic origin and attacks the principle of
the form of government as guaranteed by our Constitution. . . .

Roosevelt believed that the committee would be used mainly to attack the
New Deal and made his opposition clear, but ideological turmoil on both

the domestic and international fronts had bubbled up among many in Congress old suspicions of subversion and fears of revolutionary plots, and on May 26, 1938, by a vote of 191 to 46, Dies was given his Special Committee to Investigate Un-American Activities.

Congressman J. Parnell Thomas of New Jersey, who was immediately named to the committee and would become its chief inquisitor, made no secret of his own inclinations. The principal "un-Americanism" at issue here, he said, was communism. The Communists, he insisted, were "right in our government," and once ensconced on the committee and given the full support of Dies, its chairman, he started looking for them with a vengeance that would not be equaled in Washington until the days of Senator Joseph McCarthy. Thomas gave particular attention to the Labor Department, with its alleged sympathy for the "radical" CIO, and the WPA's Federal Theater Project, with its vaguely left-wing inclinations, particularly as expressed in its "Living Newspaper" programs. He did not much like the Federal Arts Project, either, since it gave work to a clutch of openly leftist artists like Rockwell Kent, who once managed to sneak a pitch for Puerto Rican independence into an obscure corner of a mural in the main post office building in New York City (the message was written in Icelandic, not a commonly understood language even in Manhattan, but was eventually discovered and painted out).

While Thomas lifted rocks in Washington, looking for Communists, the last piece of legislation that could truly be described as a New Deal reform measure staggered through to passage, encumbered all the way by the growing antagonism between the president and the Congress. Called the Fair Labor Standards Act, the legislation called for an end to "starvation wages and intolerable hours," as Roosevelt described them, by establishing a minimum wage and a ceiling on the number of hours people could be required to work without overtime pay. The bill was first introduced in 1937, only to be bottled up by Congressman John O'Connor, chairman of the House Ways and Means Committee, who opposed it.

The president's friends in Congress could not get the bill pried out of O'Connor's committee until well into the 1938 session, and it was not until June of that year that a conference committee worked out a compromise between the House and Senate versions of the bill. As passed, the bill outlawed the employment of child labor in interstate commerce and established a two-year period in which a minimum wage would rise to forty cents an hour and a standard work week would decline to forty hours — but was so burdened with exceptions for special industries and interests that Martin Dies was moved to offer up a satiric amendment stipulating that "within

90 days after appointment of the Administrator, she [Labor Secretary Frances Perkins, presumably] shall report to Congress whether anyone is subject to this bill." Imperfect as it was, in many ways it was the era's last legislative hurrah, the final contribution that organism of individuals and ideas called the New Deal would be able to make to the social and economic structure of the nation.

Because of his opposition to the bill, Congressman O'Connor came in for special attention from Roosevelt as he continued his attempt to rid the party of conservatives in the primary elections that year. O'Connor, in fact, was defeated, but he was the only Democrat shot down by the president's efforts. Even worse, the Republicans gained eighty-one seats in the House and eight in the Senate during the November elections. The Democrats still controlled both houses, but the margin now was perilously thin — and with an increasing disaffection between the administration and conservative and southern Democrats, Roosevelt's base of power appeared to be disintegrating. The liberal coalition, supported by the overwhelming majority of American voters for so long, was being eroded by the press of events and the increasingly diffuse and ineffective character of the administration's domestic policies. The old certainty of purpose that had captured the hearts and imaginations of millions of Americans and given them a part to play in one of the great dramas of American history seemed to have succumbed to confusion, uncertainty, and disillusion. "The people" would continue to support the president, but never again with the same fervor.

Hair-Trigger Times

Even while an increasingly intransigent Congress, eroding political power, and a quavering economy were putting great pressures on the president, international developments were becoming more and more prominent in his list of concerns. In all fairness, Dies and his committee did not confine their efforts just to ferreting out alleged Communists buried in the warrens of the New Deal. In lobbying for the creation of the committee, in fact, Dies had emphasized his plan to spend a good deal of time looking into various Nazi propaganda efforts, particularly those represented by such organizations as the German-American Bund, the principal American support group for Chancellor Adolf Hitler's Nazi party, which had come to power in Germany just a few weeks before Roosevelt's first inauguration in 1933.

There was, in fact, plenty of reason to wonder what Hitler and his fascist colleagues were up to. Indeed, Roosevelt had started worrying as

In this photograph, the grisly character of the 1935–36 war between Italy and Ethiopia is given terrible clarity. The date is May 25, 1936; the dead are civilians; the soldiers are members of Benito Mussolini's invading fascist army; the streets are those of Addis Ababa, once one of the world's great centers of civilization, major portions of which now were stinking rubble. BELOW: Mussolini reviews Nazi troops with his German counterpart, Adolf Hitler, during "Il Duce's" state visit to Munich in September, 1937, while German and Italian planes blasted Iberian cities to wreckage during the Spanish Civil War. Every day now, the deteriorating European situation troubled the minds of millions of increasingly anxious Americans. "I am afraid of all those people in Europe," one woman told an interviewer for the American Institute of Public Opinion in 1938; "they could do anything."

If American Jews were fearful about what was happening in Germany, they could find plenty of worry in their own country, thanks to numerous anti-Semitic organizations, including the German-American Bund. As this photograph of a Bund meeting indicates, this "militant group of patriotic Americans," as its leader, Fritz Kuhn, described it, equated Adolf Hitler with George Washington and vowed to oppose, among other things, "all Racial Intermixture between Asiatics, Africans, or non-Aryans . . . Alien-controlled, international so-called Labor Movements; and the Rackets of International finance." Above all, he said, it was "a great American movement of Liberation . . . in order that the dictatorship of a . . . Jewish international minority may be broken."

early as the spring of 1935. "These are without doubt the most hair-trigger times the world has gone through in your lifetime or mine," he had written to the American ambassador in Italy. "I do not even exclude June and July 1914," he added — then requested from Congress the largest peacetime defense budget in American history up to that time: $1.1 billion. What prompted his worry that spring of 1935 was the fact that Italy, solidly fascist under Benito Mussolini since the middle of the twenties, was massing troops on the border of Ethiopia, which Italy claimed as its own. Sure enough, Mussolini sent his armies into Ethiopia that October, swiftly destroying the forces of Emperor Haile Selassie and annexing the country in a little over six months, while the United States and other nonfascist powers wrung their diplomatic hands in dismay, but did nothing to stop it.

Similarly, when the Spanish Civil War erupted in July of 1936 between a Republican coalition of Communists, Socialists, and other radicals, and a Nationalist coalition of conservatives and fascists, the governments of both Italy and Germany had contributed men and materiel to the fascist side of the conflict — while those of Great Britain, France, and the United States all took refuge in the comfort of neutrality (though individual liberals, Communists, and radicals from all three nations offered their services to the Republican armies in defiance of their governments, including hundreds of Americans, black and white, who joined the Abraham Lincoln and Washington battalions and fought until the end of the war in the spring of 1939).

On the other side of the world matters were hardly better. The Empire of Japan, an island nation with few natural resources of its own, had invaded China and seized Manchuria for its raw materials in 1931. An uneasy peace had prevailed until August, 1937, when an undeclared war between the two nations began in earnest. Among several gunboats that the United States Navy sent to China to look after the interests and safety of resident American citizens and American shipping was the *Panay*, stationed on the Yangtze River. On December 12, Japanese planes unexpectedly and without known provocation attacked the *Panay*, killing one American civilian and two sailors, wounding eleven others, and sinking the boat — the whole incident dramatized in newsreels and an extraordinary series of photographs in *Life* magazine for the entire country to gasp over.

"[T]his nation wants peace," Roosevelt said in a letter of December 16, explaining why he had done nothing but send a stern message of concern to the Japanese government, asking that Emperor Hirohito be apprised of his feelings and that the government prepare a message of regret, offer full reparation, and promise not to do it again (with all of which Japan complied).

Roosevelt was entirely right about the nation's reluctance to fight over the *Panay* incident. The great bulk of the letters, telegrams, and telephone calls the White House received after the attack on the *Panay* expressed outrage — but also urged the president to do nothing in response that smacked of military action.

The overwhelming majority of Americans were dead against the idea of the United States becoming entangled in any more foreign wars; one had been enough and more than enough, thank you. Nor was the isolationist wing in Congress ready to give up the illusion that there was safety in distance. Led by a small but powerful coalition of senators — chief among them Robert M. La Follette, Jr., Burton K. Wheeler, William Borah, Gerald Nye, and Hiram Johnson — the isolationists would, with diligence and considerable success, strive for the rest of the decade to keep the walls between the United States and the troubled and violent European and Asian continents high, thick, and impregnable.

The nation did want peace, yet everywhere the hope of peace seemed to be in shorter and shorter supply. In Europe, now, Hitler finally began making the kinds of moves that many had always feared he would. In March, 1938, after Austrian Nazis forced that country's chancellor from office, Hitler sent in German troops and declared that Austria had been united with Germany in an *Anschluss*. He then demanded the Sudetenland, a part of Czechoslovakia, and on September 29 and 30, 1938, British Prime Minister Neville Chamberlain and French Prime Minister Edouard Daladier met with Hitler and Mussolini in Munich and came away with an agreement that gave Hitler what he wanted. It was, Chamberlain announced upon his return to London, waving the flimsy document in one hand, "peace for our time."

It was, in fact, peace for only a few months, and for the Jews of Austria and Germany, where life grew increasingly miserable, not even that. Between Hitler's rise to power in 1933 and the end of 1937, an estimated 129,000 Jews already had left Germany. For those who remained, what must have seemed as bad as it could get got worse in 1938. In June, the synagogues of Munich, Nuremberg, and Dortmund were destroyed on the direct orders of Hitler. Mass arrests then began in both Germany and Austria in order to expedite the seizure of Jewish property and encourage continued emigration. Then on the night of November 7, a German embassy official in Paris was assassinated by a young Jew. What followed on the evening of November 9–10 in Germany and Austria was called *Kristall-nacht*, Night of the Broken Glass, as organized mobs of Nazi thugs raged through the cities of the two countries, shattering storefronts, burning

hundreds of synagogues, looting, beating, and killing. At least twenty
thousand and perhaps as many as sixty thousand Jews were arrested and
put into concentration camps, including one called Buchenwald. No one
ever knew just how many hundreds had been shot or beaten to death. It
was the beginning of the barbarism that ultimately would evolve into "the
final solution" to "the Jewish problem."

Most of the rest of the world was numb with horror, and said so out
loud. "I myself could scarcely believe that such things could occur in a
twentieth century civilization," the president of the United States told the
press. But expressions of shock were all that Roosevelt or any other national
leader seemed able — or at least willing — to offer. At a conference of
twenty-seven European and Latin American countries that FDR had called
to address the question of Jewish emigration in July, 1938, the president's
representatives announced only that the United States would make its full
quota of 27,370 openings for Jewish immigrants available, but would not
consider raising the quota (it would have taken an act of Congress to do
so, and there was not the slightest chance that any such act would pass in
a Congress most of whose members generally were nearly as anti-Semitic
as they were racist). No other country offered anything better.

So while the Jews of Germany and Austria died and tens of thousands
were imprisoned in concentration camps every passing week, America's
doors remained closed. Roosevelt did at least recall the American ambassador to Germany on November 14, after the mayhem of *Kristallnacht;*
Hitler retaliated four days later by recalling his own ambassador. None of
this diplomatic maneuvering provided much comfort to the victims, of
course.

■■■ *In a Season of Ugliness*

To many American Jews, events in Germany and Austria must have
seemed a nearly surreal exaggeration of what was happening in this country,
where both foreign-directed and native-grown fascist movements had combined with ancestral anti-Semitism and the seemingly endless disappoint-
ments of the depression years to color much of the decade with a special
ugliness. By the end of 1938, one estimate had it, there were some eight
hundred organizations in the United States that could be described as fascist
and anti-Semitic. Most were so tiny and ineffectual as to be all but invisible
outside their immediate locality, like the Knights of the White Camellia in
West Virginia, the Militant Christian Patriots of Los Angeles, or the National
Gentile League of Washington, D. C., but all stood as particularly base

expressions of the anti-Semitism that crept through much of American society, whether of the genteel middle-class kind that restricted country club membership to gentiles, or of the religious variety that infused much of the Catholic Church with old antagonisms.

Some groups that exploited such sentiments were substantial, including the principal American propaganda arm of the Nazi government itself. At first called the Association of the Friends of New Germany, the group's fervor soon disabled it, according to a report from the New York State legislature in 1939:

> The Friends of New Germany, chiefly through the stupidity of its leaders, brought a great deal of unfavorable publicity upon the organization. Mass meetings were held with uniformed storm troopers, and Jews and Catholics were called even more vile names than those now used. Many of the meetings ended in riot and bloodshed, and as a result, a reorganization came about, and the German-American Bund came into existence with explicit instructions from Germany to carry on propaganda without antagonizing the whole country.

The Bund, formed in 1936 under the leadership of a German-born Detroit autoworker, Fritz Kuhn, attempted to forge an alliance with the more militant isolationists in Congress and went about its anti-Semitic, pro-Nazi propaganda errands with greater care through the rest of the decade, though not always without incident; a huge rally at Madison Square Garden on Washington's Birthday in 1939, for example, was interrupted when a Jewish activist named Isadore Greenbaum broke through a line of Bundist storm troopers and attempted to pummel Kuhn. In front of many newsreel cameras, Greenbaum was beaten and thrown off the stage.

Among the most prominent of the homegrown groups was the Silver Legion, headed by the peculiarly mystical William Dudley Pelley, who once informed Chairman Martin Dies during HUAC hearings that we human beings "actually choose our parents by our own free will, before entering life as infants." To Pelley and his "Silver Shirt" followers, Roosevelt himself was a Jew and the New Deal was little more than a satrapy of Jews. "There is proof — pressed down and overflowing —" he wrote at one point, "that the New Deal from its inception has been naught but the political penetration of a predominantly Christian country and Christian government, by predatory, megalo-maniacal Israelites and their agents." While the membership of his group remained minuscule throughout its life, Pelley managed to flood the anti-Semitic market with publications, including books and pamphlets issued from the Skyland Press, a newspaper called *Pelley's Weekly*, and a monthly magazine called *Liberation*.

Even noisier was the Christian Front movement — not least because it was the brainchild of the radio priest, Charles Coughlin. After his candidate and his party (and by implication, Coughlin himself) had been humiliated by the results of the 1936 presidential election, Coughlin withdrew from the sociopolitical scene for a while, confining himself largely to the spiritual care and feeding of his flock, the Radio League of the Little Flower, and the production of his own newspaper, *Social Justice*. But by the summer of 1938, Coughlin hit upon a new gimmick to enhance his position in the world — anti-Semitism. Beginning with the July 18 issue of *Social Justice*, he began publishing installments of *The Protocols of the Elders of Zion*, a pile of steaming calumny against Jews that had been around since the nineteenth century. His broadcasts now took on an oily anti-Semitic turn and he began to praise the efforts of the German-American Bund and even Pelley's Silver Shirts, while castigating the New Deal for its leftist-Communist-Jewish subversion of the government. In August, he organized his steadily declining numbers of followers into platoons of twenty-five members each to create a "Christian Front" of anti-Semitic "soldiers" to promulgate bigotry and intimidate Jews, often by physical attacks and destruction of property — an unsettling echo of events in Germany.

While it made no move to prevent Coughlin from doing his work, much of the Catholic hierarchy was dismayed by his vituperation and some of its members, like Cardinal Mundelein of Chicago, openly denounced him. In 1939, the National Association of Broadcasters finally adopted a code that prohibited the purchase of air time for controversial broadcasts (it could only be given away, at the discretion of individual stations, and only with the other side of any question being given equal time to respond). This would begin a rapid disintegration of the radio network that had brought in the bulk of Coughlin's contributions since 1930, but well into 1940, he continued to poison the air with vituperation and fill the columns of *Social Justice* with every convenient lie, nurturing the joyless fantasies and dark hatreds of his constituents.

Genius Draws No Color Line

Given the equal-opportunity nature of bigotry, there was some logic in the fact that the anti-Semitism of the era often was linked to the racism that had permeated American society for three centuries and was still alive and well in the thirties. "What Man said to 'That' Woman," a popular bit of doggerel of the day ran, "You kiss the niggers,/I'll kiss the Jews,/We'll stay in the White House/As long as we choose?" While most of the fascist and cryptofascist organizations of the thirties concentrated their hatred on Jews, many, like Pelley's outfit, had no trouble embracing an equally earnest disregard for African Americans, and some organizations, like the Black Legion, a violent quasi-military group that had erupted in the Midwest, gave the benefit of their attention almost entirely to African Americans. And while the Ku Klux Klan had declined in membership and power tremendously since the days of its renewed glory in the middle of the twenties, the bigots in billowing white robes and pointy hoods could still be seen at parades and cross burnings in various parts of the country, particularly Florida, where the organization claimed a membership of thirty thousand.

For those inclined to believe the worst, it may have seemed that racism was not even susceptible to dilution, much less obliteration. The anti-lynching bill, for example, was among those progressive pieces of legislation that died during the contentious 1938 session of the Seventy-fifth Congress — though its defeat was no personal blow to Roosevelt, who still refused to actively support it. The bill, constantly reintroduced since 1935, did not even get presented to the floor for debate until January 6, 1938. True to their convictions, intransigent Southern senators launched a filibuster that continued night and day for nearly six weeks. On January 27, Senator Robert F. Wagner and other supporters of the bill asked for a vote on cloture to end debate, but lost it, 37 to 51. The yammering in the Senate continued, Mississippi's Bilbo warning of black-and-white "amalgamation," while Louisiana's Ellender urged his colleagues to "at all cost preserve the white supremacy of America." On February 16, another cloture vote failed of the necessary two-thirds majority by 42 to 46. With the southerners threatening to talk until Christmas, the bill was withdrawn.

The NAACP's Walter White wrote a politely phrased letter of thanks to Wagner and the other senators who had tried to move the bill — but he let his bitterness show in a private letter to his friend Senator George Norris, the father of the Rural Electrification Administration and the TVA. "But what, my dear Senator Norris," White asked, "is the worth to a man of an electrically lighted home if he can be taken from that home as easily as from a cabin lighted by candles, and burned to death by a howling mob?"

The demise of the anti-lynching bill might be said to stand as a kind of dark talisman, demonstrating as it did the limits both of what could be done in the New Deal and what the New Deal — or at least Roosevelt himself — was truly committed to getting done. But even after this particularly bitter defeat, African Americans as a whole were not ready to repudiate the New Deal and would continue to find solace in the dimensions of hope that had been freed up by the Roosevelt years. In spite of all its monstrous failures and hesitancies concerning the special problems of blacks, the New Deal still *seemed* to promise so much (as no other presidential administration had ever done), and at no time in the history of the thirties did that promise shine forth more brightly, if symbolically, than on Easter Sunday afternoon in 1939.

The black contralto Marian Anderson, like that other black culture hero of the time, heavyweight champion Joe Louis, was at heart an apolitical being. Like Louis, she had been born poor and had worked desperately hard to develop her skills in a white world that was essentially hostile to her ambitions. She began singing in church choirs as a child, and at the age of twenty-six triumphed over three hundred contestants to win the Philadelphia Philharmonic competition in 1926. Thirteen years later, she was one of the most famous singers in the world, and by the time she and her manager, the colorful impresario Sol Hurok, accepted an invitation to sing at the Howard University Concert Series in the spring of 1939, her popularity ensured a crowd too big for the facilities that the university ordinarily used. Consequently, on January 9, the university's school of music applied to the Daughters of the American Revolution for the use of the DAR's Constitution Hall on April 9.

But the manager of the hall, Fred Hand, refused the university's application, telling the chairman of the concert series that the policy of the hall was not to rent space to blacks. Within a few days, the New Negro Alliance of Washington had a letter-writing effort underway, the NAACP had become involved, and more than sixty black and more than thirty white or integrated organizations had joined to form a Marian Anderson Citizens Committee that began a relentless public relations campaign designed to persuade the DAR to change its mind — or, failing that, to ensure its deserved humiliation. Letters and telegrams streamed in from such famous performers as Lawrence Tibbett and Geraldine Farrar, conductors Walter Damrosch and Leopold Stokowski, and even actress and DAR member Katharine Hepburn, who said that the refusal to let Marian Anderson sing "was a serious error in judgment on the part of the Daughters of the American Revolution, and one which jeopardizes not only the position of the organization itself, but the principles on which it was founded."

The DAR would not change its mind, not even after Eleanor Roosevelt, another lifelong member, made her feelings public. Not wishing to alienate too many more southern members of Congress who did not already despise her, she had been working quietly behind the scenes for some time, encouraging the pressure on the DAR. But by the end of February, she decided she had remained quiet long enough. On February 27, she resigned, and in her syndicated "My Day" column the next day told the world. The DAR remained unmoved.

Where, then, would the concert be held? According to his own recollection, it was Assistant Interior Secretary Oscar Chapman who first suggested the Lincoln Memorial as the appropriate site for an Easter Sunday concert. When he offered this idea to Walter White, Chapman said, White gasped, "Oh, my God, if we could have her sing at the feet of Lincoln!" Others made claim to having been the first to come up with the idea, but however it evolved, it soon earned the support of Eleanor Roosevelt and Secretary Ickes, whose Interior Department administered the monument. For political purposes, it needed FDR's approval. Ickes bearded him in his office as the president was getting ready to board a train. "I don't care if she sings from the top of the Washington Monument," Roosevelt said, "as long as she sings."

And so she did, April 9, 1939, on the steps below the great, brooding presence of the seated Lincoln, before an integrated crowd of an estimated seventy-five thousand people, the largest outdoor concert audience in the District's history. Harold Ickes introduced her. "When God gave us this wonderful outdoors," he said,

> and the sun and moon and the stars, He made no distinction of race, creed, or color. . . . Genius, like Justice, is blind. . . . Genius draws no color line. She has endowed Marian Anderson with such a voice as lifts any individual above his fellows and is a matter of exultant pride to any race. And so it is fitting that Marian Anderson raise her voice in tribute to the noble Lincoln whom mankind will ever honor.

The concert lasted a bare twenty minutes, but for the black members of the audience, especially, the experience was electrifying. Many surged toward the improvised stage in an emotional wave when it was done. Walter White spoke into the microphones to calm them, and as he did, he remembered, one girl caught his eye:

> Her hands were particularly noticeable as she thrust them forward and upward, trying desperately . . . to touch the singer. They were hands which despite their youth had known only the dreary work of manual

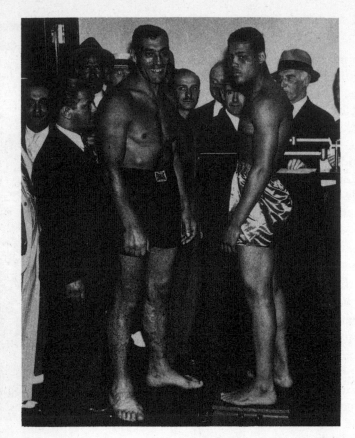

LEFT: *Joe Louis (right) weighs in with the ill-fated Primo Carnera before their fight on June 25, 1935; Carnera would be pounded into defeat in the sixth round. Like track star Jesse Owens, singer Marian Anderson, and labor leader A. Philip Randolph, the "Brown Bomber" stood for black pride — thirty years before the term became fashionable.*

Thousands of African Americans answered Howard University's call to hear Marian Anderson sing at the Lincoln Memorial on Easter Sunday, 1939. But so did thousands of white Americans, for as Interior Secretary Harold Ickes said in introducing her to the integrated crowd of 75,000 who filled the expanse between the Memorial and the reflecting pool in that great symbolic moment, ABOVE, hers was a voice that "lifts any individual above his fellows and is a matter of exultant pride to any race." As for Miss Anderson herself, pictured while singing, OPPOSITE, BOTTOM: "All I knew . . . as I stepped forward, was the overwhelming impact of that multitude. . . . I had a feeling that a great wave of good will poured out from these people, almost engulfing me. . . . It was a tremendous thing and my heart beat like mad . . . loud and strong and as if it wanted to say something."

labor. Tears streamed down the girl's dark face. Her hat was askew, but in her eyes flamed hope bordering on ecstacy. . . . If Marian Anderson could do it, the girl's eyes seemed to say, then I can, too.

■■■ *The New Deal Dismantled*

The Marian Anderson concert at the Lincoln Memorial was one of the few grace notes for the Roosevelt administration in that spring of 1939. Still carrying on its independent ways, in February the House had voted 344 to 35 to renew the Dies committee, calling it now the House Un-American Activities Committee (HUAC) and giving it a healthy appropriation of $100,000 to finance its operations. All of this was done over the spirited opposition of the New Dealers, led by Harold Ickes, who despised the committee as fervently as anyone in Washington. Roosevelt said very little about the defeat, but it must have rankled him almost as much as it did Ickes, who snarled that Congress had "surrendered to the blatant and demagogic Dies."

Congress then took on the administration's own programs. Almost precisely a year after it had given the administration $3.75 billion to prime the pump in 1938, it passed a new Relief Act that not only cut the president's comparatively modest relief appropriations request by $150 million, but, thanks to the efforts of J. Parnell Thomas and his allies, effectively killed the Federal Theater and Federal Art projects by giving them no money at all — and further stipulated that all WPA workers who had been on the federal payroll for eighteen consecutive months had to be fired. In July and August, 1939, 775,000 WPA workers were let go. What was more, late in March Congress once again refused to pass Roosevelt's reorganization bill as presented, cutting out most of the powers that he had requested and leaving him with a skeleton.

The institutional structure of the New Deal was rapidly crumbling, and rather than attempt to fight the inevitable, Roosevelt even helped with the dismantlement. Among his first acts under the limited powers granted him by the reorganization act was to take the Public Works Administration out of the Department of the Interior, restructure it as the Federal Works Administration, cut its funding to the bone, and begin the process of phasing it out.

The largest, and, arguably, the most far-reaching of all the New Deal's programs would be reduced to a bureaucratic shell in a matter of months. On June 26, 1939, departing PWA director Harold L. Ickes was given a plaque by his employees. While expressing appreciation to a single public servant, the language of the plaque also stands as a kind of eulogy for much else that was passing now, a tribute to all the hope and youthful energy that the early New Dealers had brought to Washington more than six years before. Their accomplishments may have fallen far short of their visions, but for all the splendid drones of the New Deal, the plaque seemed to say, there had been a nobility in the dreaming and a purity in the attempt that would enrich their memories forever:

> You drew the thousands of us from all walks of life, from all corners of the country, and you have welded us into a vital organization of which we are all proud. You have shown neither fear nor favor; you have neither asked nor tolerated any bending of the knee or any concessions to undue influence; and you have asked of us only one thing: that our job be well and truly done for the good of the Nation.

An era that had discovered hope in the wreckage of depression was passing away now, and another taking its place, one that would be influenced less by the domestic winds of economic trouble than by the even more terrifying uncertainties of a world that seemed hell-bent on destruction.

Waiting for the Fire

A CENTUR

1833

COM

CHI

WOR

CHAPTER TWELVE

Remember back when we had only
the depression on our minds, and
thought we were in trouble? Today
the sunshine has turned dark and
the grass sickly. The birds sing
and you think of poison gas
because they use canaries to detect
it. Nobody can plan his life a
year or six months ahead. One
hundred and thirty-five million
Americans going about their
business with a slight, steady
feeling of nausea all day long.

Bruce Bliven, editorial in
The New Republic,
August 26, 1940

Overleaf:

In 1933, the city of Chicago celebrated its centennial. But there was more to it than that, if one believed the sentiments of the fair's official guide book. "A Century of Progress," it said bravely, "intends to bring assurance that the steady march of progress has not . . . swerved aside, nor even been seriously retarded, that so-called 'recessions' are temporary, like the cloud that, for the moment, obscures the sun."

O
NE OF THE peculiarities of the years of the Great Depression was the fact that in the middle of the worst economic period Americans had ever seen, four cities somehow found the time, money, and energy to produce four world's fairs — more than during any other ten-year period in the nation's history. The first, Chicago's "Century of Progress" celebration, had opened for business on a four-hundred-acre landfill on the edge of Lake Michigan on April 29, 1933. The fair, its president, Rufus C. Dawes, said on opening day, was "the spontaneous expression of the pride of citizenship of Chicago" and, furthermore, demonstrated man's "power to prevail over the perils that beset him." Over the two years of the fair's life, thirty-eight million people came to witness its attractions, giving the city of Chicago a helpful shot of income for several months (though the fair itself lost money, as world's fairs tend to do).

Hoping to duplicate Chicago's economy-boosting success, on June 6, 1936, Texans had celebrated the hundredth anniversary of their independence from Mexico by producing the Texas Centennial Exposition in Dallas, and a smaller though related Frontier Centennial Exposition in Fort Worth. Before closing down in December, the combined expositions drew some seven million visitors, and if that appeared insignificant when compared to the Chicago fair, the celebration accomplished its principal task, according to Stanley Marcus, cofounder of the mercantile empire of Neiman-Marcus. "I've frequently said that modern Texas history started with the celebration of the Texas Centennial," he remembered, "because it was in 1936 . . . that the rest of America discovered Texas."

Then there were the two great fairs that marked the end of the decade — San Francisco's Golden Gate Exposition, which opened on February 18, 1939, and the New York World's Fair, which opened on April 30, 1939; both would run until the fall of 1940. Neither brought in anywhere near the number of people Chicago's fair had in 1933, but each stood at the cusp between two historical epochs and consequently would shine forth more brilliantly in the national memory, both burdened and enhanced by their roles as symbols.

San Francisco's exposition was designed to celebrate the completion of the Oakland-San Francisco Bay Bridge and the Golden Gate Bridge across the entrance to San Francisco Bay, two of the certifiably triumphant engineering accomplishments of the age. The fair itself was distinguished particularly by the fact that it was erected on a four-hundred-acre landfill called Treasure Island, the largest man-made island in the world, and it featured a number of technological exhibits, like "Willie Vocalite," a

The Midway of Chicago's 1933 "Century of Progress" fair featured a twin ferris wheel. Even more thrilling was the Skyride, one of whose 628-foot towers looms in the background of the view.

The completion of the Golden Gate Bridge in 1939 occasioned tremendous celebration in San Francisco. It began in February, with a seven-day "Golden Gate Bridge Fiesta," during which local realtors devised a flag that boasted of sunshine in San Francisco 66 percent of the time. Then came the Golden Gate International Exposition on Treasure Island, and then opening day of the great bridge itself on May 27, 1939, when more than 250,000 people walked across the Golden Gate Bridge from the Marin County headlands to San Francisco, a moment captured in the photograph OPPOSITE. The moment was further commemorated in poetry by its builder, Joseph Strauss: "High overhead its lights shall gleam;/Far, far below, life's restless stream/Unceasingly shall flow;/For this was spun its lithe fine form,/To fear not war, nor time, nor storm,/For Fate had meant it so."

All of the great fairs of the thirties were conceived as brave challenges: in spite of the worst that fate and circumstance might do, their promoters wanted the world to know, humankind would somehow triumph. None celebrated this audacity more self-consciously than the New York World's Fair of 1939–40. It was called "The World of Tomorrow," and one of the fair's designers said that its purpose was to "make it say to each visitor: 'No superman is going to build the world of tomorrow for you. You must build it yourself." A less fervent commentator said the fair "was the paradox of all paradoxes. It was good, it was bad; it was the acme of all crazy vulgarity, it was the pinnacle of all inspiration." ABOVE: The fair's thematic structures, the Perisphere and the Trylon, rise in the distance; TOP, the enormous National Cash Register exhibit, which rang up each day's attendance. The fair lost money, as most do, but it had never been about money; it had been about hope.

Westinghouse robot, and "Pedro the Vodor," a keyboard-operated talking machine invented by the Bell Telephone Laboratories. Another well-publicized distinction of the fair was the presence of nude fan dancer Sally Rand, who had debuted at the Chicago Fair; her show had now expanded to include a "nude ranch" populated by forty-seven cowgirls who pitched horseshoes, rode burros, and did other ranchlike activities dressed mainly in ten-gallon hats, cowboy boots, and G-strings.

The inspiration for the New York World's Fair, built on a twelve-hundred-acre Long Island refuse site called the Corona Dump five miles from downtown Manhattan, was the inauguration of President George Washington 150 years before, which the fair's leaders chose to identify as the true moment when the United States of America opened for business. The theme of the fair was "The World of Tomorrow," and it featured the definitive futuristic symbols of the age, a 750-foot-high spike called the Trylon and by its side an enormous globe called the Perisphere, two hundred feet in diameter (devotees of the Golden Gate Exposition, it was said, criticized these symbols as being faintly suggestive). The fair was crawling with its own forward-looking exhibits — a robot named Elektro, a simulated trip to the moon, and the first public demonstration of television, among others — but the most ambitious was "Futurama," a $7.5 million exhibit funded by General Motors and designed by Norman Bel Geddes. With 500,000 miniature buildings, a million little trees, and 50,000 tiny automobiles that ran like beetles over complex highway networks, the huge exhibit pictured what Bel Geddes thought America would be like in the year 1960.

If the great industrial designer's vision of the future was not entirely reliable (he predicted that his teardrop-shaped automobiles would cost only $200, for one thing), it was no more flawed than the vision of the current world that both the Golden Gate Exposition and the New York World's Fair presented. The ornate mix of Mayan, Cambodian, Burmese, Malayan, and Polynesian architectural styles that characterized most of the buildings on San Francisco's Treasure Island, for example, was called "Pacific Basin," and the fair's busy publicity machine repeatedly emphasized the wonderful unity of prosperity and cooperation that the peoples of the Pacific Rim nations enjoyed and presumably would continue to enjoy. For its part, the New York fair's own publicity people touted the beauty and hope represented by its Lagoon of Nations, its Hall of Nations, and its Court of Peace bordered by the flags of the fifty-eight foreign countries that had chosen to participate in the fair, twenty-one of which had erected their own buildings or pavilions, including Italy, the USSR, France, Great Britain, Japan, and Belgium. So had the League of Nations, that engine of universal peace that had been established (without the participation of the United States) after the first World War.

But not Nazi Germany, which had snubbed this entire brave celebration of world unity and the dream of peace — and therein could be read the true outlines of the future. "The day of world's fairs was over before we started," Leland Cutler, president of the Golden Gate Exposition, said of himself and Grover Whalen, president of the New York World's Fair, "and neither of us knew it." Adolf Hitler had no interest in the protocols of peace; neither did Benito Mussolini, even if he had authorized a building for the fair, and totalitarian dreams of conquest would soon disintegrate the fragile vision of world serenity. On March 15, 1939, German troops marched into Moravia and Bohemia, all that remained of dismembered Czechoslovakia, and occupied them with no resistance. On April 7, Italian troops crossed the Adriatic Sea and invaded Albania. On April 14, Roosevelt wired Hitler and Mussolini, asking if they would guarantee ten years of peace if he offered them the chance to talk about trade and armaments agreements; both ignored him. To further complicate the situation, on August 24 Germany and the Soviet Union announced that they had signed a non-aggression pact, throwing spectacular confusion and dismay into the ranks of the Communist Party/USA. Some diehard ideologues attempted to rationalize Stalin's move, but many more felt plainly betrayed. Malcolm Cowley spoke for a generation of idealistic young men and women when he remembered what the Soviet Union had seemed to be, but clearly was no more:

> All through the 1930s the Soviet Union was a second fatherland for millions of people in other countries, including our own. It was the land where men and women were sacrificing themselves to create a new civilization, not for Russia alone but for the world. It was not so much a nation, in the eyes of Western radicals, as it was an ideal, a faith and an international hope of salvation.

But there would be no salvation now. On September 1, Hitler issued an official declaration: "The Polish State has refused the peaceful settlement of relations which I desired. . . . Germans in Poland are persecuted with bloody terror and driven from their houses. A series of violations of the frontier, intolerable to a great Power, prove that Poland is no longer willing to respect the frontier of the Reich." None of it was true, but it did not matter. "In order to put an end to this lunacy," Hitler continued, "I have no other choice than to meet force with force from now on." At 5:45 A.M. the same day, German troops were ordered to cross over into Poland and German planes were sent to bomb airfields, villages, and cities all the way to Warsaw. Britain and France had earlier signed a pact to defend the sovereignty of Poland if she were invaded. The two nations now prepared to honor that obligation. On September 3, Joseph Kennedy, American ambassador to Great Britain, called from London, waking the president at 4:00 A.M. to tell him that Prime Minister Neville Chamberlain was about to end peace in his time with a war message to Parliament. "It's the end of the world," Kennedy cried, "the end of everything."

And so it must have seemed. After the German invasion of Poland, the swiftly conquered country was summarily partitioned between Hitler and his ally, Stalin. By the summer of 1940, Germany had invaded and occupied Denmark, Norway, Luxembourg, and Belgium, while the Soviet Union had attacked, defeated, and annexed Finland. British troops were driven to the sea at Dunkirk on the coast of northern France and only after herculean efforts were the troops evacuated before advancing German armies could annihilate them and end the war at that moment. France fell to Germany in June, leaving Great Britain as the only major power opposing Hitler's ambitions — and the little island nation was under terrible pressure. German planes began to bomb London on a regular basis at the end of the summer, and Americans soon grew accustomed to hearing the gravelly voice of Edward R. Murrow on CBS News telling them "This . . . is London," then describing what it was he was seeing, day after day, night after night, in broadcasts like this one on September 7:

> There are no words to describe the thing that is happening. . . . A row of automobiles, with stretchers racked on the roofs like skis, standing outside of bombed buildings. A man pinned under wreckage where a broken gas main sears his arms and face . . . the courage of the people; the flash and roar of the guns rolling down streets . . . the stench of air-raid shelters in the poor districts.

If it was not quite the end of everything, as Ambassador Kennedy had cried, it undeniably was the end of a world in which millions of Americans had their origins, the source of traditions that still flourished in the urban pockets where Polish-American, Irish-American, German-American, Italian-American, and other hyphenated Americans struggled for assimilation — or if not assimilation, at least acceptance. Many shared Kennedy's anguish, for in a New World in which most still had not managed to beat down the walls of prejudice and class distinctions, the Old World that had given them pride of identity now was flaming into history.

While the bombs fell on London, both of the great world's fairs in the United States finally closed. For nearly two years, each had spoken of the possibilities of tomorrow, their towers and pylons rising to the sky like hope itself, their exhibits celebrating industrial genius and technological prowess, giving millions their first glimpses of television, robotics, communications wizardry of the future. Now their closing was enveloped in the heavy sadness of finality. "The fair had been a sedative, of course," Richard Reinhardt remembered of the last moments of the Golden Gate Exposition,

> a tranquilizer for a frightened generation; we had understood this and accepted it with gratitude. We welcomed our brief oblivion and clung to our illusive innocence as long as the spell would last. In a world consumed by rage, there would be no further respites, no more innocent islands.

■■■ The Blowing of an Evil Wind

As the decade of the thirties ground to an end, then, it was not merely domestic concerns that were writing finish to the institutions of the New Deal — and to the Great Depression itself, an international economic crisis being alleviated now not by any conscious effort or specific government programs, but by the inexorable demands of war. In this country, there was less and less discussion in Congress about reform measures, relief appropriations, and public works, and much more consideration of how much to appropriate for the national defense. At Roosevelt's urging, $3.3 billion in defense spending was authorized in June, 1940, and another $8.8 billion in July; the total of more than $12 billion was four times as much money for defense as the government had ever turned loose for relief and public works projects in any preceding year.

Out of this largesse, the president called for the construction of fifty thousand warplanes, and Douglas and Lockheed in Southern California, Boeing in Seattle, Curtis-Wright in Buffalo, and other aircraft companies geared up for construction. So did the Packard Motor Car Company, which contracted with the government to build nine thousand Rolls-Royce Merlin aircraft engines a year, and the Ford Motor Company, which contracted to build four thousand Pratt & Whitney engines. Chrysler, meanwhile, began to spend $33.5 million in the production of a thousand medium tanks, while General Motors, Savage Arms, and Colt prepared space and machinery for the production of more than a hundred thousand machine guns a year. More than $2.75 billion was earmarked for the construction of a two-ocean navy of 257 ships, including 27 aircraft carriers, and shipyards from Seattle, Washington, to Newport News, Virginia, already nearing capacity, began making big plans for the expansion of facilities.

In the spring of 1940, the armed forces of this country — Army, Navy, and Marines combined — came to less than 350,000. Germany, on the other hand, had more than two million men under arms in Western Europe alone, and in an effort to bring American forces up to fighting strength, should it become necessary, on September 16, 1940, Roosevelt signed the Selective Training and Service Act, requiring men between the ages of twenty-one and thirty-five to register for military training (many young men would be rejected on the grounds of malnutrition — one sign that the work of the New Deal had not been as effective as many had believed and most had hoped). Ten days later, he announced an embargo on the shipment of scrap steel from any country in the Western Hemisphere to any country but Great Britain. This was in line with his increasingly open support of England, and polls indicated that the action was generally approved by the bulk of the American people — though not the isolationists in and out of Congress, who insisted that he was leading the country directly into the cauldron of war.

There certainly was no gainsaying Roosevelt's leanings. Two days after the outbreak of war on September 3, 1939, he had declared that the United States was a "neutral nation" in the conflict, but as early as June 3, 1940, he authorized the sale of millions of dollars worth of old war materiel, including armament and airplanes, to Great Britain, and on June 10 revised the "neutrality" pledge made in September, 1939, by announcing that the United States would henceforth operate on a condition of "nonbelligerency" — which would allow it to support the allies without actually going to war. Finally, on September 3, 1940, he agreed to give Great Britain fifty old American destroyers in exchange for the right to build American bases on various British possessions in the Western Hemisphere.

In June, 1940, Roosevelt appointed two Republicans to his cabinet — Frank Knox as secretary of the navy and Henry L. Stimson as secretary of war (Stimson had served in the same capacity for President William Howard Taft, and as secretary of state for President Herbert Hoover). These appointments were made, on the one hand, to demonstrate to Germany, Italy, and the USSR the unity of the American determination to fight if necessary, and, on the other hand, to broaden the president's own political strength when he decided to do something no other American president had ever done — seek a third term.

Roosevelt was hardly an unambitious man, but eight years of an American presidency, even in an age that moved much more slowly than our own, was an exhausting experience for anyone. "I have to have a rest," Roosevelt told Dan Tobin of the Teamsters Union at one point in 1939, saying that he was going to retire to Hyde Park at the end of his second term. "I want to have a rest." There is no reason to doubt his sincerity at the time, but by the summer of 1940 the situation in Europe

WILL ONE OF THESE
Bundles FROM Britain
BE YOUR SON?

WILL YOUR BOY BE THE NEXT UNKNOWN SOLDIER?

In early August, 1940, the Senate began debating the Selective
Service bill, while placards, OPPOSITE, TOP, were distributed
by the thousands. During debate over the draft bill, a gathering
of mothers with draft-age sons — they called themselves the
Death Watch — sat in the Senate gallery, day after day
ABOVE. Down on the floor of the Senate, debate was heated
and equally straightforward, especially when Burton K. Wheeler
of Montana got up to speak. "If you pass this bill," the old
Progressive thundered, "you slit the throat of the last
democracy still living — you give to Hitler his greatest and
cheapest victory." But the bill was passed, and October 16,
1940, was designated National Registration Day. More than
16.5 million men registered at 5,500 local stations. On October
29, the drawing of the first numbers began in Washington, D.C.
OPPOSITE, BOTTOM: FDR looks on as Secretary of War
Henry Stimson is blindfolded before reaching into the "goldfish
bowl" to pluck out the first blue capsule containing someone's
number. The number, read off by President Roosevelt, was 158.
"That's my son!" a woman in the audience shouted.

had disintegrated into such savage hopelessness that the danger to the future of democratic institutions in the whole Western World could not be denied. "All bad, all bad," he was heard to mutter while looking over each day's dispatches from various foreign fronts. Against this threat, he apparently believed, no member of his own party had emerged whose stature and experience were sufficient to protect the country, and he was not going to leave the nation in the hands of Republicans — not at that or any other time, if he could help it.

After keeping even those closest to him in the dark for months about his intentions, Roosevelt finally let his decision be known to enough of his political intimates in time for them to engineer a nomination by acclamation during the Democratic National Convention in the middle of July. Since Vice President Garner had gone after the nomination himself after making his objections to a third term known to one and all, Roosevelt chose as his running mate Secretary of Agriculture Henry Wallace — though not without much stronger opposition than that which had greeted his own nomination. To many, Wallace was the epitome of everything fuzzy-headed and illogical about the New Deal, and at one point during the convention, Governor E. D. Rivers of Georgia had asked Governor Leon C. Phillips of Oklahoma what he thought of the Wallace candidacy. "Why, he's my second choice," Phillips replied.

"Who's your first choice?" Rivers asked.

"Any son-of-a-bitch — red, black, white or yellow — who can get the nomination."

The Republicans nominated Wendell Willkie, the president of Commonwealth & Southern, who had fought with the New Dealers so persistently during the previous six years over the question of private versus public power in the Tennessee River Valley. Roosevelt and Willkie each admired the other as an individual, but the campaign was colored throughout by the shadow of war. Willkie was a staunch noninterventionist, and his campaign was built firmly around his promise to keep America out of the European conflict and his frequently voiced conviction that Roosevelt was headed straight toward war and would bring the country into it if elected.

Willkie was supported not only by the standard set of Republicans, but by the isolationist wing in Congress, as well as the America First Committee, an organization of anti-interventionists founded by a group of college students — including Gerald R. Ford, a future president of the United States — in July. General Robert E. Wood, chairman of the board of Sears, Roebuck, became the group's leader, while William H. Regnery, a Chicago textile manufacturer, furnished seed money. The committee got a major boost on September 5, when none other than Hugh Johnson, the former NRA head, gave it a resounding endorsement during his weekly radio broadcast, and it would grow to become a major irritant to Roosevelt's foreign policy, particularly during 1941, when such isolationist luminaries as Senator Burton K. Wheeler and Charles Lindbergh gave it weight and respectability.

If Roosevelt had to deal with the opposition of the isolationists and their friends, Willkie had to deal with the support of Father Charles Cough-lin and the Christian Front. When Willkie was nominated, Coughlin had praised his selection in *Social Justice*. Willkie was horrified and imme-diately issued a rejection. "I am not interested," he said, "in the support of anybody who stands for any form of prejudice as to anybody's race or religion. . . . If I understand what [Coughlin's] beliefs are, I am not only not interested in his support — I don't want it." He was a good deal happier to have the support of John L. Lewis of the CIO. Lewis and Roosevelt had fallen out over various questions of labor policy, and Lewis was convinced that the president's bid for a third term was merely a "personal craving for power," an odious ambition, he said, that was "a thing to alarm and dis-may. . . . America needs no superman." Furthermore, the labor leader believed that Roosevelt was lying when he promised repeatedly to keep America out of war. "You who may be about to die in a foreign war," he asked those young men who might be thinking of voting for FDR, "created at the whim of an international meddler, should you salute your Caesar?"

It was a long, noisy, sometimes nasty campaign, and for all his con-tinued popularity with the people, Roosevelt was by no means assured of victory. Willkie was a good campaigner and anti-interventionist sentiment around the country was very strong. Roosevelt did win in November, but when the election returns were fully analyzed, it was clear that while the president's margin of victory in the overall popular vote was still large — 55 percent to 45 percent — his margins in many individual states were so thin as to have threatened his electoral college majority of 449 to 82. As one historian has pointed out, if the Roosevelt majority of the popular vote had been cut by just 3.7 percent in every state, it would have given him only 225 electoral votes, while Willkie would have won 306 — more than enough for victory.

Narrow thing or not, Roosevelt proceeded over the next several months to act as if he had been given a mandate as overwhelming as that which the people had given him in 1936 — at least so far as war preparedness was concerned. He truly did not want war, it seems clear, but as time went on his actions demonstrated a growing conviction that the nation probably was not going to be able to avoid it, no matter how hard it might try. During his State of the Union Address on January 6, 1941, he said that only

As a selection of campaign buttons illustrates, the presidential election of 1940, when Roosevelt challenged not only his Republican opponent, Wendell Willkie, but tradition itself, was one of the liveliest in American history. It also was one of the ugliest. Willkie had so many things thrown at him during the campaign — including an office chair, a steel wastebasket, stones, and eggs — historian Geoffrey Perrett notes, that "the New York Times ran a daily box score of objects thrown and hits registered." Willkie's hopes survived the sticks and stones, but not the election; in the closest presidential race since 1916, Roosevelt won his third term. The voters, Fiorello La Guardia said, had decided they preferred "Roosevelt with his known faults to Willkie with his unknown virtues."

On September 11, a few days after a German U-boat had fired torpedoes at the USS Greer while the American destroyer was on a mail run to Iceland, the President — wearing a mourning band because his mother had died on September 7 — went on the radio for a Fireside Chat. He announced that he had ordered all U. S. Navy planes and ships to "shoot on sight" any Axis ships found violating the "sea frontier" of the United States. "When you see a rattlesnake poised to strike," he told his audience, "you do not wait until he has struck you before you crush him. . . . From now on if German or Italian war vessels enter the waters, the protection of which is necessary for American defense, they do so at their own peril."

At the end of 1940, personal income was $81.1 billion, more than $7 billion higher than any other year in the decade — and by the end of another year income would soar to $104.2 billion. The Great Depression, as an economic fact, was ended by unprecedented government spending, including billions for the vessels like the USS Atlanta, a light cruiser which slipped down the ways on September 6, 1941 — just three months before Pearl Harbor.

through the elimination of dictatorships could the "Four Freedoms" ever be won — "The first is freedom of speech and expression — everywhere in the world," he said. "The second is freedom of every person to worship God in his own way — everywhere in the world. The third is freedom from want — everywhere in the world. The fourth is freedom from fear — everywhere in the world." Two days later, he submitted his annual budget for fiscal year 1941; it called for $10.8 billion in defense appropriations and passed with little trouble. On January 10, "Lend-Lease" legislation was introduced in both the House and the Senate. The bills would give the president virtually unlimited power to supply Britain with whatever she needed to conduct the war. In spite of a bitter fight by anti-interventionists, both bills passed and were combined into a single piece of legislation that Roosevelt signed on March 12. He immediately asked for $7 billion to finance it, and Congress gave it to him.

"Dollar-a-year men" — volunteers from the world of business and industry — flocked into Washington to direct and staff a whole new set of bureaucracies designed to get the American economy and industrial matrix on a defense footing — the National Defense Advisory Commission, the Office of Production Management, the Office of Petroleum Coordination, the Office of Civilian Defense, the Office of Price Administration and Civilian Supplies, and many others, mutants and replacements of all the alphabet agencies that had given the New Deal years their institutional flavor. By the middle of 1941, the prewar economy had enhanced the financial landscape as nothing had in nearly two decades. Employment was up by more than two million jobs over the levels of 1939 and thousands of new jobs were created every day; millions of people were better off than they had been in more than ten years, even better than they had been during the boom of the twenties; manufacturing productivity blossomed, retail sales increased by more than 16 percent (automobile purchases alone rose by 40 percent); boom times were visible everywhere, from eastern seaboard ports where shipyards operated three shifts a day, to interior villages where brand-new Army bases provided tens of thousands of construction jobs and, once the bases were finished, entirely new populations of government workers who also had to be housed. Through it all flowed a rich stream of payroll spending in shops, bars, movie houses, and other business establishments.

But if there was great relief in the final dying of the Great Depression, there was little joy. The isolationists might continue to insist that America could hide behind her oceans, but to all but the most stubbornly blind it was becoming increasingly clear that if one era of national crisis was ending, another was looming quite literally over the horizon. Anyone who did not believe this could not have been listening carefully enough when President Roosevelt issued a proclamation on May 27, 1941, that should have left no doubt: "Now, therefore, I, Franklin D. Roosevelt, President of the United States of America, do proclaim that an unlimited national emergency confronts this country, which requires that its military, naval, air and civilian defenses be put on the basis of readiness to repel any and all acts or threats of aggression directed toward any part of the Western hemisphere." Newsman and radio commentator Raymond Clapper was listening, and on his own broadcast that night said good-bye to the world that had been and asked Americans to turn now to an uncertain future:

> Like lovers about to be separated by a long journey, we sit in this hour of mellow twilight, thinking fondly of the past, wondering. . . . We have had poverty, but also the hope that if the individual man threw in enough struggle and labor he could find his place. . . . In every one of us lived the promise of America. Now we see the distant fire rolling toward us. . . . It is still some distance away, but the evil wind blows it toward us.

A little over six months later, Japanese planes swept in over the unprotected Pacific Fleet stationed at Pearl Harbor in the Hawaiian Islands and bombed most of it into uselessness — and in that single act of violence provided a symbolic punctuation mark to end with absolute finality the era of the Great Depression. The people of this nation had survived one terrible passage and were now about to begin another. They came to the challenge well armed. The "new world" of which Sherwood Anderson dreamed in 1932 had come to pass. Agonies of personal financial devastation and the social, political, and economic programs of the New Deal had combined to produce a world in which the great hope of true democracy had lurched a little closer to reality; in which women, people of color, people of no previous standing in the pantheon of progress, had acquired some measure of power; in which labor had been raised up to challenge capital more effectively than ever before; and in which government and the people to be governed were newly bound in an intimacy that would never be diminished. This new world would soon be tested by war and would prove itself not merely durable, but enduring. In the end, the world of the Great Depression, molded by fear, uncertainty, determination, and a wondrous bravery, gave us the world of our own present hope — and if we shape our world half as well as did the men and women of the 1930s, we will have gone a long way toward honoring our own obligation to the future.

FURTHER READING

I t is entirely possible that no single decade in American history has been more thoroughly documented than that of the thirties. Like the era of the Civil War, which continues to fascinate us, the period of the Great Depression is a watershed in the story of this country, and even as I write the data banks of personal computers all over the nation are swiftly being filled with millions of bytes of additional information, interpretation, and analysis that will further enhance (or confuse) our understanding of the time.

The reading list that follows, then, cannot be taken for even a halfhearted attempt to be comprehensive, or even to include all of the sources consulted in the writing of *The Great Depression*. What it does attempt to do, however, is present a suitably representative mix of the indispensable histories of the past and the newest and most interesting scholarship of recent years — and to organize these sources into some sort of useful format.

— T. H. W.

General Histories of the Period

Allen, Frederick Lewis. *Since Yesterday: The Nineteen-Thirties in America, September 3, 1929–September 3, 1939*. New York: Harper & Row, 1940.

Ellis, Edward Robb. *A Nation in Torment: The Great American Depression, 1929–1939*. New York: Capricorn Books, 1971.

Furnas, J. C. *Stormy Weather: Crosslights on the Nineteen Thirties: An In-formal History of the United States, 1929–1941*. New York: G. P. Putnam's Sons, 1977.

Leighton, Isabel, ed. *The Asprin Age: 1919–1941*. New York: Simon & Schuster, 1949.

McElvaine, Robert S. *The Great Depression: America 1929–1941*. New York: Times Books, 1984.

Marquis, Alice G. *Hopes and Ashes: The Birth of Modern Times, 1929–1939*. New York: Free Press, 1986.

Parrish, Michael E. *Anxious Decades:*

America in Prosperity and Depression, 1920–1941. New York: W. W. Norton, 1992.

Peeler, David P. *Hope Among Us Yet: Social Criticism and Social Solace in Depression America.* Chicago: University of Chicago Press, 1987.

Pells, Richard H. *Radical Visions and American Dreams: Culture and Social Thought in the Depression Years.* New York: Harper & Row, 1973.

Phillips, Cabell. *From the Crash to the Blitz, 1929–1939.* New York: Macmillan, 1969.

Smith, Page. *Redeeming the Time: A People's History of the 1920s and the New Deal.* New York: McGraw-Hill, 1987.

Wecter, Dixon. *The Age of the Great Depression, 1929–1941.* Chicago: Quadrangle, 1971.

Wilson, Edmund. *The American Earthquake: A Documentary of the Twenties and Thirties.* Garden City: Doubleday, 1958.

The Crash of 1929 and Its Aftermath

Bird, Caroline. *The Invisible Scar.* New York: David McKay, 1966.

Brooks, John. *Once in Golconda: A True Drama of Wall Street, 1920–1938.* New York: Harper & Row, 1969.

Friedman, Milton, and Anna Jacobson Schwartz. *The Great Contraction, 1929–1933.* Princeton: Princeton University Press, 1965.

Galbraith, John Kenneth. *The Great Crash, 1929.* Boston: Houghton-Mifflin, 1955.

Garraty, John A. *The Great Depression: An Inquiry into the Causes, Course, and Consequence of the Worldwide Depression of the Nineteen-Thirties, as Seen by Contemporaries and in the Light of History.* New York: Harcourt Brace Jovanovich, 1986.

Klingaman, William K. *1929: The Year of the Great Crash.* New York: Harper & Row, 1989.

Leuchtenberg, William E. *The Perils of Prosperity, 1914–1932.* Chicago: University of Chicago Press, 1958.

Lisio, Donald J. *The President and Protest: Hoover, Conspiracy, and the Bonus Riot.* Columbia: University of Missouri Press, 1974.

McElvaine, Robert S., ed. *Down and Out in the Great Depression: Letters from the "Forgotten Man."* Chapel Hill: University of North Carolina Press, 1983.

Meltzer, Milton. *Brother, Can You Spare a Dime? The Great Depression, 1929–1933.* New York: New American Library, 1977.

Schlesinger, Arthur A. *The Age of Roosevelt: The Crisis of the Old Order, 1919–1933.* Boston: Houghton-Mifflin, 1957.

Smith, Gene. *The Shattered Dream: Herbert Hoover and the Great Depression.* New York: William Morrow, 1970.

Sternsher, Bernard. *Hitting Home: The Great Depression in Town and Country.* Chicago: Ivan R. Dee, 1989.

Terkel, Studs. *Hard Times: An Oral History of the Great Depression.* New York: Random House, 1970.

Thomas, Gordon, and Max Morgan-Witts. *The Day the Bubble Burst: A Social History of the Wall Street Crash of 1929.* Garden City: Doubleday, 1979.

Woodruff, Nan Elizabeth. *As Rare as Rain: Federal Relief in the Great*

Southern Drought of 1930–31.
Urbana: University of Illinois Press,
1985.

*Franklin Roosevelt and the New
Dealers*

Davis, Kenneth S. *FDR: The New York
Years, 1928–1933.* New York: Ran-
dom House, 1985.
———. *FDR: The New Deal Years,
1933–1937.* New York: Random
House, 1986.
———. *FDR: Into the Storm, 1937–
1940.* New York, Random House,
1993.
Degler, Carl. *The New Deal.* Chicago:
Quadrangle, 1970.
Freidel, Frank. *Franklin D. Roosevelt:
Launching the New Deal.* Boston:
Little, Brown, 1973.
Huthmacher, J. Joseph. *Senator Robert
F. Wagner and the Rise of Urban
Liberalism.* New York: Atheneum,
1968.
Ickes, Harold L. *The Secret Diary of
Harold L. Ickes: The First Thousand
Days, 1933–1936; The Inside
Struggle, 1936–1939; The Lowering
Clouds, 1939–1941.* Three volumes.
New York: Simon & Schuster, 1952–
1954.
Lacy, Leslie Alexander. *The Soil Sol-
diers: The Civilian Conservation Corps
in the Great Depression.* Radnor, Pa.:
Chilton, 1976.
Lash, Joseph P. *Dealers and Dreamers:
A New Look at the New Deal.* New
York: Doubleday, 1988.
———. *Eleanor and Franklin: The
Story of their Relationship, Based on
Eleanor Roosevelt's Personal Papers.*
New York: W. W. Norton, 1971.

Leuchtenberg, William E. *Franklin D.
Roosevelt and the New Deal: 1932–
1940.* New York: Harper & Row,
1963.
Loucheim, Katie, ed. *The Making of the
New Deal: The Insiders Speak.* Cam-
bridge: Harvard University Press,
1983.
McJimsey, George. *Harry Hopkins: Ally
of the Poor and Defender of Democ-
racy.* Cambridge: Harvard University
Press, 1987.
Mangione, Jerre. *The Dream and the
Deal: The Federal Writers Project,
1935–1943.* Philadelphia: University
of Pennsylvania Press, 1983.
Martin, George. *Madame Secretary:
Frances Perkins.* Boston: Houghton-
Mifflin, 1976.
Nixon, Edgar B., ed. *Franklin D. Roo-
sevelt and Conservation, 1911–1945.*
Two volumes. Hyde Park: General
Services Administration, National
Archives and Records Service, FDR
Memorial Library, 1957.
Roosevelt, Eleanor. *This I Remember.*
New York: Harper & Brothers, 1949.
Schlesinger, Arthur M., Jr. *The Age of
Roosevelt: The Coming of the New
Deal.* Boston: Houghton-Mifflin,
1958.
———. *The Age of Roosevelt: The Poli-
tics of Upheaval.* Boston: Houghton-
Mifflin, 1959.
Schwartz, Bonnie Fox. *The Civil Works
Administration, 1933–1934: The
Business of Emergency Employment
in the New Deal.* Princeton: Prince-
ton University Press, 1984.
Sherwood, Robert E. *Roosevelt and Hop-
kins: An Intimate History.* New York:
Harper & Brothers, 1948.
Sternsher, Bernard. *Rexford Tugwell and*

the New Deal. New Brunswick: Rutgers University Press, 1964.

Watkins, T. H. *Righteous Pilgrim: The Life and Times of Harold L. Ickes, 1874–1952*. New York: Henry Holt, 1990.

Wolfskill, George, and John A. Hudson. *All But the People: Franklin D. Roosevelt and His Critics, 1933–1939*. New York: Macmillan, 1969.

Political Dissidents, Left and Right

Brinkley, Alan. *Voices of Protest: Huey Long, Father Coughlin, and the Great Depression*. New York: Alfred A. Knopf, 1982.

Chalmers, David M. *Hooded Americanism: The History of the Ku Klux Klan*. New York: New Viewpoints, 1976.

Cowley, Malcolm. *The Dream of the Golden Mountain: Remembering the 1930s*. New York: Viking, 1980.

Diggins, John Patrick. *The Rise and Fall of the American Left*. New York: W. W. Norton, 1992.

Goodman, Walter. *The Committee: The Extraordinary Career of the House Committee on Un-American Activities*. New York: Farrar, Straus & Giroux, 1968.

Gornick, Vivian. *The Romance of American Communism*. New York: Basic Books, 1977.

Haywood, Harry. *Black Bolshevik: Autobiography of an Afro-American Communist*. Chicago: Liberator Press, 1978.

Healey, Dorothy, and Maurice Isserman. *Dorothy Healey Remembers: A Life in the Communist Party*. New York: Oxford University Press, 1990.

Klehr, Harvey. *The Heyday of American Communism: The Depression Decade*. New York: Basic Books, 1984.

Meyers, Gustavus. *History of Bigotry in the United States*. New York: Random House, 1943.

Mitchell, Greg. *The Campaign of the Century: Upton Sinclair's Race for Governor of California and the Birth of Media Politics*. New York: Random House, 1992.

Painter, Nell Irvin. *The Narrative of Hosea Hudson: His Life as a Negro Communist in the South*. Cambridge: Harvard University Press, 1979.

Wade, Wyn Craig. *The Fiery Cross: The Ku Klux Klan in America*. New York: Simon & Schuster, 1987.

The Labor Movement and Its Leaders

Bernstein, Irving. *The Lean Years: A History of the American Worker, 1920–1933*. Boston: Houghton-Mifflin, 1960.

——— . *The Turbulent Years: A History of the American Worker, 1933–1941*. Boston: Houghton-Mifflin, 1970.

——— . *A Caring Society: The New Deal, the Worker, and the Great Depression*. Boston: Houghton-Mifflin, 1985.

Brooks, Thomas R. *Picket Lines and Bargaining Tables: Organized Labor Comes of Age, 1933–1945*. New York: Grossett and Dunlap, 1968.

Cohen, Lizabeth. *Making a New Deal: Industrial Workers in Chicago, 1919–1939*. Cambridge: Cambridge University Press, 1990.

Dubofsky, Melvin, and Warren Van Tyne. *John L. Lewis: A Biography*.

New York: Quadrangle Books/Times Books, 1977.

Fraser, Steven. *Labor Will Rule: Sidney Hillman and the Rise of American Labor*. New York: The Free Press, 1991.

Lynd, Robert S., and Helen Merrell, eds. *Rank and File: Personal Histories by Working-Class Organizers*. Princeton: Princeton University Press, 1973.

Nelson, Bruce. *Workers on the Waterfront: Seamen, Longshoremen, and Unionism in the 1930s*. Urbana: University of Illinois Press, 1988.

Reuther, Victor G. *The Brothers Reuther and the Story of the United Auto Workers: A Memoir*. Boston: Houghton-Mifflin, 1976.

Ruiz, Vicki L. *Cannery Women, Cannery Lives: Mexican Women, Unionization, and the California Food Processing Industry, 1930–1950*. Albuquerque: University of New Mexico Press, 1987.

Agricultural Discontent

Grubbs, Donald H. *Cry from the Cotton: The Southern Tenant Farmers Union and the New Deal*. Chapel Hill: University of North Carolina Press, 1971.

Kelly, Robin D. G. *Hammer and Hoe: Alabama Communists During the Great Depression*. Chapel Hill: University of North Carolina Press, 1990.

Miller, Marc S., ed. *Working Lives: The Southern Exposure History of Labor in the South*. New York: Pantheon, 1980.

Saloutos, Theodore, and John D. Hicks. *Agricultural Discontent in the Middle West, 1900–1939*. Madison: University of Wisconsin Press, 1951.

Shover, John L. *Cornbelt Rebellion: The Farmer's Holiday Association*. Urbana: University of Illinois Press, 1965.

The Dust Bowl and Migrant Labor

Daniel, Cletus E. *Bitter Harvest: A History of California Farm Workers, 1870–1941*. Berkeley: University of California Press, 1981.

Gregory, James N. *American Exodus: The Dust Bowl Migration and Okie Culture in California*. New York: Oxford University Press, 1989.

McWilliams, Carey. *Factories in the Field: The Story of Migratory Farm Labor in California*. Boston: Little, Brown, 1939.

Stein, Walter J. *California and the Dustbowl Migration*. Westport, Conn.: Greenwood Press, 1973.

Taylor, Paul S. *On the Ground in the Thirties*. Layton, Utah: Gibbs Smith, 1983.

Worster, Donald. *Dust Bowl: The Southern Plains in the 1930s*. New York: Oxford University Press, 1979.

Women's Issues

Chafe, William H. *The Paradox of Change: American Women in the Twentieth Century*. New York: Oxford University Press, 1991.

Dubofsky, Melvin, and Stephen Burnwood, eds. *Women and Minorities During the Great Depression*. New York: Garland, 1990.

Evans, Sara. *Born for Liberty: A History of Women in America*. New York: The Free Press, 1989.

Scharf, Lois. *To Work and to Wed: Female Employment, Feminism, and the Great Depression.* Westport, Conn.: Greenwood Press, 1980.

———. and Joan Jensen, eds. *Decades of Discontent: The Women's Movement, 1920–1940.* Westport, Conn.: Greenwood Press, 1983.

Ware, Susan. *Beyond Suffrage: Women and the New Deal.* Cambridge: Harvard University Press, 1981.

African Americans, Mexican Americans, and Other Minority Groups

Acuna, Rodolfo. *Occupied America: A History of Chicanos.* New York: Harper & Row, 1981.

Adamic, Louis. *From Many Lands.* New York: Harper & Brothers, 1940.

Aptheker, Herbert, ed. *A Documentary History of the Negro People in the United States. Vol. IV: From the New Deal to the End of World War II, 1933–1945.* New York: Citadel, 1990.

Garcia, Mario T. *Mexican-American Leadership, Ideology, and Identity, 1930–1960.* New Haven: Yale University Press, 1989.

Greenberg, Cheryl Lyn. *"Or Does it Explode?": Harlem in the Great Depression.* New York: Oxford University Press, 1991.

Harris, William H. *Keeping the Faith: A. Philip Randolph, Milton P. Webster, and the Brotherhood of Sleeping Car Porters, 1925–1937.* Urbana: University of Illinois Press, 1977.

Howe, Irving. *World of Our Fathers: The Journey of the East European Jews to America and the Life They Found and Made.* New York: Harcourt Brace Jovanovich, 1976.

Kirby, John B. *Black Americans in the Roosevelt Era: Liberalism and Race.* Knoxville: University of Tennessee Press, 1980.

Myrdal, Gunnar. *An American Dilemma: The Negro Problem and Modern Democracy.* Two volumes. New York: Harper & Brothers, 1944.

Reisler, Mark. *By the Sweat of Their Brow: Mexican Immigrant Labor in the United States, 1900–1940.* Westport, Conn.: Greenwood Press, 1976.

Romo, Ricardo. *East Los Angeles: History of a Barrio.* Austin: University of Texas Press, 1983.

Rosengarten, Theodore. *All God's Dangers: The Life of Nate Shaw.* New York: Alfred A. Knopf, 1974.

Popular Culture

Barnouw, Erik. *A History of Broadcasting in the United States. Vol. II: The Golden Web, 1933–1953.* New York: Oxford University Press, 1968.

Dooley, Roger. *From Scarface to Scarlett: American Films in the 1930s.* New York: Harcourt Brace Jovanovich, 1979.

Douglas, George H. *The Smart Magazines: 50 Years of Literary Revelry and High Jinks at Vanity Fair, New Yorker, Life, Esquire, and The Smart Set.* Hamden, Conn.: Shoestring Press, 1991.

Gabler, Neal. *An Empire of Their Own: How the Jews Invented Hollywood.* New York: Crown, 1988.

Lewis, Tom. *Empire of the Air: The Men Who Made Radio.* New York: HarperCollins, 1991.

Sterling, Christopher H., and John M.

Kittross. *Stay Tuned: A Concise History of American Broadcasting*. Belmont, Calif.: Wadsworth, 1990.

The Road to War

Adams, Henry H. *Years of Deadly Peril: The Coming of the War, 1939–1941*. New York: David McKay, 1969.

Dallek, Robert. *Franklin D. Roosevelt and American Foreign Policy, 1932–1945*. New York: Oxford University Press, 1979.

Fehrenbach, T. R. *FDR's Undeclared War, 1939 to 1941*. New York: David McKay, 1967.

Ketchum, Richard M. *The Borrowed Years, 1938–1941: America on the Way to War*. New York: Random House, 1989.

Lindbergh, Anne Morrow. *War Within and Without: Diaries of Anne Morrow Lindbergh, 1939–1944*. New York: Harcourt Brace Jovanovich, 1980.

Perrett, Geoffrey. *Days of Sadness, Years of Triumph: The American People, 1939–1945*. Madison: University of Wisconsin Press, 1973.

Acknowledgments

THE GREAT DEPRESSION has been a collaborative effort from the beginning. In recognition of that fact, I must thank, first of all, the team at Blackside, Inc., in Boston — especially Henry Hampton, both the leader and the heart of that extraordinary group of people; Terry Kay Rockefeller, whose enthusiasm has been contagious and supportive; project editor Robert Lavelle, whose guidance has been indispensable and whose patience is exemplary (ditto for William Phillips, the project's editor at Little, Brown); and Michele McKenzie and her crew of interns, whose diligent research enriched not only the pictorial element of this book, but the text as well. Thanks, too, to the team of scholars — with special thanks to Robert McElvaine — who scrutinized the manuscript to discover some of my more egregious errors of fact and interpretation (any that remain in spite of their efforts are the sole and exclusive property of the author).

My participation would not have been possible without the generous cooperation of Bruno Quinson, president, and Marian Wood, executive editor, at Henry Holt and Company, who kindly granted me temporary leave from the writing of *By Chaos Out of Dream: A Portrait of the Thirties in America* in order to produce *The Great Depression.* My colleagues at The Wilderness Society have been similarly generous — as always — in allowing me the time, energy, and support to follow the Lorelei of history where it leads me.

Carl Brandt, my agent, provided his customary sharp eye, gratifying enthusiasm, and sterling advice throughout the project.

It may seem a little unusual, but I would be remiss if I did not express special gratitude to a trio of Washington, D. C., bookmen whose diligence in the discovery of materials on the Great Depression for me has been far above and beyond the call of duty, or even profit, for more than five years: Alan Fuller of Fuller & Saunders, Philip Levy of Bridge Street Books, and Andy Moursund of the Georgetown Book Shop.

My wife, Joan, has enjoyed (or at least endured) an even closer working relationship with this book than she has had with previous ones of mine; she not only read the manuscript with her usual editorial skill, but spent weeks in the warrens and cubbyholes of the National Archives, the Library of Congress, and other sources, ferreting out thousands of candidate photographs for the book. With regard to both the text and the photographs, then, her own participation in this collaboration has been as essential to the book as it has been gratefully received by its author and her fortunate husband . . .

— T. H. WATKINS

PROJECT ACKNOWLEDGMENTS

The television series, "The Great Depression," to which this book serves as a companion, was produced by Blackside, Inc., in Boston, Massachusetts. Both book and film projects were made possible through the hard work and consistent support of numerous people. The key participants were:

Publishing Project

T. H. Watkins, Companion-volume Author
Robert Lavelle, Director
Michele McKenzie, Photo Researcher and Photo Editor
Leila Fergus, Editorial Assistant
Doe Coover, Literary Agent
Joan Watkins, Maren Stange, Picture Consultants
James Green, Gerald Gill, Robert McElvaine, Susan Ware, Reviewers

Additional research and support was provided by:
Melissane Parm, Aleta Alston, as well as Dr. George J. Sanchez at the UCLA Department of History (with the students of the 1992 Minority Summer Research Program) and Carolyn Kozo (Central Los Angeles Public Library "Shades of L.A." Collection). Publishing interns included Jill Landaur, Jeffrey Zielinski, Cindy Lobel, Rhea Dunn, Dream Nefra, and Jean Cummings

Film Project

Executive Producer: Henry Hampton
Series Senior Producer: Terry Kay Rockefeller
Series Supervising Producer: Stephen Stept
Series Producer: Orlando Bagwell

Series Writer: Steve Fayer

Producers: Lyn Goldfarb, Jon Else, Dante James, Stephen Stept, Susan Bellows

Associate Producers: Leslie Farrell, Lisa Jones, Susan Levene, Tracy Strain

Editors: Lillian Benson, Jon Neuburger, Eric Handley, Howard Sharp, Marian Hunter

Archivist: Katy Mostoller

Production Manager: Michael Dick

Production Assistants: Robin Espinola, Jaison Greene, Lulie Hadad, Andreeta Hamilton, Kirsten Jones, Michael Yudell

Post Production Supervisor: Alison Bassett

Marketing and Licensing: W. Michael Greene

Director of Development: Martha Fowlkes

Business Manager: Lorraine Flynn Kiley

Funders:

The Corporation for Public Broadcasting and Public Television Stations

National Endowment for the Humanities

John D. & Catherine T. MacArthur Foundation

Lotus Development Corporation

Geraldine R. Dodge Foundation

Boston Foundation

William H. Cosby, Jr., and Camille O. Cosby

Illustration Credits

TITLE PAGE

Library of Congress.

INTRODUCTION

Pages 2–3: Courtesy of Lament Harris.

CHAPTER ONE

Pages 20–21: National Archives; page 24 (both): Culver Pictures; page 25 (top): Brown Brothers; (bottom): UPI/Bettmann; page 29 (top): National Archives; (bottom): Schomburg Center for Research in Black Culture, New York Public Library; pages 30–32: Leavenworth Photographics, Inc.; page 36: UPI/Bettmann; page 37 (both): UPI/Bettmann; page 42: UPI/Bettmann; page 43 (top): Culver Pictures; (bottom): UPI/Bettmann.

CHAPTER TWO

Pages 48–49: Archives of Labor and Urban Affairs, Wayne State University; pages 52, 53 (all): National Archives; page 58 (top): Courtesy of Archives, Great Smoky Mountain National Park; (bottom): Library of Congress; page 59: Special Collections Division, University of Washington Libraries; page 66: National Archives; page 67 (top): Brown Brothers; (bottom): Library of Congress; page 72: Courtesy of *La Opinion*; page 73 (top): Security-Pacific Collection, Los Angeles Public Library; (bottom): From the collections of the Henry Ford Museum and Greenfield Village.

CHAPTER THREE

Pages 76–77: Underwood Photo Archives, SF; page 84 (top): National Archives; (bottom): UPI/Bettmann; page 85 (top): National Archives; (bottom): Library of Congress; page 92 (top): Schomburg Center for Research in Black Culture, New York Public Library; (bottom): National Archives; page 93: UPI/Bettmann; page 96 (top): From the collections of the Henry Ford Museum and Greenfield Village; (bottom): *Detroit News*; page 97: *Detroit News*; page 104 (both): Library of Congress; page 105: National Archives.

CHAPTER FOUR

Pages 108–109: UPI/Bettmann; page 116 (top): Franklin D. Roosevelt Memorial Library; (bottom): UPI/Bettmann; page 117: Franklin D. Roosevelt Memorial Library; page 120: UPI/Bettmann; page 121 (top): The Bancroft Library, University of California at Berkeley; (bottom): Library of Congress; page 132 (both): UPI/Bettmann; page 133 (top): Library of Congress; (bottom): Franklin D. Roosevelt Memorial Library; page 135 (both): National Archives.

CHAPTER FIVE

Pages 138–139: Margaret Bourke-White, *Life* magazine © Time Warner; page 146: UPI/Bettmann; page 147 (top): Franklin D. Roosevelt Memorial Library; (bottom): La Guardia and Wagner Archives at La Guardia Community College, City University of New York; page 152 (top): Brown Brothers;

(bottom): Triborough Bridge and Tunnel Authority, Special Archives; page 153 (both): National Archives; page 158: UPI/Bettmann; page 159 (top): National Archives; (bottom): UPI/Bettmann.

CHAPTER SIX

Pages 164–165: UPI/Bettmann; page 172 (top): UPI/Bettmann; (bottom): Special collection of the University of Texas at Arlington Libraries, Texas Labor Archives; page 173: Brown Brothers; page 178 (both): The Bancroft Library, University of California at Berkeley; page 179: San Francisco Public Library; pages 182–184 (all): UPI/Bettmann.

CHAPTER SEVEN

Pages 186–187: Library of Congress; page 196 (top): Library of Congress; (bottom): UPI/Bettmann; page 197: UPI/Bettmann; page 200 (top): Library of Congress; (bottom): Dorothea Lange Collection, the Oakland Museum; page 201 (top): Visual Communications; (bottom): Library of Congress; page 204: UPI/Bettmann; page 205 (top): Library of Congress; (bottom): The Institute of Texan Cultures, *San Antonio Light* Collection; page 210 (top): Southern Historical Collection, Library of the University of North Carolina at Chapel Hill; (bottom): Wayne State Labor Archives; page 211: Southern Historical Collection, University of North Carolina at Chapel Hill.

CHAPTER EIGHT

Pages 214–215: Photograph by Leo Seltzer; page 220 (top): UPI/Bettmann; (bottom): Scurlock Studio; page 221: National Archives; page 226 (both): Library of Congress; page 227: Schomburg Center for Research in Black Culture, New York Public Library; page 232 (top): UPI/Bettmann; (bottom): Brown Brothers; page 233 (top): Library of Congress; (bottom): Culver Pictures; page 234 (top): UPI/Bettmann; (bottom): UPI/Bettmann.

CHAPTER NINE

Pages 242–243: Library of Congress; page 252 (top): Brown Brothers; (bottom): © Washington Post. Reprinted by permission of D.C. Public Library; page 253 (both): National Archives; page 256: Schomburg Center for Research in Black Culture, New York Public Library; page 257 (both): National Archives; page 260 (both): National Archives; pages 264, 265 (all): Library of Congress; page 270: National Archives; page 271 (top): Franklin D. Roosevelt Memorial Library; (bottom): Library of Congress.

CHAPTER TEN

Pages 274–275: UPI/Bettmann; page 280 (top): The George Meany Memorial Archives; (bottom): UPI/Bettmann; pages 281, 287 (all): UPI/Bettmann; page 292 (top): UPI/Bettmann; (bottom): © 1937 *Detroit News*; page 293 (top): Archives of Labor and Urban Affairs, Wayne State University; (bottom): Southern Historical Collection, Library of the University of North Carolina at Chapel Hill; page 298 (both): Library of Congress; page 299: Library of Congress.

CHAPTER ELEVEN

Pages 302–303: UPI/Bettmann; page 316 (top): UPI/Bettmann; (bottom): Underwood Photo Archives, SF; page 317: Otto Hagel, *Life* magazine © Time Warner; page 326 (top): National Archives; (bottom): UPI/Bettmann; page 327: © Scurlock Studios.

CHAPTER TWELVE

Pages 330–331: Chicago Historical Society; page 334 (top): Chicago Historical Society; (bottom): San Francisco Public Library; page 335: San Francisco Public Library; page 336 (top): Museum of the City of New York; (bottom): UPI/Bettmann; page 342 (top): Franklin D. Roosevelt Memorial Library; (bottom): UPI/Bettmann; page 343: UPI/Bettmann; page 346 (campaign buttons): Franklin D. Roosevelt Memorial Library; (photo of Roosevelt): AP/Wide World Photos; page 347: UPI/Bettmann;.

COLOR PHOTOS

Library of Congress. "Save Your Eyes" and "Protect Your Hands" by Robert Muchley, Philadelphia, Pa. "Keep Your Teeth Clean" and "Unfair to Babies," artist unknown, Rochester, N.Y.

INDEX

(Page numbers in *italic* refer to illustrations.)

Acuña, Rudolfo, 69
Adamic, Louis, 71
Adams, James Truslow, 12–13
African Americans, 70, *214–215*, 216, 218–
224, 239, 245, 322–328; as agricultural
labor in Deep South, 88–89, 203–213, *210,
211*; Anderson's Lincoln Memorial concert
and, 324–328, *326, 327*; CCC and, 137,
219–222, *221*; Communist Party/USA and,
86–91, *92*; Federal Theater Project and,
251, *256*; Great Migration of, *29*, 33, 71–74;
lynchings of, 9, 87, *214–215*, 216, 222–
224, *226, 227*, 247–248, 323–324; New
Deal and, 137, 209, 216, 218–224, *220*,
323–324; NYA and, 261; organized labor
and, 88–89, 208–209, *211*, 289, *293*; religion and, 230–231; Scottsboro case and, 89–
91, *92, 93*; Subsistence Homestead program
and, 262, *265*
Agricultural Adjustment Act (1933), 290
Agricultural Adjustment Administration (AAA),
160, 193–194, 246, 261, 290, 294, 307;
STFU activism and, 206–213
Agricultural Workers Industrial League, 86
agriculture, 55, 62, 186–213, 251, 290–301;
African-American laborers in, 88–89, 203–
213, *210, 211*; America's rural origins and,
189–190; in California, 69, *85*, 86, 195,
198–203, *201, 204, 205*, 238, 290–291,
294–295, 296–301; distribution of surplus
from, 125–126; drought and, 64–68, *67,
186–187*, 186–193, 261; farm foreclosures
and, 118–119, *121, 156, 157, 158*, 192–
193; land speculators and, 44, 190; New
Deal and, 125–126, 155–161, 190, 192,
251, 290–301; publicity about plight of laborers in, 295–301; rural displacement and,
192–203, *197, 200*; rural rehabilitation efforts and, 261–262, *264, 265*; scarcity program and, 160, 193–194, 206–213, 246,
261, 290, 294, 307; topsoil loss and, 190–
192; TVA and, 155, 162; in twenties, 44–
45, 190–191; unionism and, *85*, 86, 88–89,
199–202, *204, 205*, 206–213, *210, 211*,
290–295, *293*, 300. *See also* farmers; migrant workers; plantations; sharecroppers;
tenant farmers
Agriculture Department, U.S., 6, 68, 130, 142,
191, 192, 193, 207, 209, 296
Akron, Ohio: labor organizing in, 168
Albania, 338
Algonac Courier, 94
Allen, Florence, 127
Allen, Frederick Lewis, 143
Allen County Emergency Unemployment Com-
mittee, 70
Amalgamated Association of Iron, Steel and Tin
Workers (AA), 279–282
Amalgamated Clothing Workers of America,
168, 169, 278
Amberson, William, 206, 207–208
Amended Railway Act of 1934, 308
America First Committee, 344–345
American Association for Labor Legislation,
267
American Association for Old Age Security, 267
American Birth Control League, *37*
American Civil Liberties Union (ACLU), 90,
198, 296
American Exodus, 9–10
American Farm Bureau Federation, 290
American Federation of Labor (AFL), 46, 86,
168, 169, 171, 174, 177, 180, 185, 204,
206, 289; CIO split from, 278–282
American Guide, 254
Americanization schools, *29*
American Medical Association (AMA), 268
American Negro Labor Congress, 87
"American Plan," 45
American Red Cross, 67
American Youth Act (proposed), 259
American Youth Congress, 259
Ameringer, Oscar, 76, 80
Anderson, Marian, 324–328, *326, 327*
Anderson, Mary, 128
Anderson, Sherwood, 18, 54, 349

Anschluss, 319
anti-Semitism, 33, 34, 150, 235, *317*, 319–322, 323
Appalachia, 83; coal miners of, *164–165*, 166; hunger in, 57, *58*
apple sellers, 63, *67*, 70
Arkansas: drought in, 64–68, *67*; grass-roots activism in, 79–80
Armour, 288, 293
Armstrong, Louise V., 56, 114, 115, 126
Army, U.S., 71, 222, 340, 346; Bonus Army put down by, 102–106, 111–112
Army Corps of Engineers, 131, 144
arts: WPA and, 250–255, *256*, *257*, 314
Associated Farmers of California, 199, 290–292, 297
Association of the Friends of New Germany, 321
Atlanta: relief efforts in, 70
Auden, W. H., 306
Austria, 319–320
automobile industry: in mobilization for World War II, 340; unionization of, 277–278, *280*, *281*, 282–286, *287*. *See also* Ford Motor Company; General Motors

Bailey, Josiah, 224, 308
Baker, Newton D., 59, 149
bankers: vilification of, 13–14, 235
Bankhead-Jones Farm Tenancy Act of 1937, 296
bank holidays, 122–123
banks, 62, 235; failure of, 14, 47, *52*, 54–55, 115; in twenties, 47
Barker, J. M., 55
Bartlett, John H., 101, 102–103
Baruch, Bernard, 143
Bates, Ruby, *93*
Bel Geddes, Norman, 337
Belgium, 41, 337, 339
"Bennets, The," 238
Bennett, Harry, 94, 95, 286
Bennett, Hugh Hammond, 192
Bentley, Elizabeth, 230
Berkeley, Busby, 8
Berry, George L., 278
Bethune, Mary McLeod, 219, *220*, 224, 261
bigotry: against Catholics, 31, 33; against Mexican Americans, 68, 69. *See also* anti-Semitism; racism
Bilbo, Theodore, 224, 323
Biological Survey, 131
Birmingham, Ala.: Communist organizing in, 88
Birmingham Labor Advocate, 88
birth control, 34, *37*
Bituminous Coal Conservation Act (1933), 307
Black, Hugo, 309
Black Legion, 323

"Black Muslim" movement, 231
Blagdon, Willie Sue, 295–296
Bliven, Bruce, 283, 331
Block, Lucienne, *257*
B'nai B'rith, 34
Boeing, 340
Bolshevik Revolution of 1917, 28, 80–81, 82, 106
Bonneville Dam, 161–162, 194
Bonus Army, 98–106, *104*, *105*, 110, 111–112, 113, 130
bootleg liquor, *24*
Borah, William, 319
Bourke-White, Margaret, 10–11, 295; photos by, *138–139*
box cars: riding on, *58*, 60
Boy and Girl Tramps of America, 258
Bradley, Charles C., 157
Brandeis, Louis, 151, 240, 241, 296, 307
Bridges, Harry, 171, 175, 177–180, *178*
Brotherhood of Sleeping Car Porters, 34, 308
Browder, Earl, 82, 87, 170, 174, 225–228
Buchenwald, 320
Bunche, Ralph J., 219
Bureau of Indian Affairs, 134
Bureau of Labor Statistics, 288
Burke, Selma, *257*
Bush, George, 14
business failures, 54, 55, 57, 310
Business Week, 160, 277
Butler, J. R., 211
Byrnes, James, 224, 245

Cahill, Holger, 251
Caldwell, Erskine, 295
California: farm strikes of 1933–34 in, 199–202, *204*, *205*, 238; gubernatorial election of 1934 in, *234*, 236–239; Mexican immigrants deported from, 69–70, *72*, 195; migrant workers in, 10, 69, *85*, 86, 198–203, *201*, 290–291, 294–295, 296–301; migration to, 195–199, 290; real estate boom in, 35, 47; unionization of agricultural labor blocked in, 290–291. *See also* Los Angeles; San Francisco
"California Election News," 238–239
California Sanitary Canning Company, 291
Calloway, Cab, 90
Cannery and Agricultural Workers Industrial Union (CAWIU), 86, 199–202, *204*, 206
Cantwell, Robert, 254
capitalism, 14–15, 28, 46, 82, 91, 123, 143, 167, 225, 235, 237, 251
Capone, Al, 53
Cardozo, Benjamin, 240
Carnera, Primo, *326*
Carter, John Franklin, 6, 229

Catholics, 288; bigotry and, 31, 33, 321, 322; FDR supported by, 230, 245
Catholic Worker movement, 239
Cato, Robert, 290
Century of Progress Exposition (1933–35), *330–331*, 332, 333, *334*, 337
Chamberlain, Neville, 319, 339
Chapman, Oscar, 325
charity, *48–49*, 50, 61–68; federal initiatives and, 62–63, *66*; Hoover's views on, 50, 61–62, 63, 64, 65, 68, 124, 126; local initiatives and, 63–64, 65–68, 70; viewed as demeaning and dehumanizing, 126
Chicago: Century of Progress Exposition in (1933–35), *330–331*, 332, 333, *334*, 337
Chicago Tribune, 308
children: CCC and, 255–258; hunger among, 57, *58*; of migrant farm workers, 202, 203; as tramps and hoboes, *58*, 60–61
Childs, Marquis, 71
China, 318
Christian Front, 322, 345
Chrysler Motor Company, 277, 286, 340
CIO. *See* Committee for Industrial Organization
Civilian Conservation Corps (CCC), 17, 129–131, *133*, 137, 155, 249, 250; Native Americans in, 134; racism in, 137, 219–222, *221*; youth problem and, 255–258
Civil Works Administration (CWA), 126–127, 128–129, 134, 137, 248, 250
Clapper, Raymond, 349
closed shops, 45–46
coal miners, 48, *164–165*, 166
Cobb, Cully A., 207–208
Cohen, Benjamin, 142
collectivism, 16–17
Collier, John, 134–136, *135*, 137
Colt, 340
Comintern (Communist International), 83, 225
Committee for Industrial Organization (later Congress of Industrial Organizations) (CIO), 274, 279–282, *280*, 283, 284–285, 286, 288–289, 314; agricultural labor and, 290, 291; formation of, 278–279
Committee for Unemployment Relief, 64
Committee of One Hundred, 64
Committee on Civil Liberties, 277
Commodity Credit Corporation, 160
communism, 28, 80–81, 111, 202, 225, 230, 235, 236, 288, 318; Dies committee and, 314, 315
Communist Party/USA, 15, 28, 34, 82–98, *85*, 106, 224–228, 291; African Americans and, 86–91, *92*, *93*; agricultural labor and, *85*, 88–89, 199–202, *204*, *205*, 206, 208; marches organized by, *76–77*, 78, 83–86, *84*, 91–94, 95–98, *96*, *97*; organized labor

and, 83, *85*, 86, 88–89, 170, 174, 177, 225–228; Popular Front and, 225; Scottsboro case and, 89–91, *92*, *93*; squabbles in, 225–228; Stalin's pact with Hitler and, 338
company unions, 170
concentration camps, 320
Congress, U.S., 6, 62, 246, 296, 321, 325; anti-lynching legislation and, 87, 222, 223–224, 247–248, 323–324; bonus bill and, 98, 99, 101; defense spending and, 318, 340, 346; elections of 1934 and, 240, 245, 249, 266, 307; elections of 1936 and, 305, 306; elections of 1938 and, 312–313, 315; FDR's "court-packing" scheme and, 308, 309, 312; Muscle Shoals and, 150, 151; New Deal and, 115, 122, 123, 124, 127, 130, 136, 142, 143, 151, 160, 219, 247, 249, 250, 263, 266–267, 268, 311, 313, 314–315, 328; opposition to FDR in, 309, 312–315; outbreak of World War II and, 318, 319, 340, 341, 344, 346; Social Security Act and, 268. *See also* House of Representatives, U.S.; Senate, U.S.
Congress of Industrial Organizations. *See* Committee for Industrial Organization
Connally, Tom, 224
Constitution, U.S., 34, 224
Coolidge, Calvin, 26, 27, 69, 98, 144
Corcoran, Thomas, 142, 239, 241
corporations: in twenties, 46–47
Costigan, Edward P., 223, 224
cotton industry, 193–194, *196*, 199, *204*, *205*, 206–213; strikes against (1938–39), 291, *293*, 294
Coughlin, Father Charles E., 98, 229, 231–235, *232*, 236, 269, 272, 322, 345
Couzens, James, 70
Cowley, Malcolm, 106, 225, 338
Cox, James J., 113
crash of '29. *See* stock market crash of 1929
Creel, George, 237
Crisis, 34, 90, 261
Croppers and Farm Workers Union (CFWU), 88
Cry from the Cotton, 212
Cullen, Countee, 34
Cummings, Homer, 307
Curtis-Wright, 340
Cutler, Leland, 338
Czechoslovakia, 319, 338

Daladier, Edouard, 319
dam projects, 163; TVA and, 149–155, *153*, 162–163; in West, 148–149, 161
Daugherty, Harry, 45
Daughters of the American Revolution (DAR), 324–325
Davis, Chester, 207–208, 212

Davis, James E., 195–198
Davis, John P., 219
Davis, Kenneth S., 269
Dawes, Rufus C., 333
Dawes Severalty Act of 1887, 134, 136
Dawley, Alan, 217
Day, Dorothy, 230, 231, 296
democracy, 15
Democratic party, 91, 113, 127, 217, 218, 235, 237, 240, 245, *271*, 272–273, 306, 307; FDR's challenge to conservative wing of, 312–313, 315
Denmark, 339
depression. *See* Great Depression
De Priest, Oscar, 219
Detroit: bigotry in, 69; migration of African Americans to, 71, 74; relief efforts in, 70
Detroit Unemployed Council, 95
Dewson, Mary, 127–128
Dies, Martin, 313–315, 321, 328
Dillinger, John, 16
"ditch camps," 202
Divine, Rev. Major Jealous, 231
Don't Buy Where You Don't Work movement, 230–231
Douglas, Lewis, 129, 160, 239
Douglas, William O., 309
Douglas Aircraft, 340
Downey, Sheridan, 237
Dreiser, Theodore, 90
drought, 64–68, *67*, 186–193, 295; dust storms and, *186–187*, 188, 189, 191–192; rural displacement and, 192–193, 261
"Dry Spell Blues," 190
Dubinsky, David, 168–169, 278
Du Bois, W. E. B., 34
Dulles, Foster Rhea, 267
Dunbar, Augusta, 125
Dunjee, Rosco, 87–88
Dust Bowl, *2–3*, 4, 9–10; Lorenz's documentary on, 6–8, 9
dust storms, *186–187*, 188, 189, 191–192
Dyer, Gus W., 45
Dyer, Leonidas Carstarphen, 223

East, Henry Clay, 206–208
Eccles, Marriner, 141–142
Ecohawk, John, 136
Edison, Thomas Alva, 16
Education Department, U.S., 222
Eisenhower, Dwight D., 102
elections of 1920, 27, 113
elections of 1924, 27
elections of 1928, 27
elections of 1932, 52, 91, *108–109*, 110, 112, 113, 114, *117*, 156, *164–165*, 166, 167, 168, 225, 235
elections of 1934, 215, 217, 224, 240, 245,

249, 266, 307; California gubernatorial race, *234*, 236–239
elections of 1936, 217, 235, 269–272, *271*, 306–307, 322
elections of 1938, 312–313, 315
elections of 1940, 341–345, *348*
Electric Auto-Lite Company, 171
Ellender, Allen, 323
Ellis, Edward Robb, 249
Emergency Banking Acts of 1933, 123, 129
Emergency Relief Appropriations Act of 1935, 249
End Poverty in California (EPIC), *234*, 236–237, 238, 239
Epstein, Abraham, 267, 268, 269
Equal Rights Amendment, 34
Ethiopia, *316*, 318
Evans, Walker: photo by, *200*
"Everybody Ought to Be Rich," 40

Factories in the Field, 9–10
Fair Labor Standards Act of 1938, 314–315
Farley, James B., 113, 128, 240, 312
Farm Credit Administration, 160
Farmer, Helen, 259
Farmer-Labor party, 81
farmers: grass-roots activism of, 79–80, 118–119, *120*, *121*, 156–157, *158*, *159*, 160, 161, 190. *See also* agriculture; migrant workers; plantations; sharecroppers; tenant farmers
Farmer's Holiday Association, 118, *120*, 157, 160
Farmers Union, 156
farm foreclosures, 118–119, *121*, 156, 157, *158*, 192–193
Farm Relief Act of 1933, 160
Farm Security Administration, 7, 11, 296, 300
fascism, 225; in Europe, 315, *316*, 318, 319–320; in U.S., *317*, 320–322
Fechner, Robert C., 221, 222, 261
Federal Art Project, 250–251, 254–255, *257*, 328
Federal Council on Negro Affairs, 219, *220*
Federal Deposit Insurance Corporation (FDIC), 124
Federal Emergency Relief Administration (FERA), 124–125, 126–127, 128, 134, 137, 192, 247, 249, 261
Federal Farm Bankruptcy Act of 1934, 160
Federal Farm Board, 62
Federal Music Project, 250–251, 254–255
Federal Reserve, 123, 311
Federal Securities Act of 1933, 124
Federal Surplus Relief Corporation (FSRC), 125–126, 160
Federal Theater Project, 250–255, *256*, 314, 328

Federal Trade Commission (FTC), 181
Federal Works Administration, 328
Federal Writers' Project, 250–251, 254–255
Fifth Amendment, 224
Finland, 338
Fisher, Irving, 40
Flanagan, Hallie, 251
Flivver King: A Story of Ford-America, The, 98
Florida: real estate boom in, 35, 47
Fonda, Henry, 10
Food Control Act (1917), 44
"food riots," 80
Ford, Edsel, 286
Ford, Gerald R., 344
Ford, Henry, 16, 94, 98, 144, 169, 286; rural
  life and, 189–190; TVA and, 149–150
Ford, John, 10
Ford Motor Company, 69, 70, 71, *73,* 74, 91–
  98, *96,* 169, 277, 283, 286, 287, 340; hun-
  ger march of 1932 and, 91–94, 95–98, *96,*
  97
foreclosures, 118–119, *121,* 156, 157, *158,*
  192–193
Fortune, 6, 11, 160, 295
Fort Wayne, Ind.: relief efforts in, 70
Foster, William Z., 82, 83, 86, 225–228
"Four Freedoms," 348
Fourteenth Amendment, 224
Fowler, Gene, 63
France, 41, 318, 337, 338–339
Francisco, Don, 238
Frank, Jerome, 142, 212
Frankenstein, Richard, *287*
Frankfurter, Felix, 142, 309
Frazier, E. Franklin, 219
Frontier Centennial Exposition (1936), 333
fundamentalism, 202, 229
Furuseth, Andrew, 174
Fury, 8

Garner, John Nance, 177, 240, 307, 344
Garrison, Lloyd, *172*
Garst, Jonathan, 297
Gellhorn, Martha, 258
General Drivers and Helpers Union, 171
General Federation of Women's Clubs, 218
General Motors (GM), 57, 337, 340; strike
  against (1936–37), 277–278, *280, 281,* 283
German-American Bund, 315, *317,* 321, 322
Germany (Nazi), 315, *316,* 318, 319–320, 321,
  322, 338–339, 340–341; U.S. supporters of,
  315, *317,* 321, 322
Germany (Weimar), 41
Gibbons, Floyd, 111
Girdler, Tom, 286, 288
Glassford, Pelham G., 100, 101, 102
gold: panning for, 57–60
Gold Diggers of 1933, 8

Golden Gate Bridge: opening of (1939), 333,
  334, 335
Golden Gate Exposition (1939–40), 333–337,
  338, 339–340
gold standard, 124
Goldwyn, Samuel, 10
Gompers, Samuel, 46, 174
Goodyear Tire, 279, 282
Grand Coulee Dam, 194
Grapes of Wrath, The, 9–10, 11
grass-roots activism, 15–16, 79–107; of Afri-
  can Americans, 86–91, *92, 93;* Bolshevik
  Revolution compared to, 80–81; of Bonus
  Army, 98–106, *104, 105,* 110, 111–112,
  113, 130; of farmers, 79–80, 118–119, *120,*
  121, 156–157, *158, 159,* 160, 161, 190; of
  Mexican Americans, 34, *85,* 86; nurtured by
  Communist Party/USA, 82–98; of tenant or-
  ganizers, 79; in twenties, 34, *36, 37. See
  also* organized labor
Gray, Eula, 88
Grazing Service, 192
Great Britain, 41, 318, 337, 338–339, 341
Great Depression: causes of, 41–47, 156; docu-
  mentation of, 6–12; emotional inheritance of,
  12–19; end of, 340, 346–347, *349;* fear ex-
  perienced in, 12–13; legacy of, 347; psycho-
  logical impact of, 71–75; sense of
  connectedness to, 5–6. *See also specific topics*
Great Migration, *29,* 33, 71–74
Green, William C., 46, 167, 168, 169, 177,
  245, 279, 282
Greenbaum, Isadore, 321
"Greenbelt" towns, 262
Greenfield Village (near Dearborn, Mich.), 189
Greenway, John, 10
Grubbs, Donald H., 212
Guthrie, Woody, 10, 69, 161–162, 198

Haight, Raymond, 239
Haile Selassie, Emperor of Ethiopia, 318
Hall, Sharlot, 57–60
Hand, Fred, 324
Hapgood, Powers, 282
Happy Days, 131
Harding, Warren G., 27, 45
Harlem Theater Project, 251, *256*
Harlem Unemployed Council, *92*
Harlin, Robert, 63
Harriman, Daisy, 127
Harris, Abram L., 219
Hastie, William, 219
Hawley-Smoot Tariff Act of 1930, 41–45
Haywood, Harry, 87
Healey, Dorothy, 228, 291
Henderson, Caroline Boa, 189, 192
Herndon, Angelo, *93*
Herring, Clyde, 157

Hickock, Lorena, 124–126
Hillman, Sidney, 168, 169, 278, 288
Hinckley, Ted C., 123
Hirohito, Emperor of Japan, 318
Hiss, Alger, 142, 212
Hitler, Adolf, 225, 315, *316*, 317, 319, 320,
    338–339
hoboes, *58*, 60–61
Holman, Lee J., 171, 175
homelessness, 55–56, 60–61
Hoover, Calvin B., 208
Hoover, Herbert, 27, 39, 50, *52*, 53, 54, 81,
    91, 122, 144, 341; Bonus Army and, 98–99,
    100, 102, 103, 105, 106, 110, 111–112,
    130; charity and self-reliance as viewed by,
    50, 61–62, 63, 64, 65, 68, 124, 126; elec-
    tion of 1932 and, 110, 113, *116*, *117*, 168;
    oblivious to seriousness of crash, 51, 56
Hoover, J. Edgar, 16
Hoovervilles, *59*, 61, 118
Hopkins, Harry L., 124, 126, 127, 128, 129,
    137, 142, 239, 244, 247, *252*, 268, 306,
    311, 312; NYA and, 258; WPA and, 248–
    250
Hosmer, Helen, 297
House, Son, 190
House of Representatives, U.S., 80, 99, 101,
    122, 123, 223, 240, 245, 266, 268, 306,
    307, 312; Un-American Activities Committee
    of (HUAC), 313–314, 315, 321, 328. *See
    also* Congress, U.S.
Houston, Charles H., 219, *226*
Howard, Charles, 278
Howard University, 324
Howe, Louis, 113, 261
Hughes, Charles Evans, 240
Hughes, Langston, 34
Hull, Cordell, 119, 177
Hundred Days, 122–124, 129–130
hunger, 57, *58*, 74; soup kitchens and, *53*, 54
hunger marches, 76–77, 78; at Ford's River
    Rouge plant, 91–94, 95–98, *96*, *97*
Hurley, Patrick J., 102, 103, 111
Hurok, Sol, 324
Hurst, Willie, 295

I Am a Fugitive from a Chain Gang, 8
Ickes, Harold L., 119, 134, 138, 141, 144–
    145, 192, 219, 222, 239, 261–262, 265,
    311; Anderson's Lincoln Memorial concert
    and, 325, 327; plaque presented to, 328–
    329
immigration, 28–33, *29*; of Mexicans, 68–70,
    72, *73*, 86
income statistics, 44, 246, 309–310
"Indian New Deal," 131–136, *135*, 137
Indian Reorganization Act of 1934, 134–136
individualism, 16–17, 26–27, 269

industrial policy, 142–144, *146*
Industrial Valley, 168
Industrial Workers of the World (IWW), 83
Insull, Samuel, 39, 150
Insull Utilities Investments (IUI), 39
Interior Department, U.S., 130, 192, 197, 219,
    261, 325, 328; Guthrie's songs for, 161–162
International Labor Defense (ILD), 90, 91, *92*,
    93
International Ladies Garment Workers Union,
    168–169, *172*, 278, 289
International Longshoreman's Association (ILA),
    171, 175, 177–180
International Seaman's Union (ISU), 174, 175
International Typographical Union, 278
Iowa: activism of farmers in, 118–119, *120*,
    121, 157, *158*, *159*
Iowa Farmers Union, 118
isolationism, 27–28, 319, 320, 341, 344–345,
    346
Italy, *316*, 318, 337, 338, 341
It Happened One Night, 9

Jackson, Gardner, 212, 296
Jackson, Joseph Henry, 10
Jacobs, Lewis, 8–9
Japan, 318–319, 337, 347
Jeffries, Willye, 79
Jewish Anti-Defamation League, 34
Jews, 31, 230, 245–246, 291; anti-Semitism
    and, 33, 34, 150, *317*, 319–322, 323
Johnson, Hiram, 101, 319
Johnson, Hugh, 143–144, *146*, 177, 218, 239,
    263–266, 311, 344–345
Johnson, James Weldon, 223
Johnson, Josephine, 186
Johnson, Lyndon, 313
Johnson, Nunnally, 10
Joint Committee on National Recovery, 219
Joint Marine Strike Committee, 175, 177
Jones, Jesse, 262
Jones-Connally Farm Relief Act of 1934, 160

Kennedy, Joseph, 339
Kent, Rockwell, 314
Kester, Howard, *210*
Keynes, John Maynard, 142
Kirby, Rollin, 14
Knox, Frank, 341
Knoxville News-Sentinel, 162–163
Knudsen, William, 284, 285
Kristallnacht, 319–320
Kuhn, Fritz, 317, 321
Ku Klux Klan (KKK), *30–32*, 33, 323

Labor Advisory Board, 168
Labor Department, U.S., 130, 181, 185, 219,
    266, 314

Labor Disputes Act of 1934, 266
labor movement. *See* organized labor; strikes;
    specific unions
Ladies' Home Journal, 39–40
La Follette, Robert M., Jr., 245, 277, 319
La Guardia, Fiorello H., 145, *147*, 346
Landon, Alfred, *271*, 272, 273
Lange, Dorothea, 9–10, 297, 300; photos by,
    121, 200, 296
Lasker, Albert J., 238
Lawrence, Joseph Stagg, 38
Lazarus, Emma, 28
League of Nations, 27, 337
League of Struggle for Negro Rights (LSNR),
    87, 90
League of Women Voters, 34
Leibowitz, Samuel, *92*
Lemke, William, 272, 273
"Lend-Lease" program, 348
Lenroot, Katherine, 128
LeRoy, Mervyn, 8
Leuchtenburg, William, 18
Lewis, John L., 46, 83, 86, 167, 168, 169,
    245, *274–275*, 276, 278, 279–282, 283,
    284, 288–289, 345
Lewis, Sinclair, 27
Liberty League, 217, 272
Life, 6, 11, 318
Lilienthal, David, 151, 154
Lincoln, Abraham, 115, 312
Lindamood, Erasmus, 162–163
Lindbergh, Charles, 16, 345
Lippmann, Walter, 308
Litchfield, Paul W., 143
Living Newspaper, 251–252
Lloyd, Horatio Gates, 64
Locke, Alain, 34
Lockheed, 340
London: bombing of, 339
Long, Huey ("Kingfish"), 228–229, *232*, 236,
    237, 269–272
Longshoreman's Association of San Francisco
    and the Bay District ("Blue Book Union"),
    171, 175
Lord & Thomas, 238
Lorenz, Pare, 6–8, 9, 10, 11
Los Angeles: Mexican immigrants deported
    from, 69–70, *72*, 195; migration to, 195–
    198
Los Angeles Times, 238, 239
Louis, Joe, 324, *326*
Lovett, Edward P., *226*
Lovins, Katie, 180
Lowitt, Richard, 148
Simon J. Lubin Society, 296–297, 300
Luce, Henry, 295
Lundeberg, Harry, 180
Luxembourg, 339

lynchings, 8, 222–224, *227*; federal legislation
    against, 87, 222, 223–224, 247–248, 323–
    324; protests against, *214–215*, 216, *226*
Lynd, Helen Merrell, 57
Lynd, Robert S., 57

MacArthur, Douglas, 102, 103, 105, 111, 112
McCarran, Pat, 308
McCarran Act of 1924, 33
McCarthy, James R., 154
McCarthy, Joseph, 34
McClosky, Eddie, 106
McCormick, Anne O'Hare, 122, 140
McCormick, "Colonel" Robert, 308
McElvaine, Robert, 41
Mackay, Charles, 38
McKenney, Ruth, 168, 279
McKinley, William, 113
McKinney, Rev. E. B., 209–212, 294
McMahon, Thomas, 278
McReynolds, James, 240
McWilliams, Carey, 9–10, 70, 86, 195, 199,
    201, 202, 300
Main Street, 27
Malcolm X, 231
Manchuria, 318
Mangione, Jerre, 254
Marcantonio, Vito, 245
Marcus, Stanley, 333
Marines, U.S., 340
Marine Workers Industrial Union (MWIU),
    174–175
Marine Workers League, 174
Maritime Union of the Pacific, 175
Maurin, Peter, 230
Maverick, Maury, 245
Mayer, Arthur, 9
Mayer, Louis B., 238
Means, Gardiner, 142
Meehan, Michael J., 39
"Memorial Day Massacre" (1937), 286–288,
    287
Merriam, Frank, 176, 238–239
Mexican Americans, 28, 34, *73*, 199, 202,
    205, 288, 290, 291; deportation of, 68–70,
    72, 195; organized by Communists, *85*, 86
middle class, 13–14, 71
migrant workers, 9–10, 69, 195–203, *196*,
    201, 206–301, *298, 299*; deflected from Cal-
    ifornia, 195–198; earnings of, 203; Guthrie's
    song about, 161, 162; living conditions of,
    202, 296–297, 300; organized by Commu-
    nists, *85*, 86; publicity about plight of, 296–
    300; resentment toward, 203; unionism and,
    85, 86, 199–202, *204, 205*, 206–213, 290–
    291
Miller, Donald B., 131
Millis, Harry L., *172*

Mills, Omer, 297
Milner, Estelle, 88
Milton, George Fort, 222–223
Milwaukee Sewing Project, *253*
Minehan, Thomas, 60, 258
minimum-wage laws, 307, 308, 314–315
Minneapolis: unionism in, 171
Minnesota: Farmer-Labor party in, 81
Mississippi River Valley, 9
Mitchell, Harry Leland, 206–208, 209–212, *210*, 294
Mitchell, Jonathan, 276
Mitchell, William D., 111
Moley, Raymond, 115, 141, 239
Moore, Jake, 157
Morgan, Arthur E., 151–154
Morgan, Harcourt A., 151, 154, 155
Morgan, J. P., 13–14
Morgenthau, Henry, 119, 123, 129, 141, 239
Morrow, Dwight, 53
Moses, Robert, 145–148, *152*
movies, 6–10, *24*, 143; controversy avoided in, 8–9; documentaries, 6–8, 9; newsreels, 6, 11; in political campaigns, 238–239
Muncie, Ind.: business failures in, 57
Mundelein, George William, Cardinal, 322
Munich Pact (1938), 319
Murphy, Carl, 87–88
Murphy, Daniel E., 134
Murphy, Frank, 284, 285, 309
Murrow, Edward R., 339
Muscle Shoals, Ala., 149–151, 154
Mussolini, Benito, *316*, 318, 319, 338
Myers, Mary Conner, 212

National Association for the Advancement of Colored People (NAACP), 34, 86–87, 137, 218, 219, *226*, 261, 324; lynchings and, 87, 222, 223, 247; Scottsboro case and, 89–91
National Association of Broadcasters, 322
National Association of Manufacturers, 266, 285
National Association of Women Lawyers, 218
National Business Survey Conference, 62
National Committee for the Defense of Political Prisoners, 90
National Committee on Rural Social Planning, 296
National Consumers League, 218
National Council of Negro Women, 261
National Credit Corporation (NCC), 62
National Emergency Council, 128, 240
National Endowment for the Arts, 255
National Endowment for the Humanities, 255
National Grange, 290
National Guard, 171, 176, 177, 181, *184*, 284, 285
national health insurance, 268

National Industrial Recovery Act of 1933 (NIRA), 142–143, 144; Supreme Court and, 240, 241, 267, 290, 307; unionism and, 142, 167–168, 169–170, 171, 180, 185, 199, 206, 245, 263–266, 278, 290
National Labor Board (later National Labor Relations Board; NLRB), 142, 170, *172*, 176, 263, 266, 267, 288
National Labor Relations Act of 1935 (Wagner Act), 266–267, 277, 288, 290, 307, 308
National Labor Relations Board. *See* National Labor Board
National Miners Union, 83
national parks, 149
National Park Service, 131
National Recovery Administration (NRA), 142, 143–144, *146*, 167, 170, 175, 177, 180, 185, 239, 311; gender inequities and, 218; laxity in enforcement by, 263–266
National Resources Planning Board, 190
National Textile Workers Union, 83
National Urban League, 34, 87
National Veterans Association, 99
National Youth Administration (NYA), 17, 258–261, *260*
Nation of Islam, 231
Native Americans, 149; New Deal and, 131–136, *135*, 137
Navajo, *135*, 136
Navy, U.S., 318, 340, 347
Nazis, 315, *316*, 319–320, 321, 338–339, 340–341; German-American Bund and, 315, *317*, 321, 322
negative campaigning, 238–239
New Deal, 18, 62, 110, 115–185, 245, 313, 321, 341, 344, 349; African Americans and, 137, 209, 216, 218–224, *220*, 323–324; agriculture and, 125–126, 155–161, 190, 192, 251, 290–301; bank holidays and, 122–123; beginning of, 115–123, *132*; building human happiness as goal of, 141; collectivism espoused by, 16–17; cutbacks in, 310–311, 328; Dies committee's search for Communists in, 314, 315; diminishment of enthusiasm for, 306–307; dismantlement of, 328–329; documentation of activities of, 6, 7, 11; hope loosed by, 140, 217; human costs of, 161–163; increased power of president in, 122; industrial policy in, 142–144, *146*; labor legislation in, 263–267, 277, 288, 290, 307, 308, 314–315; leading figures of, 119, 141–142; moderate vs. radical forces in, 239; Native Americans and, 131–136, *135*, 137; organized labor and, 142, 167–180, 217; outbreak of World War II and, 340; permanent impact of, 137, 163; politics of discontent and, 214–239; pragmatic flexibility in, 129; public works programs in, 17, 142,

144–155, *147*, *153*, 161–163, 311, 328; relief programs in, 17, 124–126, 128, 137, 141, 142; rural electrification and, 149–151, 155, 161, 162, 262–263, *270*; rural rehabilitation efforts in, 261–262, *264*, *265*; Second, 242–273; Social Security and, 17, 267–269, *271*, 308, 310; Supreme Court and, 240–241, 267, 288, 290, 307; Utopian goals ascribed to, 138; women and, 127–128, 218, *220*, 239, 248, 249–250, *253*, 258; work-relief programs in, 17, 126–127, 128–131, *133*, 134, 137, 155, 218, 219–222, *221*, *242–243*, 244, 248–261, *252*, *253*, *256*, *257*, *260*, 311, 314; youth problem and, 255–261, *260*
New Negro Alliance of Washington, 324
New Orleans: orange sellers in, 63; unemployment in, 57
New Orleans *Times-Picayune*, 57, 63
New Republic, 122, 283, 306, 331
newsreels, 6, 11
New York City: apple sellers in, 63, 67; PWA money allocated to, 145–148, *147*, *152*; relief efforts in, 70
New York Post, 111
New York Stock Exchange, 38, 40, 311
New York Times, 38, 86, 111, 239, 291–292, 305, 346
New York World's Fair (1939–40), 333, *336*, 337–340
Niebuhr, Reinhold, 230, 296
Norcross, Hiram, 209
Norris, George, 150, 152, 154, 245, 261, 262, 323
Norris Dam, *153*, 154
Norway, 339
Nugent, Frank, 10
Nye, Gerald, 319

O'Connor, John, 314, 315
Oklahoma City: food riot in, 80
Old-Age Revolving Pensions, Ltd. (OARP), *233*, 236
Olson, Floyd B., 81, 119
organized labor, 86, 164–185, 217, 239, 251, 274–301; African Americans and, 88–89, 208–209, *211*, *293*; agricultural labor and, *85*, 86, 88–89, 199–202, *204*, *205*, 206–213, *210*, *211*, 290–295, *293*, 300; CIO-AFL split and, 278–282; Communist Party/USA and, 83, *85*, 86, 88–89, 170, 174, 177, 225–228; company unions and, 170; epiphany of, 282–289; FDR supported by, 245; increase in union membership and, 168–169, 180; NIRA and, 142, 167–168, 169–170, 171, 180, 185, 199, 206, 245, 263–266, 278, 290; in twenties, 24, 45–46, 167; Wagner Act and, 266–267, 277, 288,

290, 307, 308. *See also* strikes; *specific unions*
overproduction, 45, 46–47
Ovington, Mary White, 137, 223
Owen, Ruth Bryan, 127

Pacific Northwest: migration to, 194–195
Packard Motor Car Company, 340
Palmer, A. Mitchell, 28
Panay, 318–319
panhandling, 61
Parks, Gordon, 51
"Pastures of Plenty," 161, 162
Patman, Wright, 98, 99, 101
Patterson, Haywood, *92*
Payne, John Barton, 65, 68
payroll (Social Security) tax, 269, 271, 310
Peace Mission movement, 231
Pearl Harbor, 347
Pearson, Drew, 296
Pelley, William Dudley, 321–322, 323
Pennsylvania General Assembly, 64
"penny-auctions," 118–119, *121*
Pepper, Claude, 312, 313
Perkins, Frances, 119, 127, 141, 168, *172*, *173*, 177, 218, 284, 315
Philadelphia: relief efforts in, 63–64
Phillips, Leon C., 344
photography: as record of Great Depression, 5, 6, 7, 10–12
Pinchot, Gifford, 150
Pinkerton Detective Agency, 277
plantations, 65–68, 88, 193–194, *196*, 246, 294, 295; unionism and, 206–213
Plight of the Sharecroppers, The, 206–207
Plow that Broke the Plains, The, 6–8, 9
Poland, 338–339
Ponselle, Elsa, 13
Poole, Elijah (Elijah Muhammad), 231
Popular Front, 225
populism, 15
Posetta, Rose, 282
President's Emergency Committee for Employment (PECE), 62–63
President's Organization for Unemployment Relief (POUR), 62–63, *66*
price codes, 142, 143, 167
Printing Pressman's Union, 278
Progressive party, 239, 245
progressivism, 167; death of, in twenties, 26–33
Prohibition, 23, *24*
protectionism, 41–45
Protestants, 229–230, 246
Protocols of the Elders of Zion, The, 322
Public Works Administration (PWA), 17, 142, 144–155, 311, 328; legacy of, 163; New York City as beneficiary of, 145–148, *147*,

Public Works Admnistration (*continued*)
152; TVA and, 149–155, *153*, 162–163;
West transformed by, 148–149, 161
Purinton, Edward Earl, 20
Pyle, Ernie, 188

racism, 31, 33, 137, 174, 202, 206, 322–323;
in CCC, 137, 219–222, *221*; within Commu-
nist Party/USA, 87
radio, *25*, 26, *302–303*, 304, 305–306, 322
Radio Corporation of American (RCA), 39
Radio League of the Little Flower, 235, 322
Rainey, Henry, 122
Rand, Sally, 337
Randolph, A. Philip, 308
Ransome, Leon A., *226*
Raskob, John J., 39–40, 217
Rayburn, Sam, 113
Reader's Digest, 12–13
Reagan, Ronald, 14
recession of 1937–38, 309–312
Reclamation Law of 1902, 161
Reconstruction Finance Corporation (RFC), 62,
123, 124
Red Cross, 65–68, 79
Red raids of 1919, 28
Reese, Jesse, 286
Regnery, William H., 344
regulatory state, 14–15
Reinhardt, Richard, 340
Relief Act of 1938, 328
religion, 229–235; among African Americans,
230–231; depression's effects on, 229–230;
socialism and, 230, 231
Reno, Milo, 118, 120, 160
Republican party, 91, 217, 218, 240, 245,
271, 272, 273, 306, 312, 315, 344; Califor-
nia gubernatorial election of 1934 and, 237–
239
Republic Steel, 286–288, *287*
Resettlement Administration, 6, 16, 262, 296,
200
Reuther, Roy, *281*, 282–283
Reuther, Victor, 282–283
Reuther, Walter, 282–283, 286, *287*
Richberg, Donald, 141, 144, 167, 239, 263–
266
River, The, 9
Rivera, Diego, 251
Rivers, E. D., 344
Rizzo, Fiore, 134
Roberts, Owen J., 240
Robinson, Joseph, 245, 248, 309
Roche, Josephine, 127
Rogers, Will, 43
Roosevelt, Eleanor, 113, 124–125, 130, *132*,
147, 219, 224, 245, 246, 247–248, 251,
261, *264*; Anderson's Lincoln Memorial con-

cert and, 324–325; women's causes promoted
by, 127–128, 218; youth problem and, 258,
259, 260, 261
Roosevelt, Franklin D., 16, 17–18, 111–137,
116, 140, 143, *147*, 177, 184, 230, 247,
321, 325, 328; agriculture and, 156, 160,
192, 290, 296; anti-lynching legislation and,
224, 247–248, 323–324; background of,
112–113; bank holidays and, 122–123;
Bonus Army and, 111–112; building human
happiness as goal of, 141; congressional opposition to, 309, 312–315, 328; elections of
1932 and, *108–109*, 110, 112, 113, 114,
156, *164–165*, 166, 167, 168, 225, 235;
elections of 1934 and, 217, 240, 245; elections of 1936 and, 217, 269–272, *271*, 306–
307; elections of 1938 and, 312–313, 315;
elections of 1940 and, 341–345, *348*; inauguration of (1933), 114–115, *116,* 141; inauguration of (1937), 277–278; "Indian New
Deal" and, 131–136; middle course negotiated by, 239–240; New Deal begun by, 115–
123, *132*, 218; organized labor and, 167–
168, 171, 181, 185, 263–267, 289; outbreak of World War II and, 315–319, 320,
338, 339, 340, 341–346, 347, *348*; polio
suffered by, 113; race relations and, 216,
219, 224, 247–248, 323–324; recession of
1937–38 and, 309–312; relief programs and,
124–126, 137; rural electrification and, 262–
263; rural rehabilitation and, 261–262, 264;
Sinclair's gubernatorial candidacy and, 237;
Social Security and, 268, 269, 271; supported by coalition of diverse interests, 245–
246; Supreme Court and, 240–241, 307–
309, 312; TVA and, 150–151, 154; USSR
recognized by, 225; work-relief programs
and, 126–127, 128–131, *133*, 137, 145,
258; WPA and, 249, 250, 255; youth problem and, 258
Roosevelt, Theodore, 17, 112–113, 185
Rothstein, Arthur: photos by, *186–187, 196*
rubber industry, 279, 282
Rubinow, Isaac M., 267
rural electrification, 161, 262–263, *270*; TVA
and, 149–151, 155, 162
Rural Electrification Administration (REA),
262–263, *270*
Rural Rehabilitation Program, 261
Russia. *See* Soviet Union
Ryan, Joseph P., 175, 177

Sailors Union of the Pacific, 180
St. Louis: relief efforts in, 70
San Francisco: general strike in (1934), 177,
238; Golden Gate Exposition in (1939–40),
333–337, 338, 339–340; waterfront strikes
in (1934), 171–180, *178–179*

San Francisco Chronicle, 176
San Francisco Examiner, 177
San Francisco News, 297
Sanger, Margaret, 34, *37*
Sargent, John, 274
Savage Arms, 340
Schecter v. United States, 241
Schlesinger, Arthur, 219
Scottsboro case, 89–91, *92, 93*
Scottsboro Defense Committee, 91
Scottsboro Unity Defense Committee, 90
"Sears-Roebuck sales," 118–119, *121*
Seattle: Hooverville in, *59;* relief efforts in, 63, 64
Section 7(a). *See* National Industrial Recovery Act
segregation, *221,* 222
Selective Training and Service Act of 1940, 341, *342, 343*
Senate, U.S., 101, 123, 223–224, 240, 245, 247, 266, 268, 306, 307, 309, 312, 314, 315, 323, 343; Judiciary Committee of, 223–224, 309. *See also* Congress, U.S.
Sewanee Review, 154
Shahn, Ben, 257
sharecroppers, *197,* 295–296; AAA and, 193–194, 206–213; unionism and, 88–89, 206–213, *210, 211,* 291–295, *293*
Sharecroppers Union (SCU), 88–89, 206, 208
Share the Wealth Society, 228–229, 236
Sheaffer, W. A., 115–118
Sheeler, Charles, *96*
Shover, John L., 119
Silver Legion, 321–322, *323*
Simpson, John A., 156
Sinclair, Upton, 98, *234,* 236–239
sit-down strikes, 278, *280, 281,* 283–286, 288, *292,* 313
Skyland Press, 322
Sloan, Alfred P., 217, 284
Smith, Alfred E., 217, 272
Smith, Edwin S., *172*
Smith, Page, 229
Smith, Rev. Gerald L. K., 229, 272
Social Gospel, 230, 231
socialism, 81, 229, 230, 231, 236
Socialist party, 64, 224, 225, 240; agricultural labor and, 206–213, *210, 211*
Social Justice, 322, 345
Social Security, 267–269, *271,* 310
Social Security Act of 1935, 17, 268–269, 271, 308
Soil Conservation and Domestic Allotment Act of 1936, 290
Soil Conservation Service, 130, 192
Soil Erosion Service, 192
Sokoloff, Nikolai, 254
Soule, Fred, 297

soup kitchens, *53,* 54
Southern Pacific Railroad, 60
Southern Tenant Farmers Union (STFU), 206–213, *210, 211,* 290, 291–294, *293,* 296
Soviet Union, 82, 225, 337, 338, 341; Bolshevik Revolution of 1917 and, 28, 80–81, 82, 106
Spanish Civil War, 316, 318
Special Committee on Farm Tenancy, 296
speculation, 34–40; in agricultural land and commodities, 44, 190; in real estate, 35, 47, 237; in stock market, 35–40, 41
Stalin, Joseph, 85, 338, 339
Stallings, Odie, 71, 74
Stanley, Louise, 128
Statue of Liberty, 28
steel industry, *173;* unionization of, 279–282, 286–288, *287*
Steel Workers Organizing Committee (SWOC), 282
Steffens, Lincoln, 82
Stegner, Wallace, 231–235
Steinbeck, John, 9–10, *11,* 297–300
Stephenson, D. C., 33
Stephenson, Rome C., 54
Stevenson, Robert Louis, 217
Stimson, Henry L., 341, *342*
stock market: in recession of 1937–38, 311; speculation in, 35–40, 41
stock market crash of 1929, 14, 23, 40–41, *42, 43,* 82, 306, 311; economic weaknesses exacerbated by, 41–47; effects of, 51–55
Stokes, Thomas L., 103
Stone, Harlan, 240
Strauss, Joseph, 334
strikes, 34, 46, 83, 86, 88, 164, 169, 170–185, 206, 251, 279, 282, 286–288, *287,* 289, *293,* 310; of California farm workers (1933–34), 199–202, *204, 205,* 238; cotton-field (1938–39), 291, *293,* 294; by farmers, 118, *120,* 160; general, 177, 238; against General Motors (1936–37), 277–278, *280, 281,* 283; on San Francisco waterfront (1934), 171–180, *178–179;* sit-down, 278, *280, 281,* 283–286, 288, *292,* 313; by textile workers (1934), 171, 180–185, *182–184*
Stryker, Roy Emerson, 6–7
student work program, 258–259, *260*
Subsistence Homesteads, 261–262, *264, 265*
Sudetenland, 319
suffragettes, *36*
Supreme Court, U.S., 93, 240–241, 288; FDR's "court-packing" scheme and, 307–309, 312; NIRA and, 240, 241, 267, 290, 307
Sweet, Mary, 289
Swift, 288

Taft, William Howard, 341
Talmadge, Eugene, 181, 184
taxes: payroll (Social Security), 269, 271, 310
Taylor, Paul Schuster, 9–10
Taylor Grazing Act of 1934, 192
Teamsters Union, 171, 175
tenant farmers, 295–296; AAA and, 193–194,
    206–213; unionism and, 88–89, 206–213,
    210, 211, 290, 291–295, *293,* 296
Tenaycuca, Emma, *205*
Tennessee Valley Authority (TVA), 9, 16, 149–
    155, *153,* 344; accomplishments of, 154–
    155; board of, 151–154; human costs of,
    162–163
Terkel, Studs, 71
Texas Centennial Exposition (1936), 333
textile industry, 288; strikes against (1934),
    171, 180–181, *182–184*
Textile Labor Relations Board, 181, 185
Thalberg, Irving, 238
Their Blood Is Strong, 297
Thomas, J. Parnell, 314, 328
Thomas, Norman, 206, 207, *210,* 212, 224,
    279, 296
Thompson, Claude E., 125
Thomson, Virgil, 7–8
Thorton, Walton, *43*
Tobin, Dan, 341
Toland, Gregg, 10
Toledo, Ohio: unionism in, 171
"Tom Joad," 10
Toward a Soviet America, 225
Townsend, Francis, *233,* 236, 237, 268, 269,
    272
tractors, 194, *196*
Trade Union Unity League (TUUL), 83, *85,* 86,
    90, 95, 170, 174, 199
tramps, *58,* 60–61
Treasury Department, U.S., 250
Triborough Bridge (New York City), 148, *152*
Truman, Harry, 245
Tugwell, Rexford Guy, 6–7, 8, 113, 141, 239, 262
twenties, 23–55; activism in, 34, *36, 37;* agri-
    culture in, 44–45, 190–191; banking system
    in, 47, *52,* 54–55; decline of unionism in,
    45–46, 167; demise of progressivism in, 26–
    33; economic growth in, 26; immigration in,
    28–33, *29;* instability of world economy in,
    41–44; isolationism in, 27–28; life of typical
    Americans in, 23; materialism and individu-
    alism in, 26–27; overproduction in, 45, 46–
    47; reincarnation of KKK in, *30–32,* 33;
    repression in, 33–34; speculation in, 34–40,
    41, 44, 47. *See also* stock market crash of
    1929
Twentieth-Century Fox, 10
Tydings, Millard, 313
Tyson, James G., *226*

"un-Americanism:" congressional investigation
    of, 313–314, 315, 321, 328; KKK anxiety
    over, 30–31
Unemployed Citizens' League (UCL), 63
Unemployed Councils, 83, *84*
unemployment, 51, 54, 55, 56, 57, 69, 115,
    144, 194, 246, 310, 311, 312
unionism. *See* organized labor; strikes; *specific
    unions*
Union party, *271,* 272
United Auto Workers (UAW), 282–286, *287*
United Cannery, Agricultural, Packing, and Al-
    lied Workers of America (UCAPAWA), 291,
    294
United for California, 238
United Mine Workers (UMW), 169, 278, 279
United Office and Professional Workers of
    America, 288
United Rubber Workers Union (URW), 279,
    282
United States Bank, *52,* 55
United Textile Workers of America (UTW),
    180–185, *182–184,* 278, 288
Urban League, 218, 219
U.S. Steel, 286

Vann, Robert L., 219
Versailles Treaty (1919), 27, 41
voluntarism: Hoover's reliance on, 61–62, 64;
    ineffectiveness of, 63–68
"voodoo *Macbeth,*" 251, *256*
Vorse, Mary Heaton, 118

wage codes, 142, 167, 180, 218
Wagner, Robert F., 245, 246, 263, 266–267,
    323
Wagner Act. *See* National Labor Relations Act
    of 1935
Walker, Frank, 128–129
Wallace, Henry, 141, 155–156, 157–160, 193,
    207, 209–212, 296, 344
Wallace's Farmer, 44
War Department, U.S., 130
Warner Brothers, 8, 9
War of the Worlds, The, 304, 305, 306
Washington, D.C.: Bonus Army's demonstra-
    tions in (1932), 98–106, *104, 105,* 110,
    111–112, 113, 130
Washington, Naomi, 231
Waterfront Employers Association, 175–176, 177
Waterfront Worker, 175
Waters, Walter, 99, 100, 101, 102
We, Too, Are the People, 56, 126
"Weary and Willie," 238
Weaver, Robert C., 219
Webb, Rev. N. W., 209–212
Webb, Walter Prescott, 148
welfare, 17, 70, 126, 137

Welles, Orson, 251, 256, 304
Whalen, Grover, 338
Wheeler, Burton K., 113, 245, 319, 343, 345
Whitaker, Clem, 238
White, Alice, *24*
White, George H., 223
White, Walter, 223, *226*, 247–248, 323, 325–328
White, William Allen, 245
White House Conference on the Emergency Needs of Women, 128
Willard, Daniel, 56
Williams, Aubrey, 249, 258, 261, 311
Williams, Rev. Claude, 294, 295
Willkie, Wendell, 150, 344–345, *348*
Wilson, Edmund, 53, 56–57, 166
Wilson, Woodrow, 17, 26–27, 113, 122
Winant, John G., 181
Winterset, 8
women, 245; activism of, in twenties, 34, *36, 37;* dissatisfaction among, 218, *220,* 239; excluded from CCC, 258; in New Deal, 127–128; in organized labor, *281,* 283–284, 288, 289; voting rights of, 27, *36;* WPA and, 248, 249–250, *253*
Women of the Ku Klux Klan, 33
Women's Joint Congressional Committee, 218
Women's National Democratic Club, 127
Women's Trade Union League, 218
Wood, Robert E., 344
Woodin, William, 119
Woodward, Ellen, 128, 250, 253
Workers Alliance, 291
working hours and conditions, 142, 167, 314–315

workman's compensation, 268–269
Works Progress Administration (WPA), 17, *242–243,* 244, 248–255, *252,* 261, 328; arts supported by, 250–255, *256, 257,* 314; creation of, 248–249; cutbacks in, 311; flaws and inconsistencies of, 255; posters distributed by, *color inserts;* statistics on, 249; women's programs in, 248, 249–250, *253*
World of Tomorrow Exposition (1939–40), 333, *336,* 337–338, *339–340*
world's fairs, *330–331,* 332, 333–338, *334, 336,* 339–340
World War I, 26, 27, 71, 122, 143, 167; "bonuses" to veterans of, 98–106, *104, 105,* 110, 111–112, 113, 130; end of, *20–21,* 22, 23; Muscle Shoals plants and, 149–150; world economy and, 41–44
World War II, 148, 155, 161, 267, 338–349, economic boom and, *347, 348;* and end of Great Depression, *347,* 348–349; events leading to, 315–320, *316,* 338–339; isolationism and, 319, 320, 341, 344–345, *348;* U.S. mobilization for, 340–341, *342, 343,* 345–348, *347,* 349
Wright, Leroy, 89
Wright, Richard, *210,* 273

Yavapai County, Ariz.: placer mining in, 57–60
Yezierska, Anna, 242
You Have Seen Their Faces, 295
Young Communist League, 225, 259
YWCA, 218

Zanuck, Darryl F., 8, 10